THE FIGHTING AT JUTLAND

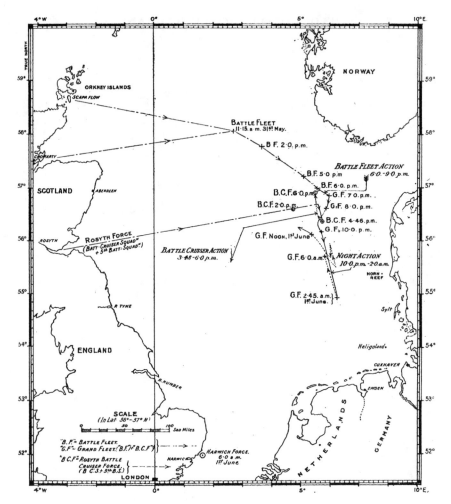

North Sea—31 May-1 June 1916.

THE FIGHTING AT JUTLAND

The Personal Experiences of Sixty Officers and Men of the British Fleet

*Edited by H W Fawcett and
G W W Hooper*

Foreword by John Roberts

NAVAL INSTITUTE PRESS
Annapolis, Maryland

Dedication
To the Memory of Those who Gave their Lives at Jutland,
31st May to 1st June, 1916

Introduction © John Roberts 2001

First published in 1921 by MacLure, Macdonald & Co, Glasgow

This edition published in 2001 in Great Britain by Chatham Publishing, 99 High Street,
Rochester, Kent ME1 1LX

Published and distributed in the United States of America and Canada by the Naval
Institute Press, Beach Hall, 291 Wood Road, Annapolis, Maryland 21402-5034

Library of Congress Catalog Card No. 2001089706

ISBN 1-55750-293-5

Manufactured in Great Britain

CONTENTS

FOREWORD

The dreadnought battleship served as the primary unit of the major fleets of the world for little more than thirty years. That is from the time that they appeared in reasonable numbers, around 1910, until the early 1940s when the aircraft carrier began to displace them from their pre-eminent position. During this time they were the yardstick by which a nation's naval strength was measured. Enormous amounts were spent on their construction and maintenance and they were seen by governments and people alike as a measure of national standing on the world stage. In fact for most of the dreadnought era they were much more of a symbol than a fighting force, and in war spent much of their time waiting for what proved to be very rare opportunities to use their guns against their own kind. The only major clash to take place between two dreadnought fleets occurred in the North Sea about 140 miles from the coast of Denmark between the British Grand Fleet and the German High Seas Fleet on 31 May-1 June 1916. It involved 151 British and 99 German warships, although the British preponderance in capital ships was less marked (28 dreadnoughts and 9 battlecruisers against 22 dreadnoughts and 5 battlecruisers).[1]

Known as Jutland (after the Jutland Bank) to the British and Skagerrack (after the passage between Denmark and Norway) to the Germans, it proved a disappointment to both sides. The

---

1 These numbers were only exceeded in October 1944 at the Battle of Leyte Gulf when 216 US (plus 2 of the RAN) and 64 Japanese vessels were engaged over a period of several days. However, this battle included a substantial contribution by aircraft (the effect of those at Jutland was less than negligible) and the US numbers are boosted by the inclusion of a large force of PT boats. The omission of the latter would just give Jutland the edge for total numbers engaged although fleet-for-fleet the US force would still have the greatest individual fleet numbers.

men of the Royal Navy and the British public had been anticipating a second Trafalgar since August 1914 but almost two
years of war had passed without fulfilment of the propaganda
which prophesied that the German Fleet would soon be sent
to the bottom of the North Sea. There was also some belief
that the Navy was not 'doing its bit' while the Army had been
suffering considerable losses on the Western Front. This sim-
plistic view ignored the strategic purpose of the Grand Fleet
in keeping Germany blockaded and its fleet contained.
Although a victory at sea would have released valuable
resources and provided a substantial advantage in morale, it
would have had little immediate effect on Germany's ability to
continue the war. It also seems to have been forgotten that
Trafalgar took place over two years after the outbreak of war
and followed a similar containment of the enemy fleets by
blockade. In addition the war against Napoleon was to continue for many more years, Trafalgar having served to limit
the Emperor's ambitions rather than bring about his defeat.

For Germany the attempt to isolate and destroy part of the
Grand Fleet had once more failed and they had been caught
and cut off from their base by the entire British battlefleet.
They had escaped from this predicament by a combination of
good tactics, good luck and the early cessation of the main
action by the intervention of nightfall. They also gained an
initial propaganda advantage. As their fleet was closer to its
base and arrived home first they were quick to release a communiqué claiming a major victory. This claim was primarily
based on the fact that the Grand Fleet's losses were greater
than those of the High Seas Fleet both in terms of ships and
men. This news arrived with the morning papers in Britain on
2 June and was believed by many as the full and unvarnished
truth. The situation was not helped by the Admiralty releas-
ing details that were honest in reporting British losses but provided little to counter the German claim to victory. In fact the
British only lost fourteen ships to Germany's eleven but
among these losses were three battlecruisers and two
armoured cruisers all of which suffered magazine explosions
and sank very quickly taking the majority of their crews with

them. As a result the British casualties in terms of officers and men were twice those of the High Seas Fleet. The initial public reaction was that the Grand Fleet had seriously failed the nation and had not lived up to the long and glorious traditions of the Royal Navy. Although these views moderated in time, Jutland permanently destroyed the Royal Navy's somewhat tabloid reputation as being almost invincible—a reputation that had evolved before the war from its historical pre-eminence in Britain's conflicts with France combined with the maintenance of the largest fleet in existence. And, it must be said, an almost universal British assumption of superiority over foreigners.

A clearer picture of Jutland has emerged over the years. Both sides could claim tactical advantages at differing stages in the battle but overall it was a strategic if inconclusive victory for the Grand Fleet. The higher British losses were largely due to serious failings in British material, particularly its ammunition. The latter also contributed to the survival of several German ships in that the British shells did not perform as they should have done. Had more care been taken over the manufacture, storage and handling of ammunition, the outcome of Jutland might have been very different, especially considering that, magazine explosions apart, the degree of damage suffered by the German capital ships was much more extensive than that of surviving British ships. In addition the operation of the fleet, while well handled on the major scale, allowing for the difficulties of control, was faulty at a detail level, showing inadequacies in, among other things, communication, night fighting and, more seriously, initiative among senior commanders.

The men of the Grand Fleet obtained a less obvious ascendancy over their enemy after Jutland for, while they maintained both their confidence and morale, that of the High Seas Fleet gradually deteriorated until it reached the point of mutiny in 1918. However, there was also an understandable feeling that their contribution at Jutland was neither appreciated nor clearly understood by the British public at large. Regardless of the outcome, which was an obvious and much regretted disappointment to many, they felt, justifiably, that they had fought as well as any of their historical forebears. This book was to a large extent an attempt to give the public a more balanced view of that battle by relating the experiences of many of those who took part. It is, moreover, a series of straightforward recollections by both officers and men that deliberately avoids references to the controversial aspects of Jutland. In fact the general conduct of the battle is only referred to in the very broadest sense and no attempt is made to either justify or condemn. It is a straightforward narrative, concentrating on personal experience, and is carefully balanced to recall events over the full length of the battle while controversial matters of tactical employment, material failures and Admiralty shortcomings are avoided completely.

Two officers who themselves saw action at Jutland— Lieutenants Harold W Fawcett and Geoffroy W W Hooper, compiled the book. First published in 1920 it contains the recollections of over sixty officers and men and for several reasons it is a unique record of the greatest naval battle of the First World War. There are many books that contain individual memories of past naval battles, but few can match *The Fighting at Jutland* for its completeness in giving a broad picture of a lengthy and complex fight. It starts with an officer from the cruiser *Falmouth* recalling an afternoon tea at Dunfermline before returning to his ship to find her preparing for sea and ends, two days later, with a description of the torpedo attack by the 12th Destroyer Flotilla on the retiring German Fleet early in the morning of 1 June. Perhaps the most important aspect of these narratives is the fact that they were set down very soon after the battle when the recollection was clear and not clouded by the passage of time. About two thirds of the entries were either generated from notes made during or shortly after the battle while the remainder were obviously produced within the period of four years between the date of the action and the publication of the book. Such detailed accounts can only be matched by official documents but these seldom provide insights into the feelings and detailed observations of those who were there—concentrating on the strict order of events, their importance to the eventual outcome and the lessons to be learnt. The human touch makes all the difference in giving some understanding of what it was like to take part in a major naval battle—with the singular exception that the reader is spared some of the more horrific effects of what occurs to humanity aboard ships struck by shells and torpedoes.

Many books have been written about Jutland, both academic and popular histories, and few have not employed Fawcett and Hooper's book as a major source of reference. The book makes no claims to historical exactness for time or position, a fact made clear by the editors in their introduction—such detail remained to be added with the publication of the official histories and much later by historians researching the official records. Despite this qualification, and the fact that the individuals involved could only recall the events within their own field of view, *The Fighting at Jutland* is remarkably clear in relating the sequence of events and is quite capable of standing alone as a history of the battle.

John Roberts
Mytchett, Surrey
2001

Publisher's Note
This edition was typeset from the complete edition of 1921. Apart from some minor stylistic changes and the elimination of chapter contents pages, the text is reproduced as originally published.

EDITORS'
INTRODUCTION

The narratives of the Fighting at Jutland which are collected in this book were all written by officers or men who were present at the battle, and they are, therefore, first-hand evidence of the detail events of the fighting.

The book is not a criticism; it is a record of personal experiences. One has often felt that a great gap would be filled in the histories of old-time naval battles if one could read true stories of all the hundred and one personal incidents of the fighting that must have occurred in the ding-dong days of old. Imagine the adventure that could be contained in a book truly describing the fighting incidents of Trafalgar! What an insight it would give us into the character and courage of the men who served Nelson. So this book of the Fighting at Jutland is an endeavour to fill a like gap for the one fleet action of the War of 1914-18.

In it all discussion of tactics and of strategy, of whether we won the battle or whether the Germans did, has been omitted, for it has been felt that the desire of all will be, not so much to read of the technicalities of the battle as of the personal experiences of the men who fought. In a personal narrative one can write many impressions of battle incidents and can refer to many details that would be out of place in official reports, so that one hopes this book will form a valuable supplement to the official histories of the action, and at the same time be of live interest to the general public as showing the experiences that men go through in modern Naval fighting.

The accuracy of times and of squadron positions or movements is not guaranteed, but is indeed in some instances sure to be at fault, for it is well known that personal records of naval battles unchecked by ships' logs, official reports, etc., are frequently inaccurate in these details. But perhaps such accuracy can justifiably be dispensed with in a book which records, not ships' movements, but personal experiences. Similarly, the small diagrams that are added to several narratives do not profess to be accurate in detail, but are included only for the purpose of illustrating the progress of the fighting.

The majority of the narratives were written very shortly after the action, or from notes made during the action; but a few were written in 1920 from memory only. A table in Appendix B gives the details of when the several narratives were written and the action station of the author, so that students may be able to judge of their value as accurate records.

In a few instances it has been thought advisable to split up a narrative and to put one part at the beginning of the book and another part later on, but as a rule the narratives are left complete in themselves as a story of one man or one ship's experiences through the action. With this exception, however, that references to certain prominent events of the battle, such as the blowing up of H.M.S. *Defence*, which was witnessed by perhaps nearly a hundred ships, has been omitted from some narratives, for the repetition became after a while wearisome without adding to our knowledge of the event. The narratives have been arranged, so far as has been convenient, in the same sequence as that in which the events they describe occurred. There have necessarily been exceptions, and there is overlapping, but, broadly speaking, anyone who reads through the sixty narratives contained in this book will be reading a history of the events at Jutland in the order in which they occurred.

For anyone who wishes to refresh his memory of the main events of the action, a brief description of the battle and a chronology of the principal events are contained in Appendix C. This, however, is not an authoritative account, but is only a *precis* of events based upon second-hand evidence.

The photographs of ships in action were all taken on 31st May, 1916, and those of damage to ships were taken immediately after the action. The illustrations in the book are drawn by an officer who was himself present at the battle.

We may conclude this introduction by expressing the hope that the book will not be too technical for the ordinary 'landlubber'. Most of us know that the bows is the front end of a ship, that port is the left-hand side and starboard the right-hand side, and that on the beam is at right angles to the fore and aft line of the ship. It is not necessary to know much more.

We also hope that the Service itself may benefit by the knowledge contained in this book, and that the Naval Officers of to-morrow who were not yet at sea when Jutland was fought, may to some little extent be inspired by the spirit that runs through these narratives of sea adventure.

We, of course, owe our principal thanks to the authors of the sixty narratives, who, placing their knowledge freely at our disposal, alone made possible the production of this book. Their willingness to assist us in all ways has made a difficult task comparatively easy. Our thanks are also due to the Admiralty for offering no obstacles whatsoever to the publication of these naval experiences.

Let us add that an underlying purpose and perhaps our justification in publishing this book (for none of us are men of letters) seems to us to be expressed in Rudyard Kipling's verse:

> 'Oh, what avails the classic bent,
> And what the cultured word,
> Against the undoctored incident
> That actually occurred.'

H. W. FAWCETT.
G. W. W. HOOPER.

THE ADMIRALTY
OFFICIAL COMMUNIQUÉ
OF THE ACTION.[1]

The Secretary of the Admiralty makes the following announcement:

On the afternoon of Wednesday, May 31st, a naval engagement took place off the coast of Jutland.

The British ships on which the brunt of the fighting fell were the Battle Cruiser Fleet and some cruisers and light cruisers supported by four fast battleships. Among those the losses were heavy.

The German Battle Fleet, aided by low visibility, avoided prolonged action with our main forces, and soon after these appeared on the scene the enemy returned to port, though not before receiving severe damage from our battleships.

The battle cruisers *Queen Mary*, *Indefatigable*, *Invincible*, and the cruisers *Defence* and *Black Prince* were sunk. The *Warrior* was disabled, and after being towed for some time had to be abandoned by her crew.

It is also known that the destroyers *Tipperary*, *Turbulent*, *Fortune*, *Sparrowhawk*, and *Ardent* were lost, and six others are not yet accounted for.

No British battleships or light cruisers were sunk.

The enemy's losses were serious.

At least one battle cruiser was destroyed, and one severely damaged; one battleship reported sunk by our destroyers during a night attack; two light cruisers were disabled and probably sunk.

The exact number of enemy destroyers disposed of during the action cannot be ascertained with any certainty, but it must have been large.

---

1 Taken from the 'Times' of June 3rd, 1916.

15

Part I

The Battle Cruiser Action

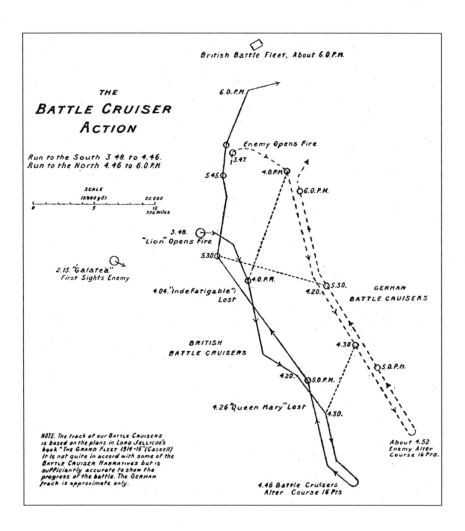

British Battle Fleet, About 6.0.P.M.

THE
**BATTLE CRUISER
ACTION**

Run to the South 3.48. to 4.46.
Run to the North 4.46 to 6.0.P.M.

SCALE
12,000 yds   20,000
0   5   10
                    sea miles

6.0.P.M

Enemy Opens Fire
3.47.
5.45.   4.0.P.M.
                    6.0.P.M.

3.48.
"Lion" Opens Fire

5.30.
2.15. "Galatea"
First Sights Enemy

4.0.P.M.   5.30.
                    4.20.   GERMAN
4.04. "Indefatigable"   BATTLE CRUISERS
Lost

BRITISH
BATTLE CRUISERS   4.30.
                    5.0.P.M.

4.20.   5.0.P.M.
4.26 "Queen Mary" Lost   4.30.

NOTE. The track of our BATTLE CRUISERS
is based on the plans in LORD JELLICOE'S   About 4.52
book "THE GRAND FLEET 1914-16" (Cassell)   Enemy Alter
It is not quite in accord with some of the   Course 16 Pts.
BATTLE CRUISER NARRATIVES but is
sufficiently accurate to show the
progress of the battle. The GERMAN
track is approximate only.

4.46 Battle Cruisers
Alter Course 16 Pts

CHAPTER I

SIGHTING THE ENEMY

Narrative from H.M.S. *Falmouth*
(Flagship of Third Light Cruiser Squadron).

The Third L.C.S., together with the First and Second L.C.S., when not employed at sea, used to lie off Charlestown, two or three miles up river of Rosyth, about four miles above the Forth Bridge. From Charlestown a pleasant four miles' country walk took one to Dunfermline, where an excellent tea could be had in the park, and on the afternoon of 30th May, a beautiful sunny afternoon, a fair number of Light Cruiser officers were having tea there and listening to the band. We had a four-mile walk back to catch our 7 o'clock boat—leave was always up at 7 o'clock—and found on arrival at the pier signs of activity in the ships, steam being raised, boats hoisted in, and the ship generally prepared for sea. Twenty hours later we were four hundred odd miles from Charlestown, and beginning the Battle of Jutland—a fact which will perhaps illustrate the suddenness with which the biggest naval action in history can develop. In sea warfare there is no lengthy process of passing from Home by transport to the overseas theatre of war, by rail to rest camp, from rest camp to reserves, and so on up to the fighting area, as there is in modern land fighting.

During the afternoon of 31st May many of us thought that it was only one of the customary sweeps that was being carried out, and that after dinner we should get the equally customary signal, 'Return to Base'. It was a glorious afternoon—one of the pleasant extremes of which North Sea weather is capable—and everybody was enjoying a bask in the sun whilst keeping handy to their action stations. The Light Cruisers were in their usual positions screening ahead of the Battle Cruisers, the Third L.C.S. being in the

19

centre, the First L.C.S. on the left wing, and the Second L.C.S. on the right wing, when quite unexpectedly, at about 2 p.m., the *Galatea*, of the First L.C.S., gave the report of enemy forces, and the Third L.C.S. closed on her to support, but I remember feeling distinctly sceptical about it, recalling the many previous false alarms we had experienced. However, we soon saw ships firing ahead, and then observed splashes falling round *Galatea*, and a little later sighted German light cruisers and destroyers which were firing at her. Whilst still out of range of our guns—I see that our range-taker was reporting 27,000 yards—one of the enemy fired a salvo at us, but the splashes fell a long way short. I remember the first impression that arose in my mind as they fired at us, bred, no doubt, by long experience of towing a target for one of our ships to fire at: 'Look out, you fool, you'll be hitting *us* if you're not careful!'

We never got into range of the Light Cruiser opponents, for they turned away to the Southward before we could close, ourselves and the First L.C.S. following in pursuit. Meanwhile, the Battle Cruisers with the Second L.C.S. had got into touch with the German Battle Cruiser Force and commenced action with them, steaming to the Southward, whilst we continued in pursuit of the Light Cruisers.

Narrative of H.M.S. *Galatea*

(Flagship of the First Light Cruiser Squadron, which first sighted the Enemy)

Late on the evening of the 30th May, H.M.S. *Galatea*, flying the broad pennant of Commodore Alexander-Sinclair, of the First Light Cruiser Squadron, with *Phaeton*, *Inconstant*, and *Cordelia* of that Squadron, and in company with the Second and Third Light Cruiser Squadrons and the Battle Cruiser Fleet, sailed from Rosyth for a sweep to the South-east. These sweeps had been carried out so many times before that no one was very excited, though those in the know were aware that the Battle Fleet was leaving Scapa in support of our force, so, apparently, there was some slight possibility of meeting an enemy force. When we were still only a short distance East of the Firth of Forth, at 3.15 a.m., the *Galatea* had a torpedo fired at her, which broke surface just on her bow, and shortly afterwards the track of another torpedo was reported crossing astern of us, but no submarine was sighted, and we continued East during the 31st May without any other excitement.

In the afternoon of the 31st we had neared the Northern fringe of the Heligoland Bight, with its mine-field, but there were no fresh rumours of German activity. About 2 o'clock the Eastern limit of the sweep was reached, and the signal to turn *en route* for home again was made, and the battle cruisers turned. But *Galatea* on the wing was late in receiving the signal, and about 2.15 was only just about to turn when a merchant ship was sighted ahead, which appeared to be stopped and blowing off steam, so the Commodore held on his course for a few minutes to have a look at her. On approaching her a little closer a destroyer, which had not at first been seen, was observed to leave her side, and at once was noted by her stump foremast and tall mainmast to be unmistakably a Hun. Action stations were at once sounded off.

I was aft on the quarter-deck quietly basking in the sun, and on hearing the bugle was in little hurry as I had heard that we were going to action stations for drill purposes sometime during the afternoon. So I strolled forward to my station—a little home-made Wireless Office on the foc'sle, more like a rabbit hutch than a W/T office, where I coded and decoded signals in action. But just as I

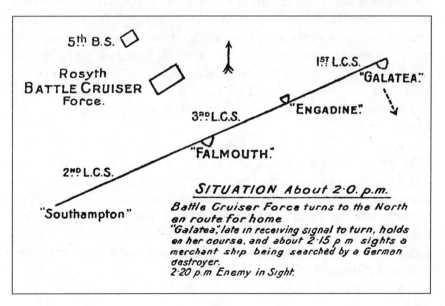

5ᵗʰ B.S.

Rosyth
BATTLE CRUISER
Force.

1ˢᵀ L.C.S.
"GALATEA."

"ENGADINE."

3ᴿᴰ L.C.S.

"FALMOUTH."

2ᴺᴰ L.C.S.

"Southampton"

SITUATION About 2·0. p.m.
Battle Cruiser Force turns to the North
en route for home
"Galatea," late in receiving signal to turn, holds
on her course, and about 2·15 p m sights a
merchant ship being searched by a German
destroyer.
2·20 p.m Enemy in Sight.

21

went up the ladder on to the foc'sle I was deafened by the report of the foc'sle 6-inch gun firing, and was almost blown down the ladder again by its blast; it was so unexpected. I nipped into my little W/T 'rabbit hutch' quicker than it takes to tell, and as I entered there rattled down the communication tube from the upper bridge, in a small brass case, the first enemy report of the Battle of Jutland:— 'Enemy in sight, consisting of one destroyer.'

The *Galatea* increased speed to 28 knots and opened fire on the destroyer. It was this first shot of the Battle of Jutland fired from the foc'sle 6-inch gun of *Galatea* at about 2.15 p.m. which had nearly blown me down the foc'sle ladder—a distinction which at the time I did not appreciate.

The first enemy report was shortly followed by several others, as first of all two German light cruisers with several more destroyers were sighted, and then more light cruisers and more destroyers, so that soon our fire was being replied to by several of the enemy. I was busy coding the several signals which were sent down to me, but could hear in between the firing of our guns, the long, drawn out whine of the enemy shells passing overhead, and a couple of crashes to port as two shells fell in the water just beyond us. Very soon afterwards there was a terrific bump just outside the little W/T room in which I was sitting, and a shell hit us below the bridge, but fortunately for all of us on the foc'sle and bridge, it did not explode, but pierced two or three decks and lodged in the port, the disengaged side of the ship, where it remained. An R.N.R. seaman saw it there a couple of minutes later, and thinking—goodness knows why—that it was one of our shells that had fallen down, tried to pick it up. It was still tremendously hot. 'Crikey, the blighter's hot!' he yelled, and let go of it with much haste, creating an incident that for some time afterwards was a standing joke in the ship.

Our range from the enemy ships was about 14,000 yards, which in 1916 was the extreme range of our 6-inch guns, and as the enemy was shooting well, we began to haul off to the North-westward, to endeavour to lead the enemy towards our battle cruisers. The Commodore signalled to the *Lion* by W/T what he was doing, and somewhat naively added, 'They all appear to be following', which was received, I believe, with some amusement in the Battle Cruisers and in the Battle Fleet, the latter now hurrying up to support but still a long way off.

| *Tiger* | *Princess Royal* | *Lion* |

Battle cruiser fleet at sea carrying out a sweep.

After this there was a lull in signals for a time, and I came out of my 'rabbit hutch' to have a look round. It was about 4.0 p.m., and our Battle Cruisers were in sight, tearing after the enemy which could be made out to consist of several battle cruisers in addition to the smaller fry. I must say it was a heartening sight to see the rapid director salvoes coming from the *Lion, Tiger,* etc., and to notice the tall columns of spray forming all round the enemy. The Germans turned and steamed South-east, our Battle Cruisers conforming, and as we had originally been on the Easterly course, the Second Light Cruiser Squadron (*Southampton,* etc.) from the starboard wing became the screen ahead of the battle cruisers, whilst we took station more or less astern. Here we remained during the run to the southward, when from about 3.45 to 4.30 the two rival battle cruiser squadrons were fiercely engaged with each other on almost parallel course. We had a very good view of the action.

The enemy were firing well, in ripple salvoes apparently, and great plumes of foam were springing up around our ships, but I could not distinguish any hits. A large barque with full sail set was lying becalmed between the two fleets about this time, and the feelings of her crew may be imagined as salvo after salvo fell in their

23

direction.[1] We in the *Galatea*, in our position astern, were steaming through the water where the German Battle Cruisers had recently passed, and I remember noticing the quantities of dead fish floating about, 'Tummy-up'—killed by the detonation of shell. About this time dense clouds of yellowish smoke rose up from the surface of the sea in the midst of the German line, and the word went round that one of the Hun Battle Cruisers had been sunk, and the sailors raised a cheer. Soon afterwards, however, we passed a number of floating brass cylinders in the water, and it was found that the enemy had been making a smoke screen by means of these cylinders, the contents of which give out a thick, impenetrable smoke when in contact with water.

About 4.30 a W/T signal from *Southampton* was intercepted, reporting that the Main High Sea Fleet was in sight to the southward and was steering to the North to close the German battle cruisers, and soon afterwards, when the enemy battleships were in sight from the *Lion*, we all turned 16 points and steered back to the northward, to draw the enemy toward the Grand Fleet. . . .[2]

Thus the action was commenced. But we must break here the *Galatea*'s narrative, for it has covered a long period of time since the first sighting of the enemy at 2.15 p.m., during which several important events have occurred. After receiving the reports of enemy in sight from *Galatea*, Vice-Admiral Beatty ordered H.M.S. *Engadine*, a seaplane carrier accompanying the battle cruiser force, to send up a seaplane to reconnoitre, and at 3.8 p.m. a two-seater 'Short' seaplane with a 225 H. P. Sunbeam engine flew off the water with Assistant Paymaster G. S. Trewin as Observer and Flight-Lieutenant F. J. Rutland as Pilot. 'The picture from the air,' says one of these officers, 'of the battle cruisers and of the *Queen Elizabeth* class battleships (5th B.S.), with their attendant light cruiser screen and destroyers, all rushing forward in what may be termed an orderly helter-skelter in a south-westerly direction to cut off the enemy, is a picture that can never be forgotten.'

---

1 Strangely enough just the same incident occurred at the Dogger Bank action on 24th January, 1915, when a Dutch sailing ship passed down between the German battle cruisers and Admiral Beatty's pursuing squadron.—*Ed.*

2 *Galatea*'s narrative is continued on page 106.

The following was their Official Report of the Flight:—

Report of Reconnaissance Flight,[3]

Carried out by 'Short' Seaplane, No. 8359, on 31st May, 1916.

H.M.S *Engadine*,
31st May, 1916.

Sir,—I have the honour to make the following report:—At 2.40 p.m. (G.M.T.), in accordance with signal and your orders, Seaplane No. 8359 was got out and proceeded to scout for enemy ships.

I was hoisted out at 3.7 p.m. (G.M.T.), and was off the water at 3.8 p.m. (Times were taken on board.)

The last information which I received from the ship was that the enemy were sighted in a N.N.E. direction, steering North.

I steered N.10, and after about ten minutes sighted the enemy. Clouds were at 1,000 to 1,200 feet, with patches at 900 feet. This necessitated flying very low.

On sighting the enemy it was very hard to tell what they were, and so I had to close to within a mile and a half at a height of 1,000 feet. They then opened fire on me with anti-aircraft and other guns, my height enabling them to use their anti-torpedo armament.

When sighted they were steering a northerly course. I flew through several of the columns of smoke caused through bursting shrapnel.

When the Observer had counted and got the disposition of the enemy and was making his W/T report, I steered to about 3 miles, keeping the enemy well in sight. While the Observer was sending one message, the enemy turned 16 points. I drew his attention to this, and he forthwith transmitted it. The enemy then ceased firing at me. I kept on a bearing on the bows, about 3 miles distant of the enemy, and as the weather cleared a little I observed the disposition of our Fleet, and judged by the course of our Battle Cruisers that our W/T had got through.

At 3.45 p.m. a petrol pipe leading to the left carburretter broke, and my engine revolutions dropped from 1,000 to 800, and I was forced to descend.

---

3 Reproduced by permission of Messrs. Longmans, Green & Co.

H.M.S. *Engadine* and seaplane.

On landing I made good the defect with rubber tube, and reported to the ship that I could go on again.

I was told to come alongside and be hoisted in. I was hoisted in at about 4.0 p.m.

The visibility at 1,000 feet was about 4 miles varying to one, and this reduced the advantage of Seaplane's height. Also, the Seaplane having to remain so close to the enemy, increased the chances of jamming the wireless. The messages, as sent, were received in H.M.S. *Engadine*, . . . but it was not known if the messages had been received until our Fleet were sighted and their course observed.

I could not keep both our Fleet and the enemy's Fleet in sight, through low-lying clouds. . . .

The speed at which things took place prevented any receiving, the Observer being busy coding and sending all the time. The enemy commenced to jam latterly.

The enemy's anti-aircraft firing was fairly good; the shock of exploding shrapnel could be felt, the explosions taking place about 200 feet away on one side, in front and astern.

I have the honour to be, SIR,

Your obedient Servant,

....

Flight Lieutenant.

CHAPTER II

THE BATTLE CRUISER RUN TO THE SOUTH

3.48 to 4.46 p.m.

Meanwhile the Battle Cruisers had worked up to full speed, had made contact with the enemy, and at 3.48 had commenced action on nearly parallel, southerly courses at a range of 14,000 to 18,000 yards. The next hour of the action was one of the most fiercely, if not the most fiercely fought periods the Battle of Jutland. During it H.M.S. *Indefatigable* and H.M.S. *Queen Mary* were blown up, with the loss of almost all hands—over 2,200 officers and men.

On a southerly course the action was continued for almost an hour, from 3.48 to 4.46 p.m., when the German High Sea Fleet was sighted coming up from the southward, and both Battle Cruiser Forces turned round 16 points, and then renewed their action on a northerly course.

The experiences of this period are described in two narratives from H.M.S. *New Zealand* and in one from H.M.S. *Princess Royal*. There is also a short description of the loss of *Queen Mary*, as seen from H.M.S. *Tiger*, her next astern, and a narrative from one of the survivors of H.M.S. *Queen Mary*. For the sake of maintaining the narrative of each ship as complete as possible, these accounts have not been broken up to describe only the events of the run South, but continue their description of the course of the Battle on past the turn to the North at 4.46 p.m. up to about 5.50 p.m., when the Battle Cruiser share of Jutland was nearly completed.

The order of the Battle Cruisers in line during the run to the South was H.M.S. *Lion* flying the flag of Vice-Admiral

Beatty, leading, followed by H.M.S. *Princess Royal, Queen Mary, Tiger, New Zealand* flying the flag of Rear-Admiral Pakenham, and H.M.S. *Indefatigable.* The ships were stationed 500 yards astern of each other, course South with alterations of about 20 to 40 degrees from time to time; their speed was 25 knots, for most of this period. A few destroyers were stationed close to the Battle Cruisers as a submarine screen, but the majority were ordered to take station ahead of H.M.S. *Lion,* and the Light Cruisers were stationed some ahead, and some on the port quarter of the Battle Cruisers.

Narrative from Officers of H.M.S. *Princess Royal*
(2nd Ship of the Battle Cruiser Line).

At 2.45 p.m. action stations, followed by the bugle 'double,' were sounded off, and all communications, instruments, etc., etc., were quickly tested. The various parties were mustered at their stations; gas masks, goggles, and life-saving belts produced, and all other final preparations for action made. Splinter mats, fire hoses, boxes of sand, stretchers, medical instruments and drugs, leak-stopping gear, shoring-up spars, spare electrical gear, spare hydraulic gear, engineers' spare gear—all these and the various other action accessories were got ready in a few minutes as nearly everything was kept permanently ready for action when at sea.

At 3.10 the *Engadine* sent up a seaplane, and at 3.32 we first sighted the enemy, 5 battle cruisers faintly distinguishable a very long distance away, accompanied by some torpedo craft. First of all their smoke, and later the outline of their masts, funnels, and the upper parts of their hulls became visible from the gun control position aloft, but from the turrets only smoke could be observed until some while later.

At 3.48,[1] having received a signal from the *Lion*, we opened fire,

---

1 The times in this narrative are reliable but they are not definitive, as recorders in different parts of the ship do not all agree in the times of their records. *Princess Royal*'s official report gives the time of opening fire as 3.48 in accord with the record taken aloft, and times quoted taken from other records are based on this being, 'zero time.' The times noted by the Midshipman in the Conning Tower do not appear to be very reliable.

Admiral Beatty's Six Battle Cruisers.   Destroyers taking up Action Stations.

Battle Cruiser Fleet Sighting the Enemy.
(Photo taken from *Champion* ahead of the Battle Cruisers)

and with her concentrated on the leading, the right-hand ship, of the five enemy battle cruisers, on a bearing Red 42. The range on our sights was then 16,000 yards, closing at a rate of about 400 yards a minute, but on seeing our shots falling over, the range was reduced by spotting corrections to 14,700 yards, with which range at 3.50 we were straddling the enemy.

They had opened fire a minute or so before us, and their first few salvoes went over. Their shells seemed to throw up a much smaller splash than ours although they were firing from 12.2-inch turrets, and we from the only slightly heavier 13.5-inch turret. Their salvoes then gradually came closer, until just as we saw the red-black burst of one of our shells hitting on the leading enemy ship, we noticed the *Lion* ahead of us hit amidships, and two minutes later, at 3.56, we were hit by two 12.2-inch shells on the port side, which temporarily knocked out our 'Argo' range-finder tower.

At 3.56 the enemy were bearing about 10 degrees abaft our port beam (Red 100)—steering approximately South, and both squadrons were firing heavily on each other at a rate and with a determination that made one think that something big must happen in a few minutes. The notes that a Midshipman stationed in the Conning Tower made during this time are rather human:—

29

'3.40. We opened fire. Their first few salvoes were over. They are getting very close. They have straddled us. No. 3 of the enemy line has been hit and is on fire. We have been hit forward. Argo tower knocked out. 'B' turret control. *Lion* on fire amidships. Went up to the bridge to find out what time we altered course, and got knocked over. M. staggered into conning tower badly burnt all over, and reported a large number of his gun's crews killed or wounded.'

Between 4 o'clock and 4.38 the Germans and ourselves ran on almost parallel courses to the southward, each endeavouring to the utmost of our ability to establish a mastery over the other. The majority of the enemy's shells appeared to fall short, throwing up columns of water nearly 100 feet high, but doing no harm, and causing little of the interference that we had at the Dogger Bank action, when the splashes coming inboard drenched the turrets and even the bridge, and seriously interfered with the gunlayers, range-takers, and spotting officers.

However, smoke and a decreasing visibility to the eastward now became two important difficulties. Our destroyers (at about 4.2) were between us and the enemy, and their smoke together with the smoke from *Lion*'s guns which was drifting across our range, was becoming a serious nuisance to our gun control. At 4.6 we altered a point to starboard, to South, to try to avoid the smoke, and for 10 minutes the range opened, until we were firing at ranges between 18,000 and 19,000 yards, or about 11 land miles. At 12 minutes past 4 we had to check fire for a while, and we turned back to South-South-East, 20 degrees more towards the enemy, to close the range. A torpedo just at this time passed right under the centre of the ship from starboard to port—*i.e.*, was fired from our disengaged side, so presumably came from a submarine, though I know of no one on board who sighted the submarine. When we had closed the enemy again slightly, to about 18,000 yards, it was pleasing to observe the 3rd ship of their line heavily on fire, but at 4.22, as a set off to this advantage, we lost the *Queen Mary*, and a few minutes later a salvo hit us abreast 'Q' turret.

At 4.24 we altered course more to port towards the enemy, on to a South-easterly course, and the range came down from 16,000 to 12,000 yards at about 4.26 (or 4.27). We were straddling the enemy and saw their leading ship hit; then our shots came short as the enemy were altering away from us, and their shots also fell short and went ricochetting overhead, 'Some with a whizz sound,' as a recorder in the director tower noted, 'or others with a sharp crashing sound, whilst splinters seemed to creak through the air, and we heard several small splinters strike the outside of the tower.'

The Midshipman in the Conning Tower at this time again had his own method of recording succeeding events:—'Just missed by a torpedo from starboard. Turrets told not to waste ammunition. Argo repaired. We are doing 28 knots now. Felt a shock. We have been hit aft by a large shell or a torpedo. 4.29. A big fire is raging in *Lion* amidships. 4.30. Ricochet skimmed over the Conning Tower. Destroyers having a go between the lines. We are fighting the whole High Sea Fleet alone, and are getting it very hot.'

This latter statement was moderately correct. At 4.36, after a turn of 20° away from the enemy to S.S.E., we lost sight of them, at a range of perhaps 16,000 to 17,000 yards, but, at the same time, sighted right ahead of us the main enemy battle fleet, which had been reported as closing towards us from the southward by our light cruiser screen a few minutes earlier.

At 4.38[2] we turned 16 points to starboard, following round in the wake of *Lion*, and re-engaged the enemy to starboard at a range of 15,000 yards, but this range quickly increased, and though at 4.48 we altered course a point towards the enemy, at 4.52 the range had become as much as 18,000 yards. Two minutes before this the 5th Battle Squadron had passed on our port hand, still steering to the southward, and we also re-passed the wreck of the *Queen Mary*.

Our target was now the right hand, *i.e.*, the rear battle cruiser, but we shifted on to the leading battle cruiser when she was visible (at 4.56), and fired 5 salvoes at her. The enemy line then altered away, and their range increased until it reached our maximum range, and we had to check fire. This was at 5.8, and we did not fire again until 5.50, when the leading battle ships of the Grand Fleet were sighted, and we had altered to starboard to close the enemy again.

After the turn to the northward, the action was much less intense than during the run to the southward. Astern of us, the 5th Battle Squadron were heavily engaged with the van of the enemy battle fleet, but in the *Princess Royal* we were out of range of these battleships, and the enemy battle cruisers had hauled off somewhat to the eastward and did not seem to be anxious to continue a close action. They were spread out over some distance, keeping bad station, and

2 The time of the 16 point alteration of Course is more probably 4.46.—*Ed.*

were firing with much less regularity and precision than an hour earlier.

This phase of the action was not very exciting, the only fear from the ship point of view being that one might get hit in the engine room, which would drop our speed, so that at once the ship would fall back and be sunk by the High Seas Fleet following us. Our whole object now was to keep the enemy battle fleet following us until we could lead them into contact with the Grand Fleet, and prevent the German battle cruisers from reporting the arrival of the Grand Fleet. From a gunnery point of view the firing was becoming very difficult, the range at 5.0 p.m. being as much as 19,000 yards, and the enemy were difficult to see. We shifted target two or three times, as one or another of the enemy could be observed, but at 5.08 we had to check fire, being unable to see a target any longer.

The notes of the Midshipman in the Conning Tower made between 4.38 and 6.0 p.m. were these:—

'4.38—Altered course 16 points to starboard owing to High Sea Fleet.

4.47—We are retiring on 5th Battle Squadron. Opened fire again. Destroyers were recalled from their action about 5 minutes ago.

4.51—5th Battle Squadron firing over our heads, going in the opposite direction.

4.54—5th Battle Squadron are turning up astern and following us.

4.57—Passed 6 survivors of a destroyer in a boat on starboard side, amid heaps of wreckage.

4.59—*Lion* hit badly aft and big fire burning.

5.00—No. 2 of the enemy's line has gone into local control. Their battle cruisers are very spread out, and there are only 4 of them; everyone seems to think that there were 5 originally. We are reduced to *Lion, P. R., Tiger, N.Z.,* and 5th Battle Squadron.

5.10—Reduced to 24 knots. Destroyers have not obeyed their recall signal, but keep dashing back to fight the enemy light cruisers and destroyers.

5.15—Lull in the action. People going out to stretch their legs and get a little fresh air. Hear that the shell which hit us forward early in the fight entered the Admiral's pantry and exploded. The whole of the Admiral's quarters is wrecked, and many people have been killed and wounded. *Indefatigable* and *Q.M.* have both blown up.

5.36—Prepare for action again.

5.42—Sighted submarine on the starboard beam.

5.43—Opened fire again.

5.44—Another submarine on starboard beam. The battle is not very furious at present.

5.55—Part of our battle fleet is in sight.

6.0—They have opened fire.'

Narrative of H.M.S. *New Zealand*
(5th Battle Cruiser in the Line)
By an Officer Stationed Aloft

At 2 p.m. on 31st May we were in 56° 30' N., 4° 47' E., steering S. 60° E. 20 knots. *New Zealand* and *Indefatigable* were 3 miles on the Port Beam of the 1st B.C.S. (*Lion*, *Princess Royal*, *Queen Mary*, and *Tiger*), when, at 2.17 p.m., the course of the Battle Cruiser Fleet was altered to N. 11° E. 19 knots. Apparently we had reached the Eastern limit of our Sweep, and were turning to the North to rendezvous with the Battle Fleet, and return to base. Everything seemed quiet and peaceful. I was Duty Control Officer on the bridge, and expected that I had the usual dull watch ahead of me, but suddenly, at 2.20 p.m., *Galatea* reported two cruisers, probably hostile, in sight. At 2.30 p.m. she reported that they were destroyers, and that she was chasing, and at 2.35 p.m. we altered course to S.S.E.

Below, in the Wardroom, the news was received with cold suspicion, and although one or two officers came on deck to have a look round, the general attitude was one of scepticism. Then came the report of a large amount of smoke, probably a fleet, bearing E.N.E., and we started to sit up and take notice. Action Stations were sounded, and as I climbed on to the rungs of the mast to go aloft a sailor asked breathlessly if the Huns were in sight, and I told him that they were. All turrets and control stations reported cleared away and correct in record time.

At 3 o'clock course was altered to East, bringing the 5th Battle Squadron on our Port Quarter just in sight of us, and a few minutes later the *Engadine*, on our port bow, hoisted out a seaplane, in which Rutland started his eventful flight. At 3.7 the enemy altered course to North West, and we increased to 25 knots and altered to N.E., and at 3.23 we sighted the German battle cruisers and their escorting destroyers on the Starboard Bow, range about 23,000 yards. At 3.30 we altered to East by South, the enemy bearing Red 25,[3] range 22,000 yards, and at this time the enemy turned round about 16 points on to a south-easterly course.

I had great difficulty in convincing myself that the Huns were in sight at last, it was so like Battle Exercise the way in which we and the Germans turned up on to more or less parallel courses and waited for the range to close sufficiently before letting fly at each other. It all seemed very cold-blooded and mechanical, no chance here of seeing red, merely a case of cool scientific calculation and deliberate gunfire. Everyone seemed cool enough, too, in the control position, all sitting quietly at their instruments waiting for the fight to commence.

At 3.40 *New Zealand* and *Indefatigable* were ordered to take station astern of our 1st B.C.S., which were on our starboard beam, and this increased the range, which at 3.48 was again 23,000 yards. At 3.53 the leading enemy battle cruiser opened fire, and a second or two later the *Lion*'s opening salvo was fired. *New Zealand* was still outside range, but at 3.57 we opened fire on the fourth ship in the enemy's line (? *Moltke*), which for some reason had her second funnel painted bright red, a great blessing, as it made her very easy to distinguish from the other enemy ships.

Shortly after opening fire the *Indefatigable*, our next astern, blew up and sank. An Assistant Paymaster, who was keeping a record of the action immediately behind me, said '*Indefatigable*— hit'; he was going to say 'sunk,' but thought it might rattle the control party.

The Captain then passed the order to engage the rear ship of the enemy's line, which we did, straddling her at once. Hits at this time were observed on both fourth and fifth ships.

At 4.22 the 5th ship was obscured by mist, and fire was shifted to the 4th ship, which was straddled almost at once, and hits were again observed. At about this time 'X' turret was hit by a heavy shell, but I knew nothing of this till later, when, during a lull, I had a telephone message from the Officer of the Turret, reporting that 'His turret had been hit by a very large brick; he thought he was dead; found he was not; and was carrying on!'

---

3 Bearing Red 25=25 degrees from right ahead on the port (left) side. Red 90 is exactly on the port beam. Green 90 on the starboard beam.

New Zealand passing last explosion of *Queen Mary*.

At about 4.35 the stern of a ship projecting about 70 feet out of the water, with the propellers revolving slowly, drifted into the field of my glasses; clouds of white paper were blowing out of the after-hatch, and on her stern I read *Queen Mary*. She passed us about 100 yards on our port beam, and a moment later there was a blinding flash, a dull heavy roar, which ceased as suddenly as it began, followed by a few seconds' silence, and then the patter of falling débris. All that was left of the *Queen Mary* was a great mushroom-shaped cloud of smoke about 600 to 800 feet high, which temporarily obscured our view of the enemy, but a few seconds later we drew clear, re-sighted the enemy, and opened fire again.

I was surprised to find that in addition to being able to follow the flight of one's own projectiles with spotting glasses, the enemy's projectiles also appeared as dots getting larger and larger, till they burst short or droned past and fell beyond us. They always seemed to be coming straight for one's eye. Ricochets were also clearly visible, turning end over end, and making a noise like the rumbling of a distant train.

A few minutes after the loss of the *Queen Mary*, the *Champion*[4] reported the enemy's Battle Fleet in sight, and at 4.45 we increased to 27 knots, and ourselves sighted the High Sea Fleet on the port bow. The battle cruisers now altered course 16 points to starboard in succession, and the enemy battle cruisers altered to a course about parallel to ours, which, as both turns were outwards, increased the range, necessitating us ceasing fire for a few minutes whilst our guns were out of range. During this time we were under the fire of German battle cruisers and of the van of the German Battle Fleet.

The 5th B.S. held on longer than the battle cruisers, and finally turned up on our starboard quarter, where they now took the brunt of the action, coming under very heavy fire from German battle cruisers and Battle Fleet.

At 4.50 we re-engaged on a battle cruiser, but for the next 20 minutes fire was intermittent as the enemy ships appeared and disappeared in the mist and smoke of battle. I particularly remember one of the *Kaiser*-class battleships appearing suddenly in strong silhouette, a magnificent target which I think several ships took advantage of, as she was practically the only heavy ship clearly visible at the time.

At 5.15 the enemy were out of range, and fire was checked.

At 5.46 fire was once more opened on a battle cruiser; two were in sight, and we engaged the second. This was probably the time when the Paymaster, who had come on deck for some fresh air and a look round, lost his trousers. He was standing on the fore superstructure when 'P' turret opened fire, and deprived him by its blast of his very necessary garment. Decency demanded an immediate retreat. . . .

From here the account is written by the Navigating Officer of H.M.S. *New Zealand.* By virtue of his station and his duties during action, a Navigating Officer is usually better able to observe the movements of the rest of his own Squadron than is a Gunnery Officer aloft, who is fully occupied the whole time in observing the enemy and controlling the gunnery of his ship. This account gives a full description

4 It was the *Southampton* which made this report.—*Ed.*

of the loss of *Indefatigable* and *Queen Mary*, as seen from H.M.S. *New Zealand*. H.M.S. *Indefatigible* was next ship astern of *New Zealand*, and H.M.S. *Queen Mary* next ship but one ahead. The distance apart of ships in the line is, as nearly as ships are able to maintain it, 500 yards.

Narrative by the Navigating Officer of H.M.S. *New Zealand*

My action station was in the conning tower, together with the Torpedo Officer, the Assistant Navigating Officer, the Admiral's Secretary, Chief Petty Officer Fitzgerald, the Chief Quartermaster, and several seamen ratings tending the voice pipes, etc. Admiral Pakenham, with his Flag-Lieutenant, was on the upper bridge, where they remained throughout the action, together with our Captain, Capt. John Green, who was wearing the Maori rush kilt or war mat, called a piu-piu, which had been given to the ship by a Maori Chief in the ship's cruise round the world in 1913-14, with the injunction that it was always to be worn by the Captain of the *New Zealand* when in action.[5]

---

5 With the gift was made a prophecy that the ship would one day be in action and would be hit in three places—on the after turret, on the fore top, and on the conning tower—but that the casualties would not be serious. At Jutland we were hit only on the after turret, and there were no casualties.

We had told the Maori chief at the time of the prophecy that what he said might come true, but that it was of no personal interest to the officers and men then in the ship, as on 1st September, 1914, we were due to pay off and a completely new set of officers and men would join the *New Zealand*. But the Maori chief was emphatic that it was the *same* officers and men who would be in the ship at the action, and he turned out to be right, for the outbreak of war stopped the ship from paying off, and many of the officers and men in her in 1913 were still in her at Jutland and later.

The rush kilt which the captain wore is made of strips of flax woven together at the top and is worn tied round the waist. The strips reach down to the knee and at intervals are dyed black, giving the appearance of a black and white kilt. A green-stone 'tiki' was also given with the kilt, and this was worn round the neck on a string of flax. Much faith was put in these mascots by the seamen, and I am sure that the word was passed round before the action began that the 'skipper' was wearing the piu-piu and tiki all right. Over a year later, on the last occasion that we sighted enemy ships during the war, on 21st (?) November, 1917, there was rather an amusing example of their faith in the mascots. Early in the morning some German light cruisers were sighted and engaged by our light cruisers, and in the *New Zealand* we went to action stations. The Admiral, the Captain (now Captain Webb), and myself were all on the upper bridge when I saw a sailor come up the ladder, peep round the corner and then disappear again.

'It's all right, he's got it on,' I heard him tell several men on the lower bridge, from which I understood that he was a scout sent out when there was a possibility of an action to make sure that the Captain actually was wearing the piu-piu and the tiki!

Shortly after receiving from one of our light cruisers a report of heavy smoke having been sighted to the East and Northeastward, the enemy became visible to us, steaming to the northward in line ahead, consisting of five German battle cruisers with various light cruisers and destroyers. A signal from *Lion* ordered us to take station astern of *Tiger*, the fourth ship of the line.

Our battle cruisers were now in single line, and Admiral Beatty led us round to a south-easterly course to get between the enemy and his base. The enemy battle cruisers had also altered their course to S.E., and were steaming at full speed. At about 3.50 the action was commenced by both sides opening fire almost simultaneously. We had only been in action a few minutes, when the Admiral's Secretary came across to where the Torpedo Officer was stationed in the conning tower and drew his attention to the *Indefatigable*. He crossed at once to the starboard side and laid his glasses on her. She had been hit aft, apparently by the mainmast, and a good deal of smoke was coming from her superstructure aft, but there were no flames visible. He thought it was only her boom boats burning. We were altering course to port at the time, and apparently her steering gear was damaged, as she did not follow round in our wake, but held on until she was about 500 yards on our starboard quarter, in full view from the conning tower. Whilst he was still looking at her through his glasses she was hit by two shells, one on the foc'sle and one on the fore turret. Both shells

The sinking of the *Indefatigable*.

appeared to explode on impact. Then there was an interval of about 30 seconds, during which there was absolutely no sign of fire or flame or smoke, except the little actually formed by the burst of the two shells, which was not considerable. At the end of the interval of about 30 seconds the ship completely blew up, commencing apparently from for'ard. The main explosion started with sheets of flame, followed immediately afterwards by a dense, dark smoke which obscured the ship from view. All sorts of stuff was blown high into the air, a 50-foot steam picket boat, for example, being blown up about 200 feet, apparently intact, though upside down.

The loss of our next astern happened so suddenly that, almost before we realised she had gone, our attention was entirely absorbed in the very fierce battle that was now progressing. The noise of our own salvoes, and the shrieking of the enemy's shells falling over or short, and throwing up great sheets of spray, left one with little time to think of anything except the work in hand. I personally was fully occupied in keeping station on our next ahead together with plotting our position on the chart, for we were being led by the Flagship along a snake-like course, to reduce the chances of being hit. The

New Zealand   *Indefatigable* explosion

Indefatigable blowing up.

enemy could be seen on our port beam at a range of about 16,000 yards, but the damage that we were inflicting on them could not be made out at this distance. For the next half-hour the battle continued on a south-easterly course, the German fire steadily growing less accurate and at times becoming quite wild, whilst we were maintaining a steady flow of salvoes.

All seemed to be going well with us, when suddenly I saw a salvo hit *Queen Mary* on her port side. A small cloud of what looked like coal-dust came out from where she was hit, but nothing more until several moments later, when a terrific yellow flame with a heavy and very dense mass of black smoke showed ahead, and the *Queen Mary*

herself was no longer visible. The *Tiger* was steaming at 24 knots
only 500 yards astern of *Queen Mary*, and hauled sharply out of the
line to port and disappeared in this dense mass of smoke. We hauled
out to starboard, and *Tiger* and ourselves passed one on each side of
the *Queen Mary*. We passed her about 50 yards on our port beam, by
which time the smoke had blown fairly clear, revealing the stem from
the after funnel aft afloat, and the propellers still revolving, but the
for'ard part had already gone under. There was no sign of fire or of
cordite flame, and men were crawling out of the top of the after turret and up the after hatchway. When we were abreast and only about
150 yards away from her, this after portion rolled over and as it did
so, blew up. The most noticeable thing was the masses and masses of
paper which were blown into the air as this after portion exploded.
Great masses of iron were thrown into the air, and things were falling
into the sea round us. There was still up in the air, I suppose at least
100 or 200 feet high, a boat which may have been a dinghy or a pin-
nace, still intact but upside down as I could see the thwarts. Before
we had quite passed, *Queen Mary* completely disappeared.

This second disaster was rather stunning, but the only sign from
the Flagship was a signal, 'Battle cruisers alter course two points to
port' —*i.e.*, towards the enemy.

The four of us now remaining continued to fire steady salvoes,
and the enemy did not appear to be able to take advantage of their
success. The spirits of our men were splendid. In spite of the fact
that they had all plainly seen the *Queen Mary* blow up, the idea of
defeat did not seem to enter their heads.

This narrative is broken here to insert *Tiger*'s description of
the loss of H.M.S. *Queen Mary*, and then a narrative of a survivor of the *Queen Mary*. It is continued on p. 51.

Loss of the *Indefatigable* and *Queen Mary*
(As seen from the Conning Tower of H.M.S. *Tiger*)

My station was in the Conning Tower, and I remember thinking
how splendid the enemy battle cruisers looked when they turned to

Queen Mary   Princess Royal   Lion

Queen Mary. Photo taken from *Tiger* about two hours before the action.

Commencement of the action as seen from *Champion*
British Battle Cruisers are behind the smoke.

41

the southward, their last ship in particular showing up wonderfully.

Both squadrons opened fire almost together, the Germans appearing to fire in ripples down their line starting from their leading ship. Their first salvo at us was about 200 yards short, and the next straddled us—one shot short, two hits (aft), and one over, the two hits temporarily knocking out 'Q' and 'X' turrets.

The next thing I remember distinctly is the Signal Boatswain reporting that the *Indefatigable* was hauling out of the line. I watched her, and thought that she must have been badly hit, as she had a list to port and thick smoke was coming from her quarter deck. A few minutes afterwards the Signal Boatswain reported that she had gone. I looked again, and all I could see was a thick cloud of smoke where she had been.

The German shooting at this time was very good, and we were repeatedly straddled, but funnily enough were not being hit very often. I remember watching the shell coming at us. They appeared just like big bluebottles flying straight towards you, each time going to hit you in the eye; then they would fall, and the shell would either burst or else ricochet off the water and lollop away above and beyond you, turning over and over in the air.

The *Queen Mary* was next ahead of us, and I remember watching her for a little, and saw one salvo straddle her. Three shells out of four hit, and the impression one got of seeing the splinters fly and the dull red burst was as if no damage was being done, but that the armour was keeping the shell out. The next salvo that I saw straddled her, and two more shells hit her. As they hit, I saw a dull red glow amidships, and then the ship seemed to open out like a puff ball, or one of those toadstool things when one squeezes it. Then there was another dull red glow somewhere forward, and the whole ship seemed to collapse inwards. The funnels and masts fell into the middle, and the hull was blown outwards. The roofs of the turrets were blown 100 feet high, then everything was smoke, and a bit of the stern was the only part of the ship left above water. The *Tiger* put her helm hard-a-starboard, and we just cleared the remains of the *Queen Mary*'s stern by a few feet.

On coming out of the smoke of the explosion, we went on to full speed and got into station astern of the *Princess Royal*. I noticed about this time that the shooting of the Germans was getting steadily worse, and I put it down to their being badly hit by our

42

squadron, because we saw several fires on board their ships, and one ship hauled out of line, due either to shell fire or else to a torpedo hit. Out destroyers had just attacked them with torpedoes.

A Survivor of H.M.S. *Queen Mary*

Narrative of Petty Officer (Gunner's Mate), E. Francis, of 'X' Turret, H.M.S. *Queen Mary*[6]

This represents a copy of a letter I sent to the Senior Surviving Officer of H.M.S. *Queen Mary*, and I am asking that whoever reads this at any time will please remember that the writer is much handier behind a pair of 13.5-inch turret guns than behind a pen.

I had the first dog watch (4.0 to 6.0 p.m.), in the battery so I made arrangements with the Gunner's Mate on watch to send a man down and let me know when it was 3.30 p.m. We lay down and had quite a comfortable sleep, having nothing on our mind to keep us awake.

At 3.30 an able seaman came down and said, 'Petty Officer Francis, it is nearly seven bells.' I thanked him, and said, 'Anything doing up top?' He said 'No.' I got up, took off my jumper, and had a wash in a bucket of water, and just as I had finished I heard in the distance a bugle sound of 'Action.' I was so surprised that I could hardly believe my ears, but the rush of feet by the door forced it upon me. I took the first hatchway up, and came up to the foremost 4-inch battery, starboard side, and raced for 'X' turret. When I got inside everyone was there. I yelled out 'Turret's crew, number.' They were correct from top to bottom, and I reported to the Lieutenant of the Turret. He said 'Test loading gear, but for goodness' sake don't let them go too rash.' The loading gear and machinery were tested, and immediately afterwards came the order to load all cages. As soon as the cages were loaded, it was reported to the Transmitting Station, and then came the order to load; the guns were loaded and brought to the half-cock and reported, and then came the order to bring the right gun to the ready, director laying and firing. Shortly after this the first salvo was fired, and we had started on the great game.

---

6 The Editors feel it their duty to point out that this narrative is not accurate in several of its statements about the action, such as the number of German ships in sight, etc.

I had no means of telling what the time was, and if I had I probably should not have looked, because getting a turret started is an anxious rushing time for a Captain of a turret; once started it is easy to keep going. Taking everything into consideration, I put it as about 3.45 or 3.55; that's as near as I can go.

The gun's crew were absolutely perfect, inclined to be a little swift in loading, but I gave them a yell and pointed out to them that I wanted a steady stride, and after that everything went like clockwork, until suddenly both rammers gave out, my gun going first. This was caused through No. 3 opening the breech before the gun had run out after firing; the carrier arm part of the breech must have hit the rammer head and slightly metal-bound it. I dropped the elevating wheel, got hold of a steel pinch bar, forced the end in behind the rammer head, at the same time putting the rammer lever over to 'Run out'; out went the rammer, and I rushed it back again, and then out again, and it went all gay once more. Then the lever was passed over to the right gun, and both rammers were once more in working order. I was pleased to get them going again, as it would have been such a damper on the crew if we had to go into hand loading.

My No. 3 said, 'Petty Officer Francis, can you see what we are up against?' Well, I had been anxious to have a look, but could not spare the time, but as soon as my gun had fired and while the loading was being completed I had a quick look through the periscope, and it seemed to me there were hundreds of masts and funnels.[7] I dropped back into my seat and laid my gun by pointer, being in director firing, and while the loading was being completed again I told them there were a few battle cruisers out, not wishing to put a damper on them in any way; not that I think it would have done so, as they were all splendid fellows and backed me up magnificently.

Up till now I had not noticed any noise, such as being struck by a shell, but soon afterwards there was a heavy blow struck, I should imagine, in the after 4-inch battery, and a lot of dust and pieces were flying around on top of 'X' turret. My attention was called by the turret trainer, A.B. Long, who reported the front glass of his periscope blocked up. This was not very important, because we were in director training,[8] but someone in rear heard him report his glass

---

7 This is an exaggeration.—*Ed.*

8 In Director firing the turret gunlayers and trainers follow pointers worked from a master position and do not have to look out through their glass at the enemy at all. The master position also fires the guns when the turret's crew have brought them to the 'ready.'

A salvo short of *Lion*   *Queen Mary* blowing up

Composite photo, roughly to scale, showing great size of smoke cloud of *Queen Mary* explosion.

foul, and without orders dashed on top and cleared it. He must have been smashed as he did it, for he fell in front of the periscope, groaning, and then apparently fell off the turret. I wish I knew his name, poor chap, but it's no use guessing. Another shock was felt shortly after this, but it did not affect the turret, so no notice was taken. The Transmitting Station reported that the third ship of the line was dropping out. First blood to *Queen Mary*. The shout they gave was good to hear. I could not resist taking a quick look at her at their request, and I saw the third ship of their line was going down by the bows. I felt the turret training a bit faster than she had been and surmised we must have shifted on to the fourth ship of the line; being in director firing no orders were required for training. I looked again, and the third ship of the line was gone. I turned to the spare gunlayer, P.O. Killick, who was recording the number of rounds fired, and asked him how many rounds the left gun had fired, and he said 30 something odd figures, I didn't catch the exact number. A few more rounds were fired, and I took another look through my periscope, and there was quite a fair distance between the second ship, and what I believe was the fourth ship, due, I think, to the third ship going under. Flames were belching up from what I believe to be the fourth ship of the line.

Then came the big explosion, which shook us a bit, and on looking at the pressure gauge I saw the pressure had failed.

Immediately after that came what I term the big smash, and I was dangling in the air on a bowline, which saved me from being thrown down onto the floor of the turret; these bowlines were an idea I had brought into the turret, and each man in the gun-house was supplied with one, and, as far as I noticed, the men who had them on were not injured in the big smash. Nos. 2 and 3 of the left gun slipped down under the gun, and the gun appeared to me to have fallen through its trunnions and smashed up these two numbers. Everything in the ship went as quiet as a church, the floor of the turret was bulged up, and the guns were absolutely useless. I must mention here that there was not a sign of excitement. One man turned, to me and said, 'What do you think has happened?' I said 'Steady every one, I will speak to Mr. Ewart.' I went back to the cabinet and said, 'What do you think has happened, sir?' He said 'God only knows.' 'Well, sir,' I said, 'it's no use keeping them all down here, why not send them up round the 4-inch guns, and give them a chance to fight it out. As soon as the Germans find we are out of action they will concentrate on us, and we shall all be going sky high.' He said, 'Yes, good idea. Just see whether the 4-inch guns aft are still standing.'

I put my head up through the hole in the roof of the turret, and I nearly fell back through again. The after 4-inch battery was smashed right out of all recognition, and then I noticed the ship had an awful list to port. I dropped back inside the turret and told Lieut. Ewart the state of affairs. He said, 'Francis, we can do no more than give them a chance; clear the turret.' 'Clear the turret,' I called out, and out they all went.

P.O. Stares was the last I saw coming up from the working chamber, and I asked whether he had passed the order to the magazine and shell room, and he told me it was no use, as the water was right up the trunk leading from the shell room, so the bottom of the ship must have been out of her. Then I said, 'Why didn't you come up?' He simply said, 'There was no order to leave the turret.'

I went through the cabinet and out through the top with the Lieutenant of the Turret following me; suddenly he stopped and went back into the turret. I believe he went back because he thought there was someone left inside. It makes me feel sore-hearted when I think of him and that fine crowd who were with me in the turret. I can only write about the splendid behaviour of my own turret's crew, but I am confident, knowing the *Queen Mary* as I did, that the highest traditions of the service were upheld by the remainder of the ship's company, from the Captain down to the youngest boy. Everyone was so keen on being in a big fight, and each member of our ship's company knew he was one of the small cog-wheels of a great machine; it was part of a man's training as laid down by our Gunnery Commander, and due to his untiring efforts to make the *Queen Mary* the splendid fighting unit I knew her to be.

I was half-way down the ladder at the back of the turret when Lieutenant Ewart went back; the ship had an awful list to port by this time, so much so that men getting off the ladder went sliding down to port. I got on to the bottom rung of the ladder, but could not by my own efforts reach the stanchions lying on the deck from the starboard side. I knew if I let go that I should go sliding down to port like some of the others must have done, and probably get smashed up sliding down. Two of my turret's crew, seeing my difficulty, came to my assistance; they were A.B. Long, turret trainer, and A.B. Lane, No. 4 of the left gun. Lane held Long at full stretch from the ship's side, and I dropped from the ladder, caught Long's legs, and so gained the starboard side. These two men had no thought for their own safety; they saw I wanted assistance, and that was good enough for them. When I got on to the ship's side there seemed to be quite a fair crowd, and they did not appear to be very anxious to take to the water. I called out to them, 'Come on, you chaps, who's coming for a swim?' Someone answered, 'She will float for a long time yet,' but something, I don't pretend to understand what it was, seemed to be urging me to get away, so I clambered up over the slimy bilge keel and fell off into the water, followed, I should think, by about five other men.

I struck away from the ship as hard as I could, and must have covered nearly 50 yards, when there was a big smash, and stopping and looking round the air seemed to be full of fragments and flying pieces. A large piece seemed to be right above my head, and acting on an impulse I dipped under to avoid being struck, and stayed under as long as I could, and then, came to the top again, and coming behind me I heard a rush of water, which looked very much like a surf breaking on a beach, and I realised it was the suction or backwash from the ship which had just gone. I hardly had time to fill my lungs with air when it was on me; I felt it was no use struggling against it, so I let myself go for a moment or two, then I struck out, but I felt it was a losing game, and remarked to myself mentally,

'What's the use of you struggling, you're done,' and actually eased my efforts to reach the top, when a small voice seemed to say 'Dig out.'

I started afresh, and something bumped against me. I grasped it, and afterwards found it was a large hammock; it undoubtedly pulled me to the top, more dead than alive, and I rested on it, but I felt I was getting very weak, and roused myself sufficiently to look around for something more substantial to support me. Floating right in front of me was a piece of timber (I believe the centre baulk of our pattern 4 target). I managed to push myself on the hammock close to the timber, and grasped a piece of rope hanging over the side. My next difficulty was to get on top, and I was beginning to give up hope, when the swell lifted me nearly on top, and with a small amount of exertion I kept on. I managed to reeve my arms through a strop, and then I must have become unconscious.

When I came to my senses again I was half-way off the spar, but managed to get back again. I was very sick, and seemed to be full up with oil fuel. My eyes were blocked up completely with it, and I could not see; I suppose the oil had got a bit dry and crusted. I managed, by turning back the sleeve of my jersey which was thick with oil, to expose a part of the sleeve of my flannel, and thus managed to get the thick oil off my face and eyes, which were aching awfully. Then I looked around, and seeing no one else, believed I was the only one left out of that fine ship's company. What had really happened was the *Laurel* had come up and picked up the remainder, and not seeing me lying on the spar had gone away out of the zone of fire, so how long I was in the water I do not know.

I was miserably cold, but not without hope of being picked up, as it seemed to me that I had only got to keep quiet and a ship would come for me.

After what seemed ages to me some destroyers came racing along, and I got up on the spar, steadied myself for a second, and waved my arms. The *Petard*, one of our destroyers, saw me and came over, but when I got up on the spar to wave to them the swell rolled the spar over, and I fell off. I was nearly exhausted again getting back. The destroyer came up and a line was thrown to me, which, needless to say, I grabbed hold of for all I was worth, and was quickly hauled up on to the decks of the destroyer. The first words I heard spoken were English, not German, and I must have managed to convince them that I was English. I remembered no more until I came to and found I was lying on what seemed to be leather settee, and someone was telling me that I was all right and not to struggle.

I could not see the faces round me, so concluded I was blind, but did not feel then that it mattered much; my thoughts flew to the fine crowd who had gone under. I cannot speak too highly of the way I was cared for on board the *Petard*, and I thank them one and all.

I was given some spirits of some sort, and then must have gone to sleep; someone came over to me and said, 'Don't get excited if you hear any shooting, but we are going to carry out an attack on a big German.' I wasn't in a fit state to worry much about attacks on Germans.

My eyes were very painful, and I must have said something about them, for I believe a young doctor came down and started to bathe them, when suddenly there was a big smash, and I was told afterwards that a shell came through, killed the doctor and eight men, and I never received a scratch. I couldn't see, and, being a gunnery man, I took the smash to be a 4-inch gun being fired; I had no idea it was a German shell.[9]

I must have gone off to sleep again, when I was wakened by some of the chaps who were taking me down to the Petty Officers' quarters, as by this time they had found out I was a Gunner's Mate. I believe in the first place I told them I was a Stoker.

Nothing happened after this of any importance, only I was in awful agony with my eyes. I was told we were steaming at greatly reduced speed to Rosyth, and arrived, as near as I can guess, about midnight on the 1st June. The Hospital Boat came over, and I was very quickly taken to Queensferry Hospital, where I was soon made nice and comfortable in bed, feeling that my troubles were over, and thanking God, Who I feel was very near me on that great day, and Who pulled me through. I fell asleep and woke up to find the doctor waiting to clean my eyes; he would not disturb me before.

After my eyes had been seen to I felt much relieved; the doctor told me to keep the bandage on and my eyes would be all right again soon. I left the Hospital on the Monday (June 5th), having previously on two days running asked the Fleet Surgeon to let me go south; I felt the groans of the burnt and wounded would have driven me mad. He told me that if I could get some clothes I could go. I met a Ward Master whom I had known some years ago, and he

9 See H.M.S. *Petard*'s narrative, page 56.

fitted me out with clothes gathered from the Hospital Staff, and made me look quite presentable. I left Edinburgh by the midnight train, and on arrival at London went to the Union Jack Club, where I had a good breakfast. I left London and arrived at the Royal Naval Barracks, Portsmouth, where I reported myself, and was allowed to proceed home. The next day I was given some clothes, and saw the doctor who advised me what to do about my eyes, and very kindly allowed me to go home on 14 days' leave. When I returned off leave I saw the doctor again, and he said, 'Your nerves are gone, you want a rest,' and sent me home for another 14 days. When I returned off leave I was feeling much better, and my eyes were nearly quite well again.

Piece of armour plate punched out by shell hitting *New Zealand*.

At the time of writing they are all right, but tire very quickly.

To finish my account, I will say that I believe the cause of the ship being blown up was a shell striking 'B' turret working chamber and igniting the shells stowed there in the ready racks, and the flash must have passed down into the magazine, and that was the finish.

Continuation of Narrative of the Navigating Officer of H.M.S. *New Zealand*

About fifteen minutes after the loss of the *Queen Mary* we saw on our port bow the German Battle Fleet coming to the rescue of their battle cruisers, and an imposing sight they looked, ship after ship in single line melting away into the haze, all showing up white, lit by the sun. Their arrival put a different complexion on the fight, and at the decided moment the *Lion* led us round on to the opposite course, and we proceeded to the north keeping at long range from the German Battle Fleet, but still continuing our fight with the German battle cruisers, which also turned to the north.

Soon afterwards, at about 4.55, the Fifth Battle Squadron, consisting of four *Queen Elizabeth* class battleships under Rear-Admiral Evan Thomas, came up to us and passed us, still steering to the south towards the enemy. Then they turned up and formed astern of us and engaged the van of the High Seas Fleet, drawing most of the fire off us on to themselves. They looked very fine as they came down past us steaming at high speed, their turrets all trained towards the enemy, and their guns cocked high up, firing strongly. Apparently our Squadron also looked pretty fit still, for one of the Navigating Officers of the 5th B.S. said to me after the action, 'The battle cruisers were a splendid sight as we passed them, firing fast and furiously, in perfect station with the blank spaces of *Queen Mary* and *Indefatigable* filled up, and seemed to be as full of fight as ever.'

We reduced speed now until we were steaming at practically the same speed as the enemy Battle Fleet, keeping at their extreme range, so that they could not properly engage us but were being enticed on to chase us to the north, until eventually we could hand them over to the Grand Fleet. This was a most interesting phase of the battle. Could we keep them following us long enough, and could we avoid being hit? We had always to think that a ship damaged enough to lose only a few knots speed would be as good as lost, for she would drop behind into the open arms of the whole German Battle Fleet. But the risk of thus drawing the enemy after us and the purpose of it were both plain to us all. The Admiral kept on asking me, 'How far off are the Grand Fleet now?' to which I would reply '60 miles'; then a little later '40 miles'; then '30' —'20'—'10.' Every

15 minutes the distance was decreasing about 10 miles, for as the Grand Fleet were coming South at about 20 knots and we were going North at about the same speed, we were closing each other about two miles every three minutes.

From 4.50 to about 5 or 5.15 we were pretty closely engaged, and the position of the *New Zealand*, now the rear of the four surviving battle cruisers, was not a very pleasant one. We felt any small hit in the engine room would cause us at once to drop astern and we should lose the ship, and during this run to the north we seemed to be more heavily fired at than were our consorts ahead.

CHAPTER III

DESTROYERS WITH THE BATTLE CRUISER FORCE

4.15 p.m. to about 5.30 p.m.

During the run to the South the 2nd L.C.S. and the destroyers attached to the Battle Cruiser Force had taken station ahead of the *Lion*, with the exception of a few of those destroyers which had not sufficient speed to gain on the battle cruisers and were left steaming abreast of them, where, incidentally, they acted as a submarine screen.

The destroyers of the 13th Flotilla were under the command of Captain (D) J. U. Farie, of H.M.S. *Champion*, and halfway through the run to the South this flotilla was ordered to make a torpedo attack upon the enemy battle cruisers. The initiation of this movement is described in Admiral Beatty's despatch, as follows:—

'Eight destroyers of the 13th Flotilla, *Nestor, Nomad, Nicator, Narborough, Pelican, Petard, Obdurate, Nerissa*, with *Moorsom* and *Morris* of 10th Flotilla, *Turbulent* and *Termagant* of the 9th Flotilla, having been ordered to attack the enemy with torpedoes when opportunity offered, moved out at 4.15 p.m. simultaneously with a similar movement on the part of the enemy. The attack was carried out in the most gallant manner, and with great determination.'[1]

It was carried out at high speed, as torpedo attacks always are, in order to lessen the time during which the flotilla was under close enemy gunfire. A position somewhere on the enemy's bow about four to five miles from them, was the goal of the flotilla, from where they could fire their torpedoes with good prospects of success. On being ordered to commence the

---

1 V. A., B. C. F.'s Despatch : Enclosure to Commander-in-Chief's Despatch.

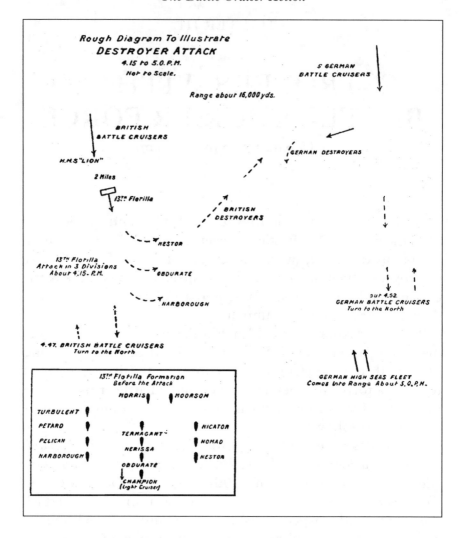

Rough Diagram To Illustrate
DESTROYER ATTACK
4.15 to 5.0.P.M.
Not to Scale.

Range about 16,000 yds.

5 GERMAN
BATTLE CRUISERS

BRITISH
BATTLE CRUISERS

H.M.S "LION"

GERMAN DESTROYERS

2 Miles

13TH Flotilla

BRITISH
DESTROYERS

NESTOR

13TH Flotilla
Attack in 3 Divisions
About 4.15. P.M.

OBDURATE

our 4.52.
GERMAN BATTLE CRUISERS
Turn to the North

NARBOROUGH

4.47. BRITISH BATTLE CRUISERS
Turn to the North

GERMAN HIGH SEAS FLEET
Comes Into Range About 5.0.P.M.

13TH Flotilla Formation
Before the Attack

MORRIS   MOORSOM

TURBULENT

PETARD   NICATOR

PELICAN   TERMAGANT   NOMAD

NARBOROUGH   NERISSA   NESTOR

OBDURATE

CHAMPION
(Light Cruiser)

54

attack they steamed ahead of the *Lion* for some little distance, and then turned sharply towards the enemy, *Nestor*'s Division leading, then *Obdurate*'s, then *Narborough*'s, and on courses roughly between east and north-east crossed the intervening space between our Battle Cruiser Line and their goal.

As our destroyers showed their intention to attack, a German Destroyer Flotilla was sent out to prevent them, and the rival destroyers met in the 'No Man's Land' and engaged each other with gunfire, the Germans apparently turning from a westerly course on to a south-westerly course, so passing our flotillas on opposite courses as we held to the northeast. The fight was not closely held by the Germans. They quickly passed, almost flashed by, and allowed our destroyers to reach their objective and fire torpedoes at the enemy battle cruisers without serious interference.

A picture of the return of some of our boats as noticed by an Officer of H.M.S. *Badger*, which was acting as submarine screen to the battle cruisers, was described in these words:—

'Another thing that caught my eye was a flotilla of our destroyers returning from a torpedo attack, led by a light cruiser, going "full out" for safety to the disengaged side of our big ships. They were closing diagonally the wake of our battle cruisers, which were on a north-westerly course. The enemy were firing accurately into the midst of this flotilla, as one might loose off a shotgun into a flight of starlings, but not one of our boats were hit, although projectiles were falling thick in the midst of them.'

But whilst the attack was in progress and the British destroyers were disputing with the German destroyers for local 'command of the sea', the German Battle Fleet arrived all unexpectedly into range from the southward, and unfortunately were so placed that they could finish off two of our destroyers which had been damaged in the fighting. *Nestor* and *Nomad* were sunk, though not before they had deliberately closed on the German Battle Fleet, together with *Nicator* and *Moorsom*, and fired their remaining torpedoes at the German Battle Line—an even more important torpedo target than the German battle cruisers.

The experiences of these attacks and of the destroyer fighting in between the Battle Cruiser Lines are contained in the following narratives from H.M.S. *Petard, Moorsom, Nicator, Nestor*, and *Nomad*. This brief description of *Nestor*'s Division attacking is taken from the narrative of H.M.S. *Galatea*, at that time stationed to the northward of our Battle Cruiser Line:

'One outstanding incident was a torpedo attack by three or four destroyers of the 13th Flotilla on the German Lines, led by Commander Bingham in the *Nestor*. *Nestor* and *Nomad* were disabled and later sunk, but the other two destroyers got away, and their escape was most spectacular. They appeared directly astern of us out of a thick cloud of funnel smoke which they were making to screen themselves, zigzagging like a couple of snipe, at times their high white bow wave the only part of them visible, and a tornado of shells were falling all round them. Apparently they would watch the flash from the ships firing at them and then put their helms over, and the place where they had been a moment before, still barely a ship's length from them, would be lashed and torn into tall pillars of water. It seemed impossible that they could escape as time after time they were obliterated from sight by salvoes, but presently their bow waves would appear again and they would emerge, only to be blotted out once more a moment later. It was a thrilling sight, and we afterwards discovered that these two destroyers got safely away.'

H.M.S *Petard* of 13th Destroyer Flotilla.

Shortly after the enemy battle cruisers were sighted, the 13th Flotilla were ordered by *Lion* to take station ahead and we proceeded to form on H.M.S. *Champion*, which took station about two miles directly ahead of *Lion*, and the flotilla formed up in three divisions in line ahead disposed abeam, astern of her.

Shortly after this the battle cruisers opened fire, and as we were directly ahead of *Lion*, we had a good view. From what I remember, the Germans straddled the *Lion* with their third salvo, and at the

A division of destroyers awaiting the order to attack.

same time I had the idea that our ships appeared to be shooting short. I was watching the *Lion* at this time, and I can remember one salvo straddling her completely; all that we could see was about twenty feet of the stem and the remainder of the ship was completely covered in spray. As the spray dropped the ship gradually came into view, but nothing seemed wrong except that there appeared to be a fire in the superstructure amidships. Shortly afterwards there was a huge explosion directly astern of *Lion*: a huge sheet of red flame which rose high in the air, gradually opening out as it rose, and I saw a large piece of metal about the size of the top of a turret go turning over and over in the air, away on the starboard side of the battle cruiser line. This must have been the explosion of *Queen Mary*.

Soon after this *Champion* ordered *Nestor*'s Division to attack the enemy with torpedoes, and I watched them turn away to port and close the enemy; then *Obdurate*'s Division followed, and shortly afterwards my Division, which was led by *Narborough*.

Petard was the third ship in the division but had become separated from the other two by H.M.S. *Nottingham* passing through the flotilla to rejoin the 2nd L.C.S., so with *Turbulent* I followed after *Obdurate*'s Division. As we steamed over towards the German line I noticed that the German Destroyer Flotilla were carrying out a similar movement towards our line; and the two flotillas appeared to more or less form into two single lines on nearly opposite courses to the battle cruisers, with the leading destroyers of each line fairly close together, and the distance apart gradually increasing the further one was stationed down the line. We opened fire on what seemed to be our opposite number at about 6,000 yards' range, and rapidly closed to about 3,000 yards. I cannot say I remember much about our shooting or about the German shooting, as I was fully occupied with handling the ship, but I remember our steaming light falling down with a crash from aloft when the halliards had been cut through by a shell. At this time Mr. Epworth, my torpedo gunner, fired a torpedo, which was set to run 6 feet deep, high-speed setting, at a bunch of four German destroyers which were close together, and the tubes' crews state they shortly afterwards noticed a very large explosion in the after part of one of them, which I hope was caused by this torpedo. Almost immediately after this we fired another torpedo at about 9,000 yards' range at the German Battle Cruiser Line, and then turned to starboard to a slightly converging, but nearly parallel, course to the German battle cruisers. We steamed ahead a little, and when about four points on their bow fired the remaining two torpedoes. By this time the German destroyers seemed to have disappeared, leaving two of their number behind, so that after firing our last torpedo we fired two or three salvoes at a German light cruiser which had closed, apparently to assist his destroyers.

Having now fired all my torpedoes, I turned towards our Battle Cruiser Line, which had by this time turned north, and was steaming towards them when we came across *Nestor*, which was also steaming in the same direction but at a reduced speed. I eased down near her and steamed alongside her for a few moments; she had obviously been hit, but there did not seem to be anything I could do for her then. About this time I caught my first sight of the German Battle Fleet coming up, bearing about south-east from us, and I can remember a long line of grey ships.

After leaving *Nestor*, we came across a huge patch of oil fuel on the sea, and H.M.S. *Landrail*[2] stopped near by with a whaler down picking up men. We also stopped on the edge of this patch and picked up one man who was swimming about; when we got him on

---

2 More probably the *Laurel*, a destroyer of the same class as *Landrail*.

board we learnt that he was the Captain of the after-turret of the *Queen Mary*.[3] We then noticed in the middle of this patch of oil that there was just showing a portion of the bilge of a ship, which was floating about a foot out of the water.

Petard then proceeded and, passing through the 2nd Light Cruiser Squadron, gradually passed up the port side of the 5th Battle Squadron, and eventually regained our flotilla astern of *Champion*. At this time I thought the German shooting was very bad, as a great number of rounds seemed to be falling anything up to 3,000 yards over the 5th B.S. However we soon got a reminder that their shooting could be accurate, when soon afterwards we saw the *Defence* blown up between the lines. . . .

Letter from H.M.S. *Moorsom*

(A Destroyer of the 10th Flotilla, from Harwich, attached to the 13th Flotilla)

At 4 p.m.[4] I went down below to have some tea, but had only just started when the alarm bell rang, and I went on deck to find all ships flying 'enemy in sight'; and there they were, five Hun battle cruisers—was never so surprised in my life. Things then began to move fairly quickly, the second battle cruiser squadron taking station astern of first B.C.S., and our party were ordered to take station ahead of *Lion*. At the same time, the Huns turned to the south-west. At about 4.15 the ball opened at 19,500 yards, by which time we were on *Lion*'s engaged bow—front row of stalls in fact—and for the first half-hour there was nothing for us to do but look on. The way the Huns picked up the range impressed me immensely, their first salvo falling within 400 yards of *Lion*, and they very soon started hitting, the *Princess Royal* actually being hit by their second salvo.

At about 4.30 the *Lion* hoisted 'Destroyers attack the van of the enemy,' a signal that I am not likely to forget in a hurry. We then went all out and started to draw ahead, in order to get into position for the attack. The first of the 13th Flotilla divisions to go in

---

3 Petty Officer E. Francis, whose narrative is on pages 43-50.

4 The time does not appear to be accurate.—*Ed.*

consisted of only three boats (*Nestor*, *Nomad*, and *Nicator*), so, being a free lance, we decided to join them. We edged slowly in towards the enemy, drawing ahead of him, and then made the routine turn in succession of 6 to 8 points in order to run down on an opposite course to the German battle cruisers and fire our torpedoes. By this time they were beginning to get busy with their secondary armaments, and had picked up the range of our turning point to a nicety—so we did not exactly follow our next ahead. I am not clear as to what *Nestor*'s lot did after this, but rather think they carried on with their attack and got it in the neck, but as the enemy's destroyers were at the same time developing their attack, we decided to abandon the idea of torpedo attacks for the moment, and engage the enemy destroyers with gunfire to break up their attack. There then followed a glorious sort of disorganised mêlée, in which the destroyers of both sides were dashing about at 30 knots in all directions, causing more anxiety to their friends than to their foes. This part of the business lasted about a quarter of an hour, during which we got rid of a good deal of ammunition at ranges varying from 2,000 to 5,000 yards. Then the Huns, having lost two of their boats, one entirely by gunfire and the other by a torpedo from *Petard* polished off by gunfire, decided that they had had enough, and returned to their own side of the street. They had shown an entire absence of the death or glory sort of business which we had always expected from them, and not more than two of them had made the least attempt to fire off their torpedoes.

We then went off on our own and made two attacks on their battleships, for I must explain that the Hun battle cruisers and main battle fleet had now made contact with each other and all were steering to the northward. I can assure you that messing about in between the lines for one and a-half to two hours was a pretty warm affair, and personally I was extremely thankful when we had got off the last two torpedoes and cleared out. They hit us once, but quite a gentlemanly knock, bringing down the mainmast and blowing the very ormolu shelter that we had on the quarter-deck over the side. The cabin flat was pretty well 'strafed,' and there were some holes in the after oil tanks, but the only casualty was one man slightly wounded. Before we left, the secondary batteries of their battleships were getting rather attentive, but their firing was not good.

On our way out we passed the wretched *Nomad* lying stopped, and one really felt rather a cad to leave them but the Captain and I came to the conclusion that it would be suicide to stand by her. We passed out ahead of the 5th B.S., which was getting it pretty hearty at the time, both from the battle cruisers and from the leading ships of the enemy's battle fleet, and as they were silhouetted against the western sky they were lovely targets, whilst the Hun ships were extremely hard to see. After we had been on the disengaged side for about half an hour or so we saw the southern wing division of the Grand Fleet coming down from the north-west, and, as far as one can gather, the whole fleet deployed across the head of the German line and steered to the eastward, until they eventually were on the east side of the Hun. We personally were out of action, as all the after oil tanks were leaking, so we retired between 9 and 10 p.m., and went to Rosyth.

I was rather amused by the remark of one of the sailors when our after shelter was knocked over the side by the Huns. The particular sailor was a defaulter, who a week before had had to spend a good deal of his spare time painting the inside of this shelter, first of all with a coat of white paint, and then with a final coat of white enamel. He was near the shelter when it went over the side, and was heard to say, 'Ha! thought so, there goes my —— White City!'

H.M.S. *Nicator*
Which attacked with H.M.S. *Nestor* and *Nomad*
(Both of the Latter Ships were Sunk by German Gunfire)

When I arrived on the bridge about 3.30 p.m. the battle cruisers were forming in single line ahead and had increased to full speed, and as we were at the tail of the line, we had to go 'all out' to take up our screening position ahead. One thought at first that it was rather unkind to make us proceed up the engaged side of the battle cruisers to take up our station, as it was quite clear that as soon as the first shots were fired at extreme range we should stand a very good chance of being hit by any shots falling short. And we weren't kept very long in suspense, because the enemy soon opened fire, but right from the start there seemed to be a remarkable lack of shorts, nearly all shots appearing to either straddle or hit, so much so that practically before the action seemed to have started the *Indefatigable* blew up just as we passed her—not a very cheering commencement. We had now got about half-way up the line, going just over 30 knots, and both lines of battle cruisers were firing at each other as rapidly as possible, but our ships were being straddled and hit much too often for anyone to be too happy about it.

We had just got abreast of the *Princess Royal*, the second ship of the line when the *Queen Mary*, her next astern which we had passed a few minutes before, had her first explosion, and shortly afterwards completely blew up and was enveloped in a huge cloud of smoke and flame. (Whether this statement is correct as to the two explosions, I do not know, but at any rate so it seemed.) When the smoke cleared there was nothing left to be seen, and for some time everyone on board the *Nicator* seemed quite stunned with horror at the sudden-ness of the thing, and at the turn that the action seemed to have taken. By this time we were abreast the *Lion* which was firing very steadily, and seemed to inspire confidence somehow in spite of the number of times she appeared to be straddled. Suddenly a huge burst of flame shot up from her, amidships, and for one ghastly moment we thought that she had gone the way of the *Queen Mary* and *Indefatigable*. However, as soon as the smoke cleared away we saw all the *Lion*'s remaining turrets fire together, and everyone on board us burst into a cheer.

Then we noticed a signal to the *Champion* (Ship of Captain (D), 13th Flotilla) flying from the *Lion* ordering the 13th Flotilla to attack, and very shortly afterwards the *Champion* hoisted the signal for the 2nd Division to deliver a torpedo attack on the enemy battle cruisers. The 2nd Division ordinarily consisted of the *Nestor*, *Onslow*, *Nomad*, and *Nicator*, but earlier on in the day *Onslow* had been detached to screen the seaplane carrier *Engadine*, so that there only remained *Nestor*, *Nomad*, and *Nicator* in the division. We started our attack in that order at about (?) 4.30 p.m.

We led out from the head of our battle cruiser line steering a south south-easterly course (the course of the two battle cruisers' lines being approximately south) at a speed of 34 knots, but shortly after the attack started *Nomad* commenced to drop behind and told us to take station ahead of her, as she could not maintain the pace.

Almost simultaneously with our attack we saw enemy destroyers coming out from the head of the German line, either to deliver a counter attack on our battle cruisers or else to beat off our attack. When we had reached a position on the enemy's bow we turned on to our attacking course, roughly north-east, and fired our first torpedo at about 9,000 to 10,000 yards' range. We were in excellent position and the torpedo, for as far as we could see its track, ran straight and doubtless least crossed the enemy line. By this time we were within gun range of the enemy destroyers, of which we could count at least eight. They were approaching at about 30 knots, two to three points off our starboard bow, and the rate at which we were closing each other was about 1,000 yards per minute, so that it was not long before we went into 'rapid independent,' our maximum rate of fire, and scored a gratifying number of hits. When at about 1,000 yards' range from us the German destroyers turned on to a south-westerly course, a practically parallel and opposite course to ours, and slightly closing.

We noticed that two of them did not turn with the others but remained stopped, one with a distinct list to starboard, whilst the firing of the remainder although very rapid was very wild, and we were not hit at all. They were now passing us at full speed at almost point-blank range, so that we were allowing the maximum deflection on the gun sights—60 knots right. This did not last long, as they were soon past us, and they turned to rejoin their battle cruisers, being engaged as they did so by the next division of our flotilla, which were following us up astern; but the Germans had left behind three of their destroyers, the crew of one of which were already taking to the boats.[5] The *Nomad* astern of us was unfortunately disabled by a hit in her engine-room, and we had to leave her.

An unfortunate accident happened to our second torpedo, for when fired it hung up half out of the tube and broke at the joint between the head and the body, the top body screws breaking but the bottom ones holding, so that the business end, with all the explosive in it, was dangling over the side. I have vivid recollections of the tubes' crew gingerly trying to bear the head off with a boat-hook as it bumped against the side with each roll of the ship. Luckily, it soon parted and fell off, again luckily just clearing the starboard propeller. Altogether a most unfortunate incident!

All this time we were under an unpleasantly hot fire from the German battle cruisers' secondary armament, and it seemed nothing short of a miracle that we escaped being hit. I put it down unhesitatingly to the way in which the Captain handled the ship, and I think everyone else on board thought that too. His idea was,

---

5 Probably only two German Destroyers were actually sunk as a result of this fighting.

and it undoubtedly saved us, to chase each salvo—that is to say, when a salvo fell short he would alter course to starboard towards it, so that after the Germans had applied an 'up' spotting correction and fired another salvo, instead of hitting us it would go over. Then we would alter to port towards where that salvo fell, and so on. Luckily we had a reserve of speed over the *Nestor*, our next ahead, so we were able to do this salvo dodging without dropping astern of station to any appreciable extent. Throughout the whole action the Captain was leaning coolly against the front of the bridge, smoking his pipe, and giving his orders to the helmsman.

By this time the German battle cruisers had turned 16 points to port. At the time we vaguely thought it was to prevent further attacks from the other divisions following us up astern, but we soon realised it was because they had effected a junction with their battle fleet, so as soon as it was seen that it was no use carrying on and chasing the enemy battle cruisers from astern, *Nestor* turned back to the west and prepared to rejoin our line.

On the way back we passed *Nomad*, stopped and apparently help-less, and we asked if we could offer any assistance but she told us to go on. Now it was for the first time that I realised that the German battle cruisers had come into touch with their battle fleet, because sighting a line of battleships on our port bow, I exclaimed to the Captain, 'Now we're all right, here is the 5th Battle Squadron.' But that moment of elation did not last long, because a closer inspection showed they were undoubtedly Germans, and, what was more, *Nestor* was converging to attack them. Very soon we were again in the thick of a perfectly hair-raising bombardment from their sec-ondary armament. We were engaging a light cruiser at the head of the line with all our guns, the range on the sights being 3,000 yards—*Nestor* was apparently going to make quite certain of his attack. At this moment, just as our sights were coming on an enemy battleship for our last torpedo, *Nestor* was hit, and we had to put our helm hard-a-port to prevent ramming him. Our torpedo gunner made frantic efforts to train the torpedo tube round to keep his sights on, but the ship was swinging so rapidly that he could not do it, and unfortunately the Captain did not realise until afterwards that the torpedo had never been fired. The *Nestor*, realising that he was out of action, ordered us to rejoin *Champion*, for apparently our recall had been hoisted for some time, and accordingly we turned and rejoined *Champion* at full speed. It seemed perfectly extraordinary that, in spite of the tornado of shells that were falling all round us, we were never hit once except by a few splinters.

Narrative from H.M.S. *Nestor*

Extract from *Falklands, Jutland and the Bight*, by Commander the Hon. Barry Bingham, V.C., R.N., Commanding Officer of H.M.S. *Nestor*, at Jutland.[6]

When the action commenced, the *Nestor* was about half a mile ahead of the battle cruisers, from which position we had the best point of vantage for observing the enemy's salvoes falling around the *Lion*. The enemy's shooting appeared good, and it was clear that he was concentrating on Admiral Beatty's flagship.

Shortly after 4 p.m. the Admiral signalled that the flotilla of destroyers ahead was to attack the enemy's battle cruisers with torpedoes. 'Captain D' in the *Champion* immediately repeated this order, adding that the *Nestor* and her division were to lead the attack.

I immediately hoisted the signal for full speed, and ordered the destroyers to form a single line astern of me. Then, shaping course a point and a half in towards the enemy, we ran full speed at 35 knots for half an hour, in order to reach an advantageous position on the enemy's bows, such as would enable me to launch the torpedo attack with the greatest possible prospect of success.

On drawing out to this position, we observed the enemy's fifteen destroyers coming out with the object of making a similar torpedo attack on our battle cruisers.

At 4.40 p.m., having reached the desired position, I turned to N. (approximately fourteen points to port), followed in succession by the rest of the destroyers, with this objective: (*a*) to frustrate the intended torpedo attack by enemy destroyers on our battle cruisers by intercepting them and bringing them to action; (*b*) to push home our torpedo attack on the enemy's battle cruisers.

The German destroyers then immediately turned on a course parallel to ours, and the destroyer action thus commenced at a range of 10,000 yards. I promptly manoeuvred to close this range.

---

6 John Murray, London, 1919. Reproduced by kind permission of the author and publishers.

At 4.45 the *Nomad*, my immediate follower, was hit in the boiler-room, and hauled out of line disabled. We in the *Nestor* got the range very quickly, and pumped in three or four salvoes from our 4-inch guns. Two German destroyers disappeared beneath the surface, and though it is unreasonable definitely to claim the credit of sinking a given ship where many are concerned, my control officer is still prepared to affirm that the *Nestor*'s guns accounted for one of them.

At 4.50 p.m. the enemy's destroyers turned tail and fled. Pursued by the British, they divided themselves into two portions, one-half of which made for the head, while the other took cover under the tail, of the German battle cruiser line. It must be remembered that, although they were numerically superior to us, the enemy's destroyers were neither so large nor so heavily armed.

The British boats promptly turned to chase the enemy's fleeing T.B.D.'s, and while I proceeded with my division, now reduced to two boats (*i.e., Nestor* and *Nicator*), after those of the enemy's destroyers, who were making for the head of the battle-cruiser line, the other two divisions of the T.B.D.'s went after the remaining, and larger, portion of the German destroyers.

Just then the enemy's battle cruisers altered course four points to port—that is, forty-five degrees to the left. Most probably this manoeuvre was prompted by the warning splashes that marked the discharge of the British torpedoes, of which the *Nestor* had just fired her first two.[7]

Thus I found myself with the solitary *Nicator* hot in the track of the fleeing destroyers, and now rapidly approaching the head of the German battle cruiser line, who were not slow in giving us an extremely warm welcome from their secondary armament. At a distance of 3,000 to 4,000 yards the *Nestor* fired her third torpedo, and immediately afterwards at 4.58 turned away eight points to starboard, in order to get clear of the danger zone and to regain the line of the British battle cruisers.

Suddenly from behind the head of the enemy's line there came a German light cruiser, who opened hot fire and straddled us. It was just about 5 o'clock when two boilers were put out of action by direct hits. From the bridge I saw at once that something of the kind

---

7 It is quite likely that one of these torpedoes actually struck the *Lutzow*. She was subsequently sunk, and her survivors at Wilhelmshaven, whilst in conversation with *Nestor*'s men, told them that a torpedo from *Nestor*'s division had struck them; this so reduced their speed that they became an easy prey to the 5th Battle Squadron's gunfire.

Nestor hit and disabled.   *Nicator.*

Nestor and *Nicator* attacking. (From a painting)

had happened. A huge cloud of steam was rising from the boiler-room, completely enshrouding the whole ship, and it was painfully apparent that our speed was dropping every second. Our speed died away gradually, until at 5.30 we came to a dead stop.

Nothing daunted, the engine-room staff applied themselves with all the means in their power to the work of setting the engines in motion. But it was all without avail. The damage was of a nature which required, above all, time. Before anything could be done, the boilers had to be cooled off, and all pipes were in the overheated condition that results from a high-speed run.

The German light cruiser, having crippled us, almost immediately turned back and rejoined her own battle cruisers.

Seeing our plight, the *Petard* (Lieutenant-Commander E. C. O. Thomson), now returning from the chase of the major portion of the German flotilla, gallantly offered a tow; but I had no hesitation in refusing an offer which would have meant the exposure of two ships to the danger that properly belonged to one.

Curiously enough, when our speed gave out, we found ourselves brought to a standstill at a spot only two miles west of the *Nomad*, our only comrade in misfortune.

But though crippled, we had guns that were still intact, and a hostile destroyer, swooping down on what she thought an easy prey, was greeted with volleys of salvoes from our invaluable semi-automatic guns. After such a warm reception, the German destroyer sheered off post-haste.

While lying helpless and broken down, we saw the opposing forces of battle cruisers retracing their tracks to the N.W., fighting on parallel courses. The rival squadrons quickly disappeared behind the horizon, engaged furiously, and we were now left with the ocean to ourselves. But it was not to be for long. Fifteen minutes later my yeoman-of-signals reported: 'German battleships on the horizon, shaping course in our direction.' This was more than I had ever bargained for, and, using my own glasses, I was dumbfounded to see that it was in truth the main body of the German High Sea Fleet, steaming at top speed in a N.W. direction, and following the wake of their own battle cruisers.

Their course necessarily led them first past the *Nomad*, and in another ten minutes the slaughter began. They literally smothered the destroyer with salvoes. Of my divisional mate nothing could be seen: great columns of spray and smoke alone gave an indication of her whereabouts. I shall never forget the sight, and mercifully it was a matter of a few minutes before the ship sank; at the same time it seemed impossible that anyone on board could have survived.

Of what was in store for us there was not now the vestige of a doubt, and the problem was how to keep all hands occupied for the few minutes that remained before the crash must come.

While the sub-lieutenant and myself were 'ditching' all charts, confidential books, and documents, the first lieutenant and the men were executing my orders in providing biscuits and water for the boats; lowering these to the water's edge; hoisting out Carley floats; and generally preparing for the moment when we should be obliged to leave the ship.

These orders were rapidly executed, and there was still time on our hands; for nothing had as yet happened. By a brilliant inspiration, Bethell[8] then suggested to me that the cables might be ranged on deck—ostensibly for use in case of a friendly tow, but in reality to keep the men busy to the last. This suggestion I readily accepted, and the hands were still thus employed when the end came.

---

8 Lieut. M. J. Bethell, 1st Lieutenant of H.M.S. *Nestor*.

From a distance of about five miles the Germans commenced with their secondary armament, and very soon we were enveloped in a deluge of shell fire. Any reply from our own guns was absolutely out of the question at a range beyond the possibilities of our light shells; to have answered any one of our numerous assailants would have been as effective as the use of a pea-shooter against a wall of steel. Just about this time we fired our last torpedo at the High Sea Fleet, and it was seen to run well.

It was a matter of two or three minutes only before the *Nestor*, enwrapped in a cloud of smoke and spray, the centre of a whirlwind of shrieking shells, received not a few heavy and vital hits, and the ship began slowly to settle by the stern, and then to take up a heavy list to starboard.

Her decks now showed the first signs of havoc amongst life and limb.

It was clear that the doomed *Nestor* was sinking rapidly, and at that moment I gave my last order as her commander— 'Abandon ship.'

The motor boat and Carley floats were quickly filled; and as the dinghy was badly broken up by shell fire, there seemed to remain for me only the possibility of a place in the whaler.

Bethell was standing beside me, and I turned to him with the question, 'Now, where shall we go?' His answer was only characteristic of that gallant spirit, 'To Heaven, I trust, sir.'

At that moment he turned aside to attend to a mortally wounded signalman, and was seen no more amidst a cloud of fumes from a bursting shell.

I clambered into the whaler, where I found about eight others waiting, and we remained alongside until the last possible moment, hailing the partially-submerged ship vigorously, in the unlikely event of any survivors being still on board. Finally we pushed off clear.

The whaler, however, had also been hit, probably at the same time as the dinghy, and before we had gone half a dozen strokes she filled and sank. We then struck out, I luckily having my 'Miranda' life-saving waistcoat on, for the well-loaded motor-boat, lying some fifty yards ahead of the *Nestor*, where some of us were pulled in, the rest supporting themselves by holding on to the gunwale.

Looking now towards the *Nestor*, we saw the water lapping over the decks, and the forecastle high in the air, still the target of the

German gun-layers, some of whose projectiles fell uncomfortably near us in the motor-boat and rafts.

In about three minutes the destroyer suddenly raised herself into an absolutely perpendicular position, and thus slid down, stern first, to the bottom of the North Sea, leaving a quantity of oil and wreckage to mark the spot where she had last rested.

As she sank, her sharp stem and stockless anchors alone visible, we gave our gallant but cruelly short-lived *Nestor* three rousing cheers and sang 'God Save the King'.

Letter from an Officer of H.M.S. *Nomad*

H.M.S. *Nomad* was sunk in this attack and the Survivors captured

As you know, we came from Rosyth with the battle cruisers, and on the afternoon of May 31st were much excited intercepting 'Fritz's' Telefunken. I think we cleared for action about 2.15 p.m., and sighted Hipper's battle cruisers about 2.30 p.m.[9] The Germans opened fire first, and our battle cruisers followed. Not long after this the 13th Flotilla, to which we belonged, were ordered to attack the enemy battle cruisers with torpedoes, and we engaged a Hun flotilla that was simultaneously moving out to attack our battle cruisers.

Five very bright minutes followed, during which it was, almost impossible to spot our fall of shot, but we saw one German destroyer which we were engaging start settling by the bow. The first hit on us smashed a big hole in our upper deck, killed all the after torpedo tube's crew, and also killed several engine-room ratings. Another hit came clean through the main steam pipe, causing a cloud of steam to rise like a thick fog, so thick that, from my position aft, I could see no part of the ship forward. The ship then gradually slowed down and finally stopped.

A few minutes after this we spotted the German main battle fleet coming up towards us from the southward. The Sub-Lieutenant and myself were for'ard on the foc'sle, preparing gear for being taken in tow on the off-chance of a ship turning up to tow us; the

---

9 Times not accurate.

Captain was busy dumping overboard confidential books, and the rest of the ship's company were going hard at the pumps and at turning out the boats, etc.

We fired our last torpedo as the leading German ship came up, but owing to damage it stuck in the tube until a hit from one of the enemy, which had now opened on us strongly, caused the ship to lurch over and the torpedo rolled out. One of our ordinary seamen, seeing the track of this torpedo, shouted out, 'Here *comes* a torpedo,' which didn't help matters any. By this time salvoes were falling all round us, as a whole German Battle Squadron were apparently using us as a target for a practice firing, and the *Nomad* was rapidly being turned into something remarkably like a Gruyère cheese. We were about 2,000 yards, as far as I can remember, from the leading German battleship when we fired the last torpedo, and so we were at practically point-blank range for their 11-inch and 12-inch guns. The ship then started sinking by the stern with a great rattle from the loose gear tumbling about in her, and then gradually disappeared, but all the men were got clear just before she sank, and, after a short swim in the sea a life-saving apparatus in the form of a German torpedo boat, so small that we could almost have taken it on with our fists, came up and picked us up out of the water. She was a single-funnel craft, with one pop-gun on the foc'sle, one torpedo tube mounted on rails, and her decks piled high with coal. However, one doesn't look a gift horse in the mouth, and in her we were taken back to Germany, and, as you probably know, we were the 'Kaiser's guests' there for the next two and a half years!

CHAPTER IV

SIGHTING THE HIGH SEAS FLEET

Whilst the 13th Destroyer Flotilla were delivering their torpedo attack and whilst the battle cruisers were still engaging the enemy battle cruisers on a southerly course, the light cruisers stationed ahead of the *Lion* sighted, to the south-south-east, enemy heavy ships 'coming up in an apparently endless procession from the south, apparently about 20 capital ships with light cruisers and masses of destroyers.'

This arrival of the High Seas Fleet, of course, altered the situation, and after receiving the reports from the 2nd L.C.S. and when he had sighted the new enemy from the *Lion*, Vice-Admiral Beatty turned his squadron from their southerly course 'right about' on to a northerly course. This enabled him to continue action with the enemy battle cruisers which also turned to the north, whilst being practically out of range of the leading German battleships. Meanwhile the 2nd Light Cruiser Squadron held on to the southward for a time, to make a closer reconnaissance of the German Battle Fleet.

The report of this period, roughly half-past four to five o'clock, was contained in Vice-Admiral Beatty's report, as follows:—

'At 4.26 p.m. there was a violent explosion in *Queen Mary*; she was enveloped in clouds of grey smoke and disappeared. Eighteen of her officers and men were subsequently picked up by *Laurel*.

At 4.38 p.m. *Southampton* reported the enemy's battle fleet ahead. The destroyers were recalled, and at 4.42 p.m. the enemy's battle fleet was sighted S.E. Course was altered 16 points in succession to starboard, and I proceeded on a northerly course to lead them towards the Grand Fleet. The enemy battle cruisers altered course shortly afterwards, and the action continued. *Southampton*, with the 2nd Light Cruiser Squadron, held to the southward to observe. They closed to within 13,000 yards of the enemy battle fleet, and came under a very heavy but ineffective fire. *Southampton*'s reports were most valuable.'

In the pages that follow are narratives from Officers of two ships of the 2nd Light Cruiser Squadron, H.M.S. *Southampton* and H.M.S. *Nottingham*, describing the experiences of their squadron when carrying out this important reconnaissance and when escaping from the 'very heavy but ineffective fire.'

Brief descriptions of the earlier incidents of the battle are also in these accounts, for they show the influence which the changing fortunes of the heavy ships had on the small ships that were in company.

Narrative of an Officer on the Fore Bridge of H.M.S *Nottingham* (2nd L.C.S.)

When fire was first opened by the battle cruisers at a range of about 15,000 yards, the enemy unluckily were very indistinct in the mist to the east of us, whereas we must have stood out clearly against the light sky and what there was of the afternoon sun in the west.

The enemy shooting was at first very short but they soon found the target, and before we had been in action ten minutes the *Indefatigable* blew up, and five minutes later the *Queen Mary* also went sky high. Our Sub-Lieutenant who was on the bridge and looking in the *Queen Mary*'s direction at the time, said that the whole ship, some 600 feet long, blew up in one terrific explosion and he saw a turret, complete, blown 200 feet into the air. When the smoke had cleared away, practically nothing remained.

We were stationed at this time about 1,500 yards on the engaged bow of the *Lion*, and roughly 13,000 or 14,000 yards from the leading enemy battle cruiser. I myself was very much occupied conning the ship, and when that could be left for a moment, looking after the

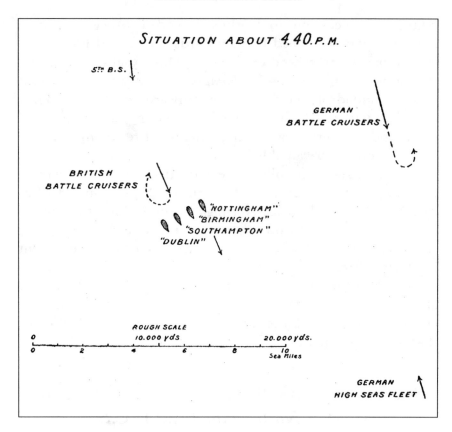

The High Seas Fleet.

signals for which I was responsible, so had little time to consider how the battle fared. Nevertheless, one had a none too cheerful feeling at the thought that two of our six battle cruisers were now at the bottom, after being hit by one salvo each, and the sooner the Grand Fleet and the 5th Battle Squadron appeared the better. Starting with six battle cruisers against five, we were now left with only four against the enemy's five.

Up till now, although actually nearer to the enemy than were our battle cruisers, we had not been fired at as the enemy had bigger fry than us to play with, and we had not fired as they were out of range of our 6-inch guns. But very soon some enemy destroyers showed signs of coming across to attack our battle cruisers, and here our gun-layers got an innings and we had the satisfaction of seeing the enemy boats hit, and the attack turned back. The worst half-hour of the day was now over (4.30 p.m.), and the 5th Battle Squadron with their 15-inch guns were already in the line astern of the battle cruisers, and beginning to make their weight felt.

But to return to the *Nottingham*; we were still about 1,500 yards ahead of our battle cruisers and roughly 13,000 yards from the enemy, when suddenly out of the mist on the port bow a line of big ships appeared. We stood on towards the enemy with the *Southampton* and the rest of our squadron to diagnose the newcomers, so as to be able to tell the Commander-in-Chief and the *Lion* exactly who was there. Soon there was no mistaking that they were the enemy Battle Fleet, and so about 4.45 we turned and followed after our big ships.

It was perhaps as well that we turned when we did, or we should probably never have got away again. We fired some long-range

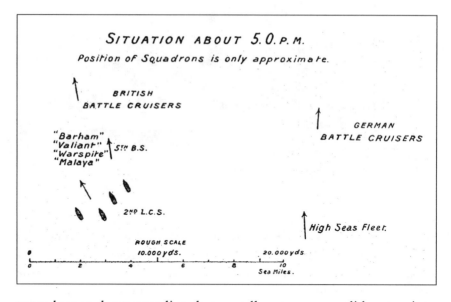

torpedoes at the enemy line, but, needless to say, we did not wait to see if they hit.[1] For the next three-quarters of an hour the German Battle Fleet had nothing to do but fire at us of the 2nd Light Cruiser Squadron—which they proceeded to do. We must have stood out clearly for them against the western sky but their shooting was so correct for elevation that with the assistance of Providence, it was not difficult to dodge the salvoes. For example, a salvo of four 11-inch shells would fall say, 200 yards over, all in a bunch as they invariably did, so that if one shell had hit us probably all would have hit. Then the next salvo would fall only 100 yards over, and the next—well, obviously something had to be done about it, or the next salvo would fall on us; there was about forty-five seconds to do it in. A little helm put on quickly and an alteration of about 20 degrees towards the last salvo, this the German would not notice and so would not allow for, and having seen his last shot fall over he would come down in his range 100 yards, and the next salvo would fall where we *had* been, but now about 50 or 100 yards short of us. Salvo after salvo we were able to dodge in this way, and although I think one may say that the man who says he enjoys a naval battle on the whole is well,—not exactly accurate, I must confess that I never had a more interesting and, in a way, really amusing half-hour than I had conning the ship at that time.

---

1 We have since been told by the post-battle umpires that our torpedo is considered to have hit.

Of course, it was no good us engaging battleships with our little 6-inch guns at 15,000 yards' range, and so, having reported the enemy, the only thing we could do was to get away as quickly as possible. Shells sometimes burst close to the ship and sent great fountains of water up the height of the mast—others would burst 100 yards short, and all the pieces would come hurtling over our heads, some hitting the ship; but we had no casualties. At times the sun would come out for a few minutes and light up the Hun out of the mist, and also dazzle him, with the result that we got some long-range shots in at him whilst he left us alone, but for the greater part of the time we were under the enemy's fire and not replying ourselves. All this time we were, needless to say, going full speed, and with the whole German main fleet following it is fortunate that nothing went wrong down in the engine-room.

When we turned to the north at 4.48, after reporting the German Battle Fleet, we were the unwilling and helpless witnesses of two of our destroyers which had taken part in a very fine attack on the German battle cruisers and had been winged in doing so, and when the battle cruisers turned to the north these two destroyers had to be left to fall right into the jaws of the German Battle Fleet. The Germans in this case picked up their crews, but only after the ships were sunk . . .

Narrative of an Officer on the Fore Bridge of H.M.S. *Southampton*

(Flagship of the 2nd Light Cruiser Squadron)

The order of the Fleet at 4.0 p.m. was *Champion*, with the 13th Destroyer Flotilla leading; then the Battle Cruisers, with 2nd L.C.S. on their starboard, the disengaged beam; and the 1st and the 3rd L.C.S. somewhere on the port side of the battle cruisers, but no longer in touch with us.

The enemy appeared to be making pretty good shooting, columns of water rising all round the battle cruisers, but, as we were on the disengaged side, we could not see any actual hits on our ships.

It was therefore a terrific shock to us when, without any warning, and apparently only a few minutes after the commencement of the action, we saw our rear battle cruiser blow up. Without perceptible noise, an immense column of smoke and flame appeared where a moment before had been the *Indefatigable*. A minute later this column of smoke cleared a little, and I saw the bows of the ship lying over in the water; then almost immediately a second explosion occurred, after which nothing further was to be seen.

Soon we had all passed on out of sight, but it was not long afterwards that the same fate overtook the *Queen Mary*. A column of smoke and flame, a few scraps of débris projected hundreds of feet in the air, a pall of smoke hanging over the sea for some minutes, and there was nothing more to be seen of her. After a short interval the *Tiger*, her next astern, was seen emerging from this smoke cloud, having apparently steamed through the same spot without meeting any obstruction.[2]

It is almost impossible to describe one's feelings on witnessing this disaster, as it was both alarming and depressing, particularly as one could not observe the results of our own fire on the enemy, but I think the principal sensation was one of astonishment that a ship should disappear in an instant without leaving a trace. One could not realise all that it meant.

Meanwhile we had been getting closer to the *Lion*, and soon afterwards it appeared as if she also was going up. She was hit in 'Q' turret and I saw for an instant a big flame over the turret, but then to our intense relief she recovered and showed no further signs of distress.

During the run south we had been steaming slightly faster than the battle cruisers, and had with *Dublin*, *Nottingham*, and *Birmingham* reached a position about two miles ahead of *Lion*, screening the battle cruisers' advance, when at 4.38 p.m. we sighted ahead the entire German High Seas Fleet coming up in an apparently endless procession from the south, about 20 capital ships, with light cruisers and masses of destroyers. Those in the *Southampton*'s control top, with the exception of the Gunnery-Lieutenant, who knew better, were convinced that the new arrivals were the British Grand Fleet, regardless of the fact that the ships were approaching from the direction of Heligoland, and it took the Gunnery-Lieutenant some little time to cure their optimism.

---

2 NOTE—*Tiger* had just avoided ramming the remains of the stern of *Queen Mary* by putting her helm hard-a-starboard, *vide* the narrative of an officer in *Tiger*'s conning tower, pages 40-43.

Lion then turned 16 points.

Southampton held her course to the southward, to make a detailed report of the composition of the enemy forces to the C.-in-C., and to deliver if possible a torpedo attack. The torpedo attack did not materialise, but the enemy report was successfully passed to *Iron Duke*, and at 4.45 p.m. we turned to the northward, being then about 14,000 yards from the centre of the enemy battle fleet.

We had not up to this time been fired on, presumably because in our approach bows on we had been taken for a friendly squadron, but as we turned and showed our four funnels, the enemy realised that we were hostile, and proceeded to make up for lost time.

The four ships of the 2nd L.C.S. were in line abreast, about ½ mile apart, and steering approximately north-west, but were well to the rear of the rest of our ships, and unsupported. The 5th Battle Squadron, *Barham*, *Valiant*, *Malaya*, and *Warspite*, had continued past the battle cruisers, and then turned up astern of them, and we now found ourselves about 3,000 yards astern of the *Warspite*. Our position during this period was unpleasantly precarious, as we were receiving the full attention of such German battleships as were unable to range on the 5th B.S. and which, therefore, had nothing better to do than pot at us. From my position in the conning tower I could not see them fire, as they were on an after bearing, but I could both hear and see the arrival of their salvoes at our end, and they were frequently much too close to be pleasant. We were straddled pretty effectively most of the time, but by the aid of much judicious zigzagging and a large amount of good luck not one of the squadron was hit.

It was at this period that the light favoured the Germans most, as our ships were silhouetted against a bright western sky, but the sun being hidden, there was no glare, whereas to the eastward there was still a dark cloudy background, against which the German ships' outlines were not clearly visible.

About 6.0 p.m. I saw a Light Cruiser Squadron appear ahead, indicating the arrival of the Grand Fleet and the C.-in-C. It was perhaps just as well that they had come, for the 5th B.S. were receiving as much attention as they wanted, and we of the 2nd L.C.S. could not expect to go on being missed by salvoes of 11-inch indefinitely. Our luck had held already for over an hour. One could not help remembering that any hit at this period sufficient to cause a reduction of speed would have meant certain destruction to the ship, as the entire German Fleet would in a very few minutes have been on top of us. . . .

This account of *Southampton* may be supplemented by a description of the period when the ship was under the fire of the German Battle Fleet, written by another Officer of the ship, and published in his book, *A Naval Lieutenant, 1914-1918*. This author, who writes under the nom de plume of 'Etienne,' and his Publishers, Messrs. Methuen & Co., have kindly given permission to reprint this extract:—

H.M.S. *Southampton* (2nd L.C.S.)

Extract from *A Naval Lieutenant, 1914–1918*, by 'Etienne'[3]

At 4.38 a very startling development took place. We suddenly saw and reported light cruisers, followed by the High Seas Fleet, bearing southeast. Sir David Beatty at once signalled to the Battle Cruiser Force to alter course 16 points (180°) in succession. The German battle cruisers were doing the same thing at the same moment.

We disobeyed the signal, or rather delayed obeying it, for two reasons—firstly, we wished to get close enough to the High Seas Fleet to examine them and report accurately on their composition and disposition; secondly, we had hopes of delivering a torpedo attack on the long crescent-shaped line of heavy ships which was stretched round on our port bow.

It was a strain steaming at 25 knots straight for this formidable line of battleships, with our own friends going fast away from us in the opposite direction. As we got closer I counted sixteen or seventeen battleships, with the four *Konig* class in the van, and the six older pre-Dreadnoughts in the rear. Seconds became minutes, and still they did not open fire, though every second I expected to see a sheet of flame ripple down their sides, and a hail of shell fall around us. I can only account for this strange inactivity on their part by the theory that, as they only saw us end on and we were steering on opposite courses to the remaining British ships, they assumed we

---

3 Reproduced by kind permission of the author and the publishers, Messrs. Methuen & Co., 36 Essex Street, London, WC.

Range-taking.

were a German light cruiser squadron that had been running away from the British battle cruisers. Only in this manner can I account for the strange fact that they allowed us to get within 13,000 yards of their line without ever firing a shot at us.

This theory is supported by the fact that when at 4.45 the calm voice of Petty-Officer Barnes on the foremost rangefinder intoned, 'Range, one, three, five double ho! Range one, three, two, double ho!' the Commodore saw that we could not get into a position for a torpedo attack, and as we would be lucky if we got out of the place we were then in, he gave the order for the turning signal, which had been flying for five minutes, to be hauled down.

Over went the helms, and the four ships slewed round, bringing our sterns to the enemy. As we turned, the fun began, and half a dozen German battleships opened a deliberate fire on the squadron.

My action station was aft, but I could hear everything that passed on the fore-bridge as I was in direct communication by voice-pipe. I heard the imperturbable Petty-Officer Barnes continuing his range-taking—'Range one, three, two, double ho! Range one, double three, double ho!' Crash! Bang! Whiz-z-z! and a salvo crumped down around us, the fragments whistling and sobbing overhead. Suddenly I heard Petty-Officer Barnes say, with evident satisfaction, 'Range hobscured!' I took a general look round, and the situation was as follows :—

81

Birmingham with a large salvo falling close to her.

Lion turning.   *Princess Royal* straddled   Destroye
                                   (head-on to camera)
Battle Cruiser Force turning from south to north on sighting the High Seas Fleet.

About three or four miles north of us our battle cruisers were steaming along making a good deal of smoke and firing steadily at what I imagined to be the German battle cruisers' distant hulls on our starboard bow. Then came a gap of two miles, between the battle cruisers and the 5th Battle Squadron. These latter four ships had passed the battle cruisers on opposite courses when Sir David Beatty turned north, and as soon as they had passed them, Rear-Admiral Evan Thomas had turned his squadron to north by west, and followed up the battle cruisers. Whilst this was going on we (Second Light Cruiser Squadron) had still been going south. When we turned to north, we found ourselves about a mile behind the last ship of the Fifth Battle Squadron.

The Fifth B.S. were a brave sight. They were receiving the concentrated fire of some twelve German heavy ships but it did not seem to be worrying them, and though I saw several shells hit the *Warspite*, just ahead of us, the German shooting did not impress me very favourably. But our own position was not pleasant. The half-dozen older battleships at the tail of the German line were too far away to fire at the Fifth Battle Squadron, and though we had gradually drawn out to 15,000 or 16,000 yards we were inside their range, and they began to do a sort of target practice in slow-time on our squadron.

I was in the after control with half a dozen men, the Sub. and the clerk. We crouched down behind the tenth of an inch plating and ate bully beef, but it didn't seem to go down very easily. It seemed rather a waste of time to eat beef, for surely in the next ten minutes one of those 11-inch shells would get us; they couldn't go on falling just short and just over indefinitely, and well, if one did hit us—light cruisers were not designed to digest 11-inch high explosives in their stomachs.

The Sub., who was practically speechless owing to his bad throat, and I agreed that we would not look at the Hun line. But we could never resist having a peep about once a minute, and somehow we always seemed to look just as two or three of the great brutes flickered flames from their guns at us, and we knew that another salvo was on its way across. We knew the time of flight was twenty-three seconds, and the Sub. had a wrist-watch with a prominent second hand—we almost agreed to throw it overboard after three-quarters of an hour's shelling; at the twenty-third second the Sub. would make a grimace, and as if in reply a series of splitting reports and lugubrious moans announced that the salvo had arrived. Frequently they were so close that torrents of spray from the splashes spattered down on the boat deck. Each shell left a muddy pool in the water, and appeared to burst on impact. We all compared notes afterwards, and decided that during this hour about fifty to sixty shells fell within 100 yards of the ship, and many more slightly farther off.

I attribute our escape, as far as we were able to contribute towards it, to the very clever manner in which our Navigator zigzagged the ship according to where he estimated the next salvo would fall. It was possible to forecast this to a certain extent as it was obvious that the Huns were working what is technically known as 'a ladder.' That is to say, the guns are fired with an increase of range to each salvo until 'the target is crossed,' and then the range is decreased for each salvo until the splashes are short of the target once again. It is thus a creeping barrage which moves up and down across the target. The best way to avoid it is to sheer in towards the enemy when the groups of tall splashes are coming towards the ship, and as soon as they have crossed over and begin once more to come towards the ship, then reverse the helm and sheer away from the enemy.

The fascination of watching these deadly and graceful splashes rising mysteriously from the smooth sea was enormous. To know that the next place where they would rise was being calculated by some Hun perched up in one of these distant masts, and that he was watching those 'leetle cruiser ships' through a pair of Zeiss binoculars—and I was watching his ship through a similar pair of Zeiss— was really very interesting. It would have been very interesting indeed if I could have been calculating the position of the splashes round his ship; but he was 16,000 yards away, and our gun-sights stopped at 14,500, so we just had to sit and hope we'd see the Grand Fleet soon. At 6.17 p.m. the news that the Grand Fleet had been sighted right ahead spread round the ship like wildfire.

CHAPTER V

EXPERIENCES IN TURRETS AND BETWEEN DECKS

Whilst a naval action is taking its course in the way of squadron manoeuvres, gunnery concentrations or delivery of torpedo attacks, the large majority of the men of each ship are occupied in putting into execution the will of the Admirals and Captains of the Fleet, without actually themselves seeing anything of the enemy.

The men in the turrets—and the crew of each turret amounts on an average to 60 or 70 men—the men between decks stationed for secondary ammunition supply or as fire and repair parties, and all the engineering complement of the ship stationed in the engine-rooms and in the boiler-rooms, are all carrying on with their work, hearing the noise of the enemy's shells as they splash in the water near the ship, hearing the noise of their own turrets firing, hearing occasionally the noise of an enemy shell hitting the ship, but neither seeing the enemy whom they are fighting nor knowing the detail results of their work. Certain small scraps of news circulate round the ship, and certain deductions can be made from orders that are given—orders for increase of speed, for firing torpedoes, for manning anti-torpedo boat armament, for 'Range 14,200, 2nd battle cruiser from the left, on fire aft—rapid fire,' etc. But it remains a fact that the majority of the men fighting a modern naval battle are not aware at the time of what is happening, who is winning, or whether other ships than their own are being damaged or not.

The following accounts therefore of events in turrets, engine-rooms, and torpedo control positions, although apparently somewhat technical will probably help the reader to reproduce in his imagination, the surroundings and the atmosphere of the men who were fighting the action of Jutland. It must always be remembered that it was the majority who were fighting under these conditions of between decks, and only the minority who were in positions above decks able to see the movements of ships.

The accounts will also confirm what other experiences of 1914-18 have taught us, that the horrors of war go hand in hand with the glory of war—such as there is of glory.

H.M.S. *Tiger*
Description of Events in 'Q' Turret

At 3.47 p.m. the 1st Battle Cruiser Squadron opened fire on the enemy battle cruisers which were then at a range of about 17,000 yards. Within a very few minutes of the commencement of the action the enemy had got the correct range, and 'Q' turret was hit by an 11- or 12-inch shell, which temporarily put both guns out of action. (Time, about 3.53.)

The shell struck the front roof plate on the edge of the centre sighting port, and burst on the top of the turret, but without penetrating. The centre sighting port hood was not seen again. Portions of the shell struck the Officer of Quarters' hood, the range finder, and the periscope, putting both the latter out of action, but all the damage inside the turret was caused by pieces of roof armour being blown inwards, no part of the shell itself ever being discovered in the turret. The fact that the shell struck the weakest point in the whole roof plate and failed to penetrate speaks well for the quality of the turret roof armour.

The Officer of Quarters was momentarily blinded by the flash of the burst and by particles of dust from the roof coming through his observation slit, but when he got into the gun-house the unwounded members of the crew appeared to be in full possession of their senses, so the stunning effect of the burst inside the turret must have been only slight. Two men were killed outright—the trainer, who

Roof of 'Q' turret, *Tiger.*

was directly under the point of impact, and the rammer number of the left gun, who was killed instantly by a piece of flying armour. The Midshipman who was standing between the two guns was mortally wounded by a fragment, and died the following day. Three of the wounded were able to carry on in the turret, and the fourth, the centre sight-setter, although badly wounded climbed down from his position unaided, and reached the dressing-station via the shell-room and handing-room. At this time all lights in the gunhouse had gone out, and the only light left was the little that filtered through the sighting ports and through the hole in the roof made by the shell. The dead and wounded were lying where they had fallen, and the screeching of pressure escaping from a damaged test cock made it extremely difficult to get orders heard and understood. As quickly as possible, however, the dead were placed to one side, the wounded

87

given first aid, and necessary substitutes were brought up from below to replace casualties.

It was then possible to ascertain the exact extent of the material damage and it was found that, although extensive, it was not sufficient to keep the turret out of action. When loading was resumed it was found that neither of the gun-loading cages would come up, as both had been jammed by fragments of armour. The left gun cage was soon put right by removing a fragment of armour; but the wire of the right gun-loading cage was seriously jammed, and that cage could not be raised until the following morning, the E.R.A. of the turret working on it during each lull in the action and through the night. So the left gun continued loading normally, and the right gun used the secondary loading method.

The firing circuits had been shot away and 'gun-layer firing' was also impossible as the telescopes were 'wooded' by part of the roof plate lying across them so that the turret was fired by percussion firing when the other guns were heard to fire, the correct elevation and bearing being maintained from the director receivers, which were fortunately undamaged.

After the action had been going on for some time the Turret Officer received a report from the handing-room that water was coming rapidly into the small magazine ('Q' turret has a large magazine on one side and a small one on the other), whereupon orders were given to transfer as much cordite as possible and then close the magazine. On going down later in a lull in the action the Turret Officer found the handing-room and shell-room crews working in several inches of water—wet but happy. It has since always been a matter of mild surprise to him, after seeing the claims for 'Clothing damaged in action,' that there could have been found room in the magazine at all for all the jumpers and flannels 'used to stop the inflow of water'!

During the action very little could be seen of what was going on outside the turret, the haze, the smoke from escorting destroyers, cordite smoke from our own guns, and spray from enemy 'shorts' making observation intermittent and difficult. It was, however, very marked the way the enemy's fire fell off after about the first forty minutes of the action. From being rapid, regular, and well directed it became intermittent and wild, and after the battle cruisers turned north few hits were scored on *Tiger*, nearly all the hits being on the port side—*i.e.*, the engaged side before the turn.

Narrative of an Officer in the Engine-Room of H.M.S. *Tiger*

I think the outstanding impression that remains regarding the Jutland Battle is the suddenness and unexpectedness of the whole incident. After one and a half years' service with the First Battle Cruiser Squadron, with almost weekly 'sweeps' into German waters, the experience had become almost monotonous, as these cruises, except for the Dogger Bank brush and a sight of an occasional Zeppelin, were almost without incident.

On 31st May, 1916, one of these cruises was in progress, and although high authorities may have known that something more than usual was on the tapis, the generality of officers and men were certainly unaware that anything was likely to happen. They were disillusioned with dramatic suddenness. About 3.45 p.m. (summer time) word was passed that enemy cruisers were in sight, and it was generally believed at first that a portion of the enemy light forces had been caught napping whilst out on a raiding expedition. Action stations were sounded, and hardly had everyone settled at their post—my particular station was the port turbine-room—when word was passed that enemy battle cruisers were in sight, and that 'Der Tag' was imminent. The accuracy of the prophecy was promptly confirmed by the firing of our big guns, and by the thuds and crashes of heavy projectiles, which told us that we were under fire of guns of considerable calibre. Previous experience enabled even those cooped up between decks to judge fairly accurately, not only which of our own guns were firing, but also the general location of the enemy hits on us.

Very early in the action an incident occurred which came very near terminating the career of the *Tiger*. A heavy thud, followed by a deafening report immediately overhead, intimated that a heavy shell had penetrated the side armour and had burst inboard. The base of the shell, forced out intact by the explosion, penetrated the upper deck and the armoured deck, and punched a neat hole in the steel bracket supporting the main steam pipe on the forward bulkhead of the port engine-room, and remained balanced overhead. Had the base of the projectile struck the pipe instead of the bracket, the whole engine-room staff would have been wiped out, and the ship completely disabled until the steam to the damaged piping was

Armour plate pierced by shell that entered *Tiger's* engine-room.

shut off, an operation which would probably have involved the vessel being destroyed by concentrated enemy fire as she drifted helpless out of the line.

The immediate consequences, however, were quite serious enough. The shell bursting in the ammunition passage killed a dozen men, set fire to the ready-use cordite in the passage, rendering it necessary to flood the midships 6-inch magazine, cut through the fresh and salt water mains, and finally the base of the shell, in penetrating to the engine-room, severed the H.P. air pressure ring main, giving the impression by the hiss of escaping air that the steam pipe itself was damaged. No examination could be made to locate the trouble, as through the hole in the deck were pouring the fumes from the burning cordite, and the engine-room was immediately filled with dense smoke, which rendered it impossible to see. Gauges, telegraphs, etc., could only be examined by the aid of flash lights and electric torches at intervals.

'Q' turret, *Lion*. Thick front armour plate pierced at junction with roof plate.
(Photo taken after plate had been removed and placed on deck)

To add to the difficulties, water from the severed mains poured through the damaged deck overhead, over the separators, and over the main steam pipes on to the platform, so that the men stationed there were subjected as the ship rolled, to alternate cascades of cold and semi-boiling water. Attempts were made to proceed to the scene of the explosions from the forward end of the engine-room, but it was found that the forward escape was blocked by wreckage. Access was finally obtained through the escape at the after end of the engine-room, and the depleted repair party, many of whom had been killed or put out of action by the explosion and fumes, set to work to plug the damaged piping in the passages.

In the engine-rooms matters gradually improved. As the cordite burnt out the smoke clouds became less dense, and matters assumed a more normal aspect. The roar of the heavy guns continued steadily the while, informing all that, whatever the general state of affairs were in the fleet, the *Tiger* was keeping her end up, while frequent bursts of firing from our 6-inch secondary armament indicated the approach of enemy destroyers or light craft. From time to time messages of varying import reached us from the upper deck. The loss of the *Queen Mary* was marked by the filling of engine-rooms with dense clouds of smoke, as the *Tiger* steamed through the area where she had been, and occasional lulls enabled hurried

91

expeditions to be made to the scene of serious damages for essential repairs to be organised and arranged for. Men in isolated posts were visited and occasional exchanges of posts arranged.

Eventually the firing gradually died away, and towards 11 p.m. word was passed that the immediate action was ended, but that action stations would be resumed at dawn, or earlier. The interval was spent in frenzied work on repairs, and some of the scenes between decks in the vicinity of shell bursts beggar description. But the most marked feature of the action that came under my personal observation was the coolness and discipline of the engine-room and artisan staff generally, under the most trying conditions, and their initiative and readiness of resource in effecting apparently impossible repairs in emergencies.

Hit on 'Q' Turret, H.M.S. *Lion*

This account shows how, on 'Q' turret of H.M.S. *Lion* being hit by an enemy shell, a chain of circumstances resulted in a serious cordite fire, which fire (and not the direct explosion of an enemy shell) almost led to the explosion of the turret magazines.

It also shows how the magazines and therefore H.M.S. *Lion* herself, with who knows what result to the British Empire, was saved from the probability of being blown up by the coolness of the Officer of Turret (Major Harvey, V.C., Royal Marines), who, although he had been mortally wounded by the explosion of the shell in the gun-house, retained the presence of mind to order the magazine party to close the magazine doors. Major Harvey was posthumously awarded the Victoria Cross for the gallantry of his conduct upon this occasion.

The Effect of a Direct Hit on 'Q' Turret, H.M.S. *Lion*

(Recorded by the Gunnery Officer of H.M.S. *Lion*)

Action with the enemy battle cruisers commenced at 3.47 p.m., G.M.T., and approximately ten minutes later, when only twelve

Flames higher than mast

Cordite flame shooting out of pierced roof of 'Q' turret, *Lion*.

rounds had been fired by 'Q' turret, an enemy shell of large calibre—11-inch or 12-inch—hit the turret and detonated inside the
gun-house, putting the turret out of action and causing, with the
cordite fire which resulted from it, about sixty deaths.

The shell struck between and above the chases of the gun at the
joint of the thick front armour plate with the front roof plate. Six
inches higher and the shell would have struck a glancing blow on the
roof plate and bounced away; 6 inches lower and it would have
struck the thick front armour plate, and in all probability have failed
to penetrate; but striking at the weak point, as it did, the shell
entered the gun-house and detonated over the centre line of the left
gun, just behind the point of balance.

The account of what occurred in the turret after the hit is
obtained from the survivors, and is as follows:

All the occupants of the gun-house proper, most of the silent-
cabinet's crew, and most of the working chamber's crew situated
directly below the gun-house, were killed or severely wounded by
the detonation of the shell in the gun-house. The Officer of the
Turret, though himself severely wounded, realised that his turret
was out of action and on fire, and also that the fire might reach the
magazine. He accordingly passed his orders by the direct voice-pipe

down to the handing-room below, to close the magazine doors and open the magazine flood valves. This order was promptly carried out, and did in fact prevent the flash from the cordite charges reaching the magazines, and so the ship from being blown up. After giving his orders to the handing-room the Officer of the Turret sent his Sergeant, who although very badly burnt and wounded was conscious and capable of movement, to make a personal report to the Captain to the effect that the turret was definitely out of action, and that the flooding of the magazine had been ordered. The Sergeant succeeded in clambering to the bridge and made his report. There were only two others of the turret's crew who escaped with their lives.

After the shell had burst in the gun-house one of the working chamber crew seems to have retained consciousness, for he climbed down the ladder-way in the central trunk of the turret to the shell-room, there to ask the Sick Berth Attendant stationed in the shell-room to go to the working chamber to render first-aid to one or two of the crew, whom, he said, 'are still alive.' He being wounded was sent up out of the shell-room *via* the handing-room and escape trunk on to the main deck, and safely reached the forward Medical Station, where he received medical attention. He was one of the survivors.

The other survivor was the Sick Berth Attendant. On receiving his summons to the turret, he proceeded thither by way of the ladder-way in the central trunk, in accordance with routine.[1] On arriving in the working chamber, which was in complete darkness, and hearing no sounds and the place being full of fumes from the burst shell, he made his way with the aid of his electric hand-lamp to the gun-house, passing up the right auxiliary shell hoist. Though very much shaken by subsequent events, he recollects that he saw daylight through the turret roof, and that the gun's crew appeared to be all dead. He therefore made his way into the silent cabinet, with the object of rendering assistance to the officers and crew there. But here the account of his actions ceases, and it can only be said that, subsequent to his arrival in the silent cabinet, the cordite fire took place, killing everyone else in the turret, handing-room, and shell-room. Some minutes after the cordite fire, and when the Fire

---

1 Full details of his actions are not available since he was burnt and rendered unconscious for some time, but his general movements and recovery from the turret are as stated.

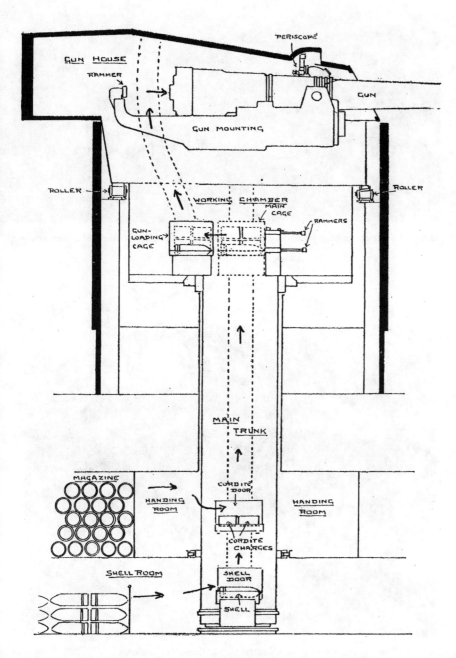

Diagram showing the relative positions of the various compartments of a turret.

13th Flotilla destroyers working ahead to attack. Remainder of salvo is over and is seen astern *Lion* being hit on 'Q' turret.

Damage to 'Q' turret, *Lion*. Taken in harbour.

Brigade had subdued the smouldering wreckage in the turret by playing hoses through the hole left open by the blown-off roof plate, and when the fumes had cleared sufficiently for them to enter the turret as a salvage party, the Sick Berth Attendant was removed from under the bodies of two dead men in the silent cabinet. No other officers or men were found alive in the silent cabinet, gun-house, working chamber, handing-room, or shell-room.

The damage and loss of life caused by the actual explosion of the German shell did not extend to the magazine handing-room and shell-room, where none of the crew were wounded, but unfortunately the whole of them lost their lives through the cordite fire which followed a few minutes afterwards.

An inspection of the 'state' in the turret, as soon after the action as was possible, indicated that this serious cordite fire originated in a curious way. The lever which controls the working of the left breech was blown to the rear *i.e.*, in the direction 'open the breech,' and accordingly the breech opened. The gun was loaded, and the shell in the gun being unseated by the shock of the hit slid down towards the breech, falling, with its cordite charge, down into the well which is in rear of the breech, and up which ammunition is supplied. (The projectile and a half-burnt powder igniter from the cordite charge were found here afterwards.) The burst of the enemy shell had started a fire in the gun-house, probably of men's clothing, or in fact of any inflammable material, and this must have reached down to the naked charge of cordite lying in the gun-well. This cordite caught fire and, burning, passed the ignition to cordite which was waiting in both gun-loading cages, and so down the main ammunition supply trunk. The resulting flash is that shown in the photogravure (opposite, above), as it took its easiest course to escape—namely, upwards through the roof of the turret by the hole made by the enemy shell burst.

The flash also passed down the main trunk into the shell-room and handing-room, and up the escape trunk into the switchboard compartment. In this latter compartment were stationed, besides the switchboard men and certain of the electrical repair party, the after medical party under the charge of a surgeon. All these men, together with the magazine and shell-room crews, were killed by the cordite fire. It is to be remarked that the clothes and bodies of these men were not burnt, and in cases where the hands had been raised involuntarily, palms forward, to protect the eyes, the backs of the hands and that part of the face actually screened by the hands were not even discoloured. Death to these men must have been instantaneous.

The absence of any burning or even charring of the paint on the handing-room or shell-room bulkhead walls is interesting. Only in the actual cordite compartments of the cages themselves is there evidence of burning fire, and even here the wooden battens are unharmed. But in the gun-house the state is quite different, the paint being burnt and charred, showing that there was open fire in addition to the cordite flash.

The uncertain effect of a shell detonation in a confined space is worth mentioning. Whilst the sights, director receiver instruments, etc., in the left and centre positions of the gun-house were wrecked, those in the right position were mechanically undamaged, even the glass of the right gun receiver being unbroken. The working chamber below also was undamaged, except as the result of the cordite fire. Where any non-inflammable material stood in the path of the flash, complete protection appears to have been provided.

The hydraulic machinery stood this very severe test admirably, and the turret and guns were able to be moved by their own hydraulic power directly after the action.

So the *Lion* was saved from the same complete explosion that had wrecked her consorts, *Queen Mary* and *Indefatigable*. It may now be interesting to hear the experiences of a battleship of the 5th B.S.—the squadron of four lately-built Dreadnoughts of the *Queen Elizabeth* class, which were under the command of Rear-Admiral Evan Thomas, and which had been following at their utmost speed in rear of the Battle Cruiser Force during the run south. Forming up after the 16-point turn at 4.46 p.m. to the southward of the battle cruisers, they took upon themelves the brunt of the action.

The following is a narrative by a young officer in the Torpedo Control Tower of H.M.S. *Malaya*, the rear ship of the 5th Battle Squadron.

Perhaps one should explain that the Torpedo Control Tower in these ships is a small, round armoured tower capable of holding five or six men with moderate comfort, and is situated abaft the funnels, just for'ard of the two after 15-inch turrets, 'X' and Y' turrets on the quarter-deck. From this tower, which contains the necessary range-finder and other instruments for calculating when to fire torpedoes, orders are passed down to the torpedo tubes to fire, or the torpedo is actually discharged by electrical mechanism in the control tower. The actual torpedo tubes in a big ship are situated in compartments below the water line, behind the protection of the armour on the ship's side. From there, of course, it is impossible to see the enemy at which one is firing, but from a torpedo control tower one can see a moderate amount of what is going on outside the ship. The Midshipman in *Malaya*'s control tower saw, and experienced, a good deal, and he remembers what he thought about it all.

A Midshipman in H.M.S. *Malaya*
(Rear Ship of the 5th B.S.)

On May 31st, 1916, I was a very Junior Midshipman of the tender age of sixteen and a quarter years, having been at sea four months. But, in spite of this short experience, we had already got more or less used to the idea of suddenly raising steam and going to sea, and on the occasion of leaving Rosyth the day before Jutland, even the 'war worn' senior midshipmen of two years' service were incapable of mustering one 'buzz' between them, and we were all bored stiff at the prospect of another uneventful sweep.

I was Midshipman of the afternoon watch on May 31st, when a signal was received which seemed to excite the small crowd on Monkeys' Island,[2] and being, like all snotties, very curious, I eventually mustered up enough courage to ask the Officer of the Watch what it was about, only to be snubbed for my pains. A few minutes later, however, the Captain sent me down to the Engineer Commander with a copy of a signal (which naturally I suppose, I read). It was from the *Galatea*, reporting two enemy ships in sight. I duly returned to the bridge, after telling the Engineer Commander that the Captain wanted steam for full speed as soon as possible.

---

2 The usual name for the Upper Bridge, from where the Captain, or the Officer of the Watch, controls the ship.

By this time I was beginning to feel slightly excited, but still did not realise what it all meant. A few minutes later the hands were piped to tea, and my excitement cooled; only, however, nearly to consume me again when, on receipt of another signal, I was told to call all officers in their cabins, and to order the bugler to sound off 'Action'. This I did, giving the officers the news that there was something exciting in the wind for a change. After this I'm afraid my extreme youth so worked me up that events followed one another in such confusion that I do not remember very clearly what happened. I remember being chased off the bridge by the Captain and proceeding to my action station in the torpedo control tower, and on getting there discovering that some of the control instruments were in the Torpedo Control Officer's cabin, so I was sent down to get them. All doors and hatches had been shut when action was sounded off, so I had to open a door to get into the cabin flat. The Chief Carpenter was the officer responsible for seeing these doors were shut, and unfortunately I met him on the way back, and in spite of all my pleadings had to leave him still convinced that it was his bounden duty to report me to the Commander for the grave offence of opening a water-tight door without permission. I spent the rest of the time until we opened fire wondering how much the punishment would be, and what was the best way of minimising the pain thereof.

I think we only realised that we were at last in for a proper action when we heard the battle cruisers firing ahead. We then began to get quite jubilant; so much so, that when a German shell landed abreast us on the port side about 500 yards short there was a positive cheer from the *Malaya*. Then we heard the other ships of our own squadron open fire, one after the other ahead of us, each salvo helped on its way by a cheer. In our torpedo control tower we were so interested in what was going on, that when *Malaya* herself opened fire the blast from 'X' turret's guns, which were only a few feet away from us, sat us down with a 'whump,' and the range-taker came down from his seat with a crash.

From this time onwards my thoughts were really more like a nightmare than thoughts of a wide-awake human being. I don't think I felt fright, simply because what was going on around me was so unfamiliar that my brain was incapable of grasping it. Even now I can only think of the beginning of the action as through a dim haze. I remember seeing the enemy line on the horizon with red specks coming out of them, which I tried to realise were the cause

100

of projectiles landing around us, continually covering us with spray, but the fact refused to sink into my brain. We were all the time rather excited, and our enthusiasm knew no bounds when we passed a sunken ship with survivors swimming around her. We never dreamt that it was one of our own battle cruisers; but it was the *Indefatigable*, and over a thousand dead men lay in her wreck. The same thing occurred when we passed the wreckage and survivors of the *Queen Mary*. Even when a man on some wreckage waved to us, we thought it must be a German wanting to be picked up. It is rather dreadful to think of now, especially as some men were not too keen on rescuing Germans after the *Lusitania* and similar atrocities, but I have often thought since how well it showed the confidence that we had in our own fleet that no one for a moment imagined that one of our own ships would be sunk so soon.

Before we turned to the North (at about 5 p.m.), we could see some of the German ships on fire, which cheered us very much. By this time we were under a very hot fire, and were zigzagging slightly to avoid it. I was very impressed by the absolute cloud of shells which landed under the next-ahead's stern as she turned 16 points, and I remember thinking what a mess her quarter deck would have been in if she had been going a few knots slower.

After the turn I had no time for anything except to plot the enemy's deflection, as we were about to fire a torpedo. The foremost tube, however, jammed, and nothing could move the bar.[3] The crew of the forward torpedo flat used some really artistic language when telling us that the starboard bar would not go out, neither by power nor by hand. We eventually fired from our starboard after tube.

All this time I was gradually getting my thoughts out of their 'dreamy' state, and was slowly beginning to realise that all these projectiles falling a few yards short and over were big ones, and that they were meant for us; and my thoughts, following their natural course, led me on to think of my life-saving waistcoat, which, like a fool, I had left in my sea-chest down below. There was no chance of getting it now.

All this time we were being thrown about by the blast of ' X' turret, and we spent quite a portion of our time in ungraceful and rather painful positions on the deck, bumping against the range-finder, plotter, and other things with sharp corners.

---

3 A part of the mechanism of a submerged torpedo tube.

The next thing of much interest that I remember was a very loud crash, followed by a sound like hail. After a short space of silent thought we disentangled ourselves, and I, being inexperienced, looked through the starboard sighting hole at 'X' turret, the roof of which had become rather like a badly-made saucer, see-sawing on top of the turret. I caught a vision of the crew inside still going strong, but my interesting report of this was cut short by a salvo from that turret, which precipitated me backwards into the arms of an able seaman, and incidentally reduced me to a state of wandering wonder for several minutes. 'X' turret had been hit by a shell on the roof, but was still in action.

Recovering from the shock of this, I was even nearer realising what was happening around us—yet was still unaware of any desire to be elsewhere—when there came a sudden shudder and lurch through the ship, a frightful din of escaping steam, and the ship took an uncomfortable list to starboard. There followed tender enquiries from the torpedo flats, switch-board, and other stations below decks as to our welfare, whether we were still alive, and also whether there were still any Huns left. To both questions we replied in the affirmative.

At this period the battle cruisers were well ahead, and the four ships of our squadron were getting the full hate of the German, fleet, which was far from pleasant. About 6.15 p.m. the *Defence* appeared between us and the enemy, on our starboard quarter, and after firing several rounds was suddenly enveloped in smoke and flames, and when these lifted, there was only a small space of smooth water where two minutes before had been a ship and her crew of 900 men. Just before this I had been thinking of the four midshipmen of my term who were in her, so it is hardly surprising that the sight of her blowing up brought home to me just what we were taking part in; what is more, it came with a distinct shock, and I had a fleeting glance of other ships having the same sudden end. I think I can truthfully say that it was at this stage of the action that I realised that the Germans were rather good shots, and also that there weren't many of us, but a deuce of a lot of them. In fact, to use another slang term, just about now I had 'wind-up'; but it was a comic feeling of being well scared and yet at the same time liking it, a feeling that I cannot quite describe in mere words. One thing I can express is the pleasure it was to see the *Agincourt* suddenly appear in sight ahead, looking more like a Brock's Benefit than a battleship, as she poured out salvoes from her broadside of fourteen 12-inch guns. After this we saw very little of the enemy, as it was very thick, and we were now the last ship in the battle line.

Shortly after 7.30 p.m. we lost touch altogether with the enemy, and a lull in the action occurred. After having a look at the damage done to 'X' turret, I went forward, and was surprised to see a large shell hole in the upper deck near No. 3 6-inch gun starboard. The lower boom stanchion was buckled out of all recognition, and the bread store was a twisted heap of wreckage. I went down to the battery, where everything was dark chaos. Most of the wounded had been taken away, but several of the killed were still there. The most ghastly part of the whole affair was the smell of burnt human flesh, which remained in the ship for weeks, making everybody have a sickly nauseous feeling the whole time. When the battery was finally lighted by an emergency circuit, it was a scene which cannot easily be forgotten—everything burnt black and bare from the fire; the galley, canteen and drying-room bulkheads blown and twisted into the most grotesque shapes, and the whole deck covered by about 6 inches of water and dreadful débris; and permeating everywhere the awful stench of cordite fumes and of war. It is hardly surprising that the nerves of many of us were shaken, especially as the men below decks and in other stations away from the actual damage had never dreamt that we had suffered such damage or casualties.

By the time it was dark we were all at our stations again. Some of the torpedo control tower's crew were lying on the deck, whilst the remainder kept a look out.

It was extraordinary how tired we all felt—too tired even to think, or even to dream about what we had gone through and seen. Men must be dead beat to sleep solidly on a hard, cold deck with the sharp corners of instruments sticking into them. Even the din of the commencement of the night attack failed to wake two of us, and we would probably have gone on sleeping till morning if someone had not trodden on our faces. At first we were really too tired to have anything but a detached interest in what was going on. It was the same 'nightmare' state as we had experienced in the early part of the day action, except perhaps there was now added a subconscious wish that it was all over, and that we could be allowed to sleep undisturbed. This feeling was stopped by a sharp action which was taking place some distance on our starboard quarter, which we could only follow by the light of occasional searchlights, gun-flashes, or the larger flashes of destroyers on fire or blowing up. We saw one large ship lighted up some distance away on our starboard quarter, probably a German cruiser, but we could not tell at the time. My memory represents the night action as a foggy haze, with occasional visions of flashes from guns, dim glimpses of destroyers, and a general medley of noises. The whole thing was a confused blur to me at the time; my mind was incapable of grasping it.

I remember we had the cheeriest breakfast party I've ever taken part in the next morning. It consisted of two officers and three men with a tin of 'bully beef,' cocoa in large quantities, and a colossal loaf of bread. But after we had finished we all became depressed again. In the gun-room it was the same, partly because all the wounded were outside.

That evening (June 1st) we buried some of the dead. There was not a soul without a lump in his throat, and quite a lot of the officers and men standing on the upper deck were very near to tears. I noticed the same thing when the dockyard maties working on board H.M.S. *Erin* cheered us on entering Invergordon.

One extraordinary effect on our nerves was that, although we were so tired, we were absolutely incapable of sleeping except for short periods with long stretches of wakefulness in between. But the most extraordinary sensation of all was that, although most of us were in a way scared, we would all have given our souls rather than have missed being in the action.

CHAPTER VI

THE BATTLE CRUISER ACTION CONTINUED

The Run to the North (4.45 p.m. to about 5.50 p.m.)
The 5th B.S. in Close Action.

We can now return to narratives that describe the continuation of the Battle Cruiser action, particularly those of the course of events from the time that the High Seas Fleet was sighted and our Battle Cruisers turned to the North at 4.46 p.m. until about 6.0 p.m. when the British Battle Fleet came into sight from the Northward.

Each fresh narrative that one reads, although it may describe the same phase of the battle as has another, appears to differ from it in 'atmosphere,' as if the intensity of modern naval action and the quick passage of events causes each person present in the battle to be left with a fresh impression of what actually occurred.

The narrative of H.M.S. *Lion*'s Gunnery Officer for example (which is the second narrative of this Chapter), describes the early events of the action wholly from a Gun Control Officer's point of view, and repictures the progress of the battle as it appeared from the foretop of the *Lion*. In reading it one realises how much each man's work must colour his impression of the fighting; probably no two men can be left with quite the same memory of a naval battle. This narrative from H.M.S. *Lion* covers the period from the opening of fire at 3.48 p.m. up to the end of the run to the North at about 6.0 p.m.

Following the *Lion*'s account, there is a narrative from a Turret Officer of H.M.S. *Malaya*, which will amplify the Midshipman's narrative in Chapter V, and show in more detail the active manner in which the 5th Battle Squadron, Admiral

Evan Thomas' magnificent squadron, supported the battle cruisers during their run to the North.

An impression of the progress of the battle between 5.0 and 6.0 p.m. received by an Officer in one of the smaller ships, is contained in the narrative of H.M.S. *Galatea*, the light cruiser that originally sighted, at 2.20 p.m., the enemy forces. During the run North she was stationed near to the battle cruisers, but, owing to the big range at which the action was being fought, and to the absence of opportunity for torpedo attack after the return of the 13th Destroyer Flotilla from their attack at about 5.0 p.m., was practically only an onlooker of the fight. This rôle of an onlooker was the lot of most of the small ships between 5.0 and 6.0 p.m.

Extract from Narrative of H.M.S. *Galatea*

1st Light Cruiser Squadron
Continued from page 24

About 4.30 a W/T signal from *Southampton* was intercepted reporting that the Main High Sea Fleet was in sight to the southward, and was steering to the north, to close the German Battle Cruisers. Soon afterwards, when the enemy battleships were in sight from the *Lion*, we all turned 16 points and steered back to the northward, to draw the Germans towards the Grand Fleet.

The new course placed the 1st L.C.S. ahead of the two fleets again, and about midway between our own and the German line, from where we had a wonderful view of the battle. It was rather thrilling. One outstanding incident was a torpedo attack by three or four destroyers of the 13th Flotilla on the German lines, led by Commander Bingham in *Nestor*. *Nestor* and *Nomad* were disabled and later sunk, but the other two destroyers got away, and their escape was most spectacular. They appeared directly astern of us out of a thick cloud of funnel smoke which they were making to screen themselves, zigzagging like a couple of snipe, at times their high, white bow wave the only part of them visible, and a tornado of shells falling all round them. Apparently they would watch the flash from the ships firing at them and then put their helms over, and the place where they had been a moment before, barely a ship's length from

Salvo falling short of *Lion*

them now, would be lashed and torn into tall pillars of water. It seemed impossible that they could escape, as time after time they were obliterated from sight by salvoes, but presently their bow waves would appear again, and they would emerge, only to be blotted out once more a moment afterwards. It was a thrilling sight, and we afterwards discovered that both these two destroyers got away.

Shortly after 5.0 p.m. I remember hearing a signalman on the bridge call out a signal from the *Lion*, which he had been reading, which ordered our squadron to make a torpedo attack on the enemy battle cruisers, the leader of which was just a little before our beam. We repeated the signal to the rest of our squadron, and crashed on to full speed to get ahead. I guessed that an attack like this in broad daylight would have only one ending for us, but off we went. However, it was found we could not get far enough ahead in time to make the attack, so it was annulled, and we resumed our position ahead of the battle cruisers.

About this time the enemy ceased fire for about 20 minutes—having lately been firing very badly, whilst our battle cruisers' fire had seemed to be very effective. Several times I watched from the port side of the signal bridge a salvo fired by *Lion*, and then went over to the starboard side and saw a quarter to half a minute later the splash of the shell as it fell near the Germans, or occasionally I thought I saw the reddish burst of a hit. The three leading enemy battle cruisers were clearly seen, the sheen of the light on their sides being quite distinct, and also the red paint on their after funnels, which acted apparently as some sort of recognition mark. Our salvoes were falling all round them, and their third battle cruiser left the line, and vanished to starboard, evidently badly hit.

We were now gradually edging the enemy round to the eastward, and about 5.45 p.m. we suddenly made out on the horizon ahead the silhouette of two of our armoured cruisers—*Defence* and *Warrior*.

I can hardly even now describe the thrill we all felt—the Grand Fleet had arrived! It was a wonderful moment, for we felt that at last the High Seas Fleet had been securely rounded up.[1] . . .

Narrative of the Gunnery Control Officer of H.M.S. *Lion*

A Gun Control Officer does not, as a rule, witness the spectacular incidents of an action, for whilst firing is in progress his eyes and mind are concentrated on the immediate business of observing and directing the fire of the armament, and during lulls in the firing he is occupied with reports of the ammunition expended, of casualties, breakdowns, etc. If the control of the gunfire is to be carried out to the best of a Control Officer's ability, he must school himself during rehearsals and practice firings to be non-susceptible to all noises and reports which are not directly connected with the gun control. This statement may sound a platitude, but the din and seeming confusion which exist in action must be realised to be appreciated. The degree of concentration which is required, and which was attained, may be indicated by the fact that in one of the battle cruisers the Control Officer was actually not aware that two out of the six ships of his own squadron, in his own line, had been blown up until after the last engagement with the enemy in the evening—three hours or more after the ships had been lost. The noise and flash of *Queen Mary* blowing up, only half a mile astern, was not taken in.

1 *Galatea*'s narrative is continued on page 137.

Action stations were sounded off at 2.43 p.m. (Greenwich time) on 31st May, and as the fleet was keeping summer time, those officers not actually on watch were at the time getting their tea, causing an unfinished tea to be the first recollection one has of the Battle of Jutland. The next meal taken was in the control position at 9.30 p.m. and consisted of a chunk of bread and a piece of ham—but the story of the Admiral's ham and the midshipman who borrowed it is well known!

Shell short of *Lion*.

From 2.43 to 3.30 p.m., 47 minutes, sounds a longish time, but occupied in receiving reports and testing the readiness of the gun machinery and communications, it seemed to pass as a very few minutes. At 3.30 p.m. the enemy battle cruisers were in sight on the port bow at a range estimated to be 23,000 yards. It is a perfect day, and all attention is concentrated on the range-finding, on the resultant range to be given to the guns, and the rate of change of range as communicated from the plotting party in the transmitting station. At 3.35 p.m. the enemy's right-hand battle cruiser, identified as one of the *Lutzow* class, being the opposite number to us in the enemy line, is given by the Captain as our target. The gun director and guns are already on this ship or on what can be seen of her, for only the masts and funnel and a part of the hull are visible above the horizon from the control top and director tower, and from the gun positions the enemy is hull down. Two ships of the same class are first and second in the enemy line, and these two ships fill the field of view of the high power glasses that we are using. Guns are at the ready, the director layer has his target, and satisfactory reports of the readings of the range-finders and of the rate in use are received from the transmitting station.

At 3.39 p.m. the order is given 'Stand-by to open fire.' At that time the enemy battle cruisers, at a range of 20,000 yards, are bearing Red 32 (32 degrees from ahead on the port side), where all four turrets can just bear, and the two lines are converging on courses which reduce the range by 400 yards a minute. At 3.45 p.m. course is altered to starboard, away, bringing the enemy broader on the beam and altering the rate of convergence, and almost immediately afterwards the enemy also alters away to bring his broadside to bear. As soon as the lines are straightened out fire will be opened. Feelings of 'intense relief after months of waiting' or of 'pleasurable excitement on the arrival of the opportunity,' which one has read of as being felt immediately before opening fire, may occur in the case of participants generally, but for the gun control staff the routine procedure dominates everything, and there is no 'small talk' in the top.

At 3.47 the enemy gun flashes are seen, and in accordance with standing orders, we immediately open fire in reply, the range at the time being 18,500 yards—10½ land miles. The Germans invariably commence action with a greater rate of fire than our ships, due to the different system of finding the gun range employed by the two Navies, consequently the first flashes of the enemy guns are followed immediately by a second, a third, and a minute later a fourth salvo. Our fourth salvo is not fired until about two and a half minutes after our first. During the time of flight of about 20 seconds before the first salvo reaches the enemy much might pass through a control officer's mind, but the one thought that is dominant is 'Splashes or no splashes?' If the salvoes fall beyond the target at such a range as 10 miles there are 'no splashes' visible to the observer, for the target covers them; but if the salvoes fall short of the target, splashes are visible. The whole of the British fire control system is based upon this observation of fall of shot-splashes. If the splashes are visible in front of the target, the range for the next salvo is increased; if the splashes are beyond the target (no splashes visible), the range must be decreased, until in due course the correct range is obtained. Then the mean position of the four or five shells of a salvo will be on the target, two perhaps being short, one over, and one hitting. This is called a straddle, and the control officer continually applies corrections to his gun range until he is straddling— that is, until he sees only two or three splashes from his four shell salvo in front of the target.

From our first salvo 'no splashes' are observed, and for two more salvoes 'no splashes,' but from the fourth salvo, fired 2½ minutes after the first, splashes are seen—*i.e.*, we have crossed from overs to shorts. From that time the control officer is making allowance for own ship altering course, judging as to enemy's course both as observed and as deduced from the plotting table in the transmitting station, receiving short reports from the T.S. and giving monosyllabic replies, overhearing quick questions and answers between the spotter and the rate-keeper, as well as general gunnery reports given and received, which are noted and acted upon, or if not of immediate interest or not requiring reply—ignored. The conversation in the gun control top runs something like this:—

'Did you see that?'

'No.'

'Down 400: close the rate 200.'

'Can't.'

'Make it one.'

'Down 400 on the plot.'

'Put it on and close 100.'

'Rate 250 closing.'

'Shoot!'

'Ship altering course to starboard, rate 200 closing.'

'Stand-by, splash.'

'Up 200'—and so on, *ad lib*.

Occasionally there is a check in this endless babble, but almost immediately it is fired into renewed activity by a sharp challenge up the voice-pipe, 'T.S.—Foretop,' to ascertain if the control position is still in action, for if there is no answer the auxiliary position must be told to take over the control. Occasionally there comes the variation of 'Hail falls,' or 'the-ship-is-picked-up-and-thrown-down-again-angrily.' Hail falling is the result of an enemy shell falling short and bursting on impact with the water, throwing a very large number of small fragments of shell high into the air which fall on the thin sheet-iron roof of the control top, making a noise like a heavy fall of hail. This was happening a number of times.

'The-ship-is-picked-up-and-thrown-down-again-angrily' is due to an enemy shell hitting the ship's armour and being unable to penetrate, when the whole of the force of detonation is imparted to the hull of the ship, and conveys to the occupants of the control top the impression stated. Once the side of the control top was struck and penetrated, but only by quite a small fragment of shell which did no harm, although the concussion was considerable. The spotter's knee was against the side of the top, and he was heard to utter one word of forcible exclamation in the midst of his gun control remarks, apparently being under the impression that his leg had been hit! Those shells which burst or detonate inside the ship did not seem to have the same effect of shaking the ship as those which burst on the armour.

At 3.57 one of the turrets is hit and put out of action, the fact being duly reported to the control top, to whom this means that the salvo will be of three guns instead of four guns for the remainder of the action, or at least until the turret is reported in action again. In point of fact that turret, 'Q' turret, was out of action finally, and the entire crew were killed.

The bearing of the enemy is now growing aft, and the range having been down to 14,500 yards at 3.54, has increased again to 16,750 at 4.01, indicating that the enemy has been altering course away slightly. The range still increases and the enemy does not fire for some ten minutes, a fact noted by the control top because there are no enemy gun flashes, and the line of view is not intermittently obstructed by columns of water thrown up by his salvoes. Some of the shell falling short burst on hitting the water and add the smoke of the burst to the spray of the columns of water, making aiming and observation of fall of shot during this period difficult, which results in a slow rate of fire from our ships. At 4.15 the enemy opens fire again, and so the running fight between the battle cruisers continues until 4.36, when the enemy, having altered course to port and being abaft the beam, has increased the range to the maximum possible for the guns, and fire is ceased. At 4.40 the enemy battle fleet has been sighted, and the battle cruiser line turns 16 points to starboard in succession.[2]

During the turn the turrets are swung round on to the opposite bow in readiness to re-engage and reports as to the amount of

---

2 This time was more probably 4.46.

Salvo falling close to *Lion.*

Photo taken from a destroyer's bridge, with signal rocket in the foreground.

ammunition expended are received in the control top and repeated to the Captain. Having completed the 16-point turn at 4.45, a further turn of 4 points is made to starboard, for both battle cruiser lines have turned outwards, thereby considerably increasing the range. Three minutes later, by which time the German battle cruisers have completed their turn, the two lines have again converged to within gun range, and fire is opened on the enemy leading ship, which is noted as being the *Von der Tann.* The range is 20,000 yards, but only eleven salvoes are fired before the bad light and mist make it possible for the enemy to pass out of sight at about 16,000 yards. At 4.48 a quantity of wreckage is passed, on which two or three men are floating, and a destroyer is standing by near to it—apparently it is the remains of the *Queen Mary*, although this is not appreciated at the time.

From 4.40 to 6 p.m. we are maintaining touch with the enemy battle fleet and leading them to our Grand Fleet, both lines steaming to the northward, but the bad light and the mist, together with the smoke of our guns firing and the smoke of enemy shells bursting, make long-range action impossible, and the action consists of a series of comparatively short bursts of firing, with longer intervals during which the enemy are not in sight.

From the turn at 4.40 p.m. until the end of the day action, the firing of our battle cruisers only consists of five separated and short engagements. From time to time the course is altered to close the enemy and search the mist and smoke-laden atmosphere for a possible target, but almost as soon as sighted and opened fire upon, the target alters course away and disappears behind a smoke screen.

At 5.08 a lull in the firing commences, during which a little incident of interest occurs. An enemy shell burst a few minutes ago in the Sick Bay, wrecking the compartment and filling it and adjacent compartment with smoke. Some of this smoke passes down a breathing pipe to 'X' turret magazine, and appearing up from behind cordite cases, makes the petty officer there hastily conclude that his compartment is on fire, which he duly reports to the officer of the turret in the gun-house above. The report reaches the control top *via* the transmitting station, '5.08, Fire in "X" magazine.' But three minutes later—sufficient time for the officer of the turret to get from his gun-house down to the magazine and back up again—the report is cancelled, '5.11, "X" magazine correct.' As these reports came through during a lull in the firing, a member of the control staff must be pardoned the interest he took in the first report, 'Fire in "X" magazine,' and the remark he made, ' Stand-by for the h—l of a bump!'

At 5.08 then the enemy were lost to sight, but were sighted again at 5.12, and again at 5.33, though insufficiently clearly to enable fire to be opened on them. The next engagement is of longer duration, and lasts from 5.39 until 6.01, at ranges varying between 13,000 and 15,000 yards. The target is noted as one of the *Kronprinz* class battleships, being the leading of two ships of the same class in close order with a third capital ship some distance astern. Ahead of the target—the leading big ship—are two ships taken to be light cruisers, each with three funnels and two masts. These are the only ships in sight at the time. Throughout this engagement the target is a very bad one, at times barely visible, so that the best point of aim is the wash at the stern of the enemy, allowance to hit the ship being made accordingly. At one time during this engagement the salvoes from another ship are noted as being directed at our target. At 5.51 it is noted 'Enemy have not been firing for some minutes, but do so now,' indicating that the mist is as disconcerting for them as it is for us, or that they have been in trouble and are unable to return the fire. At 6.01 this enemy finally passes out of sight.

This narrative is completed on page 388. As the Battle Fleet arrived and came into action before H.M.S. *Lion* was again in close contact with the enemy, several narratives from the battleships, etc., are introduced before the completion of *Lion*'s experiences.

Narrative of the 5th B.S.

(From a Turret Officer of H.M.S. *Malaya*, Rear Ship of the 5th Battle Squadron.) Summary of Notes made immediately after the Action of 31st May, 1916

Extract from the Narrative of a Destroyer screening the 5th B.S.:—

'It was a magnificent sight to watch these four splendid battleships firing their broadsides of 15-inch. There was something tremendously heartening about the look of them, and the very concussion of their broadsides was most inspiring. . . .'

At 2.30 p.m., as Officer of the Watch, I saw an intercepted signal from *Galatea* to *Lion* stating that a large amount of smoke had been sighted, apparently from a fleet under way, and shortly afterwards we heard that our light cruisers and destroyers were in touch with enemy light cruisers and destroyers. We were steaming at this time approximately east by south, and, as usual, zigzagging to avoid a possible Fritz,[3] in the order of *Barham*, *Valiant*,

---

3 'Fritz,' the customary nickname for a German submarine.

Warspite, *Malaya*, and were about 5 miles to the north of Sir David Beatty and his six battle cruisers. As this was our first intimation that any Germans were on the ocean at all, our surprise and excitement may well be imagined. Everyone woke up and became interested and excited, many coming on the upper deck or bridge to scan the horizon for a sign of the enemy. Glasses were at a premium. The pessimists still held their ground and declared that in all probability it was some wretched Hun light cruisers that would easily escape us.

3.0 p.m.—Sounded off 'Action.'

Officers and men doubled to their stations, most of them never even guessing that a German had actually been sighted, but thinking that it was merely the same old game: 'Be ready.' When I arrived in my turret ('B') I knew that the light cruisers had been in action, and that there was no time to spare. I had a hurried look round to see that all was well, and told the men what I could—viz., that we might expect to meet anything from a German light cruiser to the High Sea Fleet, and that 'B' turret had got to get off the maximum number of rounds allowed by the control. Up to date we had been favoured by good luck in practices, having no breakdowns, but we must now be ready for real action troubles and still not miss a salvo.

The men were greatly cheered by the news, and assured me that no chance would be missed to ease off a round at the Huns, and at once began to make little extra preparations, taking off superfluous clothing and so forth. They made all sorts of weird and wonderful jokes as to what would happen to any German ship unfortunate enough to come within range of our guns.

3.50 p.m.—Our battle cruisers were heard firing, so I thought it was time to get to my perch in the 'Silent Cabinet.'[4]

I saw nothing until about 4 p.m., when I sighted a German light cruiser, at which our leading ships were

---

4 A portion of the gun-house partitioned off and made sound proof, into which telephones, etc., lead from the Fire Control positions of the ship. It is used as the control position if the turret is ordered to go into 'local control', or if the communications from other positions are shot away or fail.

firing. Now things were beginning to look busy; surely we should sight something bigger soon.

About 4.10 p.m.—We turned to approx. S.S.E., and I then sighted the German battle cruisers steaming on a parallel course to us. There were five of them, and I thought their order was as follows:—Three *Derfflinger* class leading the line, followed by the *Moltke* and then the *Seydlitz*. There were light cruisers and T.B.D.s ahead and astern of them. I was sure that the last ship was the *Seydlitz* and not the *Moltke*, for I carefully compared the two, and saw that the rear ship had a raised forecastle, which is about the only way of distinguishing the *Seydlitz* from *Moltke*.

4.15 p.m.—We opened fire on the *Seydlitz*,[5] and were the last ship to commence, being the last in the line. The range was 19,000 yards, and the enemy bearing about 2 points before the beam. The visibility was then good for ranging, but I thought it bad for spotting, as the background was misty and of exactly the same shade as a splash, which made the latter difficult to distinguish.

Remembering my experiences on the Belgian Coast, I started with the intention of keeping as full notes as possible throughout the action. They would at least have been interesting for me, even if they should not prove to be of use as evidence. This I managed to do, jotting my notes down on a signal pad throughout the action, except on the occasions when I had to go down below to rectify some defect, but, by a misfortune which I shall never cease to regret, these notes became detached from the signal pad and were thrown away by an enthusiastic boy as waste paper. I had made notes of what I thought was the fate of every salvo that I saw, the target, and anything of interest. But practically the only definite thing that I remember about the fall of our shot is the fact that we hit with our fourth salvo. Most of the rest is jumbled up in my head, and I cannot pick out with accuracy the times at which various incidents happened.

---

5 This proved to be wrong and was actually the *Von der Tann*. The name has been altered accordingly to *Von der Tann* throughout the remainder of this account.

When the *Von der Tann* was hit she at once turned away about 5 points (50 or 60 degrees), but shortly afterwards resumed her course. Very soon after this I remember thinking that the enemy must be zigzagging, as on several occasions we found our shot going wrong for deflection.

During this time the enemy were firing rapidly, but, it seemed to me, wildly. We fired quickly for the first few salvoes, but as the light gradually became worse the range closed, and our firing became more deliberate. I did not have much time for observing how the shooting of the other ships fared. All I remember is that all the enemy ships seemed to be obliterated by the splashes of shell. I distinctly remember making a note that the *Von der Tann* was badly on fire soon after we hit her, and that the third ship was also on fire. The battle continued in this manner until 4.50 p.m. The visibility was rapidly becoming worse, and at times we could only see the flash of the enemy's guns. Notwithstanding this, however, the enemy must have been able to distinguish us plainly, for the horizon on our starboard side was very definite. The German battle cruisers were zigzagging rapidly, which, together with the light, probably accounts for the fact that they were not hit more often, and also for their own shooting being so erratic.

4.50 p.m.—I saw the enemy battle cruisers turning 16 points together, and looked to the southward of them to see if I could discover the reason for this manoeuvre. I saw, just distinguishable in the mist, a warship of sorts coming from the S.E. I pointed this out to the Commander, who is stationed in my turret for the purpose of conning the ship should anything happen to the main steering position and for keeping in touch with outside departments, but he did not know what to make of it. We were not long kept in suspense as to what this new ship was, for very shortly after sighting her, I saw following her a long line of others, which we soon recognised as German Dreadnought Battleships of the *Konig* and *Kaiser* classes. I could not say in what formation they were, but they appeared to be in three divisions in line ahead disposed quarterly.

Up to this time the shooting had for us been very like a 'peace battle practice'. I felt that, according to all rules of the game, the German battle cruisers ought not to remain much longer afloat. I had not up to date thought much about the danger of being hit by a projectile, except perhaps just before the action began, when my mind certainly tried to wander on to gruesome possibilities. Now, however, matters took quite a different complexion. We were closing the High Sea Fleet at a relative rate of about 40 knots, and there was every prospect of becoming engaged with them in a very short space of time. My feelings at that time are rather hard to analyse, for, as things were happening quickly, I had not enough time thinking whether I was frightened or not. I don't think I was really anxious, but I dare say that if I had stopped to think I should have been. It merely flashed across my mind that we were now in for a busy time, and probably a warm one.

4.55 p.m.—Our battle cruisers passed between us and the enemy, steaming approximately north.

I counted four, there had been six. It was then that I realised that we must have lost two, and that the wreckage that we had passed at about 4.30 must have been one of our battle cruisers. We had seen a destroyer (the *Laurel*, I believe) stopped amongst some wreckage picking up a few survivors from the water, but so small an amount of ship was left in the water that I had hoped that it was a German light cruiser, or, at the worst, if it was a ship of ours, no more than a light cruiser. The *Laurel* was about 500 yards from our line, and was under considerable fire. It was a fine sight to see her boats' crews carrying out their rescue work as though they were doing a peace evolution.

As we were on opposite courses, the battle cruisers passed us very rapidly, and we did not get much chance to see how matters were going with them. We saw the *Lion, Princess Royal, Tiger*, and *New Zealand*. They were all firing very quickly at the enemy's battle cruisers, and the only damage to them that we could pick out was at 'Q' turret in the *Lion*, which was trained away from the enemy, and appeared to have been badly hit after the

119

battle cruisers had passed us. We continued on our course on towards the enemy battle fleet for what seemed an eternity, but which in reality was only about 5 minutes.

4.59 p.m.—Then we turned 16 points to starboard in succession. I must admit to a feeling of relief when I realised that we were to turn round, though I did not like it being done in succession. When it was time for the *Malaya* to turn, the turning point was a very 'hot corner,' as the enemy had, of course, concentrated on that point. The shells were pouring in very fast, and it is doubtful whether we, the last ship of the line, could have got through without a very severe hammering if the Captain had not used his initiative and turned the ship early.

When we had turned, or rather as I was training my turret round to the starboard side, now the engaged side, I saw that our battle cruisers proceeding northerly at full speed in close action with the German battle cruisers, were already quite 7,000 or 8,000 yards ahead of us. I then realised that just the four of us of the 5th B.S. alone would have to entertain the High Sea Fleet—4 against perhaps 20.

5.15 p.m.—The enemy continued to fire rapidly at us during and after the turn, but they did not really get near until about 5.15, when their salvoes began to arrive thick and fast round us at the rate of 6, 8, or 9 a minute. From my position in the turret I could see them falling just short, could hear them going just over, and saw several times a great column of black water fall on top of the turret.

I don't know that I thought about it very much at the time, for I was trying hard to make out our target, but I expected at any moment that we should get a nasty knock, and I realised that if any one of those shells should hit us in the right place our speed would be sadly reduced, and then we should fall behind and probably be sunk.

I had counted soon after the turn the number of enemy ships firing at us, and the 9th ship was the rearmost that I thought I saw open fire. I believe that this was at times increased by the German battle cruisers joining in against us, although I cannot say that I noticed them myself.

5.20 p.m.—I saw a large column of water rise up between my guns and felt the turret shake heavily. We had been hit abreast the turret, below the water line, and so heavy was the shock that I feared that our loading gear must be damaged and so our fighting efficiency greatly impaired, although the shell had not pierced into any part of the turret. I went down into the gun-house to enquire whether all was well below, and received the report that they had been somewhat shaken, but that everything seemed all right. This proved to be over-optimistic, for when the main cage arrived in the working chamber it was found that the shell could not be withdrawn and there was a proper 'jam up.' I dashed down, and we worked like niggers to clear it. After what seemed an age, but could not really have been so very long, we managed by extemporary means to get the cage into working order again.

During this time the secondary or hand method of loading was in use for the right gun, and although five rounds had to be loaded in this manner, the turret never missed a chance to fire, which was very pleasing, as the secondary method is generally considered such a slow one. The men had to work at tremendous pressure to keep the guns going, everybody available in the turret assisting at loading the right gun, including the midshipman, armourer, torpedoman, etc. I thought their success a great credit to them.

On going back into the turret I found everyone very cheery and full of go. They had no thought that we should come off worse than the enemy, but only wanted to know how many German ships were left afloat requiring to be finished off. They were full of confidence that every shell was doing its bit, and many and varied were the benedictions they sent with each round fired. When things were at their hottest I heard one man in the gun-house call out to the others, 'Don't get rattled—you're putting your —— feet all over the —— paintwork!'

Those in the shell-room had a fairly good shock when the salvo pitched abreast them, several being actually knocked over. However, they all treated it as a joke, and their one idea was to send up as many shells as possible. I think the lot of those in the magazine was the hardest, for it is no easy job to handle cordite for a 15-inch gun, and the atmosphere down below becomes after a time extremely oppressive.

5.40.—Until about 5.40 the enemy's firing continued to be very brisk, and to fall all round us. The visibility for us had been getting steadily worse; in fact, ever since 5.15 we had rarely been able to see anything but the flashes of the German guns. We were several times hit, to what extent I could not tell, but I saw that the ship had dropped astern of station, and that we had a considerable list to starboard. Reports were continually coming in to the Commander, so we were not kept so very long in suspense as to the damage done to the ship.

I heard reports coming through of a fire, later that it was being satisfactorily dealt with; reports that certain compartments had been flooded or water was leaking into others, reports about casualties, dressing stations being full, the clearing of wounded and dead, and so on. It all came through in the most matter-of-fact way, seeming nothing out of the ordinary, as though we made and heard those sort of reports every day of our lives. The Commander had to go and investigate on two or three occasions, but as a general rule he was able to control everything from 'B' turret.

Until 6 p.m. the action continued in a northerly direction, the light gradually becoming worse and the range shorter. After 5.40 p.m. the firing became intermittent, the light being then bad for the Germans as well as ourselves. By this time the atmosphere in the 'silent cabinet' was extremely hot and uncomfortable, so the Commander and I took advantage of an unusually long pause, to get an airing on the top of the turret. The visibility was about 8,000 yards, but I could see no other ships except the other three of our squadron, which we were now overtaking again.

At 6.10 p.m. the report was passed round the ship that the Grand Fleet was in sight and would shortly deploy into action. This was extremely welcome news, for matters were not looking very cheery for us. It could hardly be hoped that we could continue to engage the German Battle Fleet for much longer without sustaining very serious damage, to say the least of it.

Part II

The Battle Fleet Action

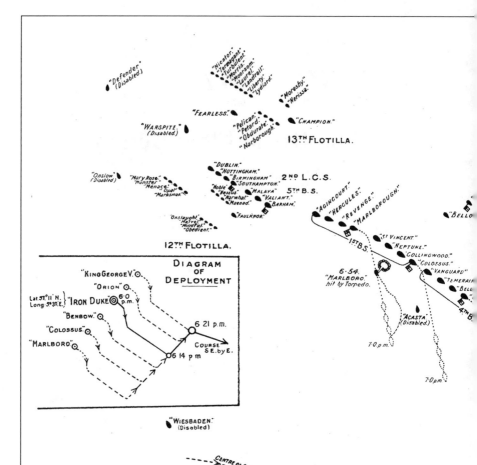

"Defender."
(Disabled)

"Nicator."
"Termagant."
"Turbulent."
"Morris."
"Laurel."
"Moorson."
"Landrail."
"Liberty."
"Lydiard."

"Moresby."
"Nerissa."

"Fearless."

"Warspite."
(Disabled)

"Pelican."
"Petard."
"Obdurate."
"Narborough."

"Champion."

13TH FLOTILLA.

"Onslow"
(Disabled)

"Mary Rose."
"Munster."
"Menace."
"Ossa."
"Marksman."

"Dublin."
"Nottingham."
"Birmingham."
"Southampton."

"Noble."
"Nessus."
"Malaya."
"Narwhal."
"Valiant."
"Nomad."
"Barham."

"Faulknor."

2ND L.C.S.

5TH B.S.

"Onslaught."
"Maenad."
"Mindful."
"Obedient."

12TH FLOTILLA.

"Agincourt."
"Hercules."
"Revenge."
"Marlborough."

"Bello

"St Vincent."
"Neptune."
"Collingwood."
"Colossus."
"Vanguard."
"Temerai
"Bell

1ST B.S.

6·54.
"Marlboro."
hit by Torpedo.

DIAGRAM
OF
DEPLOYMENT

"King George V." ⊙
"Orion" ⊙
Lat.57°.11'N.
Long.5°.39.E. "Iron Duke" ⊙ 6·0
p.m.
"Benbow." ⊙
"Colossus." ⊙
"Marlboro" ⊙

6·21 p.m.

Course
S.E.by E.

6·14 pm

"Acasta"
(Disabled)

7·0 p.m.

4TH

7·0 p.m.

"Wiesbaden."
(Disabled)

CENTRE OF GERMAN FLEET (estimated)

BATTLE FLEET ACTION,
ABOUT 7·0 P.M. 31ST MAY, 1916.
(INSET, DIAGRAM OF DEPLOYMENT AT 6·14 P.M.)

Note:- The purpose of this plan is to show, very approximately, the position of Ships & Squadre
with relation to each other during the Battle Fleet Action.

In detail the plan is not accurate, but it may be accepted as showing, for example, whether a Ship or
Squadron at 7·0 p.m. was at the Van, Rear or on the disengaged side.

The position of the Enemy with regard to our ships is not definitely established.

"IRON DUKE'S" approximate position at 7·0 p.m was Lat: 57°-04'. N Long. 6°-02'. E.

At 7·12. p.m. BATTLE FLEET re-formed Single Line-Course SOUTH: "KING GEORGE V." leading.

This Plan is principally based upon Jellicoe's "GRAND FLEET." 1914-1916'

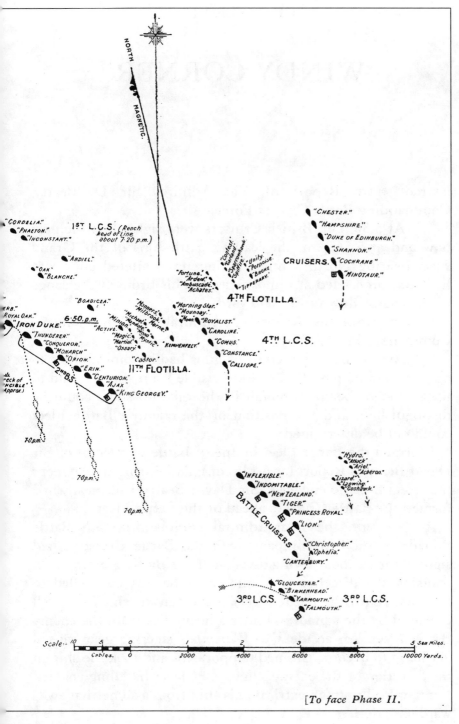

NORTH MAGNETIC.

"CORDELIA."
"PHAETON."
"INCONSTANT."

1ST L.C.S. (Reach
head of Line
about 7.20 p.m.)

"ARDIEL."

"OAK"
"BLANCHE."

"BOADICEA."

ERB."
ROYAL OAK."
IRON DUKE.   6·50.p.m.
"THUNDERER."
"CONQUEROR."
"MONARCH."
2ND BS   "ORION."
"ERIN."
"CENTURION."
"AJAX."
"KING GEORGEV."

th.
reck of
INCIBLE"
Approx.)

7.0.p.m.

7.0 p.m.

7.0.p.m.

"Hampers."
"Milbrook."
"Michael." Marne."
"Magdalena."
MINION.
"ACTIVE."
"Kempa."
"Mystic."
"Magic."
"Martial."
"Ossary."
"Castor."

"Contest."
"Garland."
"Sparrowhawk."
"Unity."
"Porpoise."
"Broke."
"Spitfire."
"TIPPERARY."

"Fortune."
"Ardent."
"Ambuscade."
"Achates."

"Morning Star."
"Mounsay."
"Noon." "ROYALIST."
"CAROLINE."
"KEMPENFELT."
"COMUS."
"CONSTANCE."
"CALLIOPE."

"CHESTER."
"HAMPSHIRE."
"DUKE OF EDINBURGH."
"SHANNON."
CRUISERS.   "COCHRANE"
"MINOTAUR."

4TH FLOTILLA.

4TH L.C.S.

11TH FLOTILLA.

"INFLEXIBLE."
"INDOMITABLE."
"NEW ZEALAND."
BATTLE CRUISERS   "TIGER."
"PRINCESS ROYAL."
"LION."

"Christopher."
"Ophelia."
"CANTERBURY."

"Hydra."
"Attock."
"Ariel."
"Acheron."
"Lizard."
"Lapwing."
"Goshawk."

"GLOUCESTER."
"BIRKENHEAD."
3RD L.C.S.   "YARMOUTH."   3RD L.C.S.
"FALMOUTH."

Scale:- 10   5   0   1   2   3   4   5 Sea Miles.
Cables.   0   2000   4000   6000   8000   10000 Yards.

[To face Phase II.

CHAPTER VII

'WINDY CORNER'

Extract from Report of Vice-Admiral Sir D. Beatty, Commanding Battle Cruiser Force:—

'. . . At 5.50 p.m. British Cruisers were sighted on the port bow and at 5.56 p.m. the leading battleships of the Grand Fleet bearing North 5 miles. I thereupon altered course to East and proceeded at utmost speed. This brought the range of the enemy down to 12,000 yards . . .'

Extract from the Report of Admiral Sir John Jellicoe, Commander-in-Chief:—

'. . . At 5.45 p.m. the report of guns had become audible to me, and at 5.55 p.m. flashes were visible from ahead round to the starboard beam, although in the mist no ships could be distinguished, and the position of the enemy's Battle Fleet could not be determined. . . .

I formed the Battle Fleet in line of battle on receipt of Sir David Beatty's Report (at 6.14 p.m.), and during deployment the fleets became engaged. Sir David Beatty had meanwhile formed the Battle Cruisers ahead of the Battle Fleet. . . .

At 6.6 p.m. the Rear-Admiral commanding 5th Battle Squadron, then in company with the Battle Cruisers, had sighted the starboard wing division of the Battle Fleet. . . . On realising the direction of deployment he was compelled to form astern (of the Battle Fleet), a manoeuvre which was well executed by the squadron under a heavy fire from the enemy Battle Fleet. An accident to *Warspite*'s steering gear caused her helm to become jammed temporarily, and took the ship in the direction of the enemy's line. . . . Clever handling enabled Captain Phillpotts to extricate his ship from a somewhat awkward situation.'

Extract from the narrative of a Light Cruiser Officer:—

'The point where all this turning took place has been called "Windy Corner." It well earned its name. Just after we arrived, the *Warspite*, which was the third ship of the 5th B.S. at that moment turning Windy Corner, for no apparent reason left her place in the line and steamed straight towards the enemy. After going some distance, until she cannot have been, we estimated, much over 5,000 yards from the enemy, she commenced to turn circles, something having gone wrong with her steering gear, with every German ship in sight firing at her. The effect was extraordinary. Columns of water from bursting shells completely surrounded her, and hid her from our sight. It seemed inevitable that she would blow up. But then, greatly to our surprise and relief, we saw her suddenly start to go ahead again, turn on a steady course towards our line and re-engage the enemy with a salvo from all her turrets, as if she was in no way the worse for her little 'stunt.'

Almost at the same time as this *Defence* had appeared in sight from ahead, had blown up in one terribly complete explosion, and *Warrior*, her next astern was badly battered, and only just able to struggle out of the action.'

Continuation of Account by a Turret Officer of H.M.S. *Malaya*, of 5th B.S.

6.20.—At about 6.20 I could just see the Grand Fleet deploying into action in magnificent style. They seemed to me to be in an ideal position almost across the head of the enemy line. I remember thinking that the position seemed so advantageous that if the light would only hold for half an hour there would be hardly a German ship left in action. 'Now,' I thought, 'our part of the work is done; we have brought the High Sea Fleet to the C.-in-C.; the Grand Fleet has deployed in exactly the correct position (between the battle cruisers and ourselves), and apparently the head of the line is even now bending to

127

| *Princess Royal* and destroyer | Splashes caused. by two shells | *Tiger* | Destroyers |

Junction of the Grand Fleet with Battle Cruiser Fleet at 'Windy Corner' about 6.15pm

starboard, crossing ahead of the enemy—the outlook is indeed good.' But matters turned out differently. When the fleet deployed the light was better than it had been for some time, but it quickly deteriorated again, so much so that only one Battle Squadron really became engaged to any extent, the rearmost one, the 1st B.S. They fired very rapidly, especially the *Agincourt*, which made a most impressive sight firing her fourteen 12-inch guns at full speed.

Although the Grand Fleet was to a certain extent in touch with the enemy until about 7.30 p.m., they never had a real chance to inflict a crushing blow. Whenever the enemy became visible, use was made of the opportunity, and undoubtedly very great damage was inflicted; but these opportunities were few and far between. At 6.30 p.m. we (the 5th B.S.) took station in rear of the 1st B.S. In doing so we must have been going too fast, for we ran up on to the last ship of the line, and were actually over-lapping each other, thereby presenting an excellent target to the 'Huns,' who were extremely quick in taking advantage of it.

At the rear of our line was a regular bunch of ships; the 5th B.S., a Light Cruiser Squadron, and a Destroyer Flotilla, gathered together in a remarkably small area, into which the enemy were concentrating all available fire. Amidst this perfect deluge of shells the light cruisers and destroyers were twisting and turning, endeavouring to avoid each other and the big ships, which themselves had to perform various manoeuvres. I cannot go into details, but suffice it to say that the general effect outdid the most imaginative picture of a Naval Battle that ever I saw. It will never cease to be a source of wonder to me that so few ships were hit and that there were no collisions. I think it must have been one of the most wonderful displays of seamanship and clear-headedness that ever existed, and as such is very comforting in these days of science and machines. One may account for the very little damage done to the rear of our line during this period by—

1. The Grace of God—for it is indeed extraordinary that so few hits were obtained, considering the number and proximity of the shells that fell amongst us.
2. That no time was lost in straightening out the muddle.
3. That the enemy's fire was drawn off us to a certain extent by the *Warspite, Defence,* and *Warrior.*

The *Warspite* received a hit which jammed her helm, or so it appeared, for when last I saw her she was heading straight for the enemy, almost obliterated by splashes but firing hard. I don't think I felt particularly troubled about her, for she seemed so very full of go. Whenever the splashes cleared 'bang' would go all her guns together.

On the other hand, it was perfectly dreadful to see the *Defence* and *Warrior.* Even when I first sighted them I felt they were doomed. They were steaming at their utmost speed between the lines, endeavouring to get clear round us—*i.e.*, round the end of the Grand Fleet—

smoking very heavily, being continuously straddled and frequently hit. They were soon badly on fire in several places, especially the *Defence*, but they continued to fire to the very last. When the Germans saw these three isolated ships the volume of fire at us considerably decreased, a great deal being concentrated on them. Suddenly the *Defence* disappeared completely in an immense column of smoke and flame, hundreds of feet high. It appeared to be an absolutely instantaneous destruction, the ship seeming to be dismembered in a second. Wreckage continued to fall into the water for quite a considerable time after the explosion, but when the smoke had subsided there was absolutely nothing to be seen where only a minute previously had been the *Defence* and her crew. The *Warrior* was just able to get clear, and the *Warspite*, after turning a complete circle, followed the line, but she eventually had to fall out and return to harbour.

Narrative of a Midshipman of H.M.S. *Warspite*

My billet was the after torpedo control tower, where were stationed also the Torpedo Lieutenant and four hands—a range-finder operator, his trainer, a man to work the plotting instrument, and the Torpedo Lieutenant's messenger. After having tested through and got everything in readiness, and imagining it was the usual kind of stunt I thought I would take a little air, so got out of the top of the control tower and went for a walk on the after superstructure. This did not last for more than five minutes or so, as the Captain spotted me, and I was told to get under cover, which surprised us all, as it was only a matter of seconds to get back inside, and up to then we had heard no news about the enemy. Soon I was joined by the Torpedo Lieutenant, who had been taking a look round the ship, and we reported to the Captain 'All correct.' As things were rather slow he rang up the Gunnery Lieutenant, who was up in the fore top, by means of a trunk call through the main exchange, and had a talk with him and asked for news. Soon afterwards we heard firing in the distance, and were informed that the action had begun and that the battle cruisers were in action. The after turrets trained on their foremost bearing, much to our disgust, as in this position each time they fired we were blown about a good deal by their blast. I should say that it was about 4.45 B.S.T. when we began firing, and soon the German salvoes began to fall short and over. After about a quarter of an hour we felt a terrific concussion aft, and the Torpedo Lieutenant remarked that we must have been hit. Soon after I went below to get some things, but I did not come across any damage. However, it can't have been long after that a shell came in down where I had been.

We had been keeping at it with our guns all this time, and could see the German cruisers and a long ripple of fire along them as they fired at us. The next thing we did was a sixteen-point turn. When during this turn our battle cruisers came along past us, we noticed that their numbers had diminished from the original 6 to 4, which was rather a shock.

Up till this time our squadron (5th B.S.) did not seem to have suffered very much, but soon after we had turned we saw a flame, which reached up as high as the upper bridge, burst out underneath the starboard side of the bridge of the ship astern, the *Malaya*. The fire then disappeared and we thought that it had been got under, but in a very short time another flame burst out, and we saw it run along the whole of the starboard battery, flames shooting out of the 6-inch gun ports and reaching as high as the masts. We expected to see her magazines go up at any time, but, thank Heavens, they did not. Things were now getting very warm, as the High Sea Fleet had turned up on the scene, and never in all my life was I so pleased as when I saw the Grand Fleet looming up on our port bow. Just at this juncture we sighted the *Defence* on our starboard bow, being badly hit. Then I saw a sight which I shall never forget. Just as we were getting abreast of her, when she was about 1,000 yards away, a large salvo fell around her; there was a small flash, and then her sides seemed to burst all ways; a terrific flame shot up and tons of smoke, her masts and funnels seemed to part all ways, and she was gone. All you could see was a huge column of smoke, on the top of which there was a black object, which looked like a gun. Thirty seconds elapsed, the smoke lifted, and for 5 seconds we saw her bottom, and then she slid down to the bottom of the sea. As far as I could see not a vestige of wreckage remained on the surface.

The next thing that struck me was the Grand Fleet deploying. Here they were in columns in line ahead, and next they were

Fifth Battle squadron in action. (From a painting)

deploying with salvoes falling amongst them. Watching them did not last for long, as suddenly we found ourselves hauling out of line and rushing towards the German line—this was when our rudder jammed. One's impression of this short time was very vivid, although aft in the torpedo control tower we did not know what was going on. All we knew was that we were in a hail of fire; in fact, so much so that the salvoes falling short and over made such splashes that a lot of water came into the tower, and we got quite wet, and could not see much owing to everything being obscured by the curtain of water caused by the falling shots. Once or twice we got a good view of the Germans, the range being only about 8,000 yards, and they seemed enormous at this distance. We thought once that our own 6-inch guns were firing, but discovered after that it was the enemy's shells bursting on our armour belt.

This had not been going on for long, when the end of the world seemed to come. The deck below me seemed to open up, and I had the sensation of falling, falling. It seemed as if I were falling into the middle of the earth with most horrible smells, though, as a matter of fact, it was only about a six-foot drop. After about a minute I recovered and looked around to see where I was, and tested my limbs all of which still worked, so I got up, and found all the rest of the crew except one man were all right but shaken. He was in a very bad condition, as both his legs were nearly shot away, so we put a tourniquet on his legs and got him some water from the mess decks, but he died within half an hour without speaking again. It transpired afterwards that our armoured tube had been hit by an 11-inch shell about 4 feet below the tower we were in, and this had naturally removed most of the tube and severed all our communications, and had so messed up the tube that it was a job to get down it.

By this time, about 7 o'clock, we had hauled out of action to make good our damage, but as we had been hit so much and night was coming on, we were ordered back to Rosyth. As I came out of the top of the tower I saw one solitary shell pitch in the water about half a mile astern, and this was the last shot of the action I saw.

ARRIVAL OF THE BATTLE FLEET AT 'WINDY CORNER'

Part of Narrative of H.M.S. *Faulknor*
Leading the 1st half of the 12th Destroyer Flotilla

H.M.S. *Faulknor*, with the 1st half of the 12th Destroyer Flotilla, came within the sound of gun-firing between 5 and 6 p.m. At that time the Flotilla were forming the Submarine Screen for the starboard Wing Column of the Battle Fleet, the 1st Battle Squadron.

About half an hour after the sound of gunfire had first been heard, the *Lion* came clearly into sight leading the battle cruisers across the van of the battle fleet screen and engaging an enemy to the southward. As she crossed the 12th flotilla's bows a considerable fire could be seen burning in her for'ard, from which rose a noticeable amount of very white smoke.

At this time there was a considerable mix-up at the rear of the battle fleet. The fleet had commenced to deploy, but the 12th

Large number of ships bunched up at 'Windy Corner'.

flotilla, stationed as the submarine screen on the original starboard, or south-west, wing, were in great doubt as to whether they could avoid collision with the destroyers stationed on the northern side of the battle cruisers, which were trying to cross our bows. Indeed, so close did they pass the Battle Cruiser Force, that the *Faulknor* had to stop engines, and several 12th flotilla destroyers had actually to go astern to avoid a collision. All the time the overs and ricochets from the German heavy ships were falling into the middle of our bunched flotilla, so that it was no pleasant situation for us, yet, miraculous though it seemed, not one ship during this period was hit even by a splinter.

The battle cruiser line was soon across our bows, and the flotilla was able to go ahead again to take up its station on the engaged side at the rear of the battle line, which, so far as we could see, had now deployed under the stern of the battle cruisers. The shell fire from the German ships seemed to pass ahead and away from us, and the battle cruisers disappeared in the mist in the same direction. For a few minutes we seemed to be out of the battle, but it was not long before we were given a vivid experience of the accuracy of the German gunfire. A group of falling salvoes seemed to be approaching towards us, and shortly afterwards columns of spray could be seen surrounding two British armoured cruisers approaching on an opposite course to that of ourselves and our battle fleet. It was evident that they were badly hit, and just as the leading ship, she was the *Defence*, came on to the *Faulknor*'s starboard bow a salvo appeared to fall all together right on her quarter-deck. In a few seconds another salvo hit her—a cloud of smoke, a flash, and no noise above the ordinary din, but nothing seemed to remain except a heavy pall of smoke. We were only about half a mile on *Defence*'s beam at the moment when she blew up, yet I do not think that a single officer in our flotilla was able to realise fully at the moment what had happened, although I think that the destruction of this ship was left to all of us as one of the most vivid impressions of the Battle of Jutland.

Part of the Narrative of H.M.S. *Obedient*
also of the 12th Destroyer Flotilla
Describing the Events at 'Windy Corner'

H.M.S. *Obedient* was one of the 12th Destroyer Flotilla attached to the 1st Battle Squadron, our duty in cruising formation being to screen the starboard wing of the fleet. At 2.30 p.m. on the 31st of May the fleet had increased speed to 18 knots, and at 3.20 the order was given 'To raise steam for full speed with all despatch.' At 5.45 p.m. flashes of gunfire were sighted on the starboard bow, and a few minutes later our battle cruisers were sighted. The visibility was poor. At 6.0 p.m. the fleet deployed to port, and the flotilla were ordered to take up their day screening position which placed us on the engaged quarter of the battle line. It was some time before the flotilla formed correctly, as there was very little room in which to manoeuvre between the fleet and the battle cruisers, the latter passing so close that *Obedient* had to stop to avoid collision with the *Lion*. For some minutes our position was very unpleasant, as the battle cruisers were heavily engaged, and the 'over' salvoes were falling amongst us. Many bits of shell fell on board but the only boat of the flotilla to be directly hit was the *Marvel*, by a 12-inch shell, in the eyes of the ship, which luckily did not burst.

Just after the battle cruisers had passed, the 5th Battle Squadron overtook us, and presented a magnificent picture, turning together to port at 25 knots to form astern of the battle line. As they turned one of them was hit on the starboard side by a whole salvo, which appeared to hit the armour and run down the side like golden liquid, but apparently without doing any harm that one could see.

By now the fleet had completed the deployment, and the flotilla had taken up their correct station, when from ahead out of the mist, there appeared the ill-fated 1st Cruiser Squadron, led by the *Defence*. When the *Defence* first appeared, steaming apparently at full speed, she did not seem to have been damaged, but she was heavily engaged and salvoes were dropping close all around her. When she was on our bow three quick salvoes reached her, the first one 'over,' the next one 'short,' and the third all hit. The shells of the last salvo could clearly be seen to hit her just abaft the after turret, and after a second a big red flame flashed up, but died away again at once. The ship heeled to the blow, but quickly righted herself and steamed on again. Then almost immediately followed three more salvoes. Again the first was 'over,' the second one 'short,' and the third a hit, and again the shell of the hitting salvo could be clearly seen to strike, this time between the forecastle turret and the foremost funnel. At once the ship was lost to sight in an enormous black cloud, which rose to a height of some hundred feet, and, quickly clearing, showed no signs of a ship at all. Just those six salvoes were seen, no more, and only the two hit, but it was a very marvellous piece of shooting. The *Defence* was just abeam of us, about 600 yards away, when she was blown up. Following her came the *Warrior*, being badly hit, and *Black Prince*, both to pass astern. All the 'over' salvoes fired at these ships fell close to us.

Up to now we had seen no enemy ships, only flashes from their guns, but at 6.30 p.m. we passed a big German ship, floating through between the lines apparently derelict. Just after the mist lifted for a minute or two to show up a few German ships, one of which was clearly seen for a time and received a fearful hammering from the battleships at the rear of our line, but then the mist covered her again.

Nothing more was to be seen for nearly an hour, though the battleships at the rear of the line occasionally fired a few salvoes. . . .

Narrative of H.M.S. *Galatea*

Continued from page 108

We were now gradually edging the enemy round to the eastward, and about 5.45 p.m. we suddenly made out on the horizon ahead, the silhouette of two of our armoured cruisers—*Defence* and *Warrior*. I can hardly even now describe the thrill we all felt—the Grand Fleet had arrived! It was a wonderful moment for we felt that at last the High Seas Fleet had been securely rounded up.

Events followed fast after this. *Defence* came down upon us, engaging three enemy light cruisers on her port bow, and cut across our bow—in fact, we had to alter course to port to avoid colliding with her—and a fine sight she was. She had been apparently newly painted, and was looking very smart, and from her housed main top-mast and her fore and main rigging she was flying large-sized white ensigns, while all her port guns were firing rapidly. My attention was taken up by something in the W/T cabin for a moment, when I suddenly heard a sailor say, 'My God, the *Defence* has gone up!' She had come under the fire of the head of the enemy's line, had been hit by several heavy salvoes simultaneously and had blown up, while the *Warrior* which was following her was badly damaged at the same time. This occurred only a few hundred yards from us, and was all over and finished in an almost incredibly short space of time.

The Grand Fleet was now well in sight, bearing down in six columns and gradually deploying to port. *Lion* and the battle cruis-ers, heavily engaged, passed us to starboard at full speed making a wonderful picture, a long cloud of smoke pouring out of a big shell hole in the *Lion*'s superstructure forward. We had been edged so far north in these manoeuvres that we now had to cross the bows of the approaching battle fleet as they were deploying, and a pretty ticklish business it was.

We were at this time in the midst of an extremely heavy fire, the whole ocean all round being torn up by shell splashes, and the noise was terrific. It was the period and position of the battle which later by common consent became known to the battle cruiser fleet as 'Windy Corner,' and certainly it was one of the most exciting periods of the day.

We went across the line at 27 knots, the squadron splitting up and getting over where best they could—a pretty piece of seamanship. Just as we were dashing across the bows of the *Agincourt* she fired a

137

salvo over us which fairly lifted us in the water. I don't know how many of her fourteen 12-inch guns she fired, but I felt as if my head was blown off.

Just as we turned up on the port, the disengaged, side of the battle fleet, a piece of shell entered the engine-room casing of *Galatea*, and put out of action one of our high-speed forced draught fans, so that our speed fell to 18 knots. There was nothing for it but to tell *Inconstant* to take the rest of our squadron (*Phaeton* and *Cordelia*) under her orders and rejoin the battle cruisers now ahead of the battle fleet, while we conducted repairs and made our way up the disengaged side of our battle fleet.

I remember noticing about this time that all the enemy 'overs' fired at our battle fleet were also falling over us, so close were we to our battle line, and I remember wondering why we did not haul out a mile or so to avoid them, as they were all 'big stuff.'

The next incident I remember is the destroyer *Acasta* drifting down disabled between the opposing fleets, and the *Galatea* going to her assistance. We went alongside her and prepared to take her in tow, a job not at all relished by the Commodore as it probably meant missing the rest of the battle. *Acasta* was badly hit in several places, and under her foc'sle oil fuel was pouring out from many holes near the water line. Fortunately, before we had time to take her in tow, *Fearless* appeared, and the Commodore gladly turned the job over to her, and we fled off after the fleet once more.

We now come to a description of the detail experiences of H.M.S. *Warspite*, the battleship which at 'Windy Corner' so extraordinarily turned away from the rest of her squadron and under jammed helm went steaming towards the enemy, surrounded and almost hidden by the shell splashes from the concentrated fire of the German fleet. It was an incident which, with the loss of H.M.S. *Defence*, will probably always be remembered as the central event of 'Windy Corner'.

H.M.S. *Warspite* was one of the latest British battleships of the *Queen Elizabeth* class, carrying eight 15-inch guns, and having also a speed of 25 knots and adequate armour protection, was more powerful than any ship of the German fleet. Indeed, equal with her sister ships *Barham*, *Valiant*, and *Malaya* (all of the 5th B.S.), she was the most powerful unit engaged at the Battle of Jutland. The following narrative is the diary of an officer stationed between decks in H.M.S. *Warspite*, and describes events in her from the time she commenced action in the early afternoon until she had to leave the line and return to base at about 6.30 p.m. She had been severely crippled by the terrible hammering she had received at 'Windy Corner,' and was, in fact, fortunate to be left still afloat. But in spite of her damage she had sufficient steaming power left to make a British harbour unassisted. Yet, when one reads the narrative of experiences on board her, one is surprised that there was left a single man alive in her to direct her course home.

Experiences in H.M.S. *Warspite*

Extracts from the Diary of her Executive Officer, who was stationed between decks in general charage of all Fire and Repair Parties

Wednesday, May 31st, 1916.

At sea and steaming to the eastward about 20 knots in single line ahead. Battle cruisers about 10 miles ahead. Usual 6-inch gun sections on watch and two turrets closed up.

2.40 p.m. Message from the Captain by his messenger 'to get the hands up at once.' At same time signal was brought to me, 'Cruiser in sight bearing north-east, probably hostile.' This was from *Galatea*, out of sight ahead. I at once sounded off 'action' and passed the word round to everybody to get cleared away as fast as possible.

Intercepted signal reporting five columns of smoke bearing north-east made from *Galatea* to *Lion*. It was pretty plain that there was something serious doing; we were now steering south-south-east. Passed the word round to everybody that we were in for the real thing, and went all round mess decks, wetted decks, put all tables and stools on the deck, and lit all 'Action Candles,' etc. Saw all doors and everything closed, and went up on deck; they were just finishing washing down the weather decks, and I sent all hands away to their stations, and went up to report everything ready. There was nothing in sight except our own ships, but we were steaming hard. Hoisted Battle Ensigns and Union Jack at after struts and masthead.

Went to my action station, 'B' turret; found everything all right, and Officer of Turret reported all correct. We were then trained on about 50 Red, and I saw we had our port sounding-boom out; I remember wishing we had got it aft, but thought it too late to worry about. It was now about 4 o'clock. Got orders to 'load and train Red 20.' Could not see anything at all, hazy and a lot of smoke about. We were steaming very hard. Wondered if our steering jackstaff would be shot away, as we had just fitted a new one. Everybody in the turret in very good spirits, and I asked G. if he had any cotton wool. He said he hadn't, and passed me a lump of cotton waste large enough to stop the ears of a donkey, which I chucked back at him; and almost at once we got the order to 'stand by.'

I made out five columns of smoke in the mist, and that was all I could see, no masts or anything else. Opened fire on light cruisers, range about 21,000 yards. Could see the fall of shot well, but could not see at all what we were firing at. Fired a few rounds by director, and saw *Barham* and *Valiant* were firing too; light cruisers were getting clearer now. Suddenly saw No. 2 column of smoke break out into a bright flame; this dropped astern, and at first I thought she was hit, but later I thought it was only a smoke box as it looked like an enormous calcium life buoy, bright flame and huge white smoke clouds drifting astern.

Found we were turning fast to starboard, and as we came round about 8 points I saw five enemy battle cruisers on port bow, about Red 40. They were steaming the same way as we were and going very hard. A mass of black smoke and I could only see their masts and the tops of their

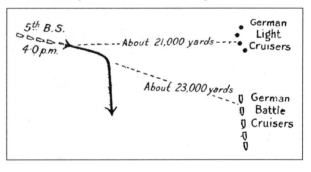

funnels above the horizon, and stern waves showing up white and very high. Opened fire on No. 5. I could not have laid on them myself; spotting frightfully hard, and we were all short; the range of the first few salvoes was, I think, 23,000 yards. Blast from 'A' turret was awfully bad, and blew salt water and dust into my eyes, which watered like blazes. I saw several of their salvoes splash short of us;

they fell into an extraordinary small spread, and made the dickens of a noise. I remember thinking how high the ricos. must be going over us. Caught sight of *Valiant* and *Barham* through the corner of my eye, and saw *Barham* straddled once or twice. I realised we were steering south and it crossed my mind whether we should meet the High Seas Fleet. They straddled us once or twice, but we had not been hit at all so far. I think they were zigzagging very much, as their deflection was very hard to pick up.

About 5.0 p.m.[1]

I suddenly saw our battle cruisers coming close by about half a mile off in the opposite direction, and I realised they had turned back. I noticed that *Queen Mary* and *Indefatigable* were adrift, but never for a moment realised they had sunk. Before this we had passed through a mass of black water with a destroyer picking up people. I heard afterwards this was *Queen Mary*. 'X' turret of *Lion* was trained towards us with guns at full elevation, several hits showing on her port side, great black splashes.

One salvo came very close, just short, smothering us with spray, and I am afraid I 'ducked' and talked to G. for a minute. We then turned 16 points in succession and trained the turret round full speed to the other beam.

Very soon after the turn I suddenly saw on the starboard quarter the whole of the High Seas Fleet; at least I saw masts, funnels, and an endless ripple of orange flashes all down the line, how many I didn't try to count, as we were getting well strafed at this time, but I remember counting up to eight. The noise of their shells over and short was deafening, like doing 'counting ship' at battle practice, that frightful crack, crack, crack, going on the whole time. Felt one or two very heavy shakes, but didn't think very much of it at the time, and it never occurred to me that we were being hit.

We were firing pretty fast on bearing about Green 120. I distinctly saw two of our salvoes hit the leading German battleship. Sheets of yellow flame went right over her mastheads, and she looked red fore and aft like a burning haystack. I know we hit her hard. Told everybody in the turret that we were doing all right and

---

1 This and subsequent times which are given in the margin, are estimated only. During the action the author lost all count of time, and he did not include any times in his original account. They are introduced here for the convenience of the reader. —*Ed.*

Warspite—armour plate pierced by shell that exploded in Boys' Mess Deck.

to keep her going; machinery working like a clockwork mouse, and no hang-up of any sort whatever.

Received message from Captain to go aft and see what was the matter, as we had been badly hit. Asked for message to be repeated, and got same through again. I thought for a few seconds 'Should I go over, or down through shell-room?' but realised I ought to get there quickly, and decided to go over the top of the turret. I didn't waste much time on the roof, as the noise was awful, and they were coming over pretty thick. As I got down the starboard ladder of 'B,' both 'A' and 'B' turrets fired, and made me skip a bit quicker. Ran down port superstructure ladder and tried to get into port super-structure. All clips were on the door, so I climbed up over second cutter. Just as I got up one came through the after funnel with an awful screech and spattered about everywhere. I put up my coat collar and ran like a stag, feeling in the deuce of a funk.

Went right down to mess deck and all along port side. All was quiet, and could see nothing wrong at all. Went right aft and down starboard bathroom lobby, up to Captain's lobby and aft to Admiral's lobby. Saw No. 6 fire brigade were all right, and came back along lobby to mess deck again. Sent telephone message to

Captain to say nothing was wrong aft as far as I could tell. As a matter of fact, we had been hit under waterline abreast capstan engine flat, but this I did not know.

I crossed the cooks' lobby and told ammunition supply parties that things were going on all right. Went through to foc'sle mess deck, and was just going forward when 12-inch shell came through side armour on boys' mess deck. Terrific sheet of golden flame, stink, impenetrable dust, and everything seemed to fall everywhere with an appalling noise. Called for No. 2 fire brigade, and they ran up from the flat below, and we got hose on, and put out a lot of burning refuse. Directly water went on to the 'glow' it vanished, and I can't say what was burning; personally, I think it was water-gas or something like it.

Several of the fire brigade were ill due to the sweet, sickly stench, but there was no signs of poison gas. The shell hole was clean, about a foot in diameter; big flakes of armour had been flung right across the mess deck, wrecking everything. Many armour bolts came away. Magazine flooding cabinet was completely wrecked, and all voice pipes and electric leads overhead were cut to pieces. Smoke was pouring up through holes in the deck, and it occurred to me that the high-angle gun magazine was very close. Told P. to stand by to flood it from middle-deck position. Water from out fire mains was pouring below, and smoke soon stopped. Everybody busy souvenir hunting, and had to put the hose over them to make them take cover below again.

About 5.30 p.m.

Went right aft port side, and aft to Captain's lobby. Found water pouring in through Admiral's scuttles, and deck aft all gone. There was about a foot of water in after cabin; billiard table untouched. Got carpenters and everybody out of it, as nothing could be done; it was obvious the side was blown in below Admiral's cabin. Stern was very deep, due to hard steaming, and water was pumping up as ship pitched.

After submerged torpedo flat reported that water was coming in to after flat; talked to them down escape hatch, and realised it was not anything really; subsequently found it was due to submerged flat hatch 'giving' a bit when burst occurred above, but no more water came down afterwards.

Captain's lobby was at this time untouched. Was just going up

Warspite—side blown out by shell exploding in Captain's lobby.

hatch to casemate lobby when I was called back and told a shell had just burst in Captain's lobby. Went aft again and found my cabin had been completely removed overboard. Lobby in an awful state, and hole about 12 feet diameter in the centre of the deck. Lot of burning débris in my cabin, which we put out; in the middle of this heap was my wife's miniature, without its case, but otherwise perfect. Sleeping cabin was not so bad, and only spattered with splinters. There were about four bursts in lobby. Trunk to steering department was wrecked, stanchions cut through, Captain's pantry in heaps, and everything in a filthy state of indescribable wreckage. Realised things were pretty warm aft and nothing could be done, so went forward again before any more arrived; holes in quarter deck and my cabin let in daylight.

Went along by No. 5 fire brigade and saw we had been heavily hit port side. Helped with fire brigade in port casemate lobby plugging cut fire mains and trying to stop water getting down ventilating trunks. Columns of water pouring through hole in deck overhead, must have been from enemy shorts. Centre line armoured door was blown off its hinges, and whole of after flat in an awful state, everything blown to pieces and spattered by splinters. The resin out of corticine makes everything in a horrid state of black, sticky, glue-like stuff when hit by shell fire.

144

A shell had come in further forward and hit 'X' turret barbette armour, killing several of No. 5 fire brigade and wounding a lot more. Water was pouring through hole in side into sergeants' mess, flooding main deck and going down shell hole to centre engine-room supply trunk. I realised we could not effectively stop hole in the side, and decided we must at all costs prevent water getting to engine-room. We plugged the supply trunk by big sheets of rubber shored down with deal flats. This, of course, stopped ventilation to engine-rooms, and they got pretty hot down below. Left marines plugging hole in ship's side with hammocks, but a lot of water was coming in and washing away all attempts at plugging.

Blast of shell momentarily put out lights, but candles were instantly re-lit, and did well. Oil lamps, as was expected, went out, and were not re-lit. Electric light bulbs broke in vicinity of shell bursts. Lot of broken glass about the deck made it awkward to get about; also sharp, jagged plates were regular death-traps. Everyone must wear leather sea boots—these are now supplied. All fire brigade and repair parties must have thick leather hedger's gloves, as it was very bad to try and handle the jagged plates.

The body of this 12-inch shell was found above the engineers' workshop, unexploded. The filling was sticking out like a chock of wood, and a couple of stokers were trying to chip the fuse out. I luckily stopped this little effort. It is extraordinary the amount of damage this one unexploded shell did; I can't help thinking that there were two shells.

Went forward along port side of mess deck and sent W. to telephone to the Captain saying things were all right. Had a cigarette the port side of cook's lobby, or rather started one to steady my feelings. Had a yarn here with the Pay., who was wandering about in a 'Kapok' waistcoat using appalling language as to when the Grand Fleet were going to turn up. Had a laugh together anyway.

Whilst there a 12-inch shell came into galley and blew down through the deck. A stoker alongside me looked up and said, 'There goes my —— dinner.'

Hopped up to battery deck port side, but found very little damage had been done, and everybody was very cheery. Went along starboard side of mess deck and made 6-inch supply parties spread out more, as they would bunch together so much. While forward was told we had been hit port side aft, so ran aft and found we had been hit under the engineers' office. It looked very bad, as a large

Warspite—hit under Engineers' office. Corner of armour plate blown away.

triangular piece had been blown out of the top corner of the main belt about a foot above water. The fresh water and oil fuel tanks had been blown to pieces, and everything in an awful state of dust, oil fuel, and mess. Engineers' office completely vanished and deck all bowed upwards. Men trying to plug the hole, but tons of water were coming in and washing them back all the time. As it was all oil fuel, they looked like a lot of goldfish swimming about. A marine remarked 'This will mean a drop of leave.'

Tried for a bit to plug and shore up with hammocks, but it was hopeless, as the force of the seas was tremendous. Decided to fill the whole compartment with hammocks, and started a strong party doing this. It eventually took nearly 600 hammocks to fill up the compartment, which effectually stopped the trouble, but not till late that night. Body of this shell was afterwards found in the bathroom.

The ventilation trunk to wing engine-room had been badly holed by this shell, and volumes of water were pouring down. Got down inside trunk, and with the Chief's assistance we plugged and shored the hole from inside the trunk with rubber sheets, and stopped water getting below. Went up to battery deck port side and looked through 6-inch control hood. Must have got a direct hit further aft with high explosive, as there was a terrific flash and shock, and I was knocked endways out of 6-inch hood, my eyes full of water and dust. G. thought I was hit, but it was only shock.

Realised it was pretty hot, and that we were getting heavily hit. Went down to mess deck again to see how the hammock party were getting on, and found they had passed a lot of hammocks in, but no signs of bottom yet. Many hammocks were lost washing out through the hole, and it didn't look promising. Crossed to starboard side and a shell burst in battery above. Sheet of flame came down through slits of sliding shutters. Told them to open the shutter with a view to going up the escape to see what had happened, but it was all aglow overhead, so shut it to again. Heard a lot of groaning on battery deck. Went forward to get up fore end, when I was told I was wanted at once, as there was a bad fire on superstructure. A fragment of shell had come through the roof of battery deck and hit the after 6-inch cordite case, containing four charges. As bad luck would have it the cartridge number had a charge half out of the case in his arms, having just received the order to load. This box and four others exploded. Whole of No. 6 gun's crew were frightfully burnt, and several more of No. 5 gun. Luckily it did not spread right along the battery, as it did in the *Malaya*, and the centre line door being shut saved the port battery. The fire was quickly put out, and never took hold of anything really.

As I passed the port war signal station I asked if they knew anything, but they knew nothing, and all their signal halliards were cut. At this time I thought our 6-inch were firing, but I realised afterwards it was only hits on us. The noise was deafening and rather nerve-shattering. You could not hear yourself speak, and had to shout in anybody's ear.

Went up to superstructure by battery deck escape and found the whole place ablaze. All fire mains were cut, and we couldn't get any water up there at all. Signalmen and messengers peering out through slot of conning tower looked like thrushes in a nest, gaping and shouting 'Put the fire out.' We eventually got a steam main connected and got water, which I got in the neck as they turned it on.

About 6.0 p.m.

The fire had started in the navigator's sea cabin, which was completely gutted; all our swimming collars, about 400 of them, which we kept hung on jack stays near here for use in emergency, were burning, the stench of rubber being perfectly awful. Smouldering wooden uprights of doors kept on breaking out again, so left marines playing the hose. Decks were all warped, and resin under corticine was crackling like burning holly. The upper deck and superstructures looked perfectly awful, holed everywhere. Everything in the fore superstructure was wrecked, and it looked like a burnt-out factory all blackened and beams twisted everywhere. I think at this time the fire had slackened, but the noise was deafening; shells bursting short threw tons of water overhead.

A 12-inch had come through after funnel, through beef-screen,[2] hit armoured grating over 'B' boiler-room, and being deflected upwards, smashed second cutter to matchwood. On its way through the beef-screen it had carried a whole sheep with it, which was wedged into the gratings; at first I thought it was a casualty. Went below again and found a second shell had come into boys' mess deck through the embrasure overhead. Looked outboard through hole in armour on ship's side: looked red, lurid, and beastly; heavy firing all round and splashes everywhere; thought we were steaming slow. Went aft the port side and saw how the plugging was getting on; there was a fair amount of water going down the centre engine-room still, and the plugs kept on washing away from the hole. Everybody was very cheery and anxious for news, which I couldn't give, as I hadn't the faintest idea what was happening. Marines of port 6-inch ammunition supply were playing cards on the deck quite happily.

Got a message that men were in the after steering compartment and could not get out, and water was gaining. I had clean forgotten all about them, and, of course, the shell into the trunk had shaken them; went aft and found the whole trunk full to the level of cabin flat. They reported by telephone that there was 18 inches of water and gaining slowly. Tried to open the door by deck plate in Admiral's lobby, but it was absolutely fixed; realised it was jammed by wreckage from above. Telephoned them to wait and that everything was all peace.

Went forward again to port side of mess deck. Two stokers came to me when I was very busy and begged me to take watches, letters, etc., found on men who had been knocked out. It struck me as so incongruous, as if it mattered a bit when we might all of us go any minute. I told them so, but they were so insistent about it. W. took charge of the things.

Men everywhere were simply splendid and all very cheery. I confess that I myself found it mighty unpleasant and unnerving,

2 Beef-screen—the stowage place for fresh meat.

Warspite at 'Windy Corner'. (From a painting)

although I had plenty to do, but for those who merely had to *wait* it must have been a thousand times worse.

The noise was perfectly appalling, and you couldn't hear at all between decks, and the worst of it was one knew *nothing*.

6.20 p.m.

The steering gear episode was rather extraordinary. I found out the details afterwards. We were turning to form astern of the Grand Fleet battle line, and the helm was apparently put over too quickly, and jammed at Port 15°.[3] We swung to starboard under *Valiant*'s stern, and continued swinging round towards the enemy, getting very close to them. We continued swinging round until we were on a westerly course, when the Captain managed to steady the ship by working the screws. I remember hearing him give some orders about the engines.

The whole leading enemy division concentrated on us during this circling, and we got very heavily hit, and everybody thought we had gone. Huns thought so too, and ceased firing, luckily for us, but they no doubt could not see us for splashes, spray, and smoke. There was a heavy pall of smoke everywhere. Terrific rumbling of heavy firing

3 Port 15° is a considerable amount of helm, sufficient to turn a ship rapidly to starboard. Port 35° is 'Hard-a-port,' the maximum amount of helm that can be put on, so that it will be understood that the *Warspite* going at full speed with 15° of helm on was taking a big and difficult to control turn to starboard—towards the enemy.

and the whole horizon lit by orange flashes everywhere; everything blurred and beastly.

I saw the *Agincourt* a long way off firing like blazes, and remember thinking she was going it pretty hard, but that's all I ever saw of the Grand Fleet.

Details of *Warspite*'s Circling at 'Windy Corner'
Explained by another Officer of H.M.S. *Warspite*

About 6.20 p.m. to 6.30 p.m.

It was just after we had sighted the battle fleet, when we were on a northerly course approaching the corner where the battle cruisers turned to starboard to take station ahead of the battle fleet, and where *Defence* was blown up after apparently being hit by two successive salvoes.

Our Admiral signalled the 5th B.S. to alter course to port, obviously intending to take station astern of the battle line. *Barham*, *Valiant*, and *Warspite* turned practically together, but *Malaya*, having fallen rather astern and being further to westward, stood on her original course. As the moment approached for *Warspite* to turn again with *Barham*, she was fast closing *Malaya* on a nearly opposite course, and the Captain, with the purpose of warning *Malaya* of his intentions, gave the order Port 20° rather earlier than was actually necessary. The helmsman, evidently thinking we were getting close, put the helm over very quickly, and a minute later, on receiving the order to put the helm back to 'Amidships,' found the helm jammed at Port 15°. The Captain's first thought was for the *Valiant*, then on our starboard hand, but we swung round to starboard clear of her stern without having to reverse engines.

An effort was then made to stop the ship swinging further to starboard, and to resume, if possible, our course to follow the battle fleet. But we were at this time coming under very heavy fire as we became the nearest ship to the enemy, and so terrific was the noise of the bursting shell that no one in the conning tower could hear the Captain's orders, added to which the Navigating Officer was temporarily blinded by our gun flash, with the result that the Captain himself had to work the telegraphs and use the voice tubes, etc. He very soon arrived at the conclusion that the only way to prevent actually running right into the enemy's line was to continue the turn to starboard, and not to attempt either to turn back to port against the action of the helm nor to wait for the other wheel and steering engine to be connected up, which had been ordered.

It was evident that no helm or engine work could possibly turn the ship back to *port* quick enough to avert disaster, due to the more and more powerful concentration of enemy fire that was being directed upon us, and, therefore, with both engines at full speed ahead, the Captain continued to swing the ship until he had made the circle to starboard and were stern to the enemy, when he checked the swing and steadied her on a westerly course by going astern with the port engine. Nothing could be seen during this turn except the bursting of shell all around us, and our guns were only able to fire in reply through breaks in the splashes.

On the receipt of the report that the steering gear was connected up to the other steering engine, course was altered at full speed to follow *Malaya* which had meantime taken up our position in the 5th B.S. line, but before getting into station we again swung rapidly to starboard in spite of the helm. This was at the time accounted for as another jam, but was subsequently proved to be due to the steering engine being connected up at Port 15° instead of at amidships, which, considering the prevailing conditions, was a mistake one could excuse. We made another circle to starboard, circling round *Warrior*, who happened to be in the way, and then, no longer being under fire, the engines were stopped to ascertain the cause of the erratic behaviour of the steering gear, and also to obtain reports as to damage received from gunfire. Various reports of damage had been received in the conning tower during this time, including one stating that the ship was sinking by the stern, but the Engineer Commander reported that all was correct in both engine-room and boiler-room, which was a great relief.

Although the after part of the ship was flooded at the water line, the submerged tube flat and other compartments below that level were practically tight, and apparently much of the water in the ship was due to our fire mains having been cut by shell fire, so pouring water about the ship. In spite of the ship having received about 30 direct hits, mostly from heavy guns, the Captain considered her still fit for further action, and we proceeded to rejoin the battle as quickly as possible, but we shortly received, in reply to our request for a position, orders to proceed to Rosyth.

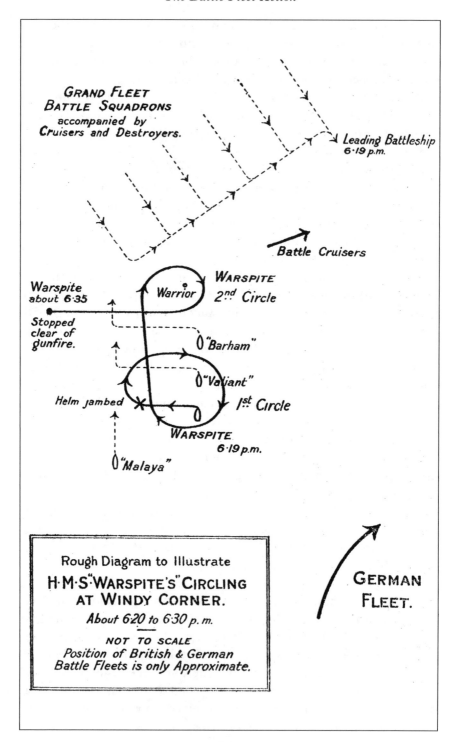

GRAND FLEET
BATTLE SQUADRONS
accompanied by
Cruisers and Destroyers.

↘ Leading Battleship
6·19 p.m.

Battle Cruisers

Warspite
about 6·35

Stopped
clear of
gunfire.

WARSPITE
2ⁿᵈ Circle

Warrior

◊ "Barham"

◊ "Valiant"

Helm jambed

1ˢᵗ Circle

WARSPITE
6·19 p.m.

◊ "Malaya"

Rough Diagram to Illustrate
H·M·S "WARSPITE'S" CIRCLING
AT WINDY CORNER.
About 6·20 to 6·30 p.m.

NOT TO SCALE
Position of British & German
Battle Fleets is only Approximate.

GERMAN
FLEET.

The exact cause of the helm originally jamming was by subsequent investigation fairly conclusively proved to be as follows:—
The two steering engines are both situated in the engine-room fitted on a vertical bulkhead. This bulkhead must have been strained by the bursting of shell in the vicinity, with the result that the steering engine in use developed a hot bearing (by becoming out of line or improperly supported or some such cause), and when the quartermaster worked the steering wheel with extra rapidity and later tried to force it over, the steering engine jammed, and it was found to be impossible to move the wheel. (The steering wheel is in the conning tower or other steering position, and operates a telemotor system which controls the steering engine in the engine-room. This engine moves the rudder.) The other steering engine, as has been said, except for being connected up incorrectly at first, worked quite satisfactorily.

To recall the time of H.M.S. *Warspite*'s arrival at 'Windy Corner,' it might be added that one's first impression on sighting the battle fleet was one of relief and admiration as previous doubts were dispelled as to how the Commander-in-Chief, in the prevailing conditions of light and visibility, would be able to deploy his enormous fleet to advantage.

The sight of our battleships deploying to the eastward and practically surrounding the head of the enemy's line, evoked the remark from the Captain, 'That is the grandest deployment I have ever seen.'

(Continuation of *Warspite*'s 'Narrative.)

8.30 p.m.

Went below and was at the port hits again, when I got a message asking could we go 16 knots, and I said, 'Yes,' or it may have been, 'What speed can you go?' and I said '16.' I don't know which it was anyway. Went aft and tried to square up the hole by port casemate lobby. Got half-a-dozen men to get the dead out of the flat below. Got a message that we were to return to Rosyth. Arranged to get the men a meal as best we could whilst keeping the guns manned. I had no idea whatever as to time, but it was then about 8.30, I believe.

Went on the upper deck and had a look round. Main derrick was shot through and lying across the picket boat, mainmast holed by a 6-inch, and boats all smashed to atoms. Compass platform was

Warspite—No. 7 6in gun starboard on the upper deck.

riddled by splinters. Big hole starboard side by 6-inch gun, which we covered over with collision mat and nailed down.

Tried to 'darken ship' as best we could, but the holes everywhere made this rather hopeless; plugged them with canvas and deck cloths. A 12-inch shell had hit the communication tube of the after director tower, sheared all rivets, and spun the tube through 180 degrees, but only one man was killed and two wounded in the tower above—rather miraculous. 'X' turret had a direct hit, looked like an 8-inch, but no damage whatever inside; in fact, they did not know they had been hit.

The boats were a comic sight; launch absolutely smashed to blazes, all Carley rafts except two small ones broken up, and no sound boat left. First picket boat had just been painted, too, and new brass rails round casings were all cut to pieces. Both ladders to quarter deck had gone, and both life buoys blown away by blast from 'X' turret.

All mainstays had been shot through except one the starboard side. Searchlights had not suffered very badly, except those on after-superstructure; they were like scrap iron. There were many holes on the quarter deck, rather death-traps.

Where shell hit the deck, planks and fastenings were removed as cleanly as if they had been shovelled away, in several places over an area of 10 or 12 square feet.

About 9.0 p.m. to midnight

Went down to an awkward fire in sick-bay; could not get along upper deck before the battery, due to dense smoke, even with respirator, etc., on; even Edes' helmet was no good; smoke absolutely thick yellow. Went up on foc'sle deck and got through skylight, which we opened to let the smoke out. Eventually got outboard on port forward embrasure with a chief stoker and a hose, and played it over the burning débris and wreckage. We had not had time before the action to strip the sick-bay, and a 12-inch had come clean through from port to starboard, completely wrecking sick-bay, which was in an awful state of confusion, due to fire and water, chemicals, broken glass, etc. Having got this fire out, went and saw fleet surgeon, who was very busy in fore distributing station. Large numbers of burnt men were in a dreadful state.

Went aft and telephoned to after steering compartment asking them how things were; they said there was 3 feet of water there and gaining slowly. As a matter of fact, this was exaggerated, as there never was more than 2 feet, but the position there certainly couldn't have been pleasant. Got door to them open about a foot, and the three men with old W. came up looking a bit shaken, but none the worse. They had been down there about eight hours, and must have been pretty anxious.

By this time one felt one wanted something inside, so repaired to the ward-room; found they had got some food of sorts going, sardines and tinned tongue; everybody was very cheery. A funny hit here; 6-inch shell had come through ward-room table, making a clean round hole, dented deck, and gone out through other side, having wrecked stove, armchair, and piano. We hope to sell the piano for a good price as a souvenir, although it has no inside left, but the outside is all right.

Thursday, June 1st

At daylight we fell the hands in and went on getting things squared up as best we could. Started carpenters on repairing first cutter, which was the only possible boat, and got mess tables, stools, etc., up to build rafts on the upper deck. Steaming 18 knots, zigzagging. Our standard compass had about 10 degrees' error after the hitting we had got. Gyro all right.

About 6 a.m. Captain sent for me and said he was certain we should be attacked by submarines, and to do all I could to get everything as ready as possible. Got 6-inch gun crews closed up and went on getting rafts, etc., built. Had a strong party plugging holes up in cabins and quarter deck aft, and used up all blankets and bedding from after cabins. Captain's cabin was about a foot deep in water. Got the 5-ton pump under way trying to pump it over, not knowing that there was a hole below the water-line.

About 8 o'clock two torpedoes were fired at us; one just crossed the bow, the other followed up astern alongside the starboard side. We increased to 21 knots and zigzagged all the time. There was nothing more to be done, as we already had double look-outs and had a lot of officers up in addition.

Decided to get all the wounded out of after medical distributing station and to close all doors in the ship. P.M.O. was splendid with this, and did it all so well. Closed all doors to locker flats, bathrooms, and everywhere, and passed the word that no door in the ship was to be opened without special permission.

About 10 a.m. opened fire on a submarine on port quarter, range about 800 yards. Port 6-inch fired about eight rounds at periscope. Captain sent me down to look at shoring by the hits port side and see how it was standing. I went and had a good look, and told him it was all right. This forenoon was, I think, about the worst part of the whole show, as everybody was very much on edge.

From then onwards nothing of special interest happened, and we came safely in. I am bound to say I heaved a sigh of relief as we passed under the Forth Bridge, and the cheers from the troops made one feel quite gulpy.

We were drawing about 35½ feet aft when we docked.

CHAPTER VIII

THE WRECKING OF ARBUTHNOT'S SQUADRON

One has now gained a general impression of what 'Windy Corner' was like, what a strange jumble of ships were there, how German shells were falling round everywhere during the five or ten minutes when the battle fleet was joining the Rosyth battle cruisers, and how everyone expected a number of ships to be hit, yet how few ships were hit. Then in a few minutes the battle fleet had deployed, and formed in battle line were moving away to the E.N.E., whilst the battle cruisers were steaming at full speed to reach a position at the van to turn aside the enemy battle cruisers to the east, and later to the southeast. At the same time the 5th Battle Squadron, still under the fire of the High Seas Fleet on their northerly course, and vigorously replying to the fire with their 15-inch broadsides, had arrived at 'Windy Corner' and, seeing the Grand Fleet deploying, had been led sharply round by Admiral Evan Thomas to form astern of H.M.S. *Agincourt*, the rear ship of the battle line. In the midst of this turn, which because of restricted space had to be a very sharp one, the *Warspite* did her extraordinary 'stunt,' and almost at the same time there came the dramatic arrival and breaking up of Rear-Admiral Arbuthnot's Cruiser Squadron, *Defence*, *Warrior*, *Black Prince*, and *Duke of Edinburgh*. Coming from their cruising position ahead of the centre of the battle fleet, *Defence* and *Warrior* were engaging as their first target a German light cruiser, which presumably was scouting ahead

157

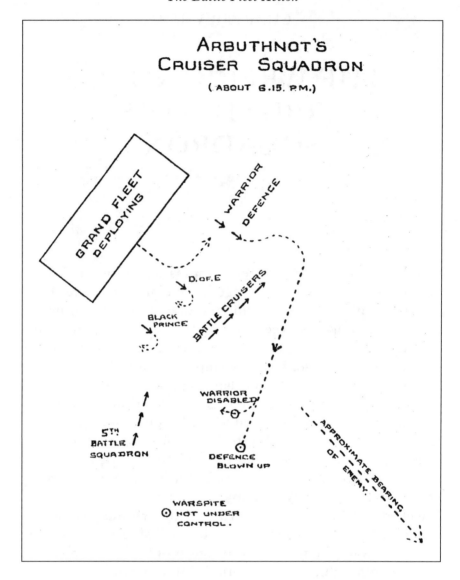

and on the port bow of the German battle cruisers. Still engaging this ship with their port broadsides, they were led down by Admiral Arbuthnot to the south-east—that is, towards the sounds of gunfire—until they sighted the *Lion* on their starboard hand. They continued to lead across *Lion's* bows down the engaged side of our battle cruisers, until closing the enemy to a terribly close range they became the target for the concentrated fire of the leading battleships and battle cruisers of the High Seas Fleet. Their dramatic arrival into action and the tragic result to them of the overwhelming German fire remains one of the outstanding features of the action of Jutland. It was witnessed distinctly by almost all ships of the battle cruiser force and by many of the battle fleet ships at the rear end of the line:—

'At about 6.15 p.m. we witnessed the action of the 1st Cruiser Squadron and the blowing up of *Defence*. We thought she had gone about a minute before she finally blew up, as she completely disappeared in a mass of spray, smoke, and flame. But she came through it apparently still intact, only to disappear a few seconds later in a tremendous belch of vivid flame and dense black smoke, from which some dark object, possibly a boat or a funnel, was hurled through space, twirling like a gigantic Catherine-wheel.' (Narrative of H.M.S. *Colossus*, battleship.)

H.M.S. *Yarmouth*, of the 3rd Light Cruiser Squadron attached to the Battle Cruiser Force, arrived from the southward at the same time, and an officer who was in her gives this description of the end of the 1st Cruiser Squadron:—

'Between 6 and 6.30 p.m. was for us the most eventful time of the whole day. First of all, the 1st Cruiser Squadron (*Defence*, etc.) broke through the centre of our squadron as we made to the eastward. The *Black Prince* crossed the bows of the *Falmouth*, our flagship, whilst the *Duke of Edinburgh* passed between *Birkenhead* and ourselves causing *Birkenhead* and *Gloucester* to alter course to port. Admiral Arbuthnot's Squadron then wheeled round to starboard on to a westerly course and opened fire on a German light cruiser which hove in sight on our starboard bow. Apparently, Admiral

159

Arbuthnot was anxious to engage any enemy that might turn up, and pressed forward with great impatience. His squadron looked a very fine sight turning and firing in succession, but almost immediately they found themselves within close range of the German battle cruisers and battleships, and before they could turn away—there was practically no direction clear to which they could turn—they were being concentrated upon by overwhelming gunfire from the enemy ships. The *Defence* and *Black Prince* were beaten and blew up,[1] *Warrior* drifted out of action helpless and in flames, and the only ship of the squadron to escape was the *Duke of Edinburgh*, which hauled away to the northward in time. . . .'

A little later, H.M.S. *Nottingham*, of the 3rd L.C.S., stationed near the rear of the Battle Cruiser Force, arrived at the scene of the 1st C.S.'s action:—

'We arrived at "Windy Corner" at about 6.15 p.m., and the first thing we sighted was a ship that looked as if she had once been a cruiser, stopped and helpless in the mist on our starboard bow. Suddenly there was a terrific explosion in her of black smoke and flame, and two minutes later nothing remained that we could see. We found out later that this was the *Defence*. Shortly afterwards the *Warrior* came struggling out of the action towards us, on fire and belching steam from a shothole near the foremost funnel, very badly damaged, but with just sufficient steaming power left to escape. . . .'

What a terrible quick change from the description, 'The squadron looked a very fine sight turning and firing in succession!'

Finally, the appearance of the last moments of H.M.S. *Defence* is described by an officer in the foretop of H.M.S *Neptune*, a battleship near the rear of the battle line:—

'A few minutes after we opened fire, the *Defence* and *Warrior* appeared on our engaged side steaming on an opposite course. The ships were practically continuously hidden by splashes, they were

---

1 H.M.S. *Black Prince* did not actually founder until several hours later.

being repeatedly hit by heavy shell, and must have been going through hell on earth. The *Defence*, which was leading, was just about abeam of the *Neptune*, and barely a mile away, when she was hit heavily and blew up in one fearful cloud of smoke and debris. The foretop fell with a sickening splash into the water, and then the *Warrior*, herself damaged, listing to starboard and in places on fire, raced over the spot where the *Defence* had been, through the smoke-cloud of her flagship's explosion.'

Mercifully this death by which the 900 officers and men of the *Defence* perished, was an instantaneous one, without probably causing them any suffering. We may remember as their epitaph, 'They pressed forward with great impatience.'

In the following chapter are narrated the experiences of H.M.S. *Warrior*, and of the seaplane carrier, H.M.S. *Engadine*, from the time when this ship took H.M.S. *Warrior* in tow and endeavoured to bring her back to harbour. H.M.S. *Warrior*, although damaged beyond repair, did not immediately blow up and sink like her sister ship, H.M.S. *Defence*, but was kept afloat by great exertions on the part of her crew until 7.30 a.m. on the following morning, June 1st. Her crew were then forced to abandon her, and she sank. There is also a narrative from H.M.S. *Duke of Edinburgh*, the only ship of the 1st Cruiser Squadron that returned safely from the action to harbour.

H.M.S. *Black Prince* was separated from other British ships and was not seen again. It is thought that she foundered during the night.

Narrative of H.M.S. *Warrior*

On the afternoon of May 31st the 2nd Cruiser Squadron, composed of *Defence* (flag), *Warrior*, *Duke of Edinburgh*, and *Black Prince*, was stationed on the starboard wing of the cruiser screen 10 miles ahead of the battle fleet, in which position it was our special duty to sight and inform the Commander-in-Chief of the position, course, and speed of the enemy's fleet should we at any time make contact with them. We were steaming to the south-east at about 18 knots, carrying out one of the frequent sweeps of the North Sea, but that afternoon the situation appeared so peaceful and the visibility was so good that I left the bridge about 2.0 p.m. to count the public money. Hardly had I returned when, at about 3 p.m., an intercepted message came from light cruisers attached to the battle cruiser fleet, reporting that enemy ships were in sight about 50 miles to the south-eastward of our position. Wireless reports were then intercepted in quick succession, 'Enemy battle cruisers in sight,' 'Enemy battle cruisers being engaged by our battle cruisers,' and so forth.

At 3.30 p.m. the signal for action stations was made by Rear-Admiral Sir Robt. Arbuthnot from the *Defence*, and when everything had been reported ready for action on board, I sent the ship's company to tea. From this time onwards intercepted signals showed clearly the reported positions, courses, and speeds of our battle cruiser fleet and of the enemy, and after tea I explained the position of affairs to the Commander, and told him to assemble all hands, inform them that an action was imminent, and give them an idea how matters stood so far as we knew them. As the men closed up at their action stations they cheered with enthusiasm.

At 5.40 p.m., while still 10 miles ahead of our battle fleet, and with speed now increased to 20 knots, gunfire was heard and gun flashes seen about 30 degrees before our starboard beam, but on a bearing west of south, instead of the bearing east of south on which, by plotting the reports of the enemy from our battle cruisers, we had calculated that we should join the action. The time also was about half an hour earlier than we had expected.

A few minutes later, on almost the same bearing as the gun-flashes, light cruisers belonging to our battle cruiser fleet were sighted, closely followed by the battle cruisers, and although no enemy ships were yet in sight, projectiles were observed to be falling round our ships—generally speaking, short of them. At about 5.47 I sighted three or possibly four enemy light cruisers about 20 degrees on my starboard bow, and I now increased speed to 21 knots to close from ½ a mile to ¼ of a mile astern of *Defence*. *Defence* then altered course about 30 degrees to port, bringing the nearest enemy cruiser—the *Wiesbaden*—on to a bearing of Green 80 (80 degrees from right ahead on the starboard side) and signalled 'Open fire, ship interval 12 seconds.' Three salvoes were fired by each of us at extreme range under the concentrated pair ship fire organisation which the squadron had worked up, but all the shot falling short, we checked fire, and *Defence* altered course directly towards *Wiesbaden*. At 6.1 p.m. the *Defence* again altered course and brought *Wiesbaden* on to a bearing 40 degrees on the port bow. Just after this the light cruisers of our battle cruiser fleet passed astern, and we came under fire from the enemy light cruisers.

Defence and *Warrior* then opened fire, and the second salvo of both ships hit the *Wiesbaden*, setting her on fire, and causing a great escape of steam on board her. In a few minutes she was seen to be stopped, but as she was still in a position favourable for firing torpedoes at our battle cruisers, we, *Defence* and *Warrior*, continued hitting her again and again with our port guns, closing her to within 6,000 yards before turning away. During this time everything seemed to be happening quite naturally and in order, with nothing surprising nor disconcerting. When both *Defence*'s and *Warrior*'s second salvoes hit the enemy, I remember remarking to the Navigator, 'We have never had a practice concentration of fire go off so smoothly and successfully.' There seemed to be plenty of time for everything; to give orders, to have them repeated, and to have them reported back executed.

As we closed the *Wiesbaden*, we passed about a mile ahead of our battle cruiser squadron, and came under a heavy fire from the enemy battle cruisers and subsequently from the enemy battleships, but, in spite of being under this heavy fire, we were for some time unable to see the enemy, as they were hidden by mist and smoke, and at no time were there more than three enemy ships visible. It was peculiarly annoying to be having the enemy's heavy salvoes falling close to us without being able either to see the ships which were firing, or make a useful report of the position, course, and speed of their battle fleet to the Commander-in-Chief—always the principal duty of a cruiser. I well remember looking back to the north-eastward, and seeing how clearly our battleships showed up in that direction against a bright skyline.

During this fighting *Warrior* was ¼ of a mile astern of *Defence*, and I twice thought that *Defence* had been hit by the enemy battle cruisers because of sudden puffs of black smoke which came from her. At 6.19 she commenced to turn away to starboard, and was then hit by two salvoes in quick succession. Then she blew up and completely disappeared. We, both of us, from 6.10 to 6.19, had been under a very heavy fire, but after the *Defence* blew up the enemy concentrated upon *Warrior*. As soon as I saw *Defence* turning away I had done the same, ordering the Navigating Officer to come with me into the conning tower to con the ship from there. A few minutes later a shell wrecked the bridge, wounded the torpedo officer for whom there was no room in the conning tower, and cut the clothing of the signal boatswain, who also had to remain outside for lack of room inside.

The *Warrior* was now between the enemy's battle fleet and our 5th B.S., about one and a half miles from the latter, and steering about 135° to starboard of their course. I decided to withdraw and try to follow the 5th B.S., but finding the *Warrior* was fast losing speed, I soon decided that it was hopeless to try to keep station on that squadron, and after giving our first antagonist, the *Wiesbaden*, two final salvoes from my starboard guns, which appeared to finish her off for she disappeared in a cloud of smoke and steam, I withdrew from the action, zigzagging to avoid the enemy's salvoes.

The *Warspite* was then about 2 miles astern of her squadron, having made a large circle towards the enemy as her steering gear had jammed. I had intended to pass astern of her, but finding that she was turning to starboard, I also turned to starboard and passed ahead of her. As she came between the *Warrior* and the enemy battle fleet she drew upon herself the fire that previously had been concentrated upon us, which undoubtedly saved the *Warrior* from being sunk then and there. This seemed to us to be a particularly gallant act on her part, and it gave us in the *Warrior* much satisfaction to see her replying with all her 15-inch guns to the enemy's fire, in spite of the fact that she was being heavily hit.

After turning away we were still under heavy fire, apparently from three, probably four enemy battleships, judging by the rapidity with which heavy salvoes fell close to us, but due to the small spread of their salvoes which fell in one huge splash, we just escaped time and again being hit although very frequently a whole salvo fell extremely close.

At 6.26 all electrical instruments and hydraulic power for the turrets failed. At 6.30 p.m. I received a report that the starboard engine-room was out of action, but in response to my orders to keep the engines going at all costs, it was reported a minute later that both engines were going ahead slow. Then at 6.35 I received a report that the main topmen's mess deck was on fire, and at 6.40 that the aft deck also was on fire; but by this time we were out of the action steering N.N.W., whilst the rest of our fleet were steering S.E. and soon were out of sight from us.

Receiving the report that all heavy guns were again ready for action in hand-gear—two turrets had been jammed by damage to the deck and there still was no hydraulic power—I ordered submarine look-out stations to be assumed, and soon afterwards a periscope was reported on the port bow, but I could not see it myself nor was any torpedo track observed.

About 6.55 the seaplane carrier, *Engadine*, was sighted to the southwest, and when we recognised her I signalled her to close and stand by the *Warrior* until we could ascertain our damage. We had been hit at least 15 times by heavy projectiles—11-inch or 12-inch—and about 6 times by smaller shells. Fires were raging so badly aft that it was impossible to get access to the engine-room; the whole main deck was full of flame, smoke, and gas from enemy shells; the upper deck was torn to pieces, and every boat was damaged beyond repair. The masts still stood, and so did the funnels, although the rigging had been shot away, and there were many holes in both masts and funnels. But the most serious damage was that caused by an 11-inch or 12-inch projectile which struck us on the water-line on the port side, passed through the after reserve coal bunker, crossed the upper part of the port engine-room, and burst as it went through the middle line bulkhead, leaving most of its gas in the port engine-room, while several large fragments of it were deflected downwards and tore a large hole in the double bottom at the after end of the starboard engine-room. On its way it carried away the transverse auxiliary steam pipe, which caused both engine-rooms to fill with steam.

The Engineer Commander was in the starboard engine-room, and described the circumstances there in the following report, which he made to me after the action:—

'At the time of the explosion I was in the starboard engine-room. The concussion was very violent, and was immediately followed by a heavy rush of water and a blowing of steam, and all the lights at the after end were extinguished. A moment's consideration convinced me that the damage was greater than could possibly be dealt with by the circulators, so I at once ordered the men to leave the engine-room . . . I decided to leave the engines running as fast as possible, and to check them if necessary by the communication valve worked from the main deck. By the time I reached the upper platform all lights had gone out, and I felt my way along the tops of the cylinders to the mid line door at the fore end, intending to get into the port engine-room, but I found the hatchway full of smoke, and, being unable to get through it, I climbed out through a large rent in the deck overhead.

Meanwhile the port engine-room had been filled with smoke and steam and the Senior Engineer Lieutenant, who was in charge there, finding it untenable, succeeded in opening the water-tight door and escaping to the starboard side. After closing the door, he found that the water was rising above the floor plates, and after a courageous but unsuccessful attempt to put the main circulating pump on to the bilge and to shut off steam, he ordered his party up on deck.

By this time, however, the ladders were inaccessible, the floor plates having been washed away, and the engines were still revolving in the water in the dark, and several of them were imprisoned beneath the upper gratings, whence four survivors were rescued more than two hours afterwards.'

The delay in rescuing them, it may be said, was largely due to the fires raging on the main deck and to the escaping steam, which prevented rescue parties from reaching the engine-room and them from escaping. Imprisoned under the engine-room gratings, they were only just rescued in time, having been nearly drowned, scalded, and suffocated.

Five or six shells burst on the main deck, and the majority of the ship's casualties occurred here. In all, there were 68 killed and 34 wounded. Another shell burst on the aft deck, and several more on the upper deck. There were many large rents in the upper deck, one 10 feet by 15 feet large, and the whole of the cabins and structure under the after shelter deck close to the main mast were completely blown away.

The effect of another shell that caused much damage, and the steps taken to cope with the damage, were described in the Commander's report to me afterwards:—

'*Hit No. 14.*—Shell went through the ship's side about 6 feet above the water-level just before 160 station, through the gunnery office, ship's office, engineers' office and workshop, store-room, lower store-room, and A. 2 (7.5-inch gun) support, striking and indenting the starboard side armour, the projectile falling back without exploding and remaining in A. 2 support. This projectile must have set fire to the gunnery office and Captain's domestics' mess by fusing circuits; it caused a hole on the port side about 12 inches in diameter, very much jagged.

The fire raged chiefly in the gunnery office and the stewards' mess adjacent ... It was impossible to bring hoses to bear on it directly, but eventually it was somewhat reduced by playing a hose through the hole in the ship's side made by the shell which had caused the fire, and after this a few men in smoke helmets managed to climb down through a coaling scuttle and gradually to extinguish the fire with buckets of water passed down from above.'

Another shell passed through the canteen store under the fo'csle, littering the upper deck in the vicinity with bacon, jams, and all sorts of eatables and stores. All the pumps except the two small Downtons and one little hand firepump were destroyed, and the Chief Carpenter and all his staff, except four, were killed, which was particularly unfortunate for their services were badly needed. But those four remaining carpenter ratings performed wonders later in the way of repairing damage, shoring up bulkheads, and making cofferdams around the rents in the deck.

While ascertaining the extent of our damage, I ordered all the spare hands to rig rafts, as the ship was taking a serious list to starboard, and soon afterwards the Engineer Commander reported to me that both engine-rooms were rapidly filling with water, and that the engines must stop before long; also that, while the fires raged and steam was escaping from several steam pipes, he could not ascertain all the damage nor our prospects of saving the ship.

I then gave orders to draw fires in the boilers and to shut off steam in the boiler-rooms, and signalled to the *Engadine* to take *Warrior* in tow. This operation was carried out very expeditiously, although our 6-inch wire towing hawser was stowed on the main deck in a position very difficult of access, due to the smoke, gas fumes, and corpses. Taking in tow was an exercise that Sir Robt. Arbuthnot had frequently made the ships of his squadron practise, and from this we now profited.

By 9 p.m. we were in tow. All the usual steering gear and communications had been destroyed, and the ship was being steered by hand from the tiller flat, with a field telephone rigged up from the bridge as communication which proved quite efficient. I directed the *Engadine* to shape course for Cromarty and to proceed at her best speed, which gave us about 8 knots at first, though this was reduced to 6 knots the next morning.

It grew dark about 9.30 p.m., and the barometer then started falling rapidly, so that our prospects of getting home were none too bright, but all hands worked with a will at stopping leaks and at shoring up bulkheads. After dark I made a personal examination of our damages, and of the steps that had been taken to cope with them. I felt that, if the weather remained fine and the sea smooth, there was a sporting chance of saving the ship, and that at any rate she would keep afloat during the dark hours; we intercepted wireless signals reporting that tugs were on their way out from Cromarty to assist us.

Every two hours the amount that the water had risen in the engine-room was reported to me. It ceased to rise from 2 a.m. to 4 a.m., but after 4 a.m. the wind and sea rapidly got up and the water gained fast. At 6 a.m., and again at 7.15 a.m., I made a tour below, as a result of which I was forced to the conclusion that nothing we could now do would save the ship. The water was gaining beyond our control, and the ship was no longer answering to the motion of the sea but was beginning to roll in a way that showed her stability was fast disappearing, due to the huge quantity of water on the main deck. I ordered the Engineer Commander, the Commander, and the Senior unwounded Lieut.-Commander to go round below and report to me their opinion of the prospect of being able to keep the ship afloat. They all agreed that at any moment she might sink, and that she could not last more than a couple of hours. The barometer was falling fast and the wind and sea were rapidly rising, so I hoisted the signal which I had previously arranged with *Engadine* to indicate to her that she was to cast off the tow and come alongside the *Warrior* for us to abandon ship.

All the wounded were got up in cots or stretchers; the ship's company were fallen in by divisions, and after all the wounded had been transferred to the *Engadine*, the men clambered on board her, one division at a time. One of the wounded was lost overboard between the two ships, but his body was recovered by Flight-Lieut. Rutland, of *Engadine*, in a most gallant manner, for which action Rutland was later rewarded the Albert Medal. It was this same officer who had reported the enemy's movements from a seaplane the previous day.

Finally the Commander reported all hands were on board the *Engadine*, and he and I then jumped on board, and the *Engadine* went astern to clear the sinking ship. As we left the old *Warrior* we gave her three hearty cheers. Every big sea washed over her decks, and water poured down through the huge rents in the upper deck on to the main deck. As all the steam pumps and all but two of the hand pumps had been destroyed by enemy shells, we had no means of coping with the volume of water pouring into the ship, and the upper deck was now only about 2 to 4 feet above water. The whole main deck was flooded, and the ship was very much down by the stern.

The behaviour of officers and men had been splendid throughout. All had worked, not only with the utmost zeal, but most cheerily, and even as if they were thoroughly enjoying themselves. As we had passed out of action and had seen our battle fleet firing with rapid regularity, we had all felt that the German fleet was going to be destroyed, and that the loss of the *Defence* and *Warrior* would be a small item compared with the loss that the German fleet would suffer. We felt that the old *Warrior* had made a gallant fight against great odds, and had disabled and almost certainly destroyed one enemy ship before she herself was disabled.

So we left the old ship with three hearty cheers, and the *Engadine* shaped course for Rosyth.

Narrative of the Commanding Officer of H.M.S. *Engadine*

Describing the Towing of H.M.S. *Warrrior*, May 31st to June 1st

After picking up our seaplane (about 4.0 p.m.) we followed the battle cruisers to the south at our best speed, during which time we had a good view of the 5th Battle Squadron going into action as they opened fire soon after passing us. I endeavoured to keep the battle cruisers in sight and followed their alterations of course as best I could, turning north when I found that they had turned in that direction at about 4.45 p.m. We were very soon passed by them some way to the eastward, so I turned to the eastward to close them again. At this period they were very indistinct, the flashes of their guns being the only guide to their position. After a comparatively short time on this easterly course, a number of ships showed up fairly distinctly right ahead, which we took to be the Grand Fleet, amongst them two cruisers being conspicuous, one of which

HMS *Engadine* towing the disabled *Warrior*.

afterwards turned out to be the *Warrior*. She was broadside on to us, and was very conspicuous at times by what appeared to be clouds of steam pouring out of the engine-room casings; and with the other ship she seemed to be drawing all the enemy's fire, so that at intervals they were hidden in the midst of smoke and splashes, and in the mist.

The most conspicuous of the two cruisers, the *Warrior*, was soon noticed to be drawing off from the action and steering to the westward towards us, but the other ships were then lost to view in the mist and smoke. Course was altered to close her, for she appeared to be damaged in the engine-room as steam was coming from her engine-room casings, and she had also a slight list to starboard, and appeared to be down by the stern.

When sure of her identity I made a signal asking if I could be of any assistance, and received a reply to stand by her, and was also informed that her engine-room and one stokehold was flooded and that she was unable to control her engines.[2] When close up to her it was evident that she was badly crippled, although not in a sinking condition. After steaming in company for two hours or so, she ordered me to take her in tow, which at about 8.0 p.m. was carried out without any difficulty as it was fortunately then perfectly calm. *Engadine* came close under *Warrior*'s port bow and sent out a

---

2 She actually signalled that she was 'unable to stop her engines', which necessarily caused some amusement in *Engadine*, particularly amongst the R.N.A.S. detachment, as it was a continual worry to make our (seaplane) engines ever start!

grass-line in a skiff and took in *Warrior*'s 6½-inch wire, bringing it inboard through a small fairlead in the starboard quarter where it was made fast round two bollards, one on the quarter and the other about 25 feet further forward. *Engadine* then went ahead, but was unable to tow with any success, owing, it was found, to *Warrior*'s helm being jammed hard over. With this righted, however, there was no further difficulty, and working up gradually to revolutions for 18 knots, a speed over the ground of 7 knots was made good, and course was shaped for Cromarty. *Engadine* was then towing by the full length of *Warrior*'s 6½-inch wire and four shackles, I think, of cable.

In the early morning of June 1st the sea and wind gradually rose, and I became anxious about our towing bollards holding as they were very light, but fortunately they showed no signs of strain. However, about 7 a.m. *Warrior* ordered me to slip the tow and come alongside to take off her crew. Tow was slipped, and a wide turn made to come up from her stern on the lee, the starboard, side. As we came past her we had a good view of her lying broadside on to the sea, a sad but impressive sight, her upper deck aft almost awash and each wave as it reached her lapping over the side. In her starboard battery all the hands were fallen in ready to abandon ship.

We came alongside her starboard side just abaft her fore-bridge. I felt anxious about holes being made in our side by boats, davits, etc., as a nasty sea was now running, but all went well, and we received nothing worse than a puncture in the stokehold from a hanging davit.

The wounded were first brought on board and accommodated in the ward-room, and then all the rest of the crew jumped across until every place in the ship was packed as close as in a tin of sardines. In transferring the wounded, owing to the motion between the ships, one man slipped off a stretcher and fell between the two ships. The Captain of the *Warrior*, who was on the bridge, gave the order that no one was to go over after him as it appeared certain that whoever went must be crushed to death immediately; but Flight Commander Rutland of my ship climbed over forward unseen, and reached the man at great risk to himself, for which gallant act he afterwards received the Albert Medal.

When all were on board we got clear of the *Warrior* without difficulty. She looked a sad sight lying there derelict and deserted, and it was obvious that she would not keep afloat very much longer.

Course was then shaped for the Firth of Forth which was reached, without incident, in the early hours of the morning of June 2nd.

This account is supplemented by that of another of *Engadine*'s officers describing the abandoning of the *Warrior*, an account which for the first time tells of the disciplined courage displayed by the crew of the *Warrior* on this occasion.[3]

The Abandoning of H.M.S. *Warrior*
A Further Narrative from H.M.S. *Engadine*

During the night a sea got up, and the *Warrior* had taken in so much water that it was decided to abandon her. The sea was bad: the little *Engadine* bobbed about like a cork, and the *Warrior* was moving in every direction as if she was loth to give up the fight, but knew that she was doomed. Her crew were fallen in on her deck, well back from the ship's side against the funnel casing, looking as indifferent to their danger as men possibly can. They had been like this all the time overnight, working for the several hours it took to get the ship in tow as calmly as if it was all an exercise, although the ship at that time was still on the battlefield open to attack by surface ship or submarine, and with all her damage from shell fire was liable to founder at any time.

The risk of *Engadine* going alongside *Warrior* to take off the crew was tremendous, but there was no hesitation on the part of the Captain, and the crew were with him to a man. The starboard side of *Warrior* was tried first, but looked too bad: so the port side was then tried, but it looked worse. The *Engadine* then lay off the starboard quarter of *Warrior*, which must have taxed the nerves of the *Warrior*'s crew to the uttermost seeing, after all they had gone through, that apparently they had now either to swim through this seaway to the *Engadine* or else go down with the ship. Those that had collected pieces of enemy shells as souvenirs, I was told, quietly

3 This account inevitably recalls the story of the sinking of the *Birkenhead* in 1852. But how strangely Time rings in her changes. The then King of Prussia caused the account of the British soldiers' and sailors' discipline to be read aloud to every regiment in his kingdom as an example of true soldierly bearing in the face of great danger.

placed them on one side, in order that they might have less weight to carry on their swim.

The *Engadine*, however, was only waiting for the *Warrior*'s yawing from side to side to steady a little before attempting to get alongside her again on the starboard side, the side which had been looked at first. After a few minutes, which must have seemed hours to the *Warrior*'s men, the *Engadine* was placed alongside, in a manner which I think was agreed by all to be a wonderful piece of seamanship. The ships were made fast together, but worked against each other most viciously; yet all the *Warrior*'s men remained steady waiting their Captain's order to abandon ship. Then the Captain gave the order, and things moved. Each man's ration of bully beef and bread was hurled on board us, and one large mass of men poured over the nettings into the ship.

At this moment the Captain considered that there was too much haste, and he ordered the bugle 'Still' to be sounded. The result was wonderful.

"Still"

Not a single man passed from the *Warrior* to the *Engadine* after this bugle was sounded, but every man fell back from the ship's side against the funnel casing, just as they would have done if the bugle call had been sounded at drill. It was a wonderful sight—an inspiring sight; a triumph of organisation, discipline, and courage combined. I am not ashamed to say it brought tears to my eyes. Every man in the *Warrior* must feel proud of being one of such a ship's company.

When the 'Carry On' was sounded, all those still left in the *Warrior* hastened to abandon ship. The wounded were got across, and finally the officers, and lastly the Captain, all of

"Carry on"

whom kept up the highest traditions and the highest standard of courage.

Three cheers were given for their old ship as we parted, and the *Engadine* left with only a small hole in the engine-room, and the boat deck a little damaged by the *Warrior*'s guns and davits. The thing that impressed me most, both during and after the action, was the wonderful morale of the officers and men.

Narrative of H.M.S. *Duke of Edinburgh*[4]

(The Only Ship of the 1st Cruiser Squadron that came back from the Action)

May 30th.—The 1st Cruiser Squadron were lying at Cromarty when, at about 6.30 p.m., the General Recall was hoisted and steam was ordered for 18 knots. At 9.45 p.m. the ships at Cromarty and Invergordon weighed and proceeded to a rendezvous where we met the remainder of the Grand Fleet from Scapa, and together we stood to the S.E. in company during the night, and also during the forenoon and afternoon of May 31st.

May 31st.—About 2 p.m. we intercepted a signal from the 4th L.C.S. reporting enemy battle cruisers steaming east, and shortly afterwards another signal reported the presence of the whole German High Seas Fleet, in two divisions, with destroyers in attendance. At 3.30 p.m. our Battle Cruiser Force reported that they had sighted the enemy, who had turned to the north, and at 3.50 reported that they were engaging the enemy.

The 1st Cruiser Squadron was at this time stationed in the 'AA' line, 16 miles ahead of the Grand Fleet, the *Defence* and *Warrior* being nearest the centre, with *Duke of Edinburgh* 8 miles on *Defence*'s starboard beam, and *Black Prince* again 8 miles on the starboard beam of *Duke of Edinburgh*.

About 5 p.m. we heard the sound of gunfire, and shortly afterwards a couple of our light cruisers, steaming at high speed, came in sight on our starboard bow standing across our course from starboard to port. It was unfortunately a misty day with haze over everything, and the visibility was only from 6,000 to 8,000 yards: the sea was calm, and there was little wind; sun only occasionally visible.

It was soon evident that the light cruisers were in action for we could see the flashes of their guns and also the splashes of the shot which were being fired at them. After a short time we could distinguish the flashes of the enemy's guns, but could not distinguish the ships.

Defence signalled us to 'Close,' and at 5.40 we altered course to port to comply with this order, increasing to full speed at the same time. The *Black Prince* did the same, but, owing to her distance

---

4 An account elaborated from notes taken during the action, and written in a journal immediately afterwards. It is practically copied from the journal.

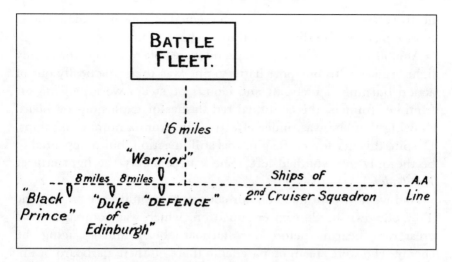

from *Defence* (16 miles), she realised apparently that it would be impossible to reach her station, and shortly afterwards she altered course away from us, presumably to take station astern of the battle fleet, and we did not see her again.

Shortly after this the *Defence* and *Warrior* both opened fire with their starboard broadsides, but it was not then possible to see at what they were firing. About this time we saw our Battle Cruiser Squadron coming up from astern, bearing a little on our starboard quarter and steering approximately the same course as ourselves, for the masts of all the ships were almost in line with each other. They were also engaging the enemy, but it was impossible to see more than the flashes of the enemy's guns. The action was driving rapidly upon us, and it soon became possible to catch occasional glimpses of light grey hulls.

The *Defence* and *Warrior* were now firing rapidly, and I could see what appeared to be four-gun salvoes straddling the *Defence*. About this time (6 p.m.) the enemy appeared to make a turn of 16 points bringing them roughly on to the opposite course to us, but they must have turned again to their original course very shortly afterwards, as on the next occasion of sighting them they were unquestionably steering a nearly parallel course to us going in the same direction as we were. They (the enemy) left one of their light cruisers behind at the turn, one of the *Augsburg* class apparently, in serious difficulty and the *Defence*, followed by the *Warrior*, turned to starboard towards her. We were then some 6 miles from *Defence*, and our fire was continually masked by the swarms of our

175

destroyers and light cruisers which seemed to appear from nowhere, to race past us, and disappear into the haze again.

At 6.08 we turned to starboard and were able to engage the enemy light cruiser with our port battery. She was then practically out of action burning fiercely aft and clouds of steam were blowing off from her funnels, the continual red flashes of explosions on board showing that she was under effective fire from a number of ships. Despite this her forecastle gun was still in action, but it appeared to be the only gun she had left. (She was probably the light cruiser *Wiesbaden*.)

Had we now continued on our course we should have crossed the T of our own battle cruiser squadron, which was coming up at a great rate, bearing before our starboard beam and engaging the enemy, who were steaming parallel to them on their starboard beam. We altered course to port accordingly to avoid masking their fire, but *Defence* and *Warrior* appeared to have crossed their track already and turned to starboard, passing down between our battle cruisers and the enemy, presumably intending to turn up again when astern so as to mask the fire of the battle cruisers for as short a time as possible. In any case it happened that at one period our battle cruisers and the *Defence* and *Warrior* were all in line between us and the enemy, to say nothing of a number of destroyers which were stationed on the disengaged side of our battle cruisers. We were thus, of course, prevented from firing, but had a good opportunity to see what was going on.

The *Lion* passed us about 600 to 800 yards away, followed by another battle cruiser of the same class (*Princess Royal*), and a third ship, which must have been the *New Zealand*. The enemy's fire seemed to be concentrated mostly on the *Lion*. I noticed that her 'Q' turret was out of action, and that there was a large hole in her port side plating on the level of the main deck through which I could see a fire burning. For about ten minutes we came in for a considerable fire consisting of 'overs' fired at the battle cruisers. Two salvoes straddled the ship and one fell over, while a number of ricochets rattled and puffed overhead. The noise of the bursting shell was tremendous, and I remember the officer in the Transmitting Station asking me up the voice pipe what was making all the row, as he knew that we were not firing. I looked at the *Defence* and *Warrior*, and saw them just circling round astern to follow the battle cruisers: they were both under a heavy fire, particularly the *Warrior*, which was hit

176

twice whilst I was looking at her. This was about 6.15 p.m. By 6.35 p.m. our battle cruisers had drawn ahead of us, and our battle fleet was coming up from our port quarter: our course was then S.E. by S. The *Defence* and *Warrior* were lost to sight astern, and the enemy seemed to have hauled off to the westward—*i.e.*, away from us. There was an interval of comparative calm, during which, at 6.38 p.m., we passed the two halves of a sinking ship, bow and stern both standing straight out of the water. A destroyer had closed her and sent a boat to pick up any survivors. This was, I learnt afterwards, the *Invincible*, with the *Badger* standing by.

At 6.47 the track of a torpedo was sighted coming directly towards us from starboard: we altered course to port, and it passed close astern of us.

All this time we were keeping station ahead of our battle fleet, which seemed to have deployed by sub-divisions, and was then in sub-divisions in line ahead, disposed quarterly to starboard. At 7.05 p.m. fire was opened again from our battle squadron, increasing in volume until, at 7.15, the action seemed fairly general. The 2nd Cruiser Squadron now appeared upon the scene, followed by the 7th Cruiser Squadron, and the *Minotaur* (Admiral Heath) took charge of the cruisers. By this time our course was south: we were apparently circling the enemy, and had succeeded in getting between them and Heligoland.

During the night the wind freshened a little from the south, but we neither saw nor heard anything, though the wireless told us that our destroyers were in action with the enemy battle fleet. During the night our fleet was steering in a southerly direction at 17 knots, and at 2 a.m. on June 1st, being then 78 miles from Heligoland, we turned to the northward by order of the Commander-in-Chief.

June 1st.—By 2.30 a.m. it was pretty light, and we went to action stations, and at 3.30 a.m. we heard firing, but it was only the 3rd L.C.S. attacking a Zeppelin. From 3 a.m. until 11 a.m. we, the cruisers, kept patrolling north and south edging gradually to the westward, but without seeing a sign of anything. At 11.15 a.m. we came in touch with our battle fleet steering to the north in its usual cruising formation. The cruisers were then spread on the 'AA' line, and we started for Scapa at 17 knots. There were no signs of the *Defence*, *Warrior*, or *Black Prince*. We heard that the *Warrior* had been taken in tow by the *Engadine* but finally abandoned, but neither *Defence* nor *Black Prince* replied to our repeated wireless calls.

Towards evening the cruisers were detached from the battle fleet to search for the *Warrior*, and to take her, if found, in tow. We swept over the area in which she had been abandoned but saw no signs of her, though we carried on the search throughout the night and during the light hours of the following day, Friday, June 2nd, being ordered also to look out for the *Broke*.

June 2nd.—During the night of June 2nd the *Cochrane* got into wireless touch with the *Broke*, and learning that she was off the Tyne we were ordered to abandon the search and return to Scapa. Very glad we were to do so too, as the wind and sea were getting up, and we were having a number of submarine scares, including reported sinking of one submarine by the *Minotaur* at about 9 p.m. on the 2nd.

June 3rd.—Once on the way to Scapa, however, the weather improved a lot, and when we arrived there at 5.30 p.m. on Saturday, June 3rd, it was a perfect northern summer's evening. The fleet lay peacefully at anchor just as usual, and racing boats' crews were away practising; one would never have imagined that the fleet were back after the first general action of the war. But as we anchored at the tail of the 2nd Cruiser Squadron after our fruitless search for the *Warrior* and realised also that neither *Defence* nor *Black Prince* had reached the base, the effect of the battle was brought home to us, and there was left little doubt in our minds that the days of the old 1st Cruiser Squadron were ended for ever.

CHAPTER IX

BATTLE FLEET ACTION

Extract from Commander-in-Chief's Despatch:—
'DETAILS OF THE BATTLE FLEET ACTION.

The First Battle Squadron, under Vice-Admiral Sir Cecil Burney, came into action at 6.15 p.m. with the enemy's Third Battle Squadron, at a range of about 11,000 yards, and administered severe punishment both to the battleships and to the battle cruisers and light cruisers which were also engaged. The fire of *Marlborough* (Captain George P. Ross) was particularly rapid and effective.

. . . The range decreased during the course of the action to 9,000 yards. The First Battle Squadron received more of the enemy's return fire than the remainder of the battle fleet, with the exception of the Fifth Battle Squadron. *Colossus* was hit, but not seriously damaged, and other ships were straddled, with fair frequency.

In the Fourth Battle Squadron—in which squadron my flagship, *Iron Duke*, was placed—Vice-Admiral Sir Doveton Sturdee, leading one of the divisions, the enemy engaged was the Third Squadron and some of the battle cruisers, as well as disabled cruisers and light cruisers. The mist rendered range-taking a difficult matter, but the fire of the squadron was effective. *Iron Duke*, having previously fired at a light cruiser between the lines, opened fire at 6.30 p.m. on a battleship of the *Konig* class at a range of 12,000 yards. . . .

The fire of the other ships of the squadron was principally directed at enemy battle cruisers and cruisers as they appeared out of the mist. Hits were observed to take effect on several ships.

The ships of the Second Battle Squadron, under Vice-Admiral Sir Thomas Jerram, were in action with vessels of the

179

Part of Grand Fleet operating in the North Sea.

Kaiser or *Konig* classes between 6.30 and 7.20 p.m., and fired also at an enemy battle cruiser which had apparently dropped back severely damaged. . . .'

Narrative from H.M.S. *Bellerophon*

(14th Ship in the Battle Line—*i.e.*, near the centre of the Line)

We were the second ship in the 4th Division of the battle fleet, next astern of *Benbow* which flew the flag of Vice-Admiral Sturdee.

At 6.0 p.m. we heard sounds of firing on the starboard bow, and almost simultaneously our battle cruisers came into sight crossing ahead of the battle fleet from starboard to port, and firing at the Germans somewhat abaft their starboard beam. The flashes of the German guns could occasionally be seen, but no ships were visible as it was fairly misty. There was quite a mix-up at this time between our destroyer screen and the battle cruiser force's light cruisers and destroyers, and several destroyers apparently had to stop. It was quite extraordinary to see what a 'lop' was set up by the wash of the two sets of ships passing each other.

As the battle cruisers cleared us (at 6.8) we deployed to the E.S.E., and at the same time sighted the head of the enemy battle fleet, but too indistinctly to engage them. The 1st Cruiser Squadron then suddenly came into sight across the bows of our battle cruisers, and passed down between the lines steering about west—a fine sight, all going full speed and firing away like fury with every gun that would bear; but a few minutes later the *Defence* was blown up.

At 6.23 we sighted a three-funnelled cruiser between us and the Hun fleet, heading west, enveloped in smoke from the foremost funnel aft, and apparently moving very slowly. We had by now just about finished deploying, and at 6.27 *Benbow* hoisted the signal for the 4th Division to open fire, and at 6.33, though we were rather doubtful as to whether the cruiser was one of our own or a German, we opened fire on her, as all other ships were firing at her, at a range of about 14,700 yards. This was, as far as I know, the first concentration firing on a large scale which had ever taken place, so the results naturally were rather disappointing. The German cruiser was quickly hidden by a solid wall of splashes, except her bow which remained just visible, but she didn't seem to suffer much, and as none of us had the faintest idea as to which salvoes were whose, fire control was rather hopeless. We therefore tried to shift our fire to the enemy battleships which were slowly crossing behind the cruiser, but they were hardly visible except for the gun flashes, and as none of the gunlayers could see them at all and we were not yet fitted up properly with director firing, we had to come back to firing at the cruiser again.

Soon after this, at 6.44, finding it impossible to spot, we checked fire. The cruiser eventually seemed to disappear in a cloud of spray, but with no explosion.

At 6.55 we had altered course by divisions to south, and there seemed to be a general lull in the firing. We trained all the turrets on to Green 70, waiting for something to turn up. Just at this time a four-funnelled cruiser, slightly on fire aft, heading north and steaming very slowly, appeared on our starboard beam and was engaged by two ships, I think by *Colossus* and *Collingwood*. They hit her by the mainmast fairly soon, but I did not see any more, as at 7.12 we

181

sighted a German destroyer about Green 35[1] heading straight towards us, and we opened fire on her with turrets at 7.14, but we only fired one salvo before she was damaged by some other ship and lay stopped between the lines on fire. At 7.16 we altered course 30° to port away from the enemy by Blue pendant—that is, all ships turning together. We were going 14 knots at this time and were altering away, I believe, to avoid the torpedoes that the enemy had fired.

At 7.17 three enemy battle cruisers suddenly appeared, steering about S. by W., bearing Green 120, 11,000 yards away, and at 7.18 we altered to south again and opened fire on the leading battle cruiser which was of the *Derfflinger* class, the second one being the *Seydlitz*, but the third I could not see clearly. The fore-top range-finder got a very good snap range of them, by using which our third salvo straddled the enemy, apparently hitting his 'X' turret with one shell between the guns, and the next salvo straddled him again. After this there were too many splashes falling round them to be able to spot with any certainty.

At 7.26 four enemy destroyers suddenly appeared ahead of and on our side of the battle cruisers, and we at once put 'A' turret and the two foremost guns on to them. These destroyers were nearly broadside on to us and were in an irregular formation, steering the same way as their battle cruisers. I gave the 4-inch guns a range of 8,500 as a rough guess, but the first shots fell a good way short. 'A' turret, in local control, was better, and managed to hit one destroyer with their third round, hitting her at about the second funnel so that her bow and stern shot up like the ends of a broken stick. Just after this the enemy battle cruisers turned away and the remaining destroyers followed suit, making at the same time a most effective smoke screen. Our remaining turrets had been put on to these boats just before this but no more hits were obtained.

We finally ceased firing at 7.30 p.m., the enemy now being totally hidden by smoke and mist.

At 8.25, after nearly an hour's lull, firing suddenly broke out again on our starboard bow, coming apparently, judging by the flashes, from three big ships. A minute or two later our 4th Light Cruiser Squadron suddenly appeared from the same direction—the visibility was now no more than 6,000 yards—with shell falling

---

1 35 degrees on the starboard bow.

short of them and the leading ship, *Calliope*, slightly on fire aft. The *Benbow* fired two salvoes in the direction of the enemy flashes, but, as far as we could see, she was the only ship of our line which fired; we ourselves could not see sufficiently clearly to fire. Anyhow, the enemy ceased fire almost at once and we saw no more of them, so the hands were now sent to get food.

At about 9.0 p.m. a star shell was fired some way away on our starboard beam, and at 9.30 we went to night defence stations, keeping three turrets manned.

During the first watch there was quite a lot of firing going on on our starboard quarter, and a cruiser seemed to be on fire pretty badly, searchlight beams, apparently from her, that showed in our direction being turned quite red by the flames. At about 11.40 p.m. there was further firing astern, and for the first hour or so of the middle watch there was intermittent firing on the port quarter, but otherwise the night passed without signs of action.

At 2.30 a.m. it was quite light though the visibility was still low, and we went to day action stations again. Shortly afterwards we turned north, but except for a ' Zepp.' nothing was sighted. We were still at action stations during the forenoon, and as the visibility was only 6,000 to 8,000 yards, we expected to bump into the Hun at any minute. I must own that at this time I was continually dropping off into a doze and waking up with a jerk, and the remainder of the fore-top crew were quite openly asleep unless roused every few minutes. But nothing happened so we finally turned north about 2.0 p.m. on June 1st, fell out from action stations, and reached Scapa Flow again on the following day, June 2nd.

Narrative from H.M.S. *Colossus*

(Leading Ship of Rear Battle Squadron (1st B.S.); 17th Ship in the Battle Line)

The *Colossus* (Capt. A. D. P. R. Pound) at Jutland was flying the flag of Rear Admiral E. F. A. Gaunt, C.M.G., as Rear-Admiral in the 1st Battle Squadron, his division consisting of *Colossus*, *Collingwood*, *Neptune*, and *St. Vincent*, stationed in the order named.

At approximately 6 p.m. the battle fleet deployed to port, thus putting the *Colossus* as leading ship of the 1st Battle Squadron and 17th ship in the line. The deployment was a most wonderful sight, but so many things were happening almost simultaneously that it is very hard to give a really connected account of what occurred. For this reason I append a chronological table of events, as taken down by the Admiral's Secretary who was on the fore-bridge throughout the action.

Two things stand out very clearly in my memory of the deployment. First, the extraordinary clearness with which we were able to see a large shell which ricochetted over, and which was painted yellow with a black band. It was, I think, the first shell to come anywhere appreciably close to us. And, second, the masterly way in which some light cruisers (I think the *Calliope*'s squadron) cut through the lines at full speed, one of them passing only a few yards across our bows as we turned to port into battle line.[2] We passed quite close to the *Lion*, which was heavily engaged, and showed plain evidence of what she had been through. She appeared to be on fire the port side forward, abreast 'A' turret.

At about 6.15 p.m. we witnessed the action of the 1st Cruiser Squadron and the blowing up of *Defence*. Almost simultaneously with *Defence*'s disappearance a heavy salvo fell just short of *Colossus*, and *Marlborough*, the flagship of our Vice-Admiral, opened fire. *Colossus* fired three salvoes at the enemy battle fleet, and four salvoes at a disabled four-funnelled enemy cruiser which gradually drew abeam from ahead, and was last seen obviously sinking, masts and funnels gone, and blazing merrily. Just after this interlude we passed close by the destroyer, *Acasta*, lying completely disabled; one of our Torpedo Gunners had lately joined her, and he and his party aft gave us a rousing cheer as we passed.

About 7 p.m. a three-funnelled enemy light cruiser passed on opposite courses to us at a range of 9,700 yards. We gave her three salvoes, and left her crippled and apparently sinking. It was just about then that we passed the wreck of *Invincible*, both ends sticking out of the water. We mistook her for a German, being unable to read her name. Meanwhile a solitary destroyer appeared making an attack on our starboard bow, and at her we fired both 12-inch and 4-inch, and she was stopped at a range of about 6,000 yards. I believe our foremost turret claimed a direct hit though we were by no means the only ship firing at her. I do not think she was able to fire her torpedoes.

---

2 Probably the *Galatea*'s Squadron, *vide* her narrative of the 'Windy Corner' period, page 137.

German Battle Cruiser *Seydlitz* on fire.

At 7.12 p.m. an enemy battle cruiser of the *Lutzow* class suddenly appeared on our starboard beam emerging out of the mist or
a smoke screen, and was followed by two other battle cruisers and
I think four battleships of the *Konig* class. At first I thought she
was steaming on an opposite course to us although she was only
10,000 yards distant, but she was really on an almost parallel
course. *Colossus* and *Collingwood* concentrated on this leading ship
which later was identified as *Lutzow*, and we fired five salvoes at
her, the final range being 8,400 yards, and bearing, I think, Green
105. Our fourth and fifth salvoes hit well and the *Collingwood* also
hit her. She then burst into flames, listed, and turned directly away
from us. Just before she finally disappeared, a light cruiser was
observed to approach her and appeared to be blotted out by a heavy
salvo of what looked like 15-inch shell, though it was impossible to
see what actually happened as she was almost out of sight, and the
other ships with her also disappeared either in a smoke screen or in
the mist.

During this action *Colossus* was being heavily shelled, apparently
by the German battle fleet on the starboard bow, although they were
invisible to us except for the flash of their guns, but, as far as I know,
the return fire of the battle cruisers we were engaging, *Lutzow* and

185

her squadron, came nowhere near us. We were repeatedly straddled across the fo'csle, and a good many splinter holes were made forward from numerous 'shorts' which burst on hitting the water. One salvo hit us direct at 7.16 p.m., two high-explosive shells of approximately 12-inch calibre landing in the after-end of the fore-superstructure, and, a third ricochetted on to the armoured pad abreast 'Q' turret, about 3 feet above the water-line after hitting the water a few feet short. I think only one shell exploded in the super-structure, but this caused a lot of minor damage and fired ten boxes of ready-use cordite at the port 4-inch guns, but fortunately these guns were not manned being on the disengaged side, and so there were not many casualties. This shell entered just abaft No. 5 star-board 4-inch gun which was in action, knocked over the marine gun's crew and slightly wounded three of them. Two of the Admiral's domestics, who were by the Admiral's sea cabin at the fore end of the port 4-inch battery instead of at their proper stations down below, were also slightly wounded by minute splinters that were almost like dust shot.

Another heavy shell from a salvo a few seconds later burst some

Damage in *Colossus*.

30 yards short abreast the fore-bridge, and flying fragments did quite a lot of damage. All the officers and men on the fore-bridge had very narrow escapes, but only Leading-Seaman Beddow, the range-taker at the fore-bridge range-finder, was hit, his right arm being practically severed just below the shoulder. He later had to have his arm amputated at the shoulder, but had it not been for the Captain of Marines who improvised a tourniquet out of a handker-chief and a bit of stick, and so stopped the flow of blood, he would certainly have bled to death.

No. 1 starboard searchlight was completely wrecked, the chart and signal houses were damaged, and two men in the fore-top were wounded; also a midshipman in the fore-top had a small splinter from this shell right through his cap, but it merely grazed his scalp. The fire caused by the shell-burst and by ignited cordite was easily got under, and by the time I got out of the conning tower (having been ordered to see the fire put out and report damage) there were only a few odds and ends, such as canvas gun-covers, etc., still smouldering. None of the 4-inch guns were put out of action, but the periscope glasses of 'P' turret were smashed and several of the boom-boats were badly knocked about.

It was while we were engaged with *Lutzow* that a second torpedo attack was made on us, this time by four enemy torpedo craft. Our 4-inch guns were put on to them, and 'A' turret also shifted target on to them for a round or two just before they turned away, at a range of 6,000 or 7,000 yards. They fired their torpedoes, but I do not think any of the four boats got back again as they were under a tremendous fire from a large number of our battleships, and they disappeared, presumably sunk. The tracks of five torpedoes were observed from us, and we had to alter course to port to avoid two of them, after which *Colossus* did not again come into action although we could see various actions being fought astern of us throughout the night, and a Zeppelin was sighted shortly after 3.30 a.m. next morning.

Various ships that had been near us during the day action reported that *Colossus* passed through a cloud of fire, spray, and smoke, and they quite thought that we were done for. I attribute our comparative immunity to the fact that we were gradually reducing speed all the time we were under fire, in order to correct our dis-tance from the rear ship of the 4th B.S. ahead of us, consequently nearly all of the salvoes fell across our stem. The German shooting was good, and their salvoes had a very small spread, but it was curious that the return fire of the ships with which we were actually engaged apparently all went considerably over us, it being the salvoes from ships out of sight of us that straddled and hit us. The actual damage we sustained was unimportant, and fortunately our sea-going and fighting efficiency was unimpaired. The superstructure was badly wrecked in the neighbourhood of the shell burst, also several cabins, and numerous splinter holes in the starboard side forward required plugging, but that was about all.

I was chiefly impressed by the fact that so large a number of heavy shells could fall so close to us without actually hitting, and to the sort of kaleidoscopic effect produced on one's mind by so many incidents occurring in so short a space of time. Our own shooting was good, and no failures of any sort occurred; there was less 'flap' than during an ordinary firing practice. The control officers aloft mistook the shell which hit us for 'P' turret firing without orders, and only realised that we had been hit when they saw the flames from the burning cordite.

Chronological Table of Events

H.M.S. *Colossus*—31st May to 1st June, 1916

3.00 p.m.	Signal 'BA' —(action stations).
5.40 "	Weather conditions:—Visibility 6 miles, sky overcast, sea calm, wind S.W. light.
	Heard heavy firing 4 points on starboard bow.
5.50 "	Our battle cruisers in sight on starboard bow firing.
5.51 "	Enemy battle fleet in sight on starboard bow.
5.57 "	Enemy battle fleet alter course to north.
6.02 "	Enemy battle fleet in sight.
6.06 "	*Lion* steam (? smoke) coming from abreast fore turret, port side.
6.10 "	5th B.S. in action.
6.13 "	Large yellow projectile with black band ricochetted over.
6.16 "	1st Cruiser Squadron on starboard quarter heavily engaged. One ship blows up.

6.18 p.m.	Salvo 200 yards short and left of *Colossus*.
6.19 "	*Marlborough* opened fire.
6.21 "	Heavy shell passed over.
6.22 "	Enemy cruiser on starboard beam disabled.
	Enemy battle fleet on starboard quarter, 12,000 yards.
6.30 "	*Colossus* fired three salvoes at enemy battle fleet.
6.32 "	*Colossus* fired four salvoes at enemy disabled cruiser mentioned above.
6.45 "	Ceased firing, nothing in sight.
6.48 "	Passed *Acasta* disabled.
6.50 "	Our course south.
7.00 "	*Colossus* fired three salvoes at three-funnelled enemy cruiser on opposite course, range 9,700 yards.
7.02 "	Passed wreck of *Invincible* on port beam, broken in two.
7.03 "	*Benbow* opened fire with 6-inch guns on enemy destroyer.
7.05 "	*Colossus* opened with 12-inch and 4-inch at destroyer, attacking on starboard bow. Hit and stopped her.
7.12 "	Suddenly observed *Lutzow* class battle cruiser 10,000 yards on starboard beam, accompanied by two other large ships. Opened fire at 9,000 yards, closing at 7.16 p.m. to 8,400 yards.
7.15 "	Fired five salvoes at *Lutzow*, observed at least four direct hits (4th and 5th salvoes), two on the waterline. Enemy burst into flames, listed, and disappeared in the flame, mist, and smoke.
	Marlborough, *Benbow*, *Neptune*, *Collingwood* all reported that *Colossus* passed through a cloud of fire, spray, and smoke, and they thought we were done for.
7.16 "	*Colossus* hit in superstructure just abaft foremost funnel by 12-inch shell, which exploded and caused fires on both port 4-inch gun decks and signal deck. Cordite chief cause of fire, which was extinguished in a few minutes. Another 12-inch, which did not explode, hit just abaft the first. Both shells only just missed the main strut of the mast.

7.17 p.m.	Heavy shell burst 30 yards short of ship in line with the forebridge. Splinters penetrated foremost funnel and all cabins forward. Wrecked S. 1 searchlight. Beddow, Leading Seaman range-taker on fore-bridge, arm practically shot off; two men wounded in fore-top; also three marines at S. 5 4-inch gun, and two domestics in Admiral's quarters.
7.25 ,,	Ceased fire.
7.35 ,,	Turned to port to avoid torpedo.
8.00 ,,	Divisions line ahead, course west. Speed, 14 knots.
8.15 ,,	Firing taking place right ahead.
8.55 ,,	Our light cruisers engage enemy destroyers on starboard beam. *Benbow* also fired.
9.05 ,,	Firing still heard, hands to night defence stations.
10.10 ,,	Firing on starboard beam lasting 4 minutes. Position, lat. 56° 26' N., Iong. 5° 57' E. Course S. Speed, 17 knots.
10.35 ,,	Observed destroyer action lasting about 10 minutes. One destroyer on fire.
11.40 ,,	Rapid and continuous firing for 15 minutes right astern.
1st June.	
2.15 a.m.	Day action stations. Visibility 2 miles. Misty, calm.
2.30 ,,	Course north.
3.17 ,,	Heavy firing on port quarter.
3.43 ,,	Zeppelin in sight, several ships fired. 'Zep.' flew off.
8.18 ,,	Passed lot of wreckage and bit of lifebuoy with 'EN' on it.
9.30 ,,	Submarines reported.
10.30 ,,	'B.J. 1' stations (*i.e.*, action stations, falling out for meals in reliefs).

Narrative of a Midshipman Stationed in the Fore-top of H.M.S. *Neptune*

(19th Ship in the Battle Line, 6th Ship from the Rear)

My action station was in the control top, some 60 or 70 feet above the upper deck, access to which could be gained either by ascending

'Away Aloft'.

an interminably long iron ladder running up the interior of the mast, or by climbing up outside the tripod by means of iron rungs rivetted on the struts. Experience of the difficulties of ascent had induced me some time ago to have made a blue jean bag, in whose capacious interior I always kept the thousand and one gadjets so essential for the proper and comfortable fighting of an action—ear protectors, binoculars, a stop watch, a pistol, a camera, a respirator, sundry scarves, woollen helmet, and so forth. It was armed with this weighty 'battle-bag' that I clambered up the starboard strut of the foremast, past the steam siren (which sizzled ominously as one approached it; it is an abominable experience to have a siren actually siren when you are near to it!), through a belt of hot acrid funnel smoke and finally into the top through the 'lubber's' hole.

The fleet was steaming in six columns of four ships each, and with the attendant destroyers, stretched as far as the eye could see.

The course was approximately south-east. The sea was fairly smooth, and the visibility about 17,000 yards. The arrival of the gunnery officer completed our crew, the manholes were shut down, and after the preliminary testing of communications had been done, the turrets were trained out on the beam, and we settled down to a long wait. If the powers that be knew that there was anything in the wind, I must say they kept it to themselves very well. The first inkling that I received that there might soon be something doing was when I noticed that some of the older ships of the 1st Battle Squadron were finding it difficult to keep up with their younger sisters in the other squadrons. Messages of encouragement and regret were passed to them, but still the fleet swept on. Shortly afterwards I noticed that several ships were flying, instead of the customary one ensign, three or four ensigns from various parts of the rigging, and, sure enough, the squeak of our halliard blocks announced that we were following suit. I don't know who started it, but in about ten minutes the air seemed to be thick with white ensigns, large and small, silk and bunting, hoisted wherever halliards could be rove.

By about 5.30 p.m. we had still seen nothing of the enemy, although we had received, and eagerly read, messages from the battle cruiser force telling us that the Germans were out and were in close action with our battle cruisers and with the 5th B.S. Soon afterwards all hands were sent to tea, and I was left alone in the fore-top as look-out, but five minutes after the last man had left, the sound of gunfire, heavy gunfire, came from the south. A minute later five columns of smoke appeared on the starboard bow and the flashes of guns became visible. All hands came running back to their stations; meanwhile the situation developed with startling rapidity.

Beatty's battle cruisers, for such the five columns of smoke proved to be, came into sight steaming at high speed to the north-east, and firing heavily towards the southward at an enemy which was out of our sight. Hood's squadron of *Invincible, Indomitable,* and *Inflexible* had gone on ahead to join Beatty. The leading ship of Beatty's squadron, *Lion* it was I suppose, seemed to be on fire forward, and the other ships all appeared to have received some damage. The noise rapidly became almost deafening. The *Lion* was leading her squadron across the front of the battle squadrons within 3 miles of the leading battleships, and accordingly the battle fleet reduced to 12 knots to allow them to cross and drive aside the

German battle cruisers. The High Seas Fleet had not yet sighted the Grand Fleet, and were still steaming towards us.

Shortly after 5 o'clock the flashes of the guns of the High Seas Fleet became visible, and the Grand Fleet commenced to deploy to port, turning to north-east and then to east-south-east, so bringing our starboard broadsides to bear on the enemy. The *Marlborough* was the battleship leading the starboard wing column of the fleet, and was, therefore, the nearest battleship to the enemy, and the first to open fire. The remainder of the fleet followed suit as soon as they had deployed. I shall not easily forget the dramatic atmosphere of the initial phase of the battle. The effect of the order 'Load' was to create a sort of stupor, everything was happening so suddenly, it all seemed too good to be true. The opening salvo of the *Marlborough* brought an end to that unpleasant period of comparative inactivity, and thereafter our hands were full. My impressions of the following hour were naturally somewhat vague, there was so much to do, and so much to see. I remember the dreary monotone of the range-finder operator calling out the ranges, I remember the gunnery officer and the Captain discussing through the voice-pipe the advisability of withholding fire until the ammunition could be most effectively used. I remember training my Dumaresq[3] on to the target—a battle cruiser of the *Lutzow* class— and working out the 'rate', which was probably much in error. I remember the ecstatic comments of the director layer in the tower below us when we had found the target and later saw that we were hitting, and I well remember the opening salvo from our guns, in earnest at last.

A few minutes after we opened fire, the *Defence* and *Warrior* appeared on our engaged side, steaming on an opposite course. The ships were practically continuously hidden by splashes, were being repeatedly hit by heavy shells, and must have been going through hell on earth. The *Defence*, which was leading, was just about abeam of the *Neptune* and barely a mile away, when she was hit heavily and blew up in one fearful cloud of smoke and débris. The fore-top fell with a sickening splash into the water and then the *Warrior*, herself damaged, listing to starboard and in places on fire, raced over the spot where the *Defence* had been only a moment before, through the smoke cloud of *Defence*'s explosion.

---

3 An instrument for calculating the rate at which two ships are opening or closing each other.

The two fleets were now heavily engaged, but the enemy were rapidly becoming more indistinct in the gathering haze, which was so soon to end the action. Whether this failure of visibility was just North Sea cussedness, or whether it was due to the heavy and continual gunfire I cannot say, but if it had not been for the flashes of the enemy's guns we should have had difficulty in picking out any target.

It is a curious sensation being under heavy fire at a long range. The time of flight seems more like 30 minutes than the 30 or so seconds that it actually is. A great rippling gush of flame breaks out from the enemy's guns some miles away, and then follows a pause, during which one can reflect that somewhere in that great 'no man's land' 2 or 3 tons of metal and explosive are hurtling towards one. The mountainous splashes which announce the arrival of each successive salvo rise simultaneously in bunches of four or five to an immense height. One or two salvoes fell short of us early in the action, and the remainder, I suppose, must have gone over as I did not see them. The *Hercules*, four ships astern of us, had been straddled on deployment, a feat which had greatly impressed me with the capabilities of the German gunnery, but, with the exception of the *Colossus* which received a 12-inch shell in the fore-superstructure and sundry small stuff round about her fo'csle, no single battleship suffered any real damage from the German's gunfire. The enemy however clearly received some punishment as two battle cruisers, which were rather closer than were their other ships, were engaged by us and by most ships of the rear squadron at one time or another, and we saw at least two of our salvoes hit, after which the two enemy battle cruisers dropped astern, to all appearances badly damaged. The warm, red glow of a 'hit' is easily distinguishable from the flash of a salvo, and is extremely pleasant to look upon.

Our fleet was stretched out in one long, single line, and presented a marvellously impressive spectacle as salvo after salvo rolled out along the line, adding to the fearful din which the enemy's shells and various other battle factors were already making. At 6.20 we were firing at 12,000 yards with common and lyddite shells. About this time the *Invincible*, which was leading the whole line, was struck by a salvo, turned nearly 180 degrees to starboard in her death agony, and lay burning and helpless. Her back was broken and her fore part was twisted round and upside down, giving her, when shortly afterwards we passed her 150 yards distant on our disengaged side, the appearance of having a swan bow. At the time we couldn't identify what ship it was.

German destroyers were now (about 6.40 p.m.?) observed ahead of the German battle cruiser *Lutzow*, and soon afterwards they turned towards us to attack. Our secondary armament opened fire and scored a hit or two, but their attack was successfully made and a number of torpedoes were fired, which gave us a few anxious minutes. One torpedo crossed the line immediately under *Neptune*'s stern, and directly afterwards two other parallel tracks were spotted which seemed to be coming straight for us. The ship was turned under full helm and our stern put towards the track of the torpedoes, but we only avoided being hit by inches.[4]

About this time several other battleships besides the *Neptune* were hauling out of the line dodging torpedoes, with the result that the line became considerably lengthened, and was irregular in places where ships were trying to regain their station. We had dropped astern, and for some seven minutes the *St. Vincent* was directly between us and the enemy, and we were unable to fire. Just after we had successfully dodged the torpedoes, we heard, or more exactly perhaps felt, a dull concussion and saw the *Marlborough* haul out of the line to port listing heavily. She had been hit by a torpedo, but a few minutes later she regained her position in the line with only a slight list, and we saw her firing again strongly.

I remember several small events which happened about now, but I cannot give the exact time of them. We fired a few rounds at a German light cruiser which was lying disabled between the lines, a target for a number of our battleships that were unable to see the enemy big ships clearly. She was in a sorry condition, minus her foremast and one funnel, blazing fore and aft and apparently almost sinking. She must have been no more than a floating shambles, and we only fired two salvoes at her. They said afterwards that she was probably the *Rostock*.

We passed a disabled destroyer on our starboard bow, very close to us, but she was one of ours—the *Acasta*. She was badly holed forward and aft and was much down by the bows, but the crew were clustered aft cheering us and the other ships as we passed, and then

---

4 The full account of this 'dodging' has been separated from the narrative and will be found in Chapter X., 'German Destroyer Attacks,' page 212.

she disappeared astern rolling heavily in the wash of the battle fleet but with her ensign still flying, apparently not 'done for' yet.

The visibility now was fast going from bad to worse. A few fires in the enemy ships and an occasional burst of firing pointed out what was presumably the German Fleet, now to the *westward* of us; but I suppose that about this time it was decided that it was impossible to continue the big ship action in the twilight and dark and, as we were between the enemy and Germany, that we should wait until the next morning. The Grand Fleet must have been practically invisible to the German ships for some little time now, for as we worked round to the eastward of them they were silhouetted against the light of the sunset whilst our background was a mass of dark cloud.

At 11.0 p.m. I got down from the top for a spell. There was an awful litter of stuff everywhere between decks, chiefly made by the shock of our broadsides dislodging loosely stowed gear. I found the gunnery lieutenant gazing into his cabin, speechless, for the electric radiator had been overwhelmed by the tin bath landing on it from above, all the drawers had shaken out, and his clothes were in a mêlée on the floor with much other odd matter. Moreover, the fire brigade party, zealous to guard against the chance of the cabin catching fire, had played their hose into the midst, thoughtfully filling the bath at the same time.

We had a comic supper in the gun-room, everybody talking at once and trying to eat at the same time. The inevitable gramophone was recovered from a temporary stowage which it had found on the deck, and well-worn tunes were once more played. About ten minutes to mid-night a messenger came in, looking as dirty and weird as a traveller from the infernal regions, to report that all hands would go to action stations again at 2 a.m. Till then we tried to sleep, but thoughts of that torpedo almost hitting us, of the *Acasta*, of the *Marlborough*, of the shapeless hump of the *Invincible*, and all the other incidents of the action, made any sleep difficult. And there was always the question paramount in our thoughts, 'When should we renew the action? Would it be at any moment now during the night, at point blank range in the darkness, or at daylight to-morrow?'

At 2 a.m. we were all back at our action stations, the same lot of us in the top as yesterday, but we met no enemy ships, only a Zeppelin airship. Soon after noon, June 1st, the ship's company were dispersed from action stations, and I descended with my 'battle-bag,' having been seventeen hours in the top. I was obsessed with a sudden desire for sleep, and lots of it, but on arrival in the gun-room I found that the same idea had apparently occurred to the others, for all the settees and chairs were full of sleepers, unshaved, unkempt, and unwashed. So I took a place on the deck.

When we got back to Scapa we had a long coaling, then had to get in ammunition, and also there was some oil fuel to see about. The papers next morning said nothing about any naval activity, and we were not allowed to mention anything of it in our letters, but three days later we received the papers of the 3rd June, and were horrified to read the Admiralty statement of our losses and the incomplete list of the German losses. When we heard that our seamen going to hospital had been jeered at and 'boo'ed' by some shore folk, it was almost too much—but to talk about that is perhaps not within my province.

Narrative of an Officer in 'A' Turret, H.M.S. *Conqueror*
(Of the 2nd Battle Squadron, 7th Ship in the Battle Line)

I had the afternoon watch on the 31st May, and when I went up on the bridge at 12.30 p.m. had no idea that we were out on anything but the usual fruitless sweep. However, before my watch was ended, at about three o'clock, we intercepted a signal saying that the battle cruisers had sighted the enemy, and at 3.30 p.m. we went on to full speed and closed up at action stations. I went down to 'A' turret and got everything tested and on the top line.

Shortly afterwards the Captain passed through to all turrets that the battle cruisers were engaged with the enemy, but were steaming a southerly course, so we all thought that there was no hope of our getting a look in.

We fell out for tea about 4.30 p.m., but closed up again at our stations at 5.30, by which time heavy firing could be distinctly heard ahead and on the starboard bow, and before very long we could see flashes stabbing the mist at intervals—a ripple of pin points of light. All guns were loaded with common shell.

At 6.05 p.m. we altered course 10° to port, and on training the turret on to about Green 30 our battle cruisers came into view, blazing away furiously into the mist, a very fine sight, *Lion* leading and *Tiger* third in the line. I could not make out the second ship, as she was hidden the whole time by the columns of water thrown up by shorts and overs. (It was H.M.S. *Princess Royal*.) *Tiger* kept disappearing from view in the same way. They were firing very fast, and projectiles also appeared to be raining down round them, although there did not appear to be many hits being made. I saw *Lion* hit once, low down, just before 'A' turret; it must have been by the shell that came right through before exploding as I saw the flash of explosion, and for some minutes afterwards flames and smoke continued to come through the hole made. At 6.08 we started to deploy to port, and when we were again on our course (E.N.E.) I saw the 1st Cruiser Squadron, steering at right angles to us, turn down to a parallel and opposite course between us and the battle cruisers. As each of the cruisers turned they opened fire at something that I could not see owing to the mist, but they made one of the finest sights I have ever seen, firing incredibly fast, and one mass of flashes from end to end.

The next picture was of a destroyer, name unknown, on our starboard bow suddenly vomiting clouds of steam from the region of her foremost funnel, and then stop. We passed her about two cables off, but she did not appear to be badly damaged, though a little down by the bow and listed over to port. (This was probably H.M.S. *Acasta*, *vide* p. 234.)

Meanwhile the spray columns had been creeping nearer to us and I heard later that we were at this time actually straddled, but I did not notice it myself. We had not yet opened fire, no target being visible.

At 6.31 we were put on to a three-funnelled cruiser which was lying stopped between the lines, and we fired at her for four minutes. She was looking exceedingly friendless and battered, burning freely, and surrounded by columns thrown up by falling shell; indeed, there were so many shells falling around her at the same time, that it was impossible to tell which was one's own salvo.

Just after ceasing fire I saw a great column of smoke rise up on our starboard quarter to about 200 feet, at which height the top slowly expanded till the whole looked like an enormous mushroom. This must have been the *Defence* blowing up, and was a most awe-inspiring sight; it appeared never to be coming down.[5]

---

5 *Defence* blew up at 6.16 p.m. It must have been some other ship.

A lull in the action.

All this time we were unable to see any of their battleships, except now and again one or two ships would be sighted for a moment in the mist, but never for long enough to fire at, although at intervals we could see that the other end of our line was blazing away merrily. About 7.0 p.m. there was a lull for a quarter of an hour with nothing to be seen, and the turrets' crews were given permission to fall out on top of the turrets to see a sunken ship, reputed to be German, which we were passing; its two ends were sticking out of the water. Not knowing then that it was the *Invincible*, we gave hearty cheers.

At 7.14 we observed German destroyers attacking the battle fleet and fired on them for eight minutes. They were making a very heavy smoke screen, and were never on the same course for more than about a minute at a time, turning, twisting, wriggling, and disappearing into their own smoke, only to reappear again almost immediately at a different place. We now turned four points away from the enemy. This destroyer torpedo attack being repelled, the turret was trained round on to what I took to be a battle cruiser of the *Derfflinger* class, but before we could open fire upon her she turned away and disappeared in the mist. Just afterwards for about half a minute I saw another large ship, very badly battered, on fire in several places and unrecognisable, but she too disappeared before we could engage her.

At 7.26 we again opened fire on attacking German destroyers, which were employing the same tactics of turning away at the

German Battle Cruiser *Seydlitz* badly damaged and down by the bow.
Taken from Ahead.

German Battle Cruiser *Seydlitz* badly damaged and down by the bow.

moment we fired and back again as soon as the salvo landed, the result for us being rather like trying to hit snipe with buckshot. But our last salvo landed in the smoke made by one particular boat, and in the midst of the splash and smoke there appeared to be débris, and when the smoke cleared away we saw an overturned destroyer where the target had been; my turret trainer swore he had seen our shot all the way until it hit her, in which he divided honours with the trainer of 'B' turret, who swore the same thing.

We ceased fire at 7.32.

Shortly after this we saw two of our light cruisers of the *Comus* class (4th L.C.S.), about 4,000 yards from us and between the lines, steaming fast on an opposite course, firing hard and being thoroughly well 'strafed.'

The second cruiser turned back when abeam of us, while the other carried on towards the end of the line in a fountain of falling shell. At 7.41 our course was south by west.

We remained in the turrets till 10.30 p.m., and then went to night defence stations, when I got a chance to get down for something to eat, and very ready I was for it too. Later on, hearing heavy firing, I went up on to the lower bridge and saw on our port quarter four ships with their search-lights trained on another ship, blazing away at her. The lights kept going on and off, but one could see this latter ship all the time, as she was burning from end to end. This lasted about five minutes, when she suddenly went out in an extra large flare. There was spasmodic firing for some time after this, but nothing to be seen.

Throughout the action the men were splendid, as one knew they would be. I have never seen such a blasé set of individuals as my turret's crew, who might have been at drill for all the excitement they displayed. There is a story of 'Y' turret, which in the first firing after deployment had their range clock going, and to keep up interest for the men down below in the magazine and shell-rooms, the ranges shown on this clock were being passed down by voice-pipe. The range was closing at a certain rate, when the turret was suddenly ordered to change their target, to go into local control and open fire on a destroyer. The Officer of the Turret forgot the clock, but the clock-worker continued to pass the ranges down which his clock, with the original decreasing rate on it, was showing—7,000—6,000—5,000—4,000—3,000—(Imagine a modern battle fleet action at a range of a mile and a half!)—two-five-double-oh—two-oh-double-oh—one-five-double-oh . . . At this stage a still, small voice floated up from the shell-room below, 'What are you going to do now? Ram the blooming thing?'

The men down below in the stokeholds were equally cheery, singing choruses from the songs of our last ship's concert most of the time, and stoking so lustily and energetically that the Engineer Officers during the action had not to encourage them in their work, but much of the time were occupied trying to restrain their ardour!

Narrative from H.M.S. *Castor*

This light cruiser, the ship of Commodore J. R. P. Hawksley, Commanding Destroyer Flotillas of the Grand Fleet, was stationed after deployment near to *King George V.*, Vice-Admiral Jerram's flagship which led the battle line. *Castor*'s narrative shows what difficulties the van of our battle fleet had in keeping touch with the enemy's battle line, and how little of the action was seen by the ships in our van.

We were screening the battle fleet on the bow of *King George V.* when we first heard that the battle cruiser force was in action, steaming to the southward. We later heard that they had turned 16 points, and that we should soon be in touch with them and with the enemy.

About 6.0 p.m. we sighted *Lion, Princess Royal, Tiger,* and *New Zealand* in action steaming on a converging course to us, so that eventually we got to within about 4,000 yards of *Lion*, but the only view we had of the Huns at this time was just the flashes of their guns. I noticed about this time a shell, that presumably was fired at our battle cruisers but was about 4,000 yards over, land on board one of the 1st Flotilla Destroyers, and she circled round with steam pouring out of her everywhere. (Probably H.M.S. *Defender.*) Also the *Chester* came close across our bows from east to west with four big holes in her along her main deck, and her ship's company cheering through the holes as she passed us.

We saw *Invincible, Inflexible,* and *Indomitable* come into action ahead of the *Lion*, and soon afterwards, with practically the first salvo fired at her, *Invincible* blew up.

The *Lion* and battle cruisers were going full speed I should think, and we were now on their disengaged side, dropping astern of them so that the battle fleet could get into touch with the enemy by forming astern of the battle cruisers. As the two remaining *Invincible* class battle cruisers were also dropping astern in order to prolong the battle cruiser line to the rear instead of remaining ahead of *Lion*, there was a considerable congestion of ships—light cruisers and destroyers—abreast the leading battle squadron.[6] However, we eventually got out clear on the engaged bow of the *King George V.* and close on the quarter of the last battle cruiser, the van battle squadron now being close in rear of the battle cruisers.

We then saw a somewhat disjointed-looking German flotilla apparently making a torpedo attack. We went out to drive them off, but only got within range of one straggler. Our Captain then wanted to go on and deliver a torpedo attack, though the German line was certainly not an ideal torpedo target as it was very much straggled out, but as soon as we formed for attack we were recalled by the C.-in-C. As it happened, that was the only chance we had of making a daylight attack. Not very long after this the enemy became entirely hidden by smoke, and the battle fleet ceased firing, but the enemy reappeared some time later and we could see some of the *Kaiser*, *Konig*, and *Heligoland* class battleships quite plainly from our advanced position; but as soon as our 2nd Battle Squadron opened fire, the smoke again obscured them.

I took this opportunity to go down and look for some food, and as soon as I got up again I saw a German flotilla apparently making a torpedo attack, so we went off to repel them. We then came in sight of the enemy heavy ships again, four battleships of the *Nassau* pre-Dreadnought class, which were firing in a desultory sort of way apparently at nothing. The 4th Light Cruiser Squadron was also close ahead of us, and as we approached the enemy fired a few salvoes at *Calliope*, but this was the last we saw of the day action as it was now getting dark, and observing that *King George V.* had altered course away from us, we deemed it necessary to follow her so as not to lose touch.

(Continued on page 351).

---

6 Note that this congestion of ships was at the *head* of the battle line. There was a similar congestion at the rear of the line at 'Windy Corner,' when the battle cruisers passed the wing of the battle fleet, to which reference has been made in previous narratives.

CHAPTER X

THE GERMAN DESTROYER ATTACKS

Which were launched against the British Battle Fleet at
about 7.10 and 7.25 p.m.

Extract from Commander-in-Chief's despatch:—

'About 7.10 p.m. a flotilla of enemy destroyers supported by a
cruiser was seen approaching *Iron Duke* bearing 60° from ahead the
starboard side. The fleet was turned away two points by the
"Preparative,"[1] and subsequently another two points, fire being
opened on the flotilla with 6-inch and turret guns at a range of about
10,000 to 8,000 yards. When at 8,000 yards the destroyers fired their
torpedoes, turning towards the rear of their line, and disappearing
in a smoke screen. No torpedoes hit. One destroyer was observed to
sink.

About 7.25 another enemy destroyer attack was observed
approaching the rear of the battle line from a bearing 120° from
ahead, 9,000 yards on *Iron Duke*'s starboard side. They were heavily engaged by the four rear divisions of the battle fleet and 5th B.S.
The 11th Flotilla and 4th L.C.S. had advanced to counter the former destroyer attack, and were in a favourable position to counter
the second attack, during which, at 7.22 p.m., they sank an enemy
destroyer. They were recalled at 7.40. In addition, this third
destroyer from the left was observed to sink, and the left-hand one
to be struck and turn bottom up, approximately at 7.35. At 7.45 p.m.
a division of the 12th Flotilla, consisting of *Obedient*, *Mindful*,
Marvel, and *Onslaught*, proceeded to attack and sink an enemy "V"
class destroyer flying a Commodore's pendant near the rear of the
5th B.S.'

---

1 A flag signal; 2 points equals 22fi degrees—*i.e.*, quarter of a right angle.

From the leading battleship to the rear battleship, the Grand Fleet battle line was more than 7 miles long. A couple of miles or more ahead of the leading ship was the Battle Cruiser Force, itself over a mile long, and the rear of the Battle Fleet was prolonged another 1 or 2 miles astern by the light cruisers and the destroyer flotillas following the 5th Battle Squadron. The whole length of the British Fleet covered a length not less than 11 or 12 miles, perhaps nearly 15 miles.

Debouching from the head of the German Fleet, the enemy destroyer flotillas came first into sight of the van of the Grand Fleet, and then of the centre, and then of the rear, as the low range of visibility opened their changing position to first this and then that part of the long battle line.

From narratives of different ships a kind of moving picture—almost a cinematograph, one might say—can be refashioned of the path of the German attacking flotillas, as at 7.10 p.m. and again at 7.25 p.m. an attack was launched, was developed, was sighted by the British Fleet, was opposed by British gunfire, fired torpedoes, and then turned back to regain the German battle line. For the next 6 or 7 minutes perhaps the German torpedoes ran their course towards the British line, then were sighted by look-outs and hastily reported to the Captains of ships, who by use of helm turned their ships to avoid them.

From the narratives of eyewitnesses one can piece together the acts of this play, the opening scene of which is described by an officer of H.M.S. *Conqueror*, one of the battleships near the head of our line.

Description from H.M.S. *Conqueror* 7th ship in the battle line:—

'At 7.14 observed enemy destroyers attacking, and fired on them for eight minutes. They were making a very heavy smoke screen, and were never on the same course for more than about a minute at a time, turning, twisting, wriggling, and disappearing into their own smoke, only to reappear again almost immediately at a different place. We now turned 4 points away from the enemy. This attack being repelled, we trained on to what I took to be a ship of the *Derfflinger* class, but before we could open fire she turned away and disappeared in the mist; just afterwards, for about half a minute, I saw another large ship very badly battered, on fire in several places, and unrecognisable . . .

At 7.26 we again opened fire on attacking German destroyers which employed the same tactics of turning away as we fired and turning back again as soon as the salvo landed, the result for us being rather like trying to hit snipe with buckshot.

But our last salvo landed in the smoke made by one particular boat, and in the midst of the splash and smoke there appeared to be débris, and when the smoke cleared away we saw an overturned destroyer where the target had been. My turret trainer swore he had seen our shot all the way until it hit her, in which he divided honours with the trainer of "B" turret, who swore the same thing. We ceased fire at 7.32.'

The second of these two German destroyer attacks commenced at about 7.25 p.m. and was observed by the battle cruisers ahead of the battle fleet, as well as by the battle fleet themselves. The following description of the start of the second attack is from the narrative of H.M.S. *Indomitable*, at this time the rear ship of the battle cruiser force, a mile or so ahead and on the engaged side of the leading battleship.

Description from H.M.S. *Indomitable*, battle cruiser ahead of the leading battleship:-

'At 7.20 p.m. we re-opened fire at the enemy battle cruisers at a range of 14,000 yards, our squadron apparently making splendid practise. . . . One big ship turned out of the line to starboard, her after part enveloped in flame, and began slowly to drop astern. The remainder emitted dense volumes of smoke, which hung above the water like a pall, through which at 7.25 p.m. we could see about a dozen destroyers racing towards our line. Orders came through for the 4-inch guns' crews to close up, and, as the first bearing was passed and the turret swung round, I could hear the staccato bark of these small guns joining in the general din. As the destroyers cleared the smoke screen, white pillars began to leap up amongst them, like giant nine-pins, to be knocked down and spring up again without ceasing as the big guns came into action. Almost half the distance had been covered by the attackers, when I saw two of these white towers of water rise simultaneously in front of the left-hand boat of the line, and as they sank no thrusting bow came through the spray, only a thinning streak of smoke. . . .

This attack was delivered abaft our beam, so that we obviously were not its target, but we could not see what result had been obtained, although afterwards we heard that it had been abortive.'

A little later than to the ships in the van, the enemy destroyers became visible to the centre and rear ships of our battle fleet, by which time the German flotilla was apparently somewhat broken up, as the result of the gunfire that had already been concentrated upon them.

The following is part of the narrative of H.M.S. *Bellerophon*, 14th ship in the battle line (near the centre):—

'At 6.55 we had altered course by divisions to south, and there seemed to be a general lull in the firing; we trained all the turrets on Green 70, and waited for something to turn up. . . .

At 7.12 we sighted a Hun destroyer about Green 35 heading straight towards us. We opened fire at her at 7.14 with turrets, but we only fired one salvo. She was damaged by some other ship and lay stopped, on fire, between the lines. At 7.16 we altered course 3 points to port, away from the enemy, by Blue pendant—*i.e.*, all ships together—we were going 14 knots at this time.

At 7.18 we altered course back to south again, and opened fire on the leading ship of three German battle cruisers, which had suddenly appeared bearing Green 120.

At 7.26 four enemy destroyers suddenly appeared ahead of and on our side of the battle cruisers, and we at once put "A" turret and the two foremost 4-inch guns on to them. These destroyers were nearly broadside on to us, and were in an irregular formation, steering the same way as the battle cruisers.

I gave the 4-inch guns a range of 8,500 as a rough guess, but the first shots fell a good way short. "A" turret in local control was better, and managed to hit one destroyer with their third round. They got her just about the second funnel and her bow and stern shot up like the ends of a broken stick. Just after this the enemy battle cruisers turned away, and the remaining destroyers followed suit, making at the same time a most effective smoke screen. The remaining turrets had been put on to these boats just before, but no hits were obtained.

We finally ceased firing at 7.30 p.m., the enemy now being totally hidden by smoke and mist.'

7.45 p.m.—12th Destroyer Flotilla Attack and Sink a German Destroyer.

As a result of the gunfire concentrated against them, one destroyer of the German attacking flotilla, in addition to the two or perhaps three others that had been sunk instantaneously in the course of the attack, was badly hit and lay stopped between the lines, drifting down not under control close past the rear of the British Battle Fleet, whilst her consorts, unable to help her, returned to the German line, and the big ships on both sides continued the main action over her head.

Four destroyers of our 12th Flotilla, which was stationed to screen the rear Battle Squadron, moved out to 'finish off' this boat. In the words of the Commander-in-Chief's despatch:— 'At 7.45 a division of the 12th Flotilla, consisting of *Obedient*, *Mindful*, *Marvel*, and *Onslaught*, proceeded to attack and sink an enemy "V" class destroyer flying a Commodore's pendant, near the rear of the 5th B.S.' The following brief extracts from narratives describe the details of this little incident. The German destroyer appears to have fought to the last with gallantry:—

Description from H.M.S. *Faulknor*:—
'The next incident (after "Windy Corner") from the *Faulknor*'s point of view was, as far as I can remember, at about 7.35 p.m., when a German destroyer was sighted passing between the two battle lines badly damaged, but with her after-gun still firing. So the 1st division of our flotilla, led by the *Obedient*, was despatched to starboard to complete her destruction, and moved off to the southward at high speed, until a few minutes later we saw them open fire on the German destroyer. A few well-directed salvoes were sufficient, and *Obedient* rejoined the flotilla after about 15 minutes, reporting that the German destroyer had been sunk. The writer was told after the action that this German destroyer continued to fire her after-gun until the last moment before she sank.'

Description from H.M.S. *Obedient*, leading the 1st Division of the 12th Flotilla:—

'Up to now we had seen no enemy ship, only flashes from the guns, but at 6.30 p.m. we passed a big German ship, floating through between the lines apparently derelict. Just after the mist lifted for a minute or two to show up a few German ships, one of which was clearly seen for a time and received a fearful hammering from the battle ships at the rear of our line, but then the mist covered her again.

Nothing more was to be seen for nearly an hour, though the battleships at the rear of the line occasionally fired a few salvoes. About 7.35 p.m. an enemy destroyer appeared ahead, apparently broken down, at any rate only steaming very slowly. The *Obedient* asked permission to attack, and the first division, *Obedient*, *Marvel*, *Mindful*, and *Onslaught*, were ordered to close and destroy her, which they did. She opened fire from her forecastle gun at us, but did not score a hit, and early on a salvo from one of us carried away this gun, the bridge and the foremast, whilst within a minute or so another salvo from *Mindful* holed her along the water line abreast her foremost funnel. Very shortly afterwards she turned slowly over on her port side and sank. Her number we were unable to see owing to it having been shot away, but the distinguishing letter was "V," and she flew a Commodore's pendant. *Obedient* rejoined the flotilla and reported that the enemy had been sunk.'

Dodging German Torpedoes.

Meanwhile some of the German torpedoes fired from the attacking destroyers or from light cruisers between the lines, or from the German heavy ships, had reached the British battle line, and various of our battleships, sighting the tracks, were forced to haul out of the line in order to dodge the torpedoes.

Quite a number of battleships were forced to this action about 7.30 p.m. as a result of the destroyer attacks of 7.10 and 7.25 p.m., but also earlier in the action other battleships near the rear had to alter course to avoid torpedo tracks. The following two narratives, of H.M.S. *Agincourt* and of H.M.S. *Neptune*, give typical descriptions of 'torpedo dodging,' and, together with the narrative of H.M.S. *Marlborough* later in the

British destroyer making a smoke screen.

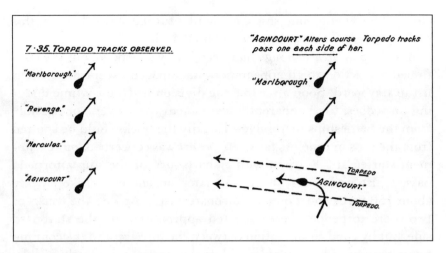

chapter, show the considerable anxiety which the German attacks caused.

Narrative of H.M.S. *Agincourt*.

'The deployment at about 6.15 placed *Agincourt* tail ship of the battle line, rather out of the action eventually, but in the meantime during the deployment we had all the fun our end. Shots had already pitched about our division, when at 6.17 *Marlborough* opened fire, and although *Agincourt*'s firing was delayed until 6.23 by our own destroyers being between us and the enemy, we then opened fire at 10,000 yards at an enemy battle cruiser. She could only just be made out, but hits were obtained on her before the mist obscured the view.

However, after this it was a regular game of "hide and seek," the enemy at times being enveloped in the mist and smoke, appearing out of it for only short intervals like rabbits running from one hole to another in a burrow, so that up to 7.50, when we eventually ceased fire, we had only four short periods of actual engagement with the enemy. It was difficult to estimate the effect of our firing, although we could tell that the third of these periods was a highly successful one in the matter of registering hits on a battleship of the *Kaiser* class. Our fourth period was at 7.25, using our secondary armament, 6-inch guns, against a destroyer attack observed to be debouching from the head of the enemy's battle fleet, and incidentally "smoke-screening" the latter very effectively. Our first few salvoes put the leading boat out of action, and we were proceeding to do the same to the second boat when the thick weather brought everything to a close. The enemy big ships evidently turned away behind this smoke screen, for they were not sighted again.

At 6.54 p.m. *Marlborough* had been hit by a torpedo, but she continued the action to all appearances undamaged except for a slight list to starboard. Soon after this the division had a busy time dodging torpedoes, fired apparently from enemy destroyers, or possibly from the battleships themselves. Luckily the tracks could be spotted from the tops in time. As far as *Agincourt* was concerned, our excitement started at 7.8, when with a sharp turn of the ship a torpedo passed just under our stern, and later on another broke surface about 150 yards short on our starboard beam. At 7.35 the tracks of two more torpedoes were reported approaching on the starboard side, but by good co-operation between the fore-top and the conning tower they were both avoided. Aloft the tracks were clearly visible, and acting on the reports from there the ship was gradually turned away, so that by perfect timing one torpedo passed up the port side and one the starboard side; after which we resumed our place in the line.

A fifth torpedo was successfully dodged by zigzagging at 7.47, but after this we had no further excitements.

We ourselves had no opportunity to fire torpedoes at the enemy, but fired 144 shells from our 12-inch turrets and from our secondary armament (6-inch guns) 111 shells.'

Extract from the Narrative of H.M.S. *Neptune*[2]

'German destroyers were now observed ahead of the German battle cruiser, *Lutzow*, and soon afterwards they turned towards us to attack. Our secondary armament opened fire and scored a hit or two, but their attack was successfully made, and a number of torpedoes were fired, which gave us a few anxious minutes. We observed a great number of tracks of torpedoes, some as far away as 2½ miles. One torpedo crossed the line immediately under *Neptune*'s stern, and directly afterwards another track was spotted which seemed to be coming straight for us. But apparently the officers on the bridge below had not seen it, and were in blissful ignorance of the danger that the ship was in. There was no time to explain, and a stentorian "hard-a-starboard" shouted down the voice pipe by the Gunnery

---

2 By a Midshipman stationed aloft. See also pages 190-197.

Lieutenant was fortunately accepted without question and put on by the helmsman. The bridge then sighted the torpedo, and emergency full speed was ordered. We began to turn rapidly, but I vividly remember how the torpedo got closer and closer. From the fore-top we were craning our necks over the metal side, while the whole top was groaning and vibrating under the strain of the ship turning at full speed with full helm on. We looked down on the tops of the turrets and the decks below, and could see our shipmates working down there quite unconscious of the immediate peril. I personally had been torpedoed once before—in the *Formidable*—and had no delusions about the situation. The ship had turned a right angle, 8 points, and the torpedo was now dead astern following exactly in our course, but going faster than our fastest speed, and coming closer and closer, until our view in the fore-top was blanketed by the mainmast and after platforms. *We* could do nothing, of course, but wait and wait, mouths open, like when one is expecting a gun to fire. Nothing happened. The time passed when it should have reached our stern and there should have been a big explosion, but still nothing happened. An enemy salvo splashed down close on our starboard bow, but nobody heeded it. Then somebody laughed, and breaking the spell, we knew that after all it was somehow all right. The miracle, for it really seemed miraculous, was accounted for in *Neptune*'s report: "Torpedo was either deflected by the wash from *Neptune*'s propellers or ran its range out. The latter is more likely."

About this time several other battleships besides the *Neptune* were hauling out of the line dodging torpedoes, with the result that the line became considerably lengthened, and was irregular in places where ships were trying to regain their station. We had dropped astern, and for some seven minutes the *St. Vincent* was directly between us and the enemy and we were unable to fire. Just after we had successfully dodged the torpedo, we heard, or more exactly perhaps felt, a dull concussion, and saw the *Marlborough* haul out of the line to port listing heavily. She had been hit by a torpedo, but a few minutes later she regained her position in the line with now only a slight list, and we saw her firing again strongly.'

German Torpedo Hit on H.M.S. *Marlborough*.

But despite the heavy gunfire concentrated against them, and in spite of the losses suffered from this gunfire, the majority of the destroyers of the German flotilla, both in the attack at about 7.10 p.m. and again in the attack at about 7.25 p.m., appear to have reached their objective (a position suitable for firing their torpedoes at the British battle line), and to have discharged a number of torpedoes. Some of these torpedoes were prevented from reaching our line by the alteration of course away from the enemy ordered by the Commander-in-Chief, and the other torpedoes were all dodged by our ships, so that no torpedo fired by the German flotilla at this time scored a hit.

Only one torpedo hit was scored on a British battleship during the whole course of the battle, and that was one from a torpedo which, running unobserved, hit H.M.S. *Marlborough*, the flagship of Vice-Admiral Burney Commanding the Rear Battle Squadron, at about 6.54 p.m.—*i.e.*, before either the 7.10 or 7.25 attacks by the German destroyer flotilla were commenced. Presumably therefore, this one effective torpedo was fired by some ship in or with the German battle line in the first half hour of the battle fleet action, or possibly by one of the detached German light cruisers that had been sighted near the British line soon after the deployment.

H.M.S. *Marlborough*, a modern super-Dreadnought of the *Iron Duke* class, in spite of her torpedo hit which later was found to have made a hole in her side 70 feet long, maintained her position in the battle line throughout the day action, and until 3 a.m. the following morning, June 1st. It will be noticed that on two occasions after she had been hit, still during the battle fleet action, she sighted torpedo tracks approaching her, but was able to manoeuvre so as to avoid them. She had dodged one torpedo just before she was hit—she did not see the track of the one that hit her and at the time thought she had been hit by a mine—and she dodged six more torpedoes afterwards. She reached the shelter of the Humber under her own steam on June 2nd. The following narrative describes her experiences during the action, including the early and late stages of the battle fleet action as well as the particular moments of the torpedo hit, and is written by an officer stationed aloft, the best position in the ship perhaps from which to observe torpedo tracks.

214

Events Noted from the Fore-top of H.M.S. *Marlborough*

(Leading Ship of the Starboard Wing Column of the Battle Fleet before Deployment; nearest Battle Ship to the Enemy at the moment of Deployment, and 21st Ship in the Line, *i.e.*, 4th from the Rear, after Deployment.)

Before 5.45 p.m., at which time four of our battle cruisers led by *Lion* came into sight on our starboard bow, in action with an unseen enemy, we had been receiving signals which gradually increased in interest and excitement from the first report of enemy light forces being sighted by one of our cruisers, until the visual signal received from *Lion* of the German battle fleet being almost within gun range of the battle fleet. I kept a record of some of the most interesting signals, of which perhaps this selection will show how our interest was gradually worked up as one after the other they received:—

2.20 p.m. *Galatea* to C.-in-C. and S.O., B.C.F.,[3] 'Enemy cruiser bearing east-south-east.'

2.30 " *Galatea* to C.-in-C. and S.O., B.C.F., 'Pursuing destroyers or cruisers.'

3.2 " C.-in-C. to Ships in company, 'Assume readiness for action. Increase speed to 18 knots. Raise steam for full speed.'

3.55 " S.O., B.C.F., to C.-in-C., 'Enemy going south. Engaging enemy. Five battle cruisers in sight.'

4.00 p.m. S.O., 2nd L.C.S., to C.-in-C., 'Enemy's battle fleet in sight steering north.'

4.04 " C.-in-C. to S.O., 3rd B.C.S. (Hood's Squadron), 'Proceed at once to reinforce battle cruiser fleet.'

4.33 " S.O., 5th Battle Squadron, to C.-in-C., 'Engaging enemy.'

4.54 " C.-in-C to Admiralty, 'Consider fleet action imminent.'

5.8 " S.O., B.C.F., to C.-in-C., 'Enemy battle fleet bearing south-east.'

5.57 " S.O., B.C.F., to C.-in-C., 'Enemy battle fleet steering north.'

---

3 Senior Officer, Battle Cruiser Force.

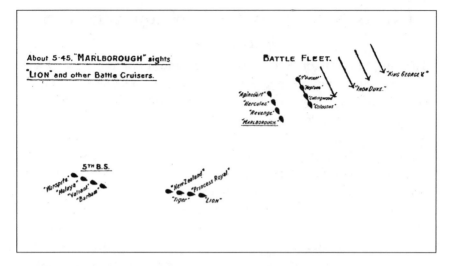

And finally at 6.15 p.m. we received this signal:-

C.-in-C.—General (to ships in company), Enemy in sight bearing S.S.E. Form line of battle S.E. by S.'

You can very well imagine the increasing excitement which the receipt of these signals produced, and long before any enemy were in sight we were all closed up at our action stations in absolute 'readiness for action.'

At 5.45 we sighted our battle cruisers on our starboard bow, and could see that they were engaging with their starboard guns an enemy that was out of sight of us. They continued on their course across our 'front,' and passed away to the (ultimate) head of the battle line.

At 6.8 p.m. we started taking ranges, and at 6.15 picked up as target an enemy battleship of the *Kaiser* class, and on her we opened fire at 6.17. She was making a good deal of smoke, but her inclination was pretty easy to determine by the trend of the smoke from the funnels and by the general look of the ship. After some alterations of range to the guns, at about 6.19 we began to hit, and when 'splash' for the fifth salvo was reported I saw four explosions with a red flame.

We fired seven salvoes at this battleship, and the fifth and last were clearly seen to hit, the fifth with a deep red flame and the last with a large cloud of greyish-coloured smoke. Our shoot was then (6.21) interrupted by a cruiser which crossed the range coming from our port side, steering practically at right angles across the line of fire, and she hid our battleship target by the smoke that was pouring from her aft, where she was badly on fire.

At 6.24 we gave her to the guns as the target: 'Green 98, cruiser, 3 funnels,' with a range of 10,500 yards, and fired five salvoes at her, but hits were not plainly distinguishable, as two or three other of our ships were also firing at her. At 6.25 our 6-inch guns joined in on this same target, but only until 6.29, when we had to cease firing for ten minutes whilst the ship was altering course, all the enemy being hidden by smoke.

Our original battleship target had appeared to turn away 8 points to starboard when the cruiser came across the range, and then became obscured, but at 6.39 we saw for a moment another—or the same?—*Kaiser* class battleship and fired one salvo at her at a range of 13,000 yards. But then she altered away to starboard and was lost. Meanwhile the cruiser which had turned towards us whilst we were engaging her lay stopped in sight of us, heavily on fire, and not replying with her guns. From 6.40 to 6.45 we had a five minutes' pause, when we could find no target for our guns—an exasperating time when one was longing to get on with the job, but could simply do nothing except curse the bad visibility and our distance from the enemy.

At 6.54 we were hit by a torpedo. We thought at the time it might have been a mine, for we saw no track of a torpedo whatsoever, but we know now for certain that it was a torpedo as bits of one were found later in the ship. It hit on the starboard side, and aloft the top swayed a lot and finally took up a list to starboard, so that I imagined one strut of the tripod mast had been shot away; but looking over the side of the top I saw that it was the whole ship that had taken a list to starboard. The shock caused some of the switches on the electrical switchboard to jump, and one of the gunnery control instruments got out of step; also some fuses of the telephone circuits went, but they were very quickly replaced.

A few minutes after we were hit we passed a destroyer, the *Acasta*, close on our port hand, flying 6 flag—'Am in danger of sinking'— and the 'Not under control' signal; she had a collision mat stretched out over her starboard quarter. I was afraid for a moment that we were going to collide with her, as we passed so close to her that from aloft she was almost hidden by our ram, and we seemed to be practically on top of her. But she came by all clear, and her men cheered as we passed.

Torpedoing of *Marlborough*.

At about 7 o'clock, when we were just getting 'square' again after the torpedo explosion, three tracks of torpedoes were seen approaching on the starboard side, all three apparently going to cross our track. The bridge were informed, and the ship was turned to port to avoid them, so that two passed ahead and one astern of us. Five or ten minutes before this some German destroyers had appeared on our starboard bow, so presumably these torpedoes, as well as the one that had hit us, came from them.

Directly after we had dodged these three torpedoes a four-funnelled cruiser of apparently the *Roon* class came into sight on our starboard beam, range 9,800 yards, bearing exactly on the beam, Green 90. She was stopped and already badly damaged, but we opened fire on her and fired four salvoes. The third and fourth salvoes hit her, opened up her sides, and revealed a deep red flame inside her hull. This was at 7.3, and two minutes later we ceased fire, as she appeared to be completely disabled, and was sinking fast.

We now sighted three battleships, and at 7.6 shifted target on to the left-hand one of them—they were ships of the *Konig* class, carrying two funnels wide apart. We opened fire at a range of 10,750 yards, and fired 14 salvoes. The sixth, the twelfth, thirteenth, and fourteenth were all distinct hits. From the sixth salvo a large cloud of grey smoke appeared near her foremast, and from the twelfth salvo two hits could be seen under her bridge, rather low down.

At 7.10 we fired a torpedo from the fore submerged tube at the disabled enemy cruiser. At 7.19 a flotilla of German destroyers appeared on our starboard quarter, approaching us, and fire was quickly opened upon them with the 6-inch battery. Also one 13.5-inch salvo was fired from the turrets. Two destroyers were hit, and the remainder immediately turned away to starboard and disappeared from sight behind a dense cloud of funnel smoke. Fourteen minutes later (7.33) the tracks of the torpedoes they had fired were observed approaching from the starboard bow and beam. The tracks were quite clear to us from aloft, and could be picked out when nearly a mile away. At once we reported to the bridge, and they altered course to starboard, so that No. 1 track, the furthest off, passed ahead of us, but Nos. 2 and 3 were nearly on top of us before the ship commenced swinging. No. 2 passed so close to the stern that we lost sight of its track from the top, and we should certainly have been hit if the stern had not been swinging away under the influence of helm; and No. 3, which I saw break surface when about 500 yards on our beam, came straight for the ship, and its track came right up against our starboard quarter—it must have been running below its depth and went right under the ship. The fact that these three were as clear as daylight, whereas no track was visible from the torpedo that had hit us at 6.54, made one think that it was a mine, not a torpedo by which we had been hit, but, as I said, other certain evidence showed that it was a torpedo.

The action for us was now finished, although we did not think so at the time. At 8 o'clock, as a result of our torpedo hit, we were reduced to a maximum speed of 17 knots, which fact was reported to the Commander-in-Chief, but we were able to keep our station leading our squadron.

At 8.15 a submarine was sighted from the bridge on the starboard side, but we did not see anything from aloft.

The course of the fleet at 8.20 was W.S.W., and at 8.32 south-west. The 3rd Light Cruiser Squadron reported that they were engaging enemy's cruisers, and at 8.40 a report from the battle cruisers stated that the nearest enemy ships were 10 to 11 miles distant, their battle cruisers and pre-Dreadnought battleships steering

S.W., speed 17 knots; but no enemy were in sight from us. At five minutes to nine some light cruisers were in sight off *Marlborough*'s starboard beam—that is, to the north-west—and some destroyers were approaching from the west. An action commenced just abaft our starboard beam, and we could see German destroyers attacking a light cruiser squadron, but nothing further happened. (This was probably the *Southampton*'s squadron, the 2nd L.C.S.)

At 9.5 the course of the battle fleet was south, and from the van battle squadron (2nd B.S.) came a report that the enemy's battle cruisers were in sight, steering south-west, but we could see no enemy our end of the line.

At a quarter past nine all destroyers were ordered to take station 5 miles astern of the battle fleet, and we took up night cruising order, expecting to be attacked by German destroyers during the night. The battle fleet squadrons were in single line, 1 mile apart, *Marlborough* leading the port, *i.e.* the easterly line, or rather the easterly but one, the actual wing column being the four ships of the 5th B.S.

During the night we saw no enemy, but there were signs of actions being fought to starboard or astern of us most of the night. There was firing on our starboard beam at 10.15 p.m., and again at 10.40; at 11.40 gunfire was reported astern, and at 12.10 a very heavy explosion, like a ship blowing up, was seen and heard, accompanied by heavy gunfire.

The ship was now settling somewhat from the effects of our torpedo hit, several compartments around the hit being flooded, and at

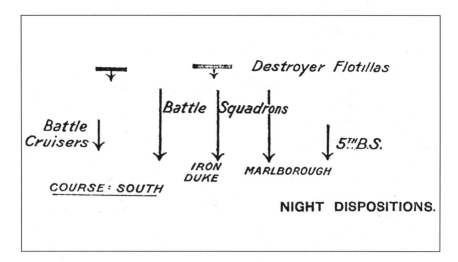

2 a.m. we were unable to keep station at 17 knots. Accordingly the Vice-Admiral signalled to *Revenge* his intention of transferring his flag to her, and at 2.15 we hauled out of the line, the light cruiser, *Fearless*, coming alongside us to take Admiral Burney off to the *Revenge*.[4] At 3 a.m. the Commander-in-Chief directed *Marlborough* to proceed 'to the Tyne or Rosyth,' and we shaped course for the Tyne.

Nothing exciting happened before 10 a.m., June 1st, except that at 4 a.m. we saw a Zeppelin passing astern of us steering east, and we unloaded our 13.5-inch guns at him, and also fired a dozen 3-inch shells from our anti-aircraft gun. He dipped suddenly after we fired, but then continued on his course apparently undamaged. Intercepted signals from various ships gave us the idea that the enemy could not be found, and there were signals from *Warrior*, *Warspite*, etc., reporting the extent of their damages, etc. Altogether the situation appeared to be rather confused, and it was difficult to tell whether we were missing any fighting or not.

At 10 a.m. we sighted two enemy submarines ahead, both with conning towers awash; shortly afterwards they dived. We altered course 8 points to port immediately, and did not sight them again, but at 11 o'clock the track of a torpedo was seen on our port side, apparently fired from one of these submarines, then almost astern of us. But it was not necessary even to alter course to avoid the torpedo, as it came past the port side and on across our bows well clear. *Fearless*, which was zigzagging ahead of us, avoided it. Our course was now West, and speed 13 knots.

At 2.15 p.m. an escort of four Harwich destroyers, which had been ordered to join us, were met, and a little later we sighted Commodore Tyrwhitt's force steering to the east, but apparently they were arriving too late for the action.

---

4 Extract from Narrative from H.M.S. *Fearless*. At daylight on June 1st a signal was made to us to proceed alongside *Marlborough* and transfer Vice-Admiral Burney and his staff to the *Revenge*. We then saw the leading ship of the line—H.M.S. *Marlborough*—haul out, and to our surprise saw that she had a heavy list, for not till then had we realised the object of the transfer of the flag. At 2.45 a.m. we went alongside the *Marlborough* and embarked the Vice-Admiral and his staff. Meanwhile the remainder of the squadron had steamed out of our sight into the fog, but as soon as the Admiral and staff were on board we shoved off, found the *Revenge*, and made a signal to her to stop, and informed her that we were coming alongside. She stopped, and at 3.10 a.m. we steamed alongside, and soon embarked the Admiral and his staff in her. We then returned to the assistance of the *Marlborough*, with orders to remain with her and escort her back to the base, which we duly did, leading her into the Humber on the morning of the second day after the battle.

About 8 p.m. on June 1st we reported our draught of water to the Commander-in-Chief, in response to his signal for information. It was now 39 feet, nearly 10 feet deeper than our normal draught at full load. The wind and sea had risen a good deal, and it was now unpleasant North Sea weather, blowing fresh, rather cold, and the sea getting up. One of our escorting destroyers, H.M.S. *Albatross*, at 11 p.m., had to separate, as she could not keep up with us in this weather.

At midnight we had to signal that the water was gaining, and that, instead of going to Rosyth which we had received an order by wireless to do, we were making for Flamborough Head at 10 knots. Under lee of the land, however, the weather moderated, and by 4 a.m., June 2nd, we were keeping the water under, and were able to signal that we did not require the tugs which were being sent to our assistance from the Humber and the Tyne. At 8.30 a.m., June 2nd, we entered the Humber and secured to a buoy; our draught of water then was exactly 40 feet.

Whilst lying in the Humber we made temporary shoring-up arrangements round the position of the torpedo hit to strengthen the adjacent bulkheads; pumped out the water and got more pumps on board. We then sailed for the Tyne under our own steam, and there went into the floating dock for proper repairs. We found that the damage done by the torpedo was far greater than we had expected, the extreme length of the hole being 70 feet, with a depth of 20 feet at the point of the explosion.

For six weeks repairs were carried out by the combined ship-building firms on the Tyne, and the opportunity was taken at the same time to make some structural alterations which were desired. One thousand workmen were employed aboard us, working day and night, so that six weeks after the battle we left the dock and rejoined the Grand Fleet up North, no worse for the torpedo hit on us, but indeed a more efficient ship than we had been before the action.

CHAPTER XI

HOOD'S BATTLE CRUISER SQUADRON

In the matter of time we must now go back a little to describe the movements of the 3rd Battle Cruiser Squadron, which, under the command of Rear-Admiral Hon. Horace Hood flying his flag in H.M.S. *Invincible*, had come into action about 5.36 p.m.

It may be recalled that this squadron, consisting of the three battle cruisers, *Invincible*, *Inflexible*, and *Indomitable*, were, at the end of May, doing exercises at Scapa Flow with the battle fleet, their place at Rosyth being taken by Rear-Admiral Evan-Thomas' 5th Battle Squadron, *Barham*, *Malaya*, *Warspite*, and *Valiant*. Accordingly the 3rd B.C.S. were in company with the battle fleet, and not with the Rosyth battle cruisers, during the early part of the action.

At 4.0 p.m. on 31st May Admiral Jellicoe ordered Hood's squadron to reinforce Vice-Admiral Beatty, and the three battle cruisers, accompanied by two light cruisers, *Chester* and *Canterbury*, and four destroyers, *Shark*, *Christopher*, *Ophelia*, and *Acasta*, went off at full speed to join Admiral Beatty's force, whose reports of his position and of the progress of the battle cruiser action were being received by wireless in the Grand Fleet.

About 5.30 p.m.—at which time that part of the action known as the Battle Cruiser run to the north was nearing its end—Hood's squadron heard sounds of gunfire to the south-westward, and at 5.36 sighted some enemy light-cruisers to the westward.[1] Hood was then some 15 or 20 miles ahead of

---

1 *NOTE.*—The authority for these and similar statements is principally the narratives in this chapter, but it is difficult to be accurate in such facts as the bearing upon which the enemy were first sighted as the evidence is scanty and occasionally contradictory.

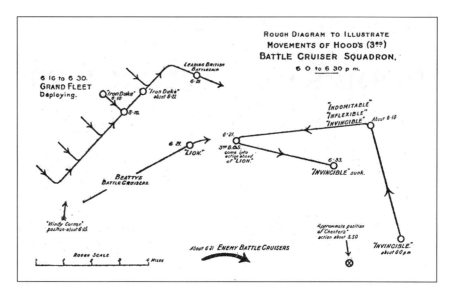

ROUGH DIAGRAM TO ILLUSTRATE
MOVEMENTS OF HOOD'S (3ʳᵈ)
BATTLE CRUISER SQUADRON,
6 0 to 6 30 p m.

the Grand Fleet, and had nearly over-run the position of the Battle Cruiser forces. An action followed with the enemy ships and with some other light cruisers that later came in sight, Hood's three battle cruisers, the Chester, the Canterbury, and the four destroyers, all being engaged. Apparently the visibility was very variable, and in certain directions was as little as 5,000 yards, or even less, and the light craft of the squadron became detached from the battle cruisers, so that several separate actions were fought by the different ships of Hood's force.

H.M.S. *Shark* was disabled and shortly afterwards sunk in this action. H.M.S. *Acasta* was damaged (we shall read in this chapter how as a result of her damage she lay stopped between 6 and 7 o'clock in the path of the Grand Fleet, and 'reviewed' them), and H.M.S. *Chester* suffered a number of casualties, but fortunately retained her full steaming powers. It is worth while stating again here that the visibility at this time was low and the situation confused; gunfire was loud, and appeared to come from the south, or from the south-west or south-east, according to the exact position of the listening ship, but this was apparently the only means of telling the exact position where Beatty's battle cruisers were in action. Just before 6.10 p.m. Hood turned to a north-west course, thinking he had over-run the position of the battle, and then at 6.10 p.m. sighted the *Lion*, followed by *Princess Royal*, *Tiger*, etc., in action with the enemy battle cruisers which were being driven aside to the east and south-east. Hood swung his squadron into line immediately ahead of the *Lion*, and at 6.21 opened fire upon the enemy battle cruisers. The course was now east.

By the time Admiral Hood had thus joined up with Admiral Beatty the latter had practically crossed the front of the Grand Fleet, having at 5.56 increased to full speed and turned more to starboard to close and drive the enemy battle cruisers away from the Battle Fleet, so that the action into which Hood now joined at about 6.21 was being fought roughly 2 miles ahead, *i.e.*, to the south-east of our leading battleship. The enemy that were being engaged were the big ships—some reports say battleships as well as battle cruisers—at the head of the enemy's battle line.

The rest of the explanation of the 3rd B.C.S.'s movements is contained in their narratives, and need only be supplemented by this extract from Vice-Admiral Beatty's despatch describing events from the time he sighted them at 6.10 p.m.:—

'I ordered them to take station ahead, which was carried out magnificently, Rear-Admiral Hood bringing his squadron into action ahead in a most inspiring manner, worthy of his great naval ancestors. At 6.25 p.m. I altered course to the E.S.E., in support of the 3rd Battle Cruiser Squadron, who were at this time only 8,000 yards from the enemy's leading ship. They were pouring a hot fire into her, and caused her to turn to the westward of south. At the same time I made a visual report to the Commander-in-Chief of the bearing and distance of the enemy battle fleet. At 6.33 p.m. Invincible blew up.

After the loss of *Invincible*, the squadron was led by Inflexible until 6.50 p.m. By this time the battle cruisers were clear of our leading battle squadron, then bearing about N.N.W. 3 miles, and I ordered the 3rd Battle Cruiser Squadron to prolong the line astern and reduced to 18 knots.'

Admiral Hood went down in the *Invincible* with the 1,025 officers and men who formed her crew. There were only six survivors.

H.M.S. *Inflexible*

The 3rd B.C.S., *Invincible, Inflexible,* and *Indomitable,* left Scapa with the Grand Fleet on 30th May, but on the way south were stationed well ahead of the Battle Fleet. We had with us two light cruisers, the *Chester* and *Canterbury,* and four screening destroyers, among which were *Shark* and *Acasta.*

About 2.30 p.m. I was taking the Midshipmen at instruction in the Captain's cabin, when the Captain's steward came in asking permission to take down the pictures and prepare the cabin for firing. 'What firing?' I asked. He replied that he did not know, but that the Captain had told him we were going to fire. Thinking that there must be something in the wind, I went up on to the bridge, and was shown some intercepted signals from *Galatea,* which made it clear that some of the enemy were out. In the meantime *Invincible* had ordered us to raise steam for full speed, and we were working up to our 25½ knots.

At short intervals more reports of the enemy were intercepted, indicating that Beatty's battle cruisers were in action with enemy battle cruisers. We were now steaming at full speed to join Admiral Beatty, and after sending the hands to tea we closed up at our action stations, though without much hope of seeing anything as the enemy were reported to be steaming away from us to the southward. In the fore-top we were kept informed of what was going on by the intercepted signals being passed up to us by voice pipe, and when there was read to us, soon after 4.30 p.m., the *Southampton*'s report of enemy battleships steering to the north, we then began to think that something might really be doing. On our present course we were closing the enemy as they came towards us at a resultant speed of about 45 knots.

Shortly before 5 o'clock we heard firing in the distance on our starboard bow, but by this time the visibility had become low and was fluctuating in different directions. The *Chester,* for example, to the westward of us, could not be seen at all. Gradually the firing became louder, and drew from our starboard bow aft to the starboard beam, then to the quarter, until we began to think that we had over-run the fight. We altered course about 12 points (a right angle and a half) in succession to starboard, bringing us to a north-westerly course, with *Invincible* leading, followed by *Inflexible,* then *Indomitable.* The firing now was slightly on the port bow. A few minutes later we sighted gun flashes, and the next minute the *Chester*, surrounded by shell splashes, came out of the mist on our port bow heading across the bows of the squadron from port to starboard, and was followed a minute later by three German light cruisers. As soon as the latter saw us they turned to starboard, to pass us on opposite courses. At 5.55 we opened fire upon them, but only had about five minutes' firing before they disappeared. *Invincible* and ourselves managed to hit one which blew up, and the *Indomitable* apparently damaged another.

After these light cruisers disappeared we could still hear a good deal of firing coming from the westward, and we started to alter in this direction. As we did so, two torpedo tracks were seen from aloft approaching us about 800 yards away, and we at once informed the bridge, who put on helm to dodge them. At the same time another torpedo, evidently at the end of its run, came slowly down our port side about 20 feet from the ship, and a little later yet another torpedo track was seen passing directly under the ship at high speed. These torpedoes had presumably been fired by the three German light cruisers, as they passed us on opposite courses whilst we were engaging them with gunfire, though a submarine may quite possibly have fired the last torpedo. One observer who saw the track of this last torpedo as it was going away after it had passed under the ship thought it was a torpedo fired by us, and could not understand at what ship we were firing. The *Invincible*'s helm jammed hard over when she was dodging torpedoes, and she turned nearly a complete circle, but without any bad effects.

Continuing to the westward, we gained touch with the advance cruisers of the Grand Fleet, *Defence*, etc., but soon lost sight of them again in the mist. The firing was now growing in volume and flashes could be seen on our port bow, so the squadron turned in succession to the southward and shortly afterwards sighted the *Lion* leading three other battle cruisers on our starboard bow. *Invincible* then led us round ahead of *Lion* on to an easterly course, and sighting the enemy as we turned, we opened fire directly afterwards. We could only see three German ships, of which the leader appeared to be of the *Derfflinger* class but was very indistinct, the next apparently a battle ship of the *Konig* class, and the third either the battle cruiser *Seydlitz* or *Moltke*. Why a battleship should be with the battle cruisers we did not understand. We opened fire at the second ship at a range of about 8,000 yards with common shell and a few

Invincible going into action (taken from next astern).

The Destruction of H.M.S. *Invincible*.

The smoke cloud of the explosion.

The wreck—bow and stern showing with destroyer *Badger* picking up survivors.

armour piercing lyddite. The common shell showed up very well when hitting and were more distinct than the armour-piercing shell bursts, although I think we hit a good many times with both types. We had quite a satisfactory 20 minutes' shooting, and I did not notice any enemy shots falling near us, although the officer of 'X' turret assured me later that we were straddled, and that he heard shell passing over his turret.

At about 15 or 20 minutes after we opened fire the *Invincible* went down, but although I was in the fore-top and we were her next astern, I saw nothing of it except the smoke and the ends of the ship sticking up as we passed by her.

At this time, 6.33 p.m., the enemy evidently altered away to the southward, and we lost touch with them. We were now leading the battle cruiser line, and we hauled round to the southward, first of all 2 points and then another 4 points, but could not regain touch. The *Lion* and her remaining three battle cruisers came up to the south-ward of us, and we were ordered to form astern of them and *Indomitable* led us round. Soon after getting in station astern of the rear ship, *New Zealand*, we sighted the enemy again through the mist, but at uncertain intervals so that we could not keep up a reg-ular gunfire. For a time the mist had cleared towards the northward, and we could see a part of the Grand Fleet deploying and opening fire, but we could not see the ships at which they were firing. A lit-tle later, an enemy destroyer flotilla came out to deliver a torpedo attack, and we fired a few salvoes at them, but they did not come close, and we saw no torpedoes. From then until about 8.30 p.m. we kept losing sight of the enemy, closing them to regain touch, firing for a few minutes, and then losing them again. Few shots came near us, although there seemed to be firing at some ship or other going on all round. I looked aft once and saw a lot of splashes falling some way astern of us in the smoke, but there did not appear to be any ships there. Also, a number of shots fell a long way over us.

About 8.30 p.m. we all felt a violent bump, which we at first thought might have been a mine or a torpedo hitting the ship, and then that we might have hit a submarine, or it may have been an enemy ship blowing up—I believe no British ship blew up at this time. At about 8.45 we seemed to lose the enemy altogether, and we did not sight them again before it finally became dark.

During the night we held on to the southward without incident, and turned to the north at about 2.30 a.m. on the 1st June. We sighted a Zeppelin shortly afterwards, and *Indomitable* fired a few rounds at it, but it kept a long way out of range. We returned to harbour on June 2nd.

Narrative of H.M.S. *Chester*
(Light Cruiser attached to Rear-Admiral Hood's (3rd) Battle Cruiser Squadron)

Extract from Commander-in-Chief's Despatch, Para. 7:-

'At 5.30 p.m. ... the 3rd Battle Cruiser Squadron ... observed flashes of gunfire and heard the sound of guns to the southwestward. Rear-Admiral Hood sent the *Chester* (Captain Robert N. Lawson) to investigate, and this ship engaged three or four enemy light cruisers at about 5.45 p.m. The engagement lasted for about twenty minutes, during which period Captain Lawson handled his vessel with great skill against heavy odds, and although the ship suffered considerably in casualties, her fighting and steaming qualities were unimpaired, and at about 6.5 p.m. she rejoined the 3rd Battle Cruiser Squadron.'

Extract from Narrative of an Officer of H.M.S. *Castor*:

'... The *Chester* came close across our bows from east to west, with four big holes in her along her main deck, and her ship's company cheering through the holes as she passed us.'

H.M.S. *Chester* had commissioned at Liverpool on 2nd May, 1916, and from there had proceeded to Scapa Flow to work up gunnery and other exercises before joining up with the 3rd Light Cruiser Squadron. We had only arrived at Scapa on 15th May, so that we were lucky to be allowed to accompany the Grand Fleet when it put to sea on the evening of the 30th May; we had returned to our anchorage only that afternoon after carrying out a battle practice.

The position we were detailed to take up in the fleet was one about 20 miles ahead of the fleet flagship, between the 3rd Battle Cruiser Squadron and the armoured cruiser screen, which was in front of the battle fleet, about 8 miles from each. For these two forces we acted as a connecting link for passing in signals, reports of the enemy, etc., to the fleet flagship.

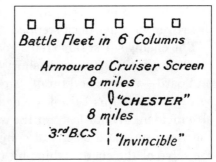

We got the first news of the enemy about 2.30 p.m., and naturally, during the succeeding three hours before we ourselves were in touch with the enemy but were intercepting the frequent reports of the action between the rival battle cruiser fleets, we were anxiously wondering whether we should arrive in time to share in the scrap. It was a beautifully clear afternoon, but soon after 5 p.m. it thickened to the south-westward and westward, and visibility in that direction decreased to 5 or 7 miles.

Owing to a discrepancy between our estimated position and that of the reports received of the fighting, we had worked out that the earliest we could meet the enemy would be 6 p.m., and that they would then probably be met on our port bow. However, at about 5.25 p.m., when we were steering a south-south-easterly course, we sighted flashes of guns to the south-west, on our starboard bow, and at once altered course to investigate, signalling to the Rear-Admiral of the 3rd Battle Cruiser Squadron the reason for our alteration. It is a point of some interest that we did not know, and now never can know, whether Admiral Hood received this signal, but I should imagine that he did so owing to his position and the course on which he was steering when we sighted him later. We were unable to communicate visually with the armoured cruisers, as we had lost touch with them when we had earlier increased speed to keep station on Admiral Hood who had been ordered to reinforce Admiral Beatty, and who consequently had increased to 24 knots.

At the same time as we turned to investigate these gun flashes, we increased to full speed, and in a very short time sighted light cruisers about 2 points on the port bow steering approximately north-north-west. Personally, I think that there were four ships there, though I believe the official despatch puts it at three. Seen dimly through the mist they appeared to be not unlike our 1st Light Cruiser Squadron. We altered to a course parallel to them, challenging at the same time, but this was somewhat superfluous as almost immediately we saw the flash of gunfire ripple along the side of the leading light cruiser, and at the same moment we sighted a destroyer with her mast stepped aft—a sure sign of a Hun.

The enemy's first salvo fell a good 2,000 yards beyond us, the second from 500 to 700 yards short, and then most of the third came on board—a very good bit of target-finding one must admit. A few seconds before this I think we had got our first salvo off, and it was also incidentally our last, for the majority of the guns' crews, and all the voice pipe and electrical communications were smashed up by the salvo of the enemy which hit us. From this point things became pretty brisk on board, the whole of the enemy light cruiser squadron concentrating on us, and several salvoes hit us. The odds were obviously more than we could stand, and as our guns were only firing spasmodically, and the range registered by our range-takers had come down to as little as 5,600 yards, the Captain decided to endeavour to fall back on the 3rd Battle Cruiser Squadron for support. We therefore altered away on to a mean course of north-east, which brought our opponents astern, and zigzagged to dodge the enemy's salvoes. The zig-zagging was done by steering into the splash of each salvo immediately after it fell, which entirely upset the deflection of the enemy, and he seldom obtained a hit after we commenced doing this, although he kept close all the time. The salvoes fell alternately first on one bow and then on the other, usually only a few yards from the forecastle. Most of the shells burst on striking the sea, and drenched everyone on the bridge with black and most unpleasant-smelling water. During our turn away we tried to get off a torpedo from the port torpedo tube, but owing to some hang-up below, it unfortunately failed to fire. We tried again later, but with the same result.

During this run our quarter-deck guns were the only guns that would bear, and they were in local control without the assistance of any fire-control instruments, so I fear that little if any damage was done to the enemy. Fortunately no part of the engine-room or boilers was damaged, and when we rang down to the engine-room the signal for emergency full speed—a movement of the pointer in quick succession from 'Full ahead' to 'Full astern'—the engineers worked the ship up to a speed of 28 knots (that is, revolutions for 28 knots), although the maximum speed made during our trials four weeks ago had been only 26½ knots. By this good work we gradually increased our range from the enemy. While we were zigzagging, a report of the helm jamming hard-a-port gave us an unpleasant moment's fright, but luckily it cleared again almost instantly, and we kept on our escaping course.

About 5.50 p.m. we sighted some large ships on the starboard bow, and, as these came clearer through the mist, we identified them as the 3rd Battle Cruiser Squadron. We passed about three cables ahead of the *Invincible*, and as we did so the latter opened fire on our late opponents, and I had the satisfaction of observing a hit obtained on one of them. We took station about half a mile on *Invincible*'s starboard bow, getting off our last few shots at the enemy across her bow, but she then made a large turn to port, and we had to alter away to starboard, where we became mixed up with the Grand Fleet destroyer flotillas, and we had some difficulty in clearing them, in the process of which we lost touch with the *Invincible*.

I think that the total number of direct hits we received was eighteen, but we also were hit by a large amount of splinters from shells bursting in the water. My own idea of affairs on the bridge was a hail storm. We had about five fires, chiefly cordite ones, but they were fairly easily got under.[2] The engine-room fortunately was not hit, although the wreckage and débris found in some spaces just above showed that the escape had been a narrow one. One high explosive shell had burst inside the foremost funnel, entering the port side and blowing out a hole about 6 feet by 8 feet large on the starboard side. This shell had also sheared the holding-down bolts of a large fan which supplies air to the foremost boiler-room, so that the engine of the fan had been moved bodily on its seat, but fortunately the steam pipes leading to it had just held it from going altogether, and a party of men handspiked it back into its place.

They said in the engine-room that their strongest desire all the time was to 'makee-look-see' what was happening, but from the time in the early afternoon when they had received a message from the Captain, 'If we wished to see any of the fun, it was time to hustle,' to the time when the ship was being badly hit and emergency full speed was ordered, the whole staff were busy at their job, and had no opportunity for sight-seeing.

The engine-room mascot, a black kitten, was taken to its action station below when action was sounded off and apparently did its duty nobly! The men down below found the gases and smoke which

---

2 H.M.S. *Chester*'s casualties were: 2 officers and 33 men killed, 3 officers and 39 men wounded.

came down the ventilating trunks directly succeeding the crash of a shell hitting the ship, to be very nauseous and unpleasant, requiring respirators to be worn all the time. But there seemed to be a divided opinion as to whether the nastiness of the antidote solution which is put on the respirators was a cure for, or a worse evil than, the nauseous taste of the gases themselves.

An example of a lucky escape in an above-deck station was the control officer in the after control position, a position abaft the funnels approximately over the engine-rooms, about 10 feet above the level of the upper deck. Two shells burst in this control position, removing the whole place except one small piece in one corner, about 2 feet square. The actual range-finder, mounted in the centre of the control position—an instrument weighing several hundredweight—was blown bodily over the side, together with every man of the crew except the Control Officer. But he, happening to be in this particular little corner that was spared, escaped with no more than a few slight burns.

The Adventures of H.M.S. *Acasta*

The destroyer, *Acasta*, one of the four boats attached to Admiral Hood's Battle Cruiser Squadron, came into action about 5.50 p.m., shortly after H.M.S. *Chester*.

H.M.S. *Acasta* attacked the enemy in company with the leader of her division, H.M.S. *Shark* (whose Captain, Commander Loftus Jones, was posthumously awarded the Victoria Cross for his gallant conduct while the *Shark* was sinking), and H.M.S. *Christopher* and H.M.S. *Ophelia*. They engaged enemy light cruisers and destroyers, and eventually the *Acasta* fired a torpedo at German battle cruisers, after which she made back to the north-westward close past H.M.S. *Lion*. (The fact of having closed unexpectedly on the German battle cruisers shows clearly that Admiral Hood's Squadron had 'over-run' the action and had sighted the enemy battle cruisers before making contact with our (Rosyth) battle cruisers.) *Acasta* was severely damaged in these attacks, and as a result of this damage lay stopped in the path of the Battle Fleet after they had deployed into battle line, and 'reviewed the fleet,' cheering each ship as they passed. This incident was referred to in Admiral Jellicoe's despatch:-

'At this time (6.45) the destroyer *Acasta* was passed in a disabled condition. She signalled that she was holed fore and aft, and unable to move her engines. In spite of her condition her ship's company were observed to be cheering as the Battle Fleet passed.'

The Adventures of H.M.S. *Acasta*
Described by her Commanding Officer

On the afternoon of 30th May the four destroyers, *Shark*, *Acasta*, *Ophelia*, and *Christopher*, were detailed to screen the 3rd Battle Cruiser Squadron (*Invincible*, *Inflexible*, and *Indomitable*), and the same evening we left Scapa Flow ahead of the main fleet and steered to the south-eastward at about 17 knots. All was peace until the next afternoon, when about 5.30 p.m. firing was heard in the distance. Later, flashes were seen ahead in the direction where *Chester* had been detached to reconnoitre. The weather was misty, and it was difficult to know what was happening, but at about 10 minutes to 6 we sighted a part of the enemy's fleet, and Commander Loftus Jones, in the *Shark*, receiving orders from Admiral Hood to proceed independently, led us into attack.

We could not clearly distinguish the various enemy ships, but we could make out several German light cruisers and a number of destroyers which evidently had sighted our 3rd B.C.S., and were commencing to make a torpedo attack on them. But when they saw us leading out they appeared to become undecided as to what our force consisted of, and as far as we could make out, turned from their torpedo attack to engage us with gunfire. The destroyers were supported by cruisers, and things very quickly became unpleasantly warm. The German shooting was undoubtedly good, their salvoes falling close together—perhaps too close together, really—but at first we were little hit, although a piece of shell scalped a signalman on our bridge and a lot of shell splinters were flying about. We afterwards picked out 30 to 40 pieces of shell from the mattresses slung round the bridge. Also, on the bridge we were all soaked through by the spray thrown up by shell, causing the sub-lieutenant to remark that 'an umbrella would be handy.'

After a while we received our first direct hit, which was right forward on the water-line, and gave us the feeling that the ship had been pushed bodily sideways. Incidentally, it spoilt the lower mess deck as a mess deck. About 10 minutes past 6, having seen that the enemy's destroyer attack was frustrated, the *Shark* turned the division to port away from the enemy, and we then saw that *Shark* herself was practically stopped, and had a quantity of steam pouring out of her engine-room, so we turned back to render any assistance possible.

We signalled to *Shark* to ask if we could be of any help, but although I passed quite close to her, we got no answer back. We saw men aft, but none for'ard. Most unfortunately at this moment we got two big ones through the after end of the engine-room, which smashed the steering engine and set alight to the engineer's store. The dynamo was wrecked, various exhaust pipes were cut, the engine-room was filled with steam, the emergency stop-valve on deck was broken, and we were left without means of shutting steam off. Everyone in the engine-room who had not been killed was forced to come up at once on deck owing to the escaping steam. I rang down 'Stop' and 'Astern,' but with no result, and it was some time before orders could be got through by word of mouth to the stokehold to shut off steam at the boilers.

Whilst turning up to close *Shark* we fired a torpedo at the leading enemy battle cruiser at a range of about 4,500 yards, and shortly afterwards an explosion was seen. Soon after passing *Shark*, with the steam sending us uncontrolled ahead, we crossed the bows of the *Lion* and very nearly caught a salvo of big stuff which was meant for her.

At about 6.30, having barged through our own destroyer flotillas ahead of the battle fleet—guided by Providence, for we had no steering gear to guide the ship with—we at last got the ship stopped, and lying there only about 200 yards from the battle line, held a very fine review of the Grand Fleet coming into action, as ship after ship they passed us. The men were very excited and cheered each ship as she passed, some to port and some to starboard, particularly the Commander-in-Chief in the *Iron Duke*. We hoisted the 'Not under control' signal, and endeavoured to tell the battleships that we were unable to move, for it would have been an ignominious end to have been run down by our own fleet. Fortunately they all dodged us.

Later, I went aft from the bridge to inspect the damage we had received. The engine-room was in an awful mess, and the store-room just abaft it absolutely wrecked and smouldering. The dynamo had ceased to exist, there was oil fuel everywhere, and the upper deck all round the after part of the engine-room was riddled with holes. We did our best to fill up the holes in the side with hammocks, canvas, etc., but it didn't make much difference. We had great difficulty in getting down to the engine-room, as there was still a lot of steam escaping, but eventually we got all the people up from there. The damage forward was not serious, and was dealt with by shoring up the bulkheads and blocking the holes with hammocks. The destruction of the dynamo left us with no lights except candles, which made repair work very difficult, especially later when it got dark, but the engine-room department did wonders particularly when it is remembered that their store-room had been wrecked, and that they were left with practically no spare parts or tools. The remarks of the artificers trying to fit a three-eighths nut on to a five-eighths bolt, by candle light in some out-of-the-way corner, working up to their waists in oil and water, were distinctly illuminating. One odd effect of being heavily engaged, which was told me by the first lieutenant, was that nobody at the after guns realised that the ship had ever been hit.

He also warned me that I should not find my cabin very comfortable now, and I found he was quite right, for two shells had gone through it completely wrecking it, and the North Sea was flowing freely in and out.

As the battleships passed us we had one very close shave from being rammed, for as *Marlborough*, leading the rear division of the battle fleet, came nearly up to us she was hit by a torpedo under her starboard bow, which threw up a big black column of spray as high as her upper turret, and she immediately listed to starboard. Apparently she was under port helm at the time, as she swung off her course and passed us on her port hand, which was lucky for us, as at the moment of being torpedoed she was heading straight for us.

After the fleet had passed, *Fearless* and *Galatea* both closed us to offer assistance, but as there were no enemy ships about, and we seemed to be still seaworthy, we did not consider it necessary to accept their help. Shortly afterwards the periscope of a submarine was reported by one of the men, and we opened a heavy bombardment on it, but it was a false scare, the periscope turning out to be only a thin spar floating upwards. Still it was an unpleasant few minutes, for we were absolutely incapable of moving.

At this time the *Warspite* was a few miles away from us steaming round in circles, her steering gear apparently damaged. She made a good target for 'U' boats, so that we were all very much on the look-out for them. Just before dark she steamed away and we were left by ourselves with no other ships in sight, feeling rather lonely.

By midnight some sort of repairs had been made to the steering engine and to the damaged steam pipes, and we started to crawl towards Scotland on a zigzag course, making 2 to 3 knots. But the steering gear was of very little use, and before long we realised that it would be impossible for us to reach harbour as we were making no real headway, and very little of the oil fuel remained fit to use. Several hands had to be employed carrying fuel forward in buckets to an undamaged tank. We knew nothing of the movements or the whereabouts of either friend or enemy, and to add to our discomfort the wind and sea were fast getting up.

During the night we heard German wireless signals close to us, but when daylight came there was nothing in sight. Later during the forenoon a destroyer was sighted coming up from the southward, and seeing her through the mist, end on, we took her to be a German, and manned the guns; but when she made the challenge, although we could not answer it having no searchlights left, we realised that she was a friend and that it was all right. She turned out to be the *Nonsuch* and took us in tow smartly, bringing us to Aberdeen, where tugs took us into the harbour at about 9 p.m. on the 2nd of June. *Nonsuch* then parted company for Rosyth.

Narrative from H.M.S. *Indomitable*

(Third and Rear Battle Cruiser of Admiral Hood's Squadron)

[The account which follows is compiled from the note-book which I kept in the fore turret of H.M.S. *Indomitable* during the action. Some slight discrepancy may be noticed in the times given, as my watch was only hastily compared with G.M.T. before the action.

The ranges given are those on the gun-sights at the time; courses during the action are only approximate. Although my field of vision through the slit in the turret hood was necessarily limited I was able to observe the enemy closely when engaged, and during lulls in the firing could obtain a comprehensive view of the general course of the fight from the top of the turret.]

The first intimation that we had of any possibility of an action was at 2.23 p.m., when *Galatea* reported enemy ships in sight, and we intercepted her signal. At that time we were stationed ahead of the battle fleet, steering S. 50° E., and zigzagging, the speed of advance being 14 knots. The wireless office could hear Telefunken signals, strength 10, very loud and strong. At 3.57 p.m. we heard from the *Lion* that they were engaging the enemy, and shortly afterwards the sounds of heavy gunfire were plainly audible, and flashes were visible on the horizon.

The weather at this time was clear, but with patches of thin mist near the horizon, and visibility of approximately 16,000 yards; the wind was S.W., force 2, and the sea smooth.

At 5.40 p.m. course was altered about 8 points to starboard, and at 5.50 p.m. *Invincible* opened fire on a three-funnelled light cruiser bearing 40° on the port bow, and was followed five minutes later by *Inflexible* and *Indomitable*, the squadron being in line ahead in that order. We could see, off the port bow, a light cruiser of the *Canterbury* class apparently stopped or moving very slowly, and heavily engaged with a squadron of four enemy light cruisers, which were advancing for torpedo attack. One of these was a four-funnelled cruiser, and seemed to be of the *Rostock* class.

Our opening range was 11,200 yards, closing by 6.0 p.m. to 8,900 yards. We had steamed between our own light cruiser and the enemy, and had severely handled them, one of the Germans disappearing in a great cloud of steam and smoke which remained for a long time over one spot, so that I have no doubt at all that she sank; and another, a three-funnelled cruiser, was badly on fire amidships, apparently stopped and settling down but I did not see her sink as we turned away to avoid torpedoes which were crossing the track. I could not see these torpedo tracks from the turret, of course, but was told afterwards that four had been sighted; one passed under the ship, one passed ahead, one a few yards astern, and one was observed by the gunnery officer to be running slowly along the starboard side of the ship a few yards off and parallel to the ship, its distinctive red head being particularly noticeable. The enemy now made off, and were attacked at 6.9 p.m. by our destroyers, with what result the smoke and haze made it impossible to observe.

The noise of firing now became like the roll of continuous thunder, and the horizon to port was filled with whirling sheets of flame. Through the mist we could distinguish the Rosyth battle cruisers hotly engaged with the enemy, whose number and class we could not

Flames shooting out of *Invincible* as she commenced to blow up. The two officer survivors were in the conning tower and spotting top.

make out. At 6.13 p.m. the *Invincible* stopped, and clouds of steam came from her exhaust pipes, but she appeared to be undamaged, and hoisting the 'Disregard' signal shortly after went ahead at 20 knots with the signal to form single line ahead flying. It was the last time I saw her as a ship.

We were now (6.20 p.m.) heavily engaged with the enemy battle cruisers and with, I think, the head of his battle line, the range being 8,200 yards, bearing 90 Green. Suddenly my left gun ceased firing. The thin metal bulkhead which had been built round the sighting position to render it, as far as possible, sound-proof prevented me from seeing what was wrong, and for a few moments I could get no reply to my enquiries from the loading officer. This was exasperating, and I began to fear that the turret had been hit although I had felt no concussion, when the welcome report came that it was only a cordite charge that had jammed and broken up.

It took but a short time to clear the jam, and two hands, with their arms full of cordite sticks, went up to the roof of the turret and threw them over the side. Both guns were in action again at 6.40 p.m., and we went into 'Independent' at a range of 8,600 yards. I think it was as well that my cabinet was sound-proof, as my loading officer told me afterwards that the left gunlayer's language was of the rare and fruity variety!

The enemy's shooting at this time was unpleasantly good, and I observed several salvoes burst alongside, and could hear the whistle of 'overs.' There was a belief that the enemy used shrapnel for a few rounds, but I cannot confirm that from personal observation. Certainly the shell splinters found on board were very small, and this may have given rise to the report. An entry in my note-book at this time reads, 'Enemy salvoes bursting close.'

At 6.35 p.m. we altered course slightly to port, reverting to controlled fire at a range of 10,750 yards. Then upon the starboard bow I saw the two ends of a ship standing perpendicularly above water, the ship appearing to have broken in halves amidships, each half resting on the bottom. My gunlayer took her for a Hun, and the crew cheered, but I could read the name *Invincible* on the stern and so knew better. Four or five survivors were clinging to floating wreckage; I have never seen anything more splendid than these few cheering us as we raced by them.

The weather now got very much thicker, and at 6.42 p.m. fire was checked, a few minutes after which the 1st B.C.S. came up, and we turned round from ahead to take station astern of them, in the order—*Lion, Princess Royal, Tiger, New Zealand, Indomitable, Inflexible.* As we turned we could see that the *Lion* had a small fire just abaft the foremast, and we learned afterwards that our arrival on the scene was most opportune, as it gave the crews of the 1st B.C.S. a brief 'stand easy,' and enabled them to put out various fires. It was generally agreed that the period 6.20 to 6.42 p.m. was the hottest part of the action, and observers in the *Princess Royal* have said that they expected every moment to see us share the fate of the *Invincible.*

We could now see the battle fleet coming up astern in three columns, and at 7.12 p.m. they re-opened fire. The spectacle was truly magnificent, tongues of flame seeming to leap from end to end of the line, but owing to the dusk and smoke we could not see what practice they were making.

At 7.20 p.m. we re-opened fire at the enemy battle cruisers at a range of 14,000 yards, our squadron apparently making splendid practice. Time after time a dull orange glow would appear on board one or other of their ships, a glow which increased and brightened, then slowly dulled; yet, in spite of these hits, the enemy's volume of fire did not seem appreciably to diminish. One big ship turned out of her line to starboard, her after part enveloped in flame, and began slowly to drop astern. The remainder emitted dense volumes of smoke, which hung above the water like a pall, and through which, at 7.25 p.m., we could see about a dozen destroyers racing towards our line. Orders came through for the 4-inch guns' crews to close up, and, as the change of bearing was passed and the turret swung round, I could hear the staccato bark of these small guns joining in the general din. As the destroyers cleared the smoke screen, white pillars began to leap up amongst them like giant nine-pins, to be knocked down and spring up again without ceasing as the big guns came into action. Almost half the distance had been covered by the attackers, when I saw two of these white towers of water rise simultaneously in front of the left-hand boat of the line, and as they sank no thrusting bow came through the spray, only a thinning streak of smoke. . . .

The 2nd Light Cruiser Squadron astern turned out to starboard and engaged the flotilla with 6-inch guns, and shortly afterwards the enemy swung round and sped back, but not before I had seen a second boat hit and destroyed.

The officer of 'X' turret told me an amusing yarn of his turret during this attack. His gunlayer was a very smart man, but not above drawing the long bow, I'm afraid, and the trainer, though an excellent trainer, was rather slow-witted. The conversation between the two was something like this:—

Gunlayer.—'Train right—Train right—Little more.'—Bang.

Trainer.—'What were you firing at?'

Gunlayer.—'Destroyer.'

Trainer.—'I can't see it.'

Gunlayer.—'No. I've sunk her. Train right—Right—Right'—Bang.

Trainer.—'I didn't see it.'

Gunlayer.—''Nother destroyer. I've sunk her. Train right again—Too much—Left a little.'—Bang.

Trainer (pathetically).—'I can't see *anything*.'

After the action I believe the gunlayer was claiming eight boats to his own gun!

The enemy now increased his range, and fire was checked at 7.40 p.m., but astern of us the firing was continuous, although it was impossible to make out the ships engaged. This lull seemed a good opportunity for sending a few men away from the turret to get food for the remainder, which was accordingly done. Shortly afterwards we passed a small skiff, painted grey, of apparently German origin, containing the bodies of two men, and round about was a quantity of wreckage and oil, but, of course, we did not stop to enquire into what it was.

At 8.20 p.m., unexpectedly, the enemy battle cruisers were again sighted closing towards us, and a few seconds later they opened fire. Most of my turret's crew had come up on top for a breath of fresh air and to hunt for splinters as souvenirs, so they tumbled back to their stations in a hurry, and by 8.26 p.m. we were hard at it again at a range of 8,800 yards. The German firing was fairly good, and we were straddled several times. Many of our squadron's salvoes hit, and large fires were observed on board several of their ships, and their speed seemed to decrease. By 8.42 p.m. they had had enough and drew off, so we ceased firing, although other ships in the squadron continued for a little time longer. At 8.44 p.m. a distinct shock and muffled explosion was felt and heard, but no damage could be discovered, nor could any definite cause be assigned to the occurrence.

At 9.0 p.m. heavy firing was heard astern, and 10 minutes later a solitary star shell was seen, followed by one heavy salvo. Firing then ceased. The south-westerly course was continued during the night, but, as far as we were concerned, nothing exciting happened during the night, apart from sighting many gun flashes from 11.45 to 12.30 a.m.

June 1st, 1916.

We 'stood to' at 2.30 a.m., a cold misty morning with the sun trying to break through, and a visibility lessening from 10,000 to 8,000 yards, or less at times. Nothing was sighted until 3.10 a.m., when a Zeppelin was observed coming up on the starboard quarter. Both my guns were loaded with armour-piercing lyddite, which are not exactly suitable shell against an airship, but I thought I would have a lap at it for luck, and fired the right gun. This had the effect of making the Zepp. turn sharply away and draw off to a greater distance on the the port beam, where at 3.33 a.m. it was engaged by our light cruisers astern, but no hits were recorded.

A signal from Admiral Beatty was received, stating that the casualties on both sides had been very heavy, that the *Lutzow* and another German battle cruiser were sunk, and that every man was to do his utmost to annihilate the enemy.

From the transmitting station we heard that the *Dublin* had reported two enemy cruisers, and at 4.50 a.m. course was altered to E.S.E. (approx.). We rejoined the battle fleet at 5.0 a.m., and at 5.40 a.m. course was altered to S.E., but nothing was sighted, and no further reports were received.

After breakfast at 7.40 a.m. I went on the bridge. The fleet continued steering on southerly courses until 10.10 a.m., when, as nothing had been seen, hope of meeting the enemy again was abandoned and course was altered to north by west, from whence the squadrons steered to their respective bases. At 11.40 a.m. we passed a black object like the bows of a destroyer showing above water, but whether she was British or German we could not discern, although during the afternoon quantities of dead German bodies were passed, all of which were floating vertically, with a cylinder looking like an anti-gas device strapped on their backs. A red life-buoy with a white letter 'S' was also seen.

Should it be my good fortune to be engaged in another action, I shall take care that only one gramophone is taken into the turret. In my turret we had two, one in the gun-house and one in the working chamber, and during every lull in the action these two were started playing simultaneously, each with a different record. The result was one of the real horrors of the war.

Narrative from H.M.S. *Badger*

The Destroyer which Rescued the Six Survivors of H.M.S. *Invincible*. H.M.S. *Invincible* was sunk at 6.33 p.m.

Commander-in-Chief's Despatch:- 'At 6.55 p.m. *Iron Duke* passed the wreck of *Invincible* with *Badger* standing by. . . .'

About 6.15 I noticed the *Invincible* and the two other battle cruisers appear out of the mist, which was thick on the disengaged side though fairly clear to the southward, and swing magnificently into line ahead of the *Lion*, opening fire as they did so. Shortly afterwards the *Defence*, *Warrior*, *Black Prince*, and one other cruiser also appeared suddenly out of the mist, and cut across the *Lion*'s bow; a few minutes later the *Defence* blew up and the others were put out of action, though I did not see exactly what happened to them.

Hardly had we recovered from the shock of this disaster—it lasted only three or four minutes—when the main Grand Fleet, with destroyers and light cruisers leading them, bore down upon us like an avalanche from out of the mist on the disengaged side. We put our helm hard over to avoid collision, and just managed to squeeze through the gap by closing the *Lion*. As the Grand Fleet deployed into line to the north-east or east-north-east, we received a signal from the *Lion*, 'Pick up survivors from wreck on starboard side,' where we could see what appeared to be the bow and stern of a light cruiser sticking up out of the water.

Assuming this to be a German wreck and that we should have prisoners to pick up, I sent to have an armed guard detailed, and warned our doctor to be ready to tend wounded prisoners. A few minutes later I received exactly similar orders from the Captain. In the meantime, we had cut through a gap between the battle cruisers, and were heading towards the wreck in 'No Man's Land,' between the two fleets. As we neared the wreck we could see the water all round thick with flotsam and jetsam, mainly composed of floating seamen's kit bags, with a few hammocks scattered amongst them. We also spotted a raft, on which were four men, and on the bridge they spotted two other survivors in the water. By orders from the Captain I lowered and sent away the whaler, with our gunner in charge armed with a service revolver. The Captain brought the ship alongside the raft, and I waited with the doctor and the armed guard ready to receive German survivors. Judge of my surprise, when the raft was almost alongside, to see a Commander R.N., a Lieutenant R.N., and two seamen ratings on it. In my surprise I forgot to dismiss the armed guard, who, no doubt considering that it was that for which they were there, wanted to seize on the unfortunate survivors as we hauled them on board. However, I quickly sent the guard away and apologised to the Commander, who only treated it as a good joke. It was a great shock to us when he made us understand that the wreck we were near was the remains of the battle cruiser *Invincible*, and that we were picking up the only six survivors from her ship's company of a thousand men.

The Commander was really marvellously self-possessed. I can hardly understand to this day how a man, after going through what he had, could come on board us from the raft as cheerily as if he was simply joining a new ship in the ordinary course of events. He laughed at the armed guard, and assured us that he hadn't a scratch on his whole body, and that he had merely—as he put it—stepped into the water when the fore-top came down.

The Lieutenant was rather more shaken, and small wonder, for he had been in the conning tower when the ship blew up, and had had to climb out of it and scramble up the sloping deck to the bridge screens, where he was almost immediately engulfed in the water. He told us that he was sucked down once or twice by eddies and had almost given up hope, when he at last broke surface, and with the aid of a floating kit-bag propelled himself to the raft on which the Commander was already seated. The two seamen from the raft appeared to be quite all right, but I did not get an opportunity of questioning them as to their experiences. Of the two men picked up from the water, one, a private of marines, was badly burnt, and later suffered great pain, though he eventually recovered. He told us later that he was in some cabinet at the rear of a turret, but remembered nothing about the explosion until he found himself in the water.

As we were hoisting our boat in again, the Germans apparently spotted us, and dropped a few shells round us, but after steaming slowly round the wreckage to make sure that there was no more survivors, we rang down full speed, and made off to rejoin our flotilla with the *Lion*.

CHAPTER XII

SIDE SHOWS

Whilst our battleships in their long battle line were engaging the German fleet, and our battle cruisers at the van were engaging the ships at the head of the enemy's line, and whilst destroyers on both sides were engaged in torpedo attacks on the rival battle fleets, a certain few British and German ships were hotly engaged in some action or other which can best perhaps be classified under the heading of 'Side Shows.' Such an action on the German side was that of the *Wiesbaden* or of the *Rostock*, light cruisers that became isolated from their big ships' support and, lying between the battle lines at close range to our ships, were heavily concentrated upon until they were reduced to burning wrecks. Such an action also was that of our 1st Cruiser Squadron, the *Defence, Warrior*, etc., which by themselves were so fiercely and unfortunately engaged during the first moments of the battle fleet action; and again such were the actions of the attached ships of Admiral Hood's Squadron, *Chester, Shark, Acasta*, etc., whose actions were apart from the main fleet action, although they were being fought at the same time as (6.0 to 6.20 p.m.), and quite close to the position of the main action.

In addition there were certain ships such as the minelayer *Abdiel* which had their own specialised work to do apart from the fleet action. The narratives of some of these 'side shows' which have not already been described are collected in this Chapter.

One ship which had a 'side show' of peculiar intensity (and gallantry) all to herself was H.M.S. *Onslow*. She was a destroyer of the 13th Flotilla, one of the two Rosyth destroyers which had been detached before the action to work as

247

submarine screen with the seaplane carrier, *Engadine*. She rejoined the Rosyth battle cruiser force just after their turn to the north at 4.45 p.m., too late to join in the torpedo attack which the rest of the 13th Flotilla were at that time carrying out on the German battle cruisers and on the recently sighted German battle fleet. *Onslow* however, with *Moresby*, her pair ship, found opportunity to carry out a torpedo attack by themselves during the Battle Cruiser run to the north.

Then, on the junction between the Battle Cruiser force and the Grand Fleet *Onslow* sighted a German light cruiser, broken down, but only about 6,000 yards from the *Lion*, in a position to fire torpedoes at our battle cruiser line, and so *Onslow* went off on her own to finish off this damaged light cruiser before any torpedoes might be fired. Continuing from this action she made a torpedo attack upon German battle cruisers, in which she was damaged, and shortly afterwards, still on her own, she went in again to attack German battleships which, by the quick changes of the battle, had been placed in a favourable position for being attacked by torpedo. Here *Onslow* fired her last torpedo, and was again badly damaged by the enemy's gunfire so that she could hardly creep out of gun range of the enemy before her engines stopped, and she lay helpless by herself in the midst of the action, not far, as it happened, from where *Warspite* was doing her 'Windy Corner' stunt. But she still floated and eventually was towed back to harbour by another crippled destroyer, H.M.S. *Defender*. The following is the full narrative of these doings, written by an officer of H.M.S. *Onslow*:—

H.M.S. *Onslow*

Early in the afternoon *Onslow* and *Moresby*, of the 13th Destroyer Flotilla, had been detached from screening the 1st B.C.S. to screen the seaplane carrier, *Engadine*. At about 3.30 p.m., when the *Engadine*'s seaplane had returned to her, the Commanding Officer of the *Engadine* gave us permission to rejoin the 1st B.C.S., then some distance to the S.S.E., steering a southerly course, and we proceeded at full speed to rejoin them.

At about 4.45 p.m., when still a mile or so astern, we noticed, much to our surprise, that the battle cruiser squadron was altering course 16 points, so we also turned and found ourselves ahead of the fleet steering north, approximately 3 miles on the engaged bow of the *Lion*. This was a good position from which to make a torpedo attack, especially as no protective cruisers or destroyers could be seen ahead of the enemy battle cruisers, so the Captain decided to take the opportunity to attack, and with the *Moresby* we closed in towards the enemy. Shortly afterwards, however, four enemy light cruisers appeared ahead of the German battle cruisers, and observing us in a conspicuous position closing the enemy, opened a very heavy and accurate fire on us and on *Moresby*. The Captain, seeing that it would be impossible to get into close range against this gunfire, decided to reserve his torpedoes for a more favourable opportunity. *Moresby*, however, fired one torpedo, which was afterwards proved to have scored a hit on the rear enemy battle cruiser.

At 5.5 p.m. we retired towards the *Lion* under very heavy fire from the enemy, and as they were outside the range of our 4-inch guns, we experienced the helpless feeling of being concentrated upon, expecting every moment that the next salvo would sink us, whilst we were unable to make any reply. *Moresby* separated from us in order to avoid making a double target, and under cover of a smoke screen we managed to regain our battle cruiser line without damage, although the impact caused by salvoes of shells hitting the water and bursting very close to the ship had made our engine-room department think that we had been hit repeatedly.

We were now again on the engaged bow of the *Lion*, watching the action between the rival battle cruisers with deep interest, for in this position we had a better view of the action than almost any other ship. The battle cruisers were firing heavily at one another at a range of about 14,000 yards, and the noise of the salvoes firing and bursting was incessant and terrific, but we could see little of the effect of the fire. After a glorious clear afternoon, the visibility had now become rather indifferent, and a mist was creeping up. *Lion* and *Tiger*, of the four surviving battle cruisers, seemed both to have suffered somewhat, but as the enemy were gradually drawing off to the eastward to increase the range, we hoped that the damage our battle cruisers had done to them was more severe. At 5.45 p.m. the Grand Fleet cruisers were sighted on our port bow, and a very welcome sight they were, I can assure you, for knowing that the Germans had their entire battle fleet out in support, this recent run to the north-ward had been rather an anxious journey.

At 5.50 p.m. we sighted the first battle squadron, and *Lion* imme-diately started to close the enemy, turning to the eastward, and rapidly reduced the range. The German battle cruisers also made a big turn to the east, and a little later to a course about S.E. Just as our battle cruisers were conforming to this last alteration, we sighted a broken-down enemy light cruiser only about 6,000 yards from the *Lion*, in a position to fire torpedoes at our battle cruiser line. We were suitably placed on the engaged bow of the *Lion* for repelling such an attack, and at once went off to try and stop this fir-ing of torpedoes, and at a range of 4,000 to 2,000 yards, or less, engaged the light cruiser, firing 58 rounds of which I am sure a number must have hit. At one time we came so close that, with a range of only 1,900 yards on the gun sights, our shots were still not falling short. The enemy cruiser replied vigorously, but with little success. Her firing was very much easier to endure than the firing which we had suffered an hour previously, when we had simply to sit still under a heavy 'bombardment' unable to make any reply. I should not say perhaps that this cruiser's fire exercised *no* strain upon us, for one man of my gun's crew, for example, was found shel-tering behind a flimsy bit of canvas, apparently acting on an exten-sion of the ostrich principle that, if he was out of sight of the enemy, their shell could not hit him! But his nervousness had its use, for when shown what a fool he was the men laughed at him, and it served to steady the gun's crew, who went on firing the whole time just as coolly as if they were at target practice.

We now saw that the enemy battle cruisers had made another turn, so that we were now brought 45 degrees on their port bow at only about 11,000 yards from them—an ideal position for a torpedo attack—so the Captain closed the enemy, and when 8,000 yards from the leading enemy battle cruiser gave the signal to the torpedo tubes to fire, and turned the ship to port to being the sights on. Unfortunately, just at this moment the ship was struck amidships by a heavy shell, and was enveloped in clouds of escaping steam. In the confusion only one of our four torpedoes was fired, although the Captain understood that all four torpedoes had gone. He sent the sub-lieutenant aft to the tubes to find out exactly what had hap-pened, and this officer, finding out at the tubes that there were still three torpedoes left, and sighting at the same moment our old friend the German light cruiser, now a couple of miles away on our beam, himself aimed and fired a torpedo at her. This torpedo hit the light cruiser below the conning tower and exploded. The Sub. then returned to the bridge and reported the fact that we still had two torpedoes left, and at the same moment the writer of this account came for'ard to report to the Captain that the ship was in no immediate danger of sinking, for although our speed had dropped from 30 knots to a miserable 10 immediately we were hit, the engineer officer reported that we should be able to keep up this speed for some little time. It was not a very pleasant speed, though, at which to be cruising about within 3 miles of an enemy battle cruiser squadron that were sending an unpleasant number of shells splashing round us.

Receiving these reports, the Captain abandoned his intention of creeping out of range of the enemy before being hopelessly crippled, and decided to go in again and make use of the two remaining torpedoes by delivering a final attack on the enemy's line of battle, which at this time was re-appearing out of the mist above 8,000 yards away.

Again we were on the enemy's bow in a good position for torpedo attack. The Captain explained to me his reasons for going into attack after being partly crippled, in case I might be a survivor and he himself killed, so that I should be able to justify his decision and answer any charge of foolhardiness. He pointed out that his policy was sound, as we were in a position of torpedo advantage, and if we cleared out without firing our two last torpedoes they would be wasted, for we were far too damaged to take any part in the action later on. The probability was that the ship would be lost, as our reduced speed made us an easy target, but what was one destroyer more or less compared to a torpedo hit on one of the enemy battle line? So we steered in again towards the enemy.[1]

The sub-lieutenant was sent aft again to supervise the firing of the torpedoes, and soon after coming under fire again we fired the two torpedoes, noticing that they started their run satisfactorily and

---

[1] The Commander-in-Chief in his despatch of the action included this extract from Vice Admiral Beatty's report:- '*Onslow* was possibly the destroyer referred to by the Rear-Admiral commanding 3rd L.C.S.: "Here I should like to bring to your notice the action of a destroyer (name unknown) which we passed close in a disabled condition soon after 6.0 p.m. She apparently was able to struggle ahead again, and made straight for the *Derfflinger* to attack her." '

more than probably crossed the enemy battle line, although it was impossible to follow their track by eye very far.

About this time I noticed some black smoke coming up from the ship's side abreast of the mainmast, and thinking that there might be a small fire there, I sent down my messenger to investigate. Presently he came back grinning from ear to ear to tell me, 'Your cabin has gone, sir,' which subsequent investigation proved to be quite correct. A shell, after passing through three or four bulkheads, not to mention the ward-room gramophone, had selected my cabin as a suitable place in which to burst, and had, almost literally, removed the whole place, with every imaginable possession of mine that had been there.

The deck above and below was torn away, and nearly the whole of the ship's side had disappeared. The Captain's cabin, the ward-room, the cabin flat, etc., all presented a sorry appearance, being entirely wrecked and inches deep in a messy mixture of oil fuel and salt water.

Meanwhile the Captain had, as he put it in his official report, 'retired at greatly reduced speed . . . proceeding to close H.M.S. *Champion*, with the idea of rejoining the 13th Flotilla,' but owing to two shells exploding in No. 2 boiler-room, the ship gradually lost speed, and then stopped whilst we were still some way short of the battle line. Just before this we observed near us one of our battle-ships stopped and surrounded with water spouts, apparently about to be sunk, although she was replying to the enemy's fire with all her guns—an inspiring sight. We afterwards discovered that it was the *Warspite* doing her famous stunt at 'Windy Corner.' Two of her officers afterwards told us that we in the *Onslow* presented an equally remarkable appearance, roaming about all alone between the battle lines belching forth vast clouds of steam, and we were given credit in some quarters for having put up a smoke screen in front of the *Warspite*. But this we did not do deliberately, as the *Warspite* was firing so lustily herself that we thought she might not like it.

The Engineer Officer now arrived on the bridge to report that he could only steam for a few more minutes, as the main feed tank was holed and all the water in the reserve feed tanks was used up. Hardly had he spoken when we gradually lost headway and lay stopped, still within range of the enemy. A few minutes before, our 13th Flotilla, led by *Champion*, had come dashing past us and had asked if we wanted assistance, but as they all looked too healthy to be employed assisting us, the Captain had replied 'No.' But now, when the ship was stopped, we would have changed the answer to 'Yes' if it had been possible, but it was not, for we had no signalling apparatus left, and the flotilla were now out of hailing distance. Meanwhile we were busy trying to stop up the holes in the ships' side with our collision mats, which proved to be rather a ludicrous proceeding as the holes were larger than the mats. We also got ready for'ard to be taken in tow, in the hopes of some other ship turning up to tow us.

The battle was now surging away from us, and, to our surprise, the *Warspite* also seemed to have come to life again and disappeared to the south-east.

I remember, as the battle lines receded, how remarkable was the calm in contrast to the continuous noise of gunfire, the shriek of shells passing overhead, and the roar of steam escaping from our engine-room, which had deafened us for the last half-hour. Now that every engine in the ship was stopped and the two battle fleets were out of sight, the sudden stillness was very weird, even though we could still hear the gunfire of the battle closer than we quite liked. It seemed like having fallen off the top of a noisy, rumbling motor 'bus and being left lying in the road in a reactionary calm, too injured to move, but wondering all the time when another 'bus was coming along to finish us off.

A quarter of an hour after our engines stopped, at 7.15 p.m., the *Defender* came in sight, closed us, and asked if she could be of any assistance. She also was a lame duck, having been reduced to a speed of 10 knots by a 12-inch shell ricochetting into her foremost boiler-room, so, as she was of no further fighting use for that day, our Captain accepted her offer, and she proceeded to take us in tow.

There then started the long journey home of two lame-duck destroyers, which Rudyard Kipling has written of under the title, 'The Cripple and the Paralytic.' I am not able to compete with Rudyard Kipling as a descriptive author, and anyhow there is really not much to be said about it, except that it was a somewhat uncertain and distinctly uncomfortable voyage. The taking in tow was enlivened by a few large splashes arriving near us, I don't know where from, and by the apparent probability of the general action returning to our neighbourhood at any moment. The Captain directed *Defender* to shape course west by north as soon as we were in tow, and just as dusk was falling we left the scene of our adventures at rather less than 6 knots' speed, still hearing occasional

253

bursts of firing to the southward. I must mention here that, in spite of the heavy damage to the ship, our casualties were only three men killed, which was really an astonishingly light number considering all the damage we had received. Two of these three men we buried next morning, according to the custom of the sea.

About 9 p.m. we had a mild scare, the after look-outs reporting a large ship overhauling us, but, to our relief, it proved to be the *Warspite*, which signalled to us, 'Take station astern; speed 16 knots,' and then rapidly disappeared on the port bow. We were not 16 knotters.

A fresh sou'westerly breeze was now gaining force every hour and the barometer was falling fast. Three times the tow parted, and eventually we found that the only tow that was proof against the continual jerks of the two ships plunging in the short, steep sea, was a span composed almost entirely of chain cable. But after a time the Engineer Officer raised enough steam in the boilers, by using salt water, to enable the steering engine to be worked, and this was a great assistance in preventing the ship from yawing violently from side to side as she had been doing. Most of the hands at this time were employed in transferring oil fuel from one tank to another in any little pot or pan that could be collected—the only means left of getting the fuel to the boilers, as the pipe system was out of order, and only the for'ard tank had any oil left in it. We were still able to receive W/T signals, although we could not send any, and we intercepted one signal from *Champion* giving directions for a division of 13th Flotilla to search for *Onslow*, but neither ourselves nor *Defender* (which was able to signal) could tell *Champion* where we were, as we did not know ourselves, and, our sextants all being smashed up, we could not find out.

We continued towards Aberdeen during the 1st June, but that evening intercepted a signal reporting a division of enemy destroyers steering a course and speed which apparently would take them right past our position. However, we had all our guns still intact and plenty of ammunition left, and made arrangements with *Defender* that we would occupy the Huns if we met them whilst she tried to make good her escape. But our anxiety over this was unnecessary, as some days later we heard that the scare was a false one, the division of destroyers being a British one wrongly reported as Germans.

In spite of the wind continuing to freshen, the tow held throughout the night of 1st June without further trouble, and on Friday,

June 2nd, we got under the lee of Scotland, and at 1 p.m. that day were met by tugs off Aberdeen and taken safely into harbour. There we remained being repaired for the next two months.

The Narrative of H.M.S. *Defender*

A Destroyer attached to the Rosyth Battle Cruiser Force, which, after being hit and badly damaged by a German 12-inch Shell during the 'Windy Corner' Period, hauled out of the action, met H.M.S. *Onslow*, and towed her back to harbour

H.M.S. *Defender* had been detached from the 1st Flotilla, and was attached to the Harwich Flotilla for duty with the 3rd Battle Squadron at Sheerness, but was carrying out periodical docking and refit at Leith, near Rosyth, which was only completed at noon on the 30th May.

After completing with oil and ammunition at Rosyth on that day, instead of getting sailing orders to return to Harwich, we were very much astonished to be told to raise steam for full speed and join the *Fearless* and the six remaining boats of the 1st Flotilla for duty with the Rosyth force. We sailed with *Fearless* and the flotilla about 9.30 p.m. on 30th May, and were stationed as anti-submarine screen to the 5th Battle Squadron. We had no intimation on board of what we were doing or even of the composition of our own forces out. The first news we received of anything out of the ordinary was a semaphore message about 3.45 on Wednesday, 31st May, from our Captain (D.) in the *Fearless* stating that the enemy had been sighted. However, as we could not see any enemy it did not excite us very much, until we saw the 5th B.S. increase to full speed and hoist a signal to destroyers 'Get out of the way.' We then realised something was up, and very soon afterwards sounds of firing were heard ahead from the battle cruisers.

We formed, by signal from *Fearless*, on the starboard, *i.e.*, the disengaged quarter of the last ship in the 5th B.S. line, the *Malaya*, where we were held in readiness for any attack. Nothing of the enemy could be seen except the flashes of his guns, but in the distance we saw the loss of the *Indefatigable* and the *Queen Mary*.

It was next seen that the battle cruisers led by the *Lion* had turned 16 points, and were steaming to the North on an opposite course to the 5th B.S., and as they had no destroyers with them, Captain D. turned the 1st Flotilla to their course, and we received a signal to form an anti-submarine screen ahead of the battle cruisers. *Defender*'s billet should have been half a mile ahead of the *Lion*, but the *Lion* was doing a jolly good 25 and we had not got the legs of her. However, we had a good lead and were the leading boat of the flotilla, the whole lot of which were racing for the positions, but could not get ahead of the *Lion*. *Defender* got to about half a cable (100 yards) on the port beam of the *Lion*, with *Acheron* just outside. We could see that the *Lion* had received some damage to 'Q' turret, and men were working round it putting things right again, for at the time they were out of range of the enemy.

Defender getting a shell in her foremost boiler.

Our next move (at about 6.0 p.m.) was a signal from the *Lion*— 'Prepare to renew the action'—and almost at once we saw the leading ships of the battle fleet coming in from our port bow. *Lion* turned to starboard to close the range on the enemy, but the leading destroyers of the battle fleet which had not yet got the deployment signal, nearly collided with us, but we held on to our course and they went under our stern out of it.

As we closed the range, the Germans started to drop the shells about, and salvo after salvo, meant for the *Lion*, fell beautifully all round us. At about 6.30 p.m. we took a ricochet 12-inch shell, which came in sideways into the foremost boiler-room and lodged in the bottom of the ship under the boiler without exploding. It tore a hole about 8 feet wide in the side of the ship, cut steam pipes, and started an oil fuel fire. Naturally, our speed dropped at once, and it was obvious that we could do no good where we were, so we turned out and passed between the two fleets until it got a bit clearer. We then turned again and stopped to take stock of the damage. By great exertion and extreme bravery, the boiler-room party had shut the stop valves, and the oil fuel fire, which had raged furiously, was put out with sand. The collision mat was got over the hole in the side, and acted well in checking the entry of any more water. It was found that the main steam pipe had not been cut, and that we had one boiler left and the engines intact, and with one boiler a speed of 15 knots, or perhaps more in an emergency, could be guaranteed.

A destroyer, which afterwards proved to be the *Onslow*, was seen some distance off, stopped and apparently in a worse plight than ourselves, so we closed her and offered assistance. This was at once accepted, as she had a 5-degree list, no steam, and no steering gear left, and about three large holes in her. We started to get her in tow, but very nearly made a mess of it owing to some cruisers coming into view, which looked as if they were Germans going to put an end to both of us. We luckily got the *Onslow*'s wire in in time, and started to clear out of it—course, west for England.

About 9 p.m. that night—Wednesday, 31st—a large ship was seen coming up astern, but on being challenged she proved to be the *Warspite*, also homeward bound. We asked if we might keep with her for protection, but unfortunately she was too fast for us, and disappeared into the darkness without giving us our position. Both of us had wanted a position badly, as during the fighting no very accurate reckoning had been kept, and our compasses had no doubt been put out of adjustment.

In the middle watch the wind got up, and unfortunately we did not ease speed in time, so the tow parted. But the *Onslow* had got some steam by this time, and said she could struggle on by herself, but at daylight it was seen that it was hopeless and she was hardly making any way through the water so it was decided to take her in tow again, using *Defender*'s wire. Some little time was taken to prepare for this, and also it was necessary for *Defender* to steam stern to wind to adjust her collision mats, which had become displaced in the rising sea. But eventually the *Onslow* got in tow again, and we were just going well ahead when the towing slip of *Defender* snapped clean in two. This meant further delay and getting some cable from the fo'csle aft, but at last *Onslow* was in tow again with *Defender's* wire secured to a shackle of cable round the pedestal of *Defender's* after 4-inch gun.

The weather got steadily worse, which gave us cause for anxiety as we wanted to take a sight of the sun, being very uncertain of our position, and whenever we tried to get a sounding we lost every lead owing to the heavy rolling of the ship. Also our anxiety was increased by the very alarming reports received from time to time from the *Onslow*, from which it really seemed that we should fail to get her in, and that she would sink while still in tow. To slip our make-shift towing gear in a hurry would have been impossible for us, and the chance of saving her crew would have been very remote. The weather was anxiously studied, and, as the *Onslow* had no barometer left, she was asking us for frequent readings in the hopes that we had seen the worst of it and that a turn for the better was coming. But our speed went down and down until we could hardly keep steerage way.

Just before dark we intercepted a wireless signal from one of our destroyers which was apparently ahead of us, stating that she had sighted four German destroyers steaming back towards Heligoland, and from the course and position she gave of them, we estimated that they would pass close to us. A couple of lame birds would have been easy meat for them, so *Onslow* decided to alter up to the northward to give them as wide a berth as possible, but as we were so uncertain of our position, we were still left rather anxious that we might run across them. However, we didn't meet them.

Next morning, Friday, 2nd June, the weather got a little better, and about 10 o'clock, to our great relief, we made out Tod Head, and shaped course for Aberdeen which we reached about 1.0 p.m., when a couple of tugs picked up the *Onslow* from us just outside the breakwater, and took her into harbour.

As there was no reason for *Defender* to enter, we shaped course for the Firth of Forth, and made fast alongside the destroyer depot ship, *Woolwich*, that night, from where in due course we moved into dockyard and there refitted the ship and gave leave to the crew.

H.M.S. *Abdiel*, Minelayer

Extract from Lord Jellicoe's Book, 'The Grand Fleet, 1914-16.'[2]

'At 9.32 p.m. a signal was made to the Mine-laying Flotilla Leader, *Abdiel* . . . to proceed to lay a mine-field in a defined area some 15 miles from Vyl Lightship,[3] over which it was expected the High Seas Fleet would pass if the ships attempted to regain their ports during the night via the Horn Reef. The *Abdiel* carried out this operation unobserved in the same successful manner as numerous other similar operations have been undertaken by this most useful little vessel; from the evidence of one of our submarines, stationed near the Horn Reef, which reported on return to her base having heard several underwater explosions between 2.15 and 5.30 a.m. on June 1st, it was judged that some enemy ships had struck mines. . . .'

Letter from H.M.S. *Abdiel*

Abdiel had no active part as far as fighting was concerned in the Battle of Jutland, and one cannot make a good yarn out of it. Up to the time of meeting the Germans we were working with the 4th Light Cruiser Squadron, stationed 5 miles ahead of the Battle Fleet and steaming in line abreast, ships a mile apart. When the fleets sighted each other and the deployment signal was made, the 4th L.C.S. went off to their station ahead of the line; but *Abdiel* remained where she was until the fleet had nearly completed deploying, by which time the 'overs' from the Germans, strafing two of our four-funnelled cruisers about half a mile south-west of us and the three battle cruisers led by *Invincible* about half a mile to the south-east of us, came buzzing about and bursting round us. I,

---

2 Page 375. Cassell's Edition 1919. The extract is taken from this book instead of from the official despatch because the reference to *Abdiel*'s operation in the despatch, probably in order to preserve secrecy, was confined to this:- '*Abdiel*, ably commanded by Commander Berwick Curtis, carried out her duties with the success which has always characterised her work.'

3 Vyl Lightship:—Position 55° 24' N, 7° 45' E, just south of Horn Reef off the Jutland coast, and about 72 miles north of Heligoland.

therefore, legged it round the head of our battle line, which had finished deploying, and managed to get through four lines of destroyers taking up their position ahead of the fleet, and finally got to my battle position half a mile or so on the disengaged beam of the *Iron Duke*. Here we remained until dusk.

At about 9.30 p.m. I got orders to proceed to a position south of Vyl Lightship and lay a line of mines. We, therefore, went off at 32 knots, passing on our way several ships in the distance, and also a flotilla of sorts which were making a great deal of smoke, but as we were not making any smoke ourselves, we presumably were not seen. We reached our position about 1 a.m., and laid the mines, then returned to Rosyth for another load, passing south of the big North Sea mine area.

Abdiel was not hit during the battle, and did not have any action with any Hun destroyer or big ships, but we got a very good view of the whole show between 6 and 8 p.m. We had 80 ordinary mines and 10 Leon mines on board, all primed, so perhaps it is just as well that we weren't hit.

The ship did exactly what she was intended to do, justified her existence, and that's all there is to it.

Narrative of a Submarine

It is perhaps easy for there to be misconception in the mind of civilians or even in the minds of trained naval officers, as to what share submarines had in the Battle of Jutland—or might have had if this or that had happened. Actually their share was very slight, and possibly they had no effective share at all beyond the threat of their presence, which may have influenced squadron movements. Many people who appreciate the great influence which submarines had upon other phases of the naval war during 1914-1918 may be surprised at this, and may be led to think that by some error none of our submarines were near the scene of the action, and had no share in the battle because they were kept in harbour and not allowed within hundreds of miles of where the battle was being fought.

The following letter, however, which may be considered as a typical narrative for any one of the half-dozen or so British submarines that were out in the Heligoland Bight during 31st May, will show that some of our submarines were near to the Grand Fleet on 31st May, but simply did not share in the surface-ship action, because it was not within their powers to do so. They were patrolling submarines stationed in particular areas, and they could not at a moment's notice be transferred to another area, for in 1916 wireless communication with submarines was not yet highly developed. If enemy ships came into or near these areas the submarines had their opportunity, but they could not co-operate more directly than that in the surface-ship action. Later in the war specially designed submarines for working with the fleet were built and were employed in fleet duties, but at the time of Jutland they were not yet completed. It may, therefore, remove misconception if the following narrative is read as a typical account of the opportunities, or rather lack of opportunities, which our submarines actually had in the Battle of Jutland.

If it is disappointing to read that our submarines were given no opportunity of torpedoing the German Fleet, one can remember that the German submarines also had no direct share in the action, although at the time it was thought that one or two of them had attacked our battle cruisers, and that one had been rammed and sunk during the battle fleet action. Later evidence suggests that this was false.

Letter from a Submarine Officer
On Patrol off Horn's Reef Light Vessel in the Vicinity of the Scene of the Battle during 31st May and 1st June

I am afraid that one cannot say much about our experiences during the Battle of Jutland, as none of us knew anything about Jutland until our return to harbour four or five days after. During the 30th May my boat, and either two or three other submarines, received orders to proceed to sea that evening to take part in an operation in the vicinity of the Vyl Light Vessel on the night of 1st June. Late that afternoon, 30th May, a 'flap' started, and the remainder of the submarine flotilla were ordered to sea, but our party were ordered still to carry out the original operation, as it was not known what the flap was about.

We proceeded to sea about 8 p.m., and a very careful look-out was kept, and W/T masts kept up longer than usual, as I personally thought it might be another Yarmouth raid on. However, we had a very uneventful trip, and neither saw nor heard anything.

About 11.30 p.m. on 31st May we should have made the Horn's Reef Light Vessel, but failing to do so, I decided we must be to the westward, and altered course to the eastward, and later to the southward. Just as we picked up the light at midnight, the look-out, pointing vertically overhead, sang out, 'Do you think that is a Zeppelin, sir?' I looked up and saw a man put his head out of the car of a Zepp., so I blew the hooter and dived to the bottom. As we were settling down on the bottom after adjusting the trim of the boat, there was a very loud noise, as if an explosive sweep was being towed up astern of us. I noticed on glancing round from the diving gauge in the direction from which the noise was coming that one of the crew had his hand on the very spot where I had mentally decided it would strike us, and I wondered if we should hear the clang of the impact before the explosion. However, it passed away forward without contact.

Shortly afterwards the crew fell out from diving stations, and a little later loud explosions were heard at intervals, apparently all round us as if the vicinity was being depth-charged. However, I decided not to shift, as I considered it just as likely we might get one while shifting as by remaining where we were; also, it was of the utmost importance to save the battery, as the following night we had orders to be on the bottom out of the way of our own surface craft, and to come up at dawn and to keep diving patrol and attack any enemy vessels which might have been enticed out. It was, therefore, important that we should start operations with the battery as fully charged as possible, and at the same time not give our position away by being on the surface charging longer than was absolutely necessary during daylight. With this in view, and having ample time in which to reach our billet, we remained on the bottom until next morning when the tide being favourable we rose and proceeded to our billet diving at periscope depth. Shortly after rising a destroyer was sighted, but she turned away before we could identify her or get within range. During that day and the next we sighted several hostile submarines homeward bound, but only succeeded in getting within range of one, who turned away immediately after the torpedo was fired. We completed our time on patrol and returned to Harwich without further incident.

Sorry I can't tell you anything more, but that is all that there is, and, as I said previously, we knew nothing of Jutland until our return to harbour. When the torpedo lieutenant of the depot ship greeted us with the news and asked how many ships we had got, we thought that he was pulling our legs.

CHAPTER XIII

CRUISERS DURING THE BATTLE FLEET ACTION

Not very dissimilar to the work of those ships whose narratives we have grouped under the title of 'Side Shows' was the work of the cruisers attached to the battle and battle cruiser fleets during the time of the main action.

As everyone knows, a cruiser is too lightly armoured and too lightly gunned a ship to take its place in the battle line with the heavy ships. Cruisers are the modern equivalent of Nelson's frigates, the 'eyes of his fleet,' and their principal duty is, as it was then, to scout.

We have read of how *Galatea*, *Southampton*, and others carried out their scouting work in the first stages of the action, discovering and reporting first the German battle cruisers and then the German battle fleet. Also, how *Chester*, *Defence*, etc., carried out the same duty for Jellicoe's battle fleet, scouting ahead of the big ships as they closed to 'the sounds of gunfire,' and made touch with Beatty's already engaged battle cruisers and with the enemy. But during the battle fleet action there was naturally small opportunity or need for scouting work, and the rôle of the cruisers became a waiting one, with an occasional opportunity to engage one of the enemy's cruisers or the enemy's torpedo craft attacking our battle fleet, or to fire torpedoes at the enemy's heavy ships. The only real difference between the work of the cruisers and of the 'side shows' ships was that the cruisers retained their squadron organisation, and except for mishaps fought their various small actions three or four ships together.

The following narratives will give an idea of the experiences of the cruisers, very varied experiences which seem to have cropped up quickly and unexpectedly, at any odd moment from the time the first Grand Fleet battleship came into action at 6.17 pm., until the last big-gun shot was fired at about 9.0 p.m. As over thirty cruisers were present at the battle fleet action, it will be understood that all experiences cannot be described here, but the following are perhaps representative ones. Many cruisers which the deployment placed on the disengaged flank of the battle line found no opportunity for getting into action at all, so, to their disappointment, they have no fighting experiences to record.

One cannot help drawing particular attention to the exploit of *Falmouth* and *Yarmouth*, of the 3rd Light Cruiser Squadron, under the command of Rear-Admiral T. D. W. Napier, in attacking with their light 6-inch guns the five times larger and more powerful battle cruisers, *Derfflinger* and *Lutzow*, 'with impunity to themselves,' as Admiral Beatty's despatch stated, 'thereby demonstrating that the fighting efficiency of the enemy had been seriously impaired.'

WORK OF THE 2nd LIGHT CRUISER SQUADRON

Narrative from H.M.S. *Southampton*, Flagship of the 2nd L.C.S.

Continued from the description on page 80 of the original sighting of the High Seas Fleet at 4.38 p.m., and the escape of the 2nd L.C.S. to the northward under the heavy fire of the leading German battleships.

About 6.0 p.m. I saw a light cruiser squadron appear ahead, indicating the arrival of the Grand Fleet and the C.-in-C. It was perhaps just as well that they had come, for the 5th B.S. were receiving as much attention as they wanted, and we could not expect to go on being missed by salvoes of 11-inch indefinitely. Our luck had held already for over an hour. One could not help remembering that any hit at this period sufficient to cause a reduction of speed of a few

265

knots would have meant certain destruction to the ship, as the entire German fleet would in a very few minutes have been on top of the ship. It was at this period, 5.0 to 6.0 p.m., that the light favoured the Germans most as our ships were silhouetted against a bright western sky, whereas to the eastward there was still a dark, cloudy background, against which the German ships' outlines were not clearly visible.

I now observed that the leading German ships were hauling off to starboard, showing that they realised the vital change in the situation. Our line began to trend in the same direction. We actually sighted the leading battleships of the Grand Fleet at 6.17 p.m., but some minutes before this the leading enemy ships had disappeared in the mist, steering in a north-easterly direction.

The 5th B.S. had now joined up at the rear of the Grand Fleet, which had deployed into battle line to the eastward, and we remained astern of the 5th B.S., so that events in the van could not be seen from where we were, and at our end there was for the time being a distinct lull. But the action soon became general along the line, the two fleets gradually turning towards the south-eastwards, which brought us abreast of the rear of the German battle fleet. It was rather refreshing to watch the battleships firing after the somewhat too exciting events of the past hour.

The next incident for us occurred about 6.45 p.m., when we saw a three-funnelled German cruiser drifting helplessly between the lines, listing over and on fire. We did not know at the time that it was the *Wiesbaden*, which had already been unmercifully 'strafed' and was in a sinking condition. The 2nd L.C.S. went in to finish her off, but she was covered by the rear ships of the enemy's fleet, which cunningly waited until we were as close as about 12,000 yards from them and then let rip at us. We had already opened fire on the *Wiesbaden* with some effect, but we were not anticipating the salvoes of 11-inch which began to arrive around us. We had a remarkably warm ten minutes before we regained our position astern of the 5th B.S., but again not one of the squadron was hit, although the people on the bridge were drenched by the splash from an 'over,' and in the conning tower we were smothered by water from a shell which pitched a short distance ahead of the ship. Further aft, I am told, shells were falling on both sides with rather alarming persistence.[1]

At about 7.30 p.m. the enemy C.-in-C. apparently decided that he had had enough of the action, whereat a few destroyers crept out from their line, and in five minutes obliterated it entirely by a smoke screen, the rear ships at the same time turning away 8 points together. This manouvre was extremely well executed, and, as we were unused to smoke screens in those days, all that we knew was that the enemy had disappeared in a south-westerly direction.

One small incident occurred at this time which was cheering to us who had seen little except our own fleet's casualties. A solitary German destroyer appeared at a range of about 9,000 yards, damaged, and left stranded on the wrong side of his smoke screen. He was evidently partially disabled, but we gave him a few salvoes, and had the satisfaction of hitting him in the engine-room. A few minutes later some of our destroyers arrived to add the final touch, and he vanished.

A period of calm succeeded this as it gradually grew dark, broken only at about 8.30 p.m. by a rather feeble attack by a few German destroyers on the 5th B.S. This we easily drove off at a long range and again scored several hits on one destroyer.

At dusk the Grand Fleet took up their night cruising stations, the 5th B.S. being stationed astern of the other battle squadrons, and we of the 2nd L.C.S. astern of them. . . .

---

1 The following is an extract from the narrative of an officer of H.M.S. *Nottingham* describing this incident:— 'After leaving "Windy Corner" we again followed the 5th B.S., which were now bringing up the rear of the battle line, until our Commodore in *Southampton* sighted what in the mist appeared to be a disabled German battleship. Doubtless he thought that a torpedo would help her in her disabilities. We turned to starboard towards this ship, opening fire on her with our 6-inch guns as we closed in towards torpedo range, when suddenly from out of the mist close behind her came an absolute rain of shells. We could not tell what it was that we had run into here, but apparently it must have been the tail of the German battle line now given an opportunity for a last flick before they turned away and made off to the Southward.

There was nothing for us to do but retire back towards our fleet. As the *Southampton* turned a salvo of big shells landed all around her, and the *Dublin* turning in her wake was missed only by inches. We turned before our time inside the wake of *Dublin* and just missed the salvo which, falling exactly at the other's turning-point, would have obliterated us. We then had another enjoyable ten minutes dodging salvoes from German battleships as we slowly regained the rear of our battle-line.'

THE 4TH LIGHT CRUISER SQUADRON

Narrative from H.M.S. *Calliope*, Flagship of the 4th L.C.S.

The 4th Light Cruiser Squadron accompanied the battle fleet from Scapa to the scene of operations. Our cruising position before deployment was 4 miles ahead of the battle squadrons, and subsequently, when the battle fleet deployed to port, we formed part of a large number of light cruisers and torpedo craft stationed on the starboard (engaged) bow of the leading battle squadron to repel hostile torpedo attacks, or attack in our turn if ordered.

During deployment, being slightly nearer the enemy than were the battle fleet, we had a good view of two of the *Defence* class (we never discovered which two), part of Sir Robert Arbuthnot's Squadron, heavily engaged with an enemy quite invisible to us. Very soon after this, we passed the German light cruiser, *Wiesbaden*, disabled and in flames. The whole battle fleet engaged her till she finally sank, though when we passed her she had still one gun in action.

The deployment of the battle fleet was a wonderful sight, and although we were too far away to watch the detailed movements of each squadron, we had a good view of it. From our distance the whole fleet seemed to be mixed up for a few minutes in apparently inextricable confusion, and then quite suddenly to be formed in one long, regular line, on the starboard bow of which we took station, and whose rear end we could not see in the mist. Just after deployment we saw the destroyer *Acasta* in a very bad way, down by the head, on fire, and not under control, coming from the direction of the firing; she passed astern of us and ahead of the approaching battleships. Shortly afterwards, about 6.15 as far as I remember, we sighted the squadron of battle cruisers, under Rear-Admiral Horace Hood, which had come from Scapa with the battle fleet. As they were stationed well ahead of the battleships they got into action first, and had joined the Rosyth battle cruiser force which were heavily engaged with an enemy quite invisible to us. But we were not wholly unconcerned in the affair, as we were getting some of the 'overs' rather too close to be pleasant, being about a mile on the battle cruisers' disengaged beam. As we watched, we saw an enormous flash burst out from the *Invincible*, followed by a large volume of grey smoke, which eddied up in the form of a cumulus cloud, and when it disappeared her two halves were distinctly visible, standing upright in the water, and probably resting on the bottom.

Subsequently we had an excellent view of the actual battle fleet action from our station on the leading battle squadron's engaged bow, and specially noticed one of the German *Kaiser* class battleships with her bridge and forepart enveloped in brilliant red flames. Our squadron were detailed during this interval to assist in beating off the German destroyers' determined torpedo attack, and it was then that we opened fire for the first time. This attack was probably the finest spectacular display that we saw in the whole action; the destroyers were at times completely hidden by the splashes caused by the secondary armaments of the battle cruisers and battleships, as well as those of our own guns, and twice we saw one sink. The first seemed to disappear suddenly; the second stopped and sank slowly by the head, pouring out steam. These were the only two that we had time or oportunity to notice, but there must have been many others.

We rejoined the battle fleet after the attack was beaten off, and were in our station during the big circling movement made by our fleet. Much later, about 8.15 p.m., while we were on a southerly course, we proceeded with the *Constance* to attack some destroyers which appeared on our beam at extreme visibility (about 10,000 yards), but as quickly vanished again. We chased them, and shortly sighted the German battle fleet proceeding also on a southerly course. We turned on to a course parallel to them after closing to about 8,500 yards, to fire a torpedo. We were not fired at previous to our turning, possibly because they could not make us out as friend or enemy, but they proceeded to rectify their error as soon as we turned, and got our range quickly, straddling us before we got our submerged torpedo tube flooded.

Having fired our torpedo, we turned and proceeded full speed, zigzagging 2 points each way on an easterly course to join our own ships, which were by this time out of sight.

We were in sight of the German battleships for perhaps 10 minutes, and under fire during this time from two *Kaiser* class battleships and one *Heligoland*, whose shooting was very accurate, and only our high speed and zigzagging saved us from annihilation. As it was, we seemed to be in the middle of splashes, and the noise of the bursting shell and flying fragments was absolutely deafening.

We were hit five times in all, three of which did serious damage to personnel. One shell, bursting against the breech of the port after 4-inch gun, smashed the fittings and gun shield and killed practically all the gun's crew, the notable exception being the sight-setter—a corporal of marines—who had the gun between him and the burst and only suffered a slight scalp wound.

The second hit on us burst near No. 3 4-inch gun under the bridge, disabled the gun, killing and wounding some of the crew, and fragments of this shell penetrated the deck of the lower bridge and wounded a signalman and a bugler.

The third shell penetrated the upper deck, and burst in the boys' mess deck, almost in the middle of the after dressing station, killing some and wounding many others, including the staff surgeon.

For the last five minutes that we were under fire we were in sight of our own ships, although the two battle fleets were invisible to each other, and we were told afterwards that at times we were hidden in spray from the splashes. Altogether, we had 10 killed and 23 wounded, some seriously. We were ordered to take station on the port beam of the battle fleet for the night, and in the morning resumed our cruising station ahead during the search for disabled enemy ships.

On reaching Scapa afterwards, we were ordered in first, instead of waiting for the battle fleet to enter, to land our wounded. Our dead we buried at sea the morning after the action, the Commodore leaving the bridge for a few minutes to read the burial service, the one time he was ever known to leave the bridge at sea.

H.M.S. *Caroline* (4th L.C.S.)

A rough account of experiences in H.M.S. *Caroline* at Jutland, May 31st. (As written out immediately on return from action.)

3.30 p.m. Exercised action and prepared for a scrap.

About 5.40 p.m. we sighted smoke on the starboard bow, and shortly afterwards heard sounds of firing in that direction; then the 2nd Light Cruiser Squadron and 1st Light Cruiser Squadron, with battle cruisers behind, came across our bows heavily engaged. We turned and followed, and being on the disengaged side of battle cruisers got all the German 'overs' among us, three or four shots falling just short and just over, and two destroyers astern of us got hit. We were all badly bunched, light cruisers and destroyers together, and it took some time to deploy and get clear, so it was lucky that more damage was not done to us. A little later the *Invincible* blew up ahead of us, and after this we deployed out and were on the engaged side of the battle fleet, but action near us broke off, although heavy firing could be heard and seen in the rear.

At this time one enemy cruiser appeared to be sinking by the stern, and after a few minutes she vanished completely. We also passed a German destroyer floating upside down. Shortly afterwards the fleets drew together again, and our battle fleet opened a heavy fire, *Iron Duke*'s squadron firing right over us. We next went ahead and moved out towards the enemy, to stop a torpedo attack which they were launching, and opened fire on a German destroyer. We had a very exciting few minutes dodging a torpedo, which came straight for us running on the surface, and then appeared to follow us round, missing our stern by inches. Another torpedo passed just ahead of

Signalmen using ten-inch arc-lamp

us. About this time we rammed something, and as a submarine had been seen just previously right ahead of us, we hoped we had got her. The destroyer we were firing on disappeared; several people say she went down, but it is hard to judge in the mist, although a lot of our shots appeared to be falling all round her.

After this there was a lull, and we started edging over towards the enemy again until we made out a line of ships in the mist—we were stationed just ahead of *King George V.*, leading the van battle squadron. They challenged us by flash-light, but made a wrong challenge, and when we saw this, and also were able to make out their cranes, which only Germans carry, we reported them as enemy, and at a range of about 5,200 yards fired both our torpedoes.

271

Royalist, astern of us, also fired one torpedo. We then turned away at full speed, and made smoke to cover ourselves. The ships we fired at were battleships of the *Deutschland* class, we thought, and immediately we turned they opened fire on us, firing star shells once or twice. They straddled us at once and for about the next eight minutes with 11-inch shell, but we were not hit although we had some close shaves, one shell passing between the wireless and upper deck, and spray from the splashes fell on the upper deck several times. A torpedo passed close to us at this time, and we twice bumped into something below surface.

After this we took up station for the night, rejoining our flagship, *Calliope*, which had taken her division away previously to make a torpedo attack separate from us. We heard heavy firing astern of us about 10 p.m., and again about midnight, but we saw nothing more except for a large flare-up—a sheet of flame some way off. We were, of course, at action stations all the night and morning, sleeping at our stations.

At daylight there were no signs of the enemy, and though search was made all the morning they could not be found, and they must have got back to their ports. At 4.30 p.m. on June 1st we packed up from action stations and returned to base.

The conditions during the action were considered trying, as when we were first engaged and under fire we were too far off to be able to retaliate, and also were masked by other ships. Except for firing at a destroyer and for making one torpedo attack, we did not get an opportunity of taking much hostile action. The behaviour of the ship's company was excellent; they were very cool, and cheered each time a hit was observed on the enemy.

From observations on board, it appeared that just after the *Invincible* blew up, an enemy cruiser was heavily hit, and was sinking by the stern; otherwise, except for seeing a destroyer bottom up, and noticing another destroyer we engaged getting it fairly hot, and noticing some hits on enemy's battleships, not much could be seen of results.

The smoke screen which we made with funnel smoke after our torpedo attack seemed very effective. But we were very lucky on this occasion, as the enemy got the range of *Royalist* and ourselves with their first salvo, and straddled us well, yet we were not hit.

Some special points that were noticed were that our guns seemed to be hitting, while German shells were all falling short; the distinctive black smoke when enemy shells exploded; the small splash the enemy shells made compared to ours; and that the noise of the enemy shell bursting over the ship sounded exactly like a heavy gun firing.

The 3rd Light Cruiser Squadron

Extract from Vice-Admiral Commanding Battle Cruiser Force's report, quoted in Commander-in-Chief's despatch (para. 7):—

'From the report of Rear-Admiral T. D. W. Napier, M.V.O., the 3rd Light Cruiser Squadron, which had maintained its station on our bow well ahead of the enemy, at 6.25 p.m. attacked with the torpedo. *Falmouth* and *Yarmouth* both fired torpedoes at the leading enemy battle cruiser, and it is believed that one torpedo hit, as a heavy underwater explosion was observed. The 3rd Light Cruiser Squadron then gallantly attacked the heavy ships with gunfire, with impunity to themselves, thereby demonstrating that the fighting efficiency of the enemy had been seriously impaired. Rear-Admiral Napier deserves great credit for his determined and effective attack. *Indomitable* reports that about this time one of the *Derfflinger* class fell out of the enemy's line.'[2]

Narrative from H.M.S. *Falmouth*, Flagship of the 3rd L.C.S.

From 5.0 to 6.0 p.m. our battle cruisers and the 5th B.S. were being engaged by the greater part of the German fleet, and I must admit that I was extremely glad when we saw the leading ships of our battle fleet screen appear over the horizon. Once sighted, the approach

---

2 Comparative strength of *Falmouth* class and *Derfflinger* class:—

	Type	Size	Broadside Guns	Armour	Speed	Crew
Falmouth or *Yarmouth*	Light Cruiser	5,250 tons	Five 6"	About 4" armour	25 knots	400 men
Derfflinger or *Lutzow*	Battle Cruiser	26,000 tons	Eight 12"	12" armour	28 knots	1125 men
			Twelve 5.9"			

of the battle fleet seemed rapid. The 4th Light Cruiser Squadron ahead of the battle ships raced through our line, and turned up on to our course, and the 1st Cruiser Squadron, *Defence*, etc., went right through and on towards the enemy, where they were lost. There was handling of ships at full speed in that ten minutes of crossing the battle fleet's front such as had never been dreamt of by seamen before, and that no ship was lost by collision speaks volumes for the skill of commanding officers. The 3rd L.C.S. became divided during this time, *Yarmouth* only being left with *Falmouth*, but *Canterbury* joined us, and *Birkenhead* and *Gloucester* were near to us abreast the 3rd Battle Cruiser Squadron (*Invincible*, etc.). *Falmouth* was now leading the entire line.

Almost immediately after clearing the head of our battle fleet, we were ordered to attack detached enemy light cruisers, but for the moment we could not see any. However, we closed in to starboard towards the enemy, and at seven minutes past six opened fire on a light cruiser which had already been severely damaged by the 3rd B.C.S. This German light cruiser certainly put up a very plucky fight, for she was obviously sinking, one funnel was knocked away, and probably all her guns were out of action except her forecastle gun, which was steadily firing. We fired on her till she dropped out of range astern. Then two other light cruisers appeared on our starboard bow, firing at our Scapa destroyers coming down from ahead, and we opened fire on them, setting one on fire, again probably only a smoke box, but they promptly retired.

The 3rd B.C.S. had now—it was about 6.15—turned up on our port quarter ahead of Admiral Beatty's four battle cruisers, and were engaging *Derfflinger* and *Lutzow*. *Derfflinger* was being splendidly hit, and there was a big explosion forward. She dropped astern, and it looked as though one of the foremost turrets was destroyed. *Lutzow* then led their line, and at a range of between 5,000 and 6,000 yards *Falmouth* opened fire on her, apparently with some success, and also fired a torpedo. *Lutzow* was hit amidships by a torpedo, which may possibly have been from *Falmouth*, though it may have been fired by the gallant *Shark* before she sank.

After being fired on by *Falmouth* for several minutes, *Lutzow* directed her secondary battery on to us, and after two or three salvoes gained a hit on *Falmouth*'s fore-mast, which, though it only scored the mast and did not explode, cut the voice pipes from the fore-top, and a ricochet came in aft. As the position had now become unhealthy for a small ship, *Falmouth* drew off. Just about this time *Invincible* blew up on our port quarter. All the time that *Falmouth* had been in action with *Lutzow*, the head of our battle line had been working round towards the German fleet, their course altering from N.E. to east, on to S. 80° E., S.E. by S., south at 7 o'clock, then south-west, and at 8 o'clock west.

At 8 p.m. we were ordered to 'sweep to the westward and locate head of enemy line before dark.' At 8.8 we sighted, and until 8.38 engaged four light cruisers, but then some enemy battle cruisers arrived in support of the light cruisers, and we retired. This was our last action of the day. It is perhaps worthy of note that the enemy were firing shrapnel during this evening action.

At 9.15 we went to night stations, which gave an opportunity for a few of the less important members to get some sort of rest. Well shall I remember retiring on the deck down below dead weary, and half-awake, half-asleep, with a slow realisation forming of what had been taking place. I was extremely glad to get any sort of sleep, for the majority did not have the luck to get any.

We went to day action stations again just after 2 a.m., and at dawn gained touch with other light cruisers. One or two torpedo tracks were reported by look-out men, but whether real or imaginary we could not tell. About 3.15 a Zeppelin appeared, and was engaged with gunfire at about 14,000 yards—in those days we did not carry an aeroplane.

For the rest, a gradual gaining touch with the whole fleet, a fruit-less sweep for the enemy, and finally the return to base. After coal-ing and ammunitioning, the 3rd L.C.S. were sent out again for three days to search the battle area for traces of the abandoned *Warrior*, which was reported to be still floating water-logged and derelict. We swept to and fro for three days, sighting more than one torpedo, and here and there pathetic floating relics of what once had been a ship; otherwise nothing.

Narrative of H.M.S. *Yarmouth*, of the 3rd L.C.S.

In H.M.S. *Yarmouth* we had been close spectators of the loss of H.M.S. *Defence* at about 6.15 p.m., but very shortly afterwards we were able, in a slight measure, to revenge her loss.

The light cruiser which she and the other ships of the 1st C.S. had been engaging was left badly damaged, and *Falmouth* and *Yarmouth* now opened fire upon her to finish her off. At the same time, however, two German battle cruisers were observed approaching from the southward getting uncomfortably close, but just when they had opened fire upon us with a salvo of heavy stuff, which fell only just short, *Invincible*, *Inflexible*, and *Indomitable* arrived on the scene from the northward and engaged the enemy's attention. The German battle cruisers and our 3rd B.C.S. turned on to a parallel course, Admiral Hood, who led the squadron in the *Invincible*, being on our port quarter about 2,000 yards away, with the enemy only about 6,000 to 7,000 yards from us on our starboard bow. Also, on our starboard bow was a cluster of five or six British destroyers carrying out a torpedo attack on the German battle cruisers, which were heavily firing on our destroyers with their secondary armament of 5.9-inch guns. We saw two of our T.B.D.'s put out of action and drop astern (?*Shark* and *Acasta*).

Then about three German light cruisers appeared in sight ahead of the German battle cruisers, and these we engaged at a range of 8,000 to 11,000 yards. At about 6.20 *Invincible* blew up.[3] Two officers and a few men were picked up by a destroyer, though no one who witnessed the explosion would have believed that anyone could have lived through it.

Meanwhile, we were under fire from the three enemy light cruisers, and also occasional 5.9 salvoes from the German battle cruisers were fired at us, besides a few 12-inch 'shorts' meant for *Invincible*, which came close to our stern.

Hoping to close the enemy light cruisers, we drew ahead of *Inflexible* and *Indomitable*, but our opponents turned away to starboard, and we shifted our fire on to the leading German battle cruiser. She was a topping target, and it was very pleasant to see salvo after salvo of our 6-inch hitting her, which must have considerably worried their bridge and personnel on the upper deck, and perhaps accounted for the poor reply which they made to our fire with their 5.9 guns.

We continued east-south-easterly till 6.45 p.m., then south-easterly till 7.0 p.m., when the speed of the fleet was reduced to 15 knots

---

3 Actual time was 6.33.

by general signal. At 7.5 p.m. *Birkenhead* and *Gloucester* rejoined us, and at the same time the 1st L.C.S. were coming up astern; course was altered to south-west. At 7.45 p.m. we were ordered to sweep to the westward to try to locate the head of the enemy's line, and were in the process of spreading south, at one mile intervals from *Falmouth*, when at 8.20 p.m. five enemy light cruisers were observed bearing north-north-west, steering about south-west. They were followed by two battle cruisers—presumably the two we lost sight of after 6.30—which were being engaged by our battle cruisers. We at once formed single line and engaged the light cruisers at about 7,000 yards' range. Their salvoes were all short, and ours may have been as bad, for it was impossible to spot now under the almost hopeless light conditions. The enemy drew off, and we never saw them again.

Throughout the action I personally was so busy conning the ship from the upper bridge and endeavouring to keep in my head an idea of the relative positions of squadrons, that I did not appreciate until afterwards the effect that the action had upon other officers and men. Our men were wildly excited at seeing the light cruiser, *Pillau* (? *Wiesbaden*), so hopelessly knocked out by our fire and the fire of Arbuthnot's squadron, and ammunition was sent up the hoists with so much enthusiasm and energy as to accumulate a dangerous amount at the top. As it happened, we were merely splashed by salvoes close to us, and heard much hissing of splinters over our head but were never hit, and so perhaps cannot talk much about action experience, although we had a good many close shaves. The men in the engine-room and stokeholds all thought that we had been hit several times, as the heavy shells falling short felt to them like a bump on the ship.

During the night everyone was pretty weary, and there was not much opportunity for rest. I had half-an-hour's rather doubtful sleep on the chart-house table, while the Captain slept on the settee.

At daylight, however, we were all keen enough, and it was awful how the sense of disappointment came over us as the day passed on and we finally altered course for home, feeling that, although we had badly damaged and driven the enemy into his ports, we still had not met him full and square with our main fleet.

The excitement on board to learn what the Grand Fleet had actually done was intense, for from 6 p.m. onwards we had heard very heavy and more or less continuous firing, and we felt certain that heavy damage must have been inflicted, both upon the enemy and upon our own fleet. We all felt a wonderful confidence that our heavier guns and the good shooting of our battle fleet would have given us the advantage.

In the forenoon we sighted the Grand Fleet, apparently undiminished and undamaged, and could hardly credit it. Apparently only the *Warspite* and *Marlborough*, of all the Dreadnought battle fleet, had fallen out.

We feared, according to intercepted signals, that *Queen Mary* and *Indefatigable* had sunk, though, as we did not actually see them blow up ourselves, we did not learn this for certain until we arrived in harbour. Whilst coaling, some of us were putting our heads together trying to make something connected out of what seemed a most complicated puzzle, when we were ordered to sea again to search for *Warrior*, and so, already just about worn out with fatigue, we put to sea again for another three days.

Impressions of the Jutland Battle, 31st May, 1916

Seen from the Compass Platform of H.M.S. *Cochrane*, 2nd Cruiser Squadron

This narrative shows how the ships at the van, although unusually close to the enemy according to contemporary standards, had the greatest difficulty in getting into action with any German heavy ships.

When we left Scapa on the afternoon of the 30th May, no one thought that we were in for anything more than the usual North Sea sweep. As a matter of routine, we went to action stations next forenoon, but it was not till we were ordered to raise steam for full speed that we began to think that there might possibly be something doing. *Cochrane* was the left-hand ship of the cruiser screen which was spread across the head of the battle fleet, which was in cruising formation of six columns. The four ships of our squadron (2nd C.S.) were in line abreast, about three miles apart, and the same distance ahead of the fleet, joining with the 1st Cruiser Squadron (*Defence, Warrior, Black Prince*, and *Duke of Edinburgh*), which formed the westerly half of the cruiser screen.

By the various signals which were intercepted during the afternoon we began to expect that we might at last really see something of the Hun, and calculated that they ought to be sighted about tea-time. I remember thinking that three miles seemed a very long distance to be away from our supports in the existing weather conditions, for the visibility was very low, and one could not help wondering if it was intended to keep us spread ahead of the fleet until enemy ships were actually sighted. However, about 5 o'clock heavy gun firing could be distinctly heard ahead, and at the same time we were ordered to form line ahead on our flagship, the *Minotaur*. *Cochrane* became No. 2 in the line, next astern of the *Minotaur*; then came the *Shannon*, then the *Hampshire*.

By the time we had all formed up we were about two miles on the port bow of the head of the battleship line. The first thing we actually saw appertaining to the Hun was an empty brass cartridge case, which we passed floating vertically, and shortly afterwards we sighted some of our battle cruisers, but lost sight of them again soon after. We then began seeing flashes on the starboard bow, but before we could make out who was who, we saw a big explosion, which at the time we all thought must have been a German ship going up, but, from what we know now, it was probably the *Invincible*. The under-water shock from this explosion was most noticeable; we all remarked on it on the bridge, and it was felt very distinctly by the people stationed below.

About 7 o'clock we again sighted our own battle cruisers, and could also make out the hulls of some of the enemy, but they were too indistinct for us to determine what ships they were. We had a very good view of what the German's shooting was like at that time, and the general impression was that they were not doing very well. A lot of shots seemed to be more than a thousand yards short, and others as much as that over. We thought we saw a hit or two on our ships occasionally, but it was very difficult to be sure.

All this time we were steering a course to follow the battle cruisers, which made us gradually close the leading battleship of our line, the *King George V*. Between our squadron of four cruisers and the leading battleship were two flotillas of destroyers with their flotilla cruisers, I should think nearly forty ships in all, and these unfortunates were being slowly squeezed in between us and the battle fleet, until eventually it began to look as if some of the destroyers were bound to bump each other. But the situation was saved by the battle fleet reducing speed to 15 knots, and we shot ahead at 21.

279

Our squadron then took up a position about midway between the battle fleet and the battle cruisers, and we were expecting to come under fire at any moment. The range closed to the neighbourhood of 10,000 yards, which was well within range of our guns, only unfortunately the gun-layers could not see the target from the turrets, although from the bridge and spotting-top it was moderately plain. The ship was not then fitted with director firing, though an *extempore* laying director had been fitted out on board. But to use this meant that, although the elevation and firing could be controlled from aloft, the gun-layers in the turrets had to be able to see the target sufficiently to keep on for training. For some reason or other, probably because they were too busy with our battle cruisers, the Germans did not fire at us. We all noticed that, although all our battle fleet were firing hard, no German shots could be seen falling anywhere near them. I suppose this was probably when our ships were driving off a destroyer attack, and were not within sight of the enemy battle fleet, though it rather puzzled some of us at the time.

After this we gradually drew ahead of the battle fleet, until we lost sight of them, and eventually got to a position about a mile on the port (disengaged) quarter of our battle cruisers; but then they altered course away, and we had to conform to their movements, and we never got any opportunity to fire before darkness came on. It was very disappointing that we never actually opened fire, entirely due to the low visibility, and after it was all over we all wished we had attempted to try what could be done by training the guns to a fixed bearing, and opening fire by the home-made director as the bearing swing on; but perhaps it was just as well that we did not, as it would hardly have been much use, and might only have drawn the Huns' attention to us. After all, it is not usually considered advisable for an armoured cruiser to get within 10,000 yards range of an enemy battleship.

Part III

Night Action

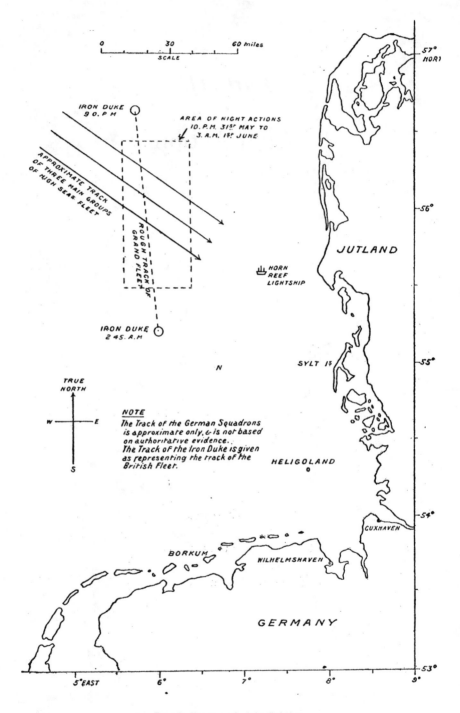

Rough diagram of night fighting.

PART III

NIGHT ACTION

During the night of 31st May to 1st June, 1916, there were few men in the British Fleet—or probably in the German fleet either—who had a clear conception of what was happening around them. It was almost impossible that they should do so in the darkness and jumble of the night fighting. But now, four years after the event, it is not very difficult to analyse the several engagements and obtain a clear idea of the general course of the fighting.

At the close of the day action on the 31st May the German fleet was some 15 to 20 miles to the westward of the British fleet—that is, the British fleet was *between the German fleet and Germany*. It was understood that there were two paths by which the German fleet could return to their bases; one, by making the Horn Reef Light Vessel and then proceeding down a swept channel close to the coast of Schleswig-Holstein to Cuxhaven; the other, by proceeding direct towards Heligoland.

At 9 p.m., the British battle fleet disposed in four divisions, with the battle cruiser fleet and crusier squadrons stationed on the flank of the battle squadrons, shaped course south. In rear of the battle squdrons were stationed the destroyer flotillas of the fleet, and also one light cruiser squadron, the 2nd L.C.S. (Note that they were in rear of the battle squadrons.)

The German fleet chose the Horn Reef route for their passage home, and steered roughly on a south-easterly course to make the Horn Reef Light Vessel.[1] They were apparently in

1 The *Abdiel*, mine-layer, at 9.32 p.m., was ordered to lay a minefield near to the Horn Reef Light Vessel. See *Abdiel*'s narrative on page 259.

three separate columns, Dreadnought battleships in one, pre-Dreadnought in another, and battle cruisers in a third, the three columns some distance apart, each accompanied by their own light forces.[2] On this south-easterly course the German squadron ran into the British destroyer flotilla astern of the battle fleet, and from soon after 9 p.m. on 31st May until 2 a.m. the following morning, these German squadrons fought intermittently with British destroyers and light cruisers as they crossed their path. In this simple fact of the Germans on their homeward course crossing the British light forces steering to the southward in rear of the British battle fleet, lies nearly all the explanation of the 'strategy' of the night fighting at Jutland that the ordinary person requires to know.

Our destroyer flotillas were not detached to seek out the German fleet, but were in such a geographical postion that the German fleet *en route* for Horn Reef came into contact with them. The German fleet did not meet any of our big ships, but the night fighting lay wholly between our light craft and the three divisions of the German fleet astern, to the northward, of our battle fleet. Our big ships did not come into action at all, although they constantly saw astern of them the gun-flashes, searchlights, and explosions of the destroyer flotillas in action.

The positions of the several fights are difficult to place exactly without first very carefully analysing all possible records, but, as one fight had little influence on another, this is of small importance to us. It is really sufficient to know that there were three main night actions. The action of the 2nd Light Cruiser Squadron at about 10.20 p.m.; the actions of *Tipperary*'s flotilla from about 11.30 p.m. onwards; and the attack on a German battle squadron by the 12th Destroyer Flotilla at daybreak on June 1st.

Under a fourth heading, 'Other Incidents of the Night,' to include two small actions by H.M.S. *Castor*, in company with the 11th Flotilla, at 10 p.m. and at 12.15 a.m., and an action by the 13th Flotilla in which H.M.S. *Turbulent* was lost, can

2 Information on this point is not authoritative, but it is understood from second-hand sources that this was the disposition of the German Fleet.

really be grouped all the remaining actions of the night. There were no other squadron actions.

But more interesting for the reader to appreciate than the cause of the fighting is the conditions of that fighting, the atmosphere of it as experienced by the British flotillas and light cruisers. The uncertainty, the continuous strain of looking-out, the anxiety to know if a ship is friend or foe, the responsibility of opening fire, the completely blinding effect of light in one's eyes after long darkness; all these must be experienced to be fully appreciated, though they can be guessed at by anyone who pictures the inevitable difficulties and the strain of fighting in pitch darkness. The night fighting that did take place, although it resulted almost entirely from the accidental passage of the German fleet through the rear of the British fleet, and although it had no governing influence on the result of the battle, probably comprises the most intensive fighting, and makes the most interesting telling of all that occurred at Jutland. The following narratives tell of the fighting, of the atmosphere of it, and the adventures of those who fought.

CHAPTER XIV

LIGHT CRUISER ACTION ABOUT 10.20 P.M.

Narrative of the Navigating Officer of H.M.S. *Nottingham*

Which was 3rd Ship in the 2nd Light Cruiser Squadron Line
during the Night Action at about 10.20 p.m.

(*Continued from page 77*)

At 9.15, whilst it was still just twilight, we had a short action with German destroyers, of which the *Southampton* later claimed to have sunk one; but they disappeared in the mist and failing light before we could come to decisive range. Firing was still going on ahead of us, but no enemy ships were in sight, and for a while we had time to think of food and such things. Personally, I had been on the bridge since 2 p.m. with no extra clothing on, and I don't think that I had every felt so cold before, but one cannot send people down to one's cabin to fetch overcoats in the middle of the Battle of Jutland. It was a relief now to get into a greatcoat and to sit down on the bridge for a few minutes and munch a sandwich.

About 9.50, when we were steaming south, heavy firing and gun-flashes could be heard and seen on the starboard bow, which we learnt afterwards was the German battle cruisers fighting our destroyers which they met in the darkness, but we did not know what it was at the time.

All was quiet for a time, and we kept undisturbed on our course until someone on the bridge sighted a ship on our starboard beam, which was obviously a three-funnel German cruiser of the distinctive *Stettin* class. She was not more than 2 miles away, silhouetted

286

against the evening sky, and so was lit up to some extent while we remained in darkness, but the gun-layers had some difficulty in picking her up from the level of the deck, although from the bridge we could see her clearly. It was not until she made a challenge of coloured lights at us that our first gun was got off, but it acted as a very good reply to her challenge and scored a direct hit.

There then followed some ten minutes of such incessant firing, blinding flashes of guns, waving of searchlights, and constant alterations of course, that I had my work cut out to keep the ship in station astern of *Southampton* and *Dublin*, and I am afraid I cannot really do justice to any description of what happened, but it was a remarkable experience. As we fired our first gun, fully a dozen searchlights were switched on to our line from the ship we had first sighted and from others with her, and immediately some sixty odd guns opened fire. Both ourselves and the enemy—we assumed afterwards that there were five enemy light cruisers—were firing with remarkable rapidity, and the noise became terrific, whilst every time that our foc'sle gun fired we on the bridge were almost blinded by its flash.

The range can have been little over 2,000 yards, which is almost point-blank range for 6-inch guns, and moreover, it was obvious that we and the enemy were on greatly converging courses, so I asked the Captain if we should alter away a little, and he told me to do so.

After two minutes of action the *Southampton* was badly on fire abreast her funnels, which lit the whole ship up, making her a most excellent target for the enemy. The *Dublin*, our next ahead, altered 8 points away almost at once, and we did not see her again, and the *Birmingham*, astern of us, also turned away. We thought that the *Southampton* with so many searchlights on her and badly on fire must in a minute be sunk, as she was so conspicuous a target. Coming third in the line, we did not receive the same attention from the enemy as did the *Southampton* and *Dublin*, and although searchlight were switched on to us and shells whistled all round, were were not hit. I think that fact that we were burning no searchlights saved us.

Then suddenly, almost as suddenly as the action had commenced, and quite inexplicably, the Germans switched off all their searchlights and vanished into the night, and the action was over. Why they did so, when *Southampton* was being so heavily hit, we could not understand, but we have always hoped that it was because we hit them well with our gunfire, and we hope that one ship was sunk by a torpedo fired from *Southampton*. The *Southampton*, Commodore Goodenough's flagship, soon got her fire under control, and we closed up upon her and for the rest of the night continued steaming to the southward unmolested and unmolesting.

At 2 a.m. we were well to the southward, near to the Heligoland Bight mine-fields, and altered round to a northerly course until 9 a.m., when we swept up and down in the hopes of regaining touch with the enemy, but without success, and at 10 a.m. we shaped course for Rosyth. I now had time to read through the signals, which yesterday had come through at the rate of about three a minute, and could endeavour to make some review of the battle we had fought. We could feel pretty satisfied with the individual part which *Nottingham* had played, and although it was not very cheering to think over the ships and men that we knew we had lost (particularly the men of our own squadron), we knew that at least we 'held the ring' at the end of the action, and that the Germans must surely have suffered heavily if they would not renew the action at daylight. At any rate, thinking over in cold blood all the enemy's salvoes which, by the grace of God, we had successfully dodged, we felt pretty thankful that we were still alive.

Narrative of the Torpedo-Lieutenant of H.M.S. *Southampton*

(Flagship of the 2nd Light Cruiser Squadron)

(This is a continuation of the Narrative printed in Part I., p. 80, and Part II., p. 267)

At dusk the Grand Fleet took up their night cruising stations, the 5th B.S. being stationed astern of the other battle squadrons, and the 2nd L.C.S. were astern of them.

In the *Southampton* we went to night action stations, and the word was passed round for the starboard guns' crews to be in immediate readiness for action on that side, whilst the port crews lay down to rest alongside their guns ready to take over the watch at midnight.

In this manner we proceeded quietly south for about an hour. At

2nd L. C. S. in action with enemy light cruisers at 10.15pm. (From a painting)

about 9.0 o'clock a brief action took place on our starboard beam, but it was impossible to see who was engaged, although several destroyers steaming at high speed were visible in the beams of searchlights. The firing was very heavy for a few minutes, then ceased as suddenly as it began.

Soon afterwards something appeared on our starboard bow, and closing rapidly turned out to be a number of destroyers. Fortunately we did not open fire, as they proved to be friendly, and they turned up on a parallel course and were soon lost to sight ahead.

The gathering on the *Southampton*'s upper bridge was now considerable, including the Commodore, with his flag lieutenant and his secretary, the Commander, Navigator, Gunnery lieutenant, Torpedo lieutenant, and some ten ratings forming the range-finder crew, messengers and men tending the gunnery and torpedo communications, etc. In addition to this, on the lower bridge were two sub-lieutenants, majority of the signal ratings, and two searchlights' crews. We always steered from the lower conning tower when at action stations, the Navigator conning the ship by voice pipe from

289

the upper bridge, which, as events turned out, was fortunate, as the conning tower armour saved the steering gear from being wrecked.

At about 10.15 there appeared on our starboard beam, scarcely 1,500 yards distant, a line of five ships steering in the same direction as ourselves. We inspected them carefully from the bridge, and the officers in the after control position also observed and reported their presence to us.

The next few minutes were full of suspense, the newcomers being as unwilling to disclose their identity as were we; meanwhile cautionary orders were passed to the guns and searchlights, and I gave orders to flood the starboard torpedo tube ready for firing. Then the two squadrons almost simultaneously decided that the other was hostile and opened a violent fire.

Each of the five German ships switched on two groups of lights and opened fire, at least three ships very speedily concentrating on *Southampton*, which, with her searchlights burning, made an excellent target, the others finding and engaging the *Dublin*, our next astern. Neither *Nottingham* nor *Birmingham* showed any lights, with the result that they remained undiscovered and were enabled to pour in a heavy fire on the enemy at almost point-blank range.

The next few minutes can only be described from a purely personal point of view, and my impressions are naturally confined to events in my immediate vicinity. Down at the guns the conditions were infinitely worse than on the bridge, where we were comparatively sheltered by the splinter mats rigged round the bridge rails. On the bridge the full glare of the searchlights of the leading enemy ship was on us, and we could see nothing, but I had already received enough impression of the general direction of advance of the enemy for the purpose of torpedo fire, so I passed down an order to the torpedo flat and waited impatiently for a reply. When it came through—the report 'ready'—I fired at a group of hostile searchlights, which were the only things visible.

The Commodore came over to my side of the bridge and asked me if I had fired. I told him I had, and that the tube's crew were reloading. There was nothing for me to do at the moment, and I began to look round. It was impossible to distinguish the firing of our own guns from the noise of bursting shells; I remember a continuous screaming noise, apparently caused by 'overs,' but I could see nothing of the results of our own firing owing to the glare of searchlights. I received no definite impression of the ship being struck by shell, only of a confused uproar. I did not find out the true state of affairs on deck until it was all over. I observed that a fire had started on board somewhere aft, which was soon hidden by another which shot up just abaft the bridge nearly to the fore-top. Our firing and the enemy's too now became desultory, and there were brief periods of calm, when there was little else to do but watch the fire, which was within a few feet of the after bridge screens, and, having seen three ships blow up earlier in the day, I wondered how long it would be before we should make the fourth, and what it would feel like. It was hot on the bridge, like standing in front of a boiler with the furnace door open. The doctor, who was down below, told me afterwards that his chief anxiety at this moment was to know whether the deck would split and let him through, or whether he would have to open it with his head when the ship went up.

But the enemy had apparently been hit as much as we had, and were glad of any pretext for breaking off the action, and just as we had made up our minds that another few minutes would surely see the end of the *Southampton*, the searchlights from the leading enemy ship suddenly went out, and she sheered off to starboard. She had been torpedoed and was sinking, though we did not know it at the time. The remainder of the Germans followed the motions of their leader, switched off their lights, and disappeared to the westward.

We held our course to the southward, and within a few minutes our fires were under control. They had done comparatively little damage to the ship, being entirely cordite fires amongst ammunition in rear of the guns, and had not caused an explosion. But the flash had passed below to the ammunition passages, and only the prompt action of those on the spot in closing down the hatches and in deal-ing with the situation when in most cases the fire hoses were shot away, probably saved the ship. There were many severe casualties from burning amongst these men below.

Gradually we collected ourselves and our squadron together, and began to take stock of the situation. The whole action had in reality lasted no more than four minutes, though it seemed very much longer, but in that time our casualties had been very severe, 35 men killed or died of wounds, and 1 officer and 54 men wounded, and our broadside had been reduced from five 6-inch guns to two.

On the upper bridge the range-taker had been killed and another seaman badly wounded by a splinter, but, considering the number of people up there, we were surprisingly lucky. On the lower bridge three were killed and several wounded.

The real havoc was along the upper deck amongst the gun's crews, and in the passages where the ammunition supply parties were stationed. The three midship guns' crews in the starboard battery had been wiped out. The casualties of these three guns were 11 killed and 16 wounded, 27 out of a total of 33. The guns of the disengaged side were not much better off, losing 6 killed and 14 wounded out of a similar total of 33.

The forecastle and quarter-deck guns were untouched, but nearly all the voice pipes had been destroyed, and communication with the control had ceased soon after the action started. The casualties of the searchlights were severe, all the crew of the after pair of lights being killed, a direct hit on one searchlight removing it bodily, and the other light was completely wrecked. The funnel, masts, and protective matresses round the bridge and control positions were riddled with splinters, and there were 10 direct hits on the ship's side, but only 3 of these were anywhere near the water-line and though they caused considerable damage inboard, there was never any danger to the stability of the ship.

After the action the medical staff were sadly busy. Divided into two parties at opposite ends of the central passage along the main deck, they worked throughout the night under the most appalling conditions. The dressing station was an ill-ventilated bathroom situated just over the boiler-rooms, measuring perhaps 8 feet square and hardly 6 feet high. An operating table was in the middle, and the deck as well as the passage outside was a litter of mangled men laid out in rows by the first-aid parties. Add to this a foul atmosphere thick with chloroform, and the painfully depressing sight of numbers of badly wounded men waiting their turn for attention, and the rest may be left to the imagination.

As each case was passed through the doctor's hands and his wounds were dressed he was removed to the ward-room, though this soon became overcrowded, and all officers' cabins were requisitioned. Several cabins were wrecked, and there was a good deal of water about dripping through from the deck above, where fire mains were burst and water was lying or flowing about. This did not add to the comfort of the wounded, but the holes were soon effectively stopped, and by the morning everyone had been made as comfortable as possible.

On deck there was an immense amount of work to be done in clearing away wreckage, organising and extemporising communications, etc. Guns' crews were made up as far as possible from stokers and anyone else available, but we were really in no condition to fight another action, and we earnestly hoped to be left alone until daylight at least.

The Commander and the Gunnery lieutenant went round doing what they could, and eventually reduced the chaos to something like order. I remained on the bridge in case of another attack, the torpedo armament being undamaged.

At 11.30 p.m. there was heavy firing with searchlights burning some 5 miles astern, which lasted a few minutes, but then there was silence again. Some time later there was firing again in the same direction, which left us wondering who was fighting, but hoping sincerely that, whoever it was, he would keep his action to himself.

Late in the night we increased to 20 knots, and at daybreak we were close to the 5th B.S. The dawn was misty, visibility not more than 7,000 yards, and about 5.0 a.m. we passed through the whole British fleet. Squadrons were being reformed and re-stationed, and we joined the battle cruisers, which we had not seen since the 16-point turn early in the action of the previous day. The day passed slowly without incident. We cruised south as far as the enemy minefield, then back through the area covered the day before, but saw nothing except the bows of a destroyer floating vertically, and close to this an enormous patch of oil.

By the evening there was nothing to be gained by remaining in these waters, and we started for our base. During the night the wind freshened, and we had a little trouble with some of the shores and plugs over the holes in the side, se we eased down to make good the damage, but not before a certain amount of water had come into the ward-room, which caused some distress to the wounded.

Owing to this reduction of speed, we did not reach the Firth of Forth until some hours after the rest of the fleet, but it was most cheering to receive such a warm welcome—the battle cruisers cheered us as we passed, which we felt tremendously—and after evacuating our wounded we proceeded into the dockyard for repairs.

Extract from *A Naval Lieutenant, 1914–1918*

By 'ETIENNE,' an Officer of H.M.S. *Southampton*[1]

... At about 10 p.m. searchlights criss-crossed on the far western horizon; they rose and fell, turned and twisted, and finally fixed their implacable and relentless light on a group of destroyers. Fascinated, we watched the destroyers rushing up the bright paths of light. The white splashes gleamed all round them, and then a great red lurid stain started in one of the attacking craft and spread to a vast explosion of fierce white flame, beside which the cruel searchlights seemed pale. Instantly the searchlights were extinguished, the attack was over, and once more all was dark. .... The sudden disappearance of all signs of this attack ever having been made, left a curious feeling of emptiness in the atmosphere.

I groped my way on to the bridge and had a chat with B., the Gunnery lieutenant, as a result of which he arranged that, in the event of night action, he would control the guns from the fore-bridge, and I would be in general charge aft. A moment later a signalman and R.I., the navigator, suddenly whispered, 'Five ships on the beam.'

The Commodore looked at them through night glasses, and I heard a whispered discussion going on as to whether they were the enemy or the 3rd Light Cruiser Squadron. From their faint silhouettes it was impossible to discover more than the fact that they were light cruisers. I decided to go aft as quickly as possible. On the way aft I looked in at the after control, where H.B. said to me, 'There are five Huns on the beam. What on earth is going on?'

They were evidently in as much doubt as us, for, as I got down into the waist by the mainmast, a very great many things happened in a very short time. We began to challenge; the Germans switched on coloured lights at the fore yardarms. A second later a solitary gun crashed forth from the *Dublin*, which was next astern of us. Simultaneously I saw the shell hit a ship just above the water-line and about 800 yards away. As I caught a nightmare-like glimpse of her interior, which has remained photographed on my mind to this day, I said to myself: 'My G——, they are alongside us.'

At that moment the Germans switched on their searchlights and we switched on ours. Before I was blinded by the lights in my eyes

1 By kind permission of the author and of the publishers, Messrs. Methuen & Co., Ltd.

I caught sight of a line of light grey ships. Then the gun behind which I was standing answered my shout of 'Fire!'

The action lasted 3½ minutes. The four leading German ships concentrated their lights and guns on the *Southampton*, the fifth, and perhaps the fourth as well, fired at the *Dublin*. The *Nottingham* and *Birmingham*, third and fourth in our line, with great wisdom did not switch on their lights, and were not fired at. In those 3½ minutes we had 89 casualties, and 75 per cent. of the personnel on the upper deck were killed or wounded. . . .

The range was amazingly close—no two groups of ships have ever fought so close in the history of this war. There could be no missing. A gun was fired and a hit obtained; the gun was loaded, it flamed, it roared, it lept to the rear, it slid to the front; there was another hit.

But to load guns there must be men, flesh and blood must lift the shells and cordite, and open and close the hungry breeches. But flesh and blood cannot stand high explosives, and there was a great deal of high explosive bursting all along H.M.S. *Southampton*'s upper deck from her after screen to the fore-bridge.

The range was so close that the German shots went high, just high enough to burst on the upper deck and around the after super-structure and bridge. And in a light cruiser *that's* where all the flesh and blood has to stand.

So in a very few seconds my guns stopped firing, all through lack of flesh and blood—it was a great pity. In fact, the sergeant-major, with a burnt face, and myself seemed to be the only bits of flesh and blood left standing.

Where on earth were the others?

Why had the men on each side of me fallen down in such funny heaps? It was curious, very curious; as a matter of fact, daylight revealed that it wasn't so very remarkable. The really remarkable thing was that the sergeant-major, with his burnt face, and myself were still standing about and representing flesh and blood.

One shell burst on the side just below the gun, and the fragments had whipped over the top of the low bulwark and mowed the men down as standing corn falls before the reaper. Another shell burst on the searchlight just above us and hurled the remains of this expensive instrument many feet. Three men who looked after it and had guided its beam on to the enemy died instantly.

The fragments from this shell descended upon 'the waist' like hail, and scoured out the insides of the gun-shields of the two

6-inch, manned by marines, one gun each side. And then I seemed to be standing in a fire. The flash of some exploding shell had ignited half-a-dozen rounds of cordite.

A shell exploding in the half-deck had severed the connection to the upper deck fire main. I put my head down a hatch and shouted for a good hose. The wine steward came up on deck with one, someone turned on the water down below, and the fire was quickly out. . . .

Then it became lighter than the day.

I looked forward.

Two pillars of white flame rose splendidly aloft. One roared up the fore-mast, the other reached above the tops of the second and third funnels. This them was the end! The heat warmed the cheek. It was bad luck, just after we had got the small fire aloft extinguished. But there could be no doubt; the central ammunition hoist was between those two funnels.

What was it going to feel like to blow up?

Let me see—how had the *Queen Mary* looked?

Of course, we were a smaller ship, perhaps we would blow up in a gentler manner. Might as well take one's greatcoat off, just in case one fetched up in the water. I took it off.

What ought one to do?

Could not be more than a few seconds now. What could one do in a few seconds.

Could not fire a gun—no men.

Fascinating sight, those two pillars of white flame.

By heaven, the centre one had turned red, it wavered, it decreased in height; it grew again, but the spell was broken, and I rushed to the ladder which led from the waist to the boat deck in order to get up to the fire and assist. I ran a few steps and tripped up over a heap of bodies. I got up, tried not to tread on soft things, and arrived on the boat deck.

The firing had ceased, the Commander and H. B. were at the central fire. It suddenly went out, so did the foremost one.

Everything was pitch black.

Where were the Germans?

Nothing but groans from dark corners. ...

It is after the firing is over that the real horror of a night action begins. We did not know where the Germans were, our guns' crews were practically non-existent, the voice pipes and telephones to the guns were in shreds. We simply had to have time to reorganise, so we didn't dare show a light.

Yet the upper deck was strewn with dead and wounded. One stumbled on them as one walked. By the aid of discreetly struck matches and shaded torches the upper deck was searched. I heard a groan, and came upon a poor boy named Mellish. He could only say, 'My leg—my arm.' Another man and myself got him down one of the two steep hatches that led to the lower deck. His injuries were sickening, but with a smile he said: 'It's no good worrying about me, sir,' and then he died. I don't think he felt any pain.

I went up to the bridge to see B. about reorganising the men left for guns' crews and rigging up temporary communications. As I passed the chart-house a well-known voice called me in. It was the Commodore.

He told me to go down to the fleet surgeon and find out what our casualties were. And once more I went below.

I went down the foremost hatch and along the central passage— nick-named the twopenny tube—which in this class of ship runs down the centre of the ship above the boiler and engine-rooms. There was about 6 inches of water in this passage, which had slopped in from some holes almost exactly on the water-lines.

The operating-room—at the after end of this passage—was the stokers' bathroom. Imagine a small room which a shore-goer might hesitate to use as a dark room in his house, it might get so stuffy. The size of this room was about 8 feet high, 12 feet broad, and 12 feet long. The centre of the room was occupied by a light portable operating table. A row of wash basins ran down one side, and the steel walls streamed with sweat. Four bright electric lights were fixed to the roof, but with its faults the stokers' bathroom had some advantages. It had a tiled floor and a drain in the corner.

Stepping carefully between rows of shapes who were lying in lines down each side of the passage-way, I put my head inside the narrow doorway.

Bare-armed, the fleet surgeon and C., the young doctor, were working with desperate but methodical haste. They were just taking a man's leg off above the knee, so I did not interrupt. When they had finished and the patient had been carried out, I gave the P.M.O. the Commodore's message, whilst his assistants went outside to get another man.

'About 40 killed and 40 or 50 wounded,' he said.

I thanked him, and went back to the bridge. . . .

I told the Commodore what I had learned. He made a remark. I realised we were only one light cruiser in a very big fleet.

I went aft again and down to the ward-room. The mess presented an extraordinary appearance. As it was the largest room in the ship, we placed all the seriously wounded cases in it. The long table was covered with men, all lying very still and silently white.

The young doctor was in charge, and as I came in he signalled to the sick-berth steward to remove one man over whom he had been bending. Four stokers, still grimy from the stokehold, lifted the body and carried it out.

Two men were on the top of the sideboard, others were in arm-chairs.

A hole in the side admitted water to the ward-room, which splashed about as the ship gently rolled. In this ankle-deep flood, blood-stained bandages and countless pieces of the small débris of war floated to and fro. All the wounded who could speak were very cheerful, and only wanted one thing—cigarettes. The most dreadful cases were the 'burns'—but this subject cannot be written about.

An hour's work on deck connected with the reorganisation of the guns' crews, the impressment of stokers off watch for this duty, and the testing of communications followed. Then H. B. and myself decided we'd sit down somewhere. . . .

We had just lain down when fresh gun-firing broke out right astern, and everyone was on the *qui vive* with a jump. It died down—I wasn't sorry; we were not as ready for action as we could have wished.

We increased speed to 20 knots, and as dawn slowly grew the ghostly shapes of some battleships loomed out of the mist. I heard a pessimist on the upper bridge hazard the opinion that we were about to take station astern of the German battle fleet, but as the light grew brighter we saw that we had rejoined the British fleet.

Complete daylight enabled us to survey the damage.

The funnels were riddled through with hundreds of small holes, and the decks were slashed and ripped with splinters. There were several holes along the side, but the general effect was as if handfuls of splinters had been thrown against the upper works of the ship. The protective mattresses round the bridge and control positions were slashed with splinters. The fore-mast, the rigging, the boats, the signal lockers, the funnel casing, the main mast—everything was a mass of splinter holes.

Our sailors firmly believed, and continued to do so up to the day on which I left the ship, that we had been deluged with shrapnel. It was certainly surprising that anyone on the upper deck remained unhit.

Narrative from H.M.S. *Dublin*
Of the 2nd L.C.S., next Ship astern of H.M.S *Southampton*

Until about 10.30 p.m. the movements of H.M.S. *Dublin* were closely connected with those of our flagship, H.M.S. *Southampton*, so that the account concerning the latter ship will also have covered the incidents in which *Dublin* took part.

Shortly after 10 p.m. a squadron of five ships was sighted on our starboard beam converging on our squadron. Orders were promptly passed round the quarters to prepare to engage whilst we awaited a reply to our challenge, which was eventually forthcoming by the strange ships switching on coloured recognition lights, and a moment later simultaneously switching on searchlights and opening fire. We at once switched on our searchlights and opened fire at a range that could not have been more than 800 yards.

After an engagement of about 5 to 10 minutes, the *Southampton*, ahead of us, was seen to be heavily on fire, and a heavy explosion appeared to take place in one of the enemy ships, after which they evidently turned away, ceased fire, and were lost sight of in the darkness.

Meanwhile the ship had been hit about 20 times, but fortunately no vital damage had been done, and the shot holes were soon plugged and the litter of débris put more or less ship-shape. Between decks a large fire, which nearly necessitated the foremost magazine being flooded, and several small fires had started, but, being promptly dealt with, they were successfully extinguished by the stokers' fire brigade parties working under the general direction of the Commander. The men in these parties entered fully into the zest of turning hose on to anything and everything. The mess decks were for a time in darkness except for the glare from smouldering woodwork, etc., for the electric light had failed generally, and the auxiliary lights had been unable to stand the shock of shells striking the hull or bursting in the interior of the ship. But the results which affected us most seriously at the time were the destruction of the charts and data giving the ship's position, and the temporary disablement of our wireless installation. Otherwise we were soon in fighting condition again.

It would appear that a certain amount of confusion is inevitable in even the best disciplined ship during a night action, and in the *Dublin* this confusion was accentuated by the fact that, during this short engagement, many voice pipes and nearly all the telephone and fire control cables were damaged, which greatly hindered the passing of orders, etc. Moreover, a shell which struck the chart-house mortally wounded the Navigating officer and killed or wounded all the signalmen stationed on the upper and lower bridges, in consequence of which an alteration of course by the *Southampton* was not observed, and very soon after we had lost sight of the enemy we discovered that we were separated from our own squadron. We held on the same course, approximately south, for some hours, but without regaining touch with any of our own ships, and as we were uncertain of our position within 30 to 40 miles owing to the charts and data giving the ship's position having been destroyed and our Navigator being killed, we altered course 16 points about daylight, considering that we must by then be near the British mine-fields off the Heligoland Bight. We afterwards learnt that our main fleet had altered course to a similar direction at about the same time.

Constant gun-firing was heard throughout the hours of darkness, and the horizon at times was vivid with searchlight flares and gun flashes. The early morning hours were again hazy, with considerable patches of mist and light fog, but it was a great relief to everyone to leave the night behind, as recent events had been trying to all our nerves. Yet, although we had a raw and comparatively young ship's company—for the ship had been in commision barely two months—the men all appeared anxious to see something of the enemy again at daylight. Just after we had turned to the north, as dawn broke, some German ships suddenly appeared out of the fog about 2,000 yards on our starboard beam steaming south at high speed. The enemy vessels appeared to be the armoured cruiser *Roon*, with three destroyers, but they only remained in sight for a minute or two, and before we had turned and headed south they had disappeared in the mist. At the same time, the mist clearing on our port side, we saw the *Champion* and a few of our destroyers, and to them we endeavoured to signal the presence of the enemy, whilst we altered course to overtake the enemy, and if possible get into a favourable position for a torpedo attack. But they were not seen again.

The guns' crews had scarcely left their guns for the last 12 hours, and some of the youngsters were obviously rather tired and done up, so that as soon as it was full daylight we relieved the crews by watches to get a spell off. Our wireless installation got working again about 3 a.m., and we were able to ascertain the position of the *Iron Duke* and the *Lion*, but as we were in doubt as to our own position, this did not help us much in finding them.

During the two or three hours succeeding daylight we passed through large quantities of floating wreckage, hammocks, bodies, etc., pointing to several ships having been sunk during the night. In passing through some of this wreckage an alert signalman reported that he saw a hand waving from a spar some distance away, and on closing we were fortunately able to rescue a stoker belonging to the *Tipperary*, who informed us that his ship had been sunk four or five hours previously. He was a man of very fine physique, or otherwise could not have survived so many hours in the water, and later on in the day he seemed none the worse for his experience. The ship's company displayed intense interest in the rescue, quite making up their minds that we were picking up a German, and I think were rather disappointed when the first few words uttered by the stranger after being hauled on board were unmistakably English.

Later in the morning we found the disabled *Sparrowhawk*, or rather what remained of her, for she had been cut in half and had neither bow nor stern left. The *Marksman* was endeavouring to take her in tow, and as our assistance was not required we stood on to the northward, and about 8 a.m., quite by chance, sighted and joined up with our battle fleet. We found that our dead-reckoning position was about 30 miles in error, which was not really excessive, considering the high speed and constant change of course made during the various stages of the action.

CHAPTER XV

THE ADVENTURES OF *TIPPERARY*'S FLOTILLA

The 4th Destroyer Flotilla, of which *Tipperary* was the leader and *Broke* the half-leader, was in the very heart of the night fighting at Jutland, and had perhaps, on this night, as many fighting adventures as has ever fallen to the lot of one small squadron of ships.[1]

Engaged at about 11.30 p.m. by three or four German cruisers at very close range, the *Tipperary* herself was irreparably damaged, her next astern, *Spitfire*, was also badly hit, and the rest of the flotilla in the confusion of the action separated one from another. *Spitfire*, by herself after this action, was seeking to rejoin her flotilla, when quite suddenly a German cruiser tried to ram her. She quickly put her helm hard over and went full speed ahead, thereby just avoiding the cruiser's ram. but by so little that, 'with an awful crash the two ships met end on, port bow to port bow,' and the German cruiser surged down our port side, clearing everything before her, boats and even davits being torn out of their sockets, and all the time firing her guns just over our heads.' But so close were the two ships together that the German could not depress his guns sufficiently to hit the *Spitfire*, yet the blast of the guns firing

---

1 I think, however, that it is proper to point out, and the Flotilla would wish it pointed out, that these adventures must be read as adventures, and it must not be inferred that they had a great influence on the Battle of Jutland. They did not, for the Flotilla did not sink more than one, possibly two, enemy ships. The ships of the 4th Flotilla were mostly small oldish destroyers, and together formed no more than a very small fraction of the total strength of the Grand Fleet. As was natural, the work they did was no more than that of which such a small Force was capable. Their adventures, however, certainly exceeded those of all the battleships put together.

'literally cleared everything before it; our mast came tumbling down, our for'ard searchlight found its way from its platform above the fore-bridge down on to the deck, and the foremost funnel was blown back till it rested neatly between the two foremost ventilation cowls like the hinging funnel of a penny river steamer.'

Sixty odd feet of plating from the German cruiser's fo'csle was left in *Spitfire*'s side as a memento of this incident.

A little later another extraordinary incident occurred, perhaps the strangest of all the strange incidents of Jutland.

The *Spitfire*'s crew were just recovering from their ramming match with the German cruiser, and most of the ship's company were collected aft, when suddenly there was a cry from nearly a dozen people at once, 'Look out! I looked up, and saw a few hundred yards away, on our star-board quarter, what appeared to be a battle cruiser on fire, steering straight for our stern. To our intense relief she missed our stern by a few feet, but so close was she to us that it seemed that we were actually under her guns, which were trained out on her star-board beam. She tore past us with a roar, rather like a motor roaring up hill on low gear, and the very crackling and heat of the flames could be heard and felt. She was a mass of fire from fore-mast to main-mast, on deck and between decks. . . . flames were issuing out of her from every corner. She appeared to us to be a battle cruiser, as her funnels were so far apart, but afterwards it transpired that quite possibly she was the unfortunate *Black Prince* with her two centre funnels gone. Soon afterwards, about midnight, there came an explosion from the direction in which she had disappeared.'

These were two of *Spitfire*'s adventures.

Meanwhile *Broke* had collected together some of the scattered flotilla, and had almost immediately come into action, either with the same group of German ships again, or with a fresh ship, possibly a battleship. *Broke* was very badly hit, losing 47 men killed and 36 wounded out of a crew of about 190, her steering wheel was shot away by a shell, and not under control she swung out of the line. *Sparrowhawk* was her next astern, and swinging in the same direction in order to bring the sights of her torpedo tube to bear upon the enemy, crashed into the swinging *Broke* before it was possible to avoid collision. The force of the collision hurled a few men of the *Sparrowhawk* across on to the deck of the *Broke* (where later they were met with the not unnatural query, ' Who the h—l are you?') and amidst clouds of escaping steam, smoke, and the splashes of shells, the two destroyers lay locked hard and fast together. Each ship thought that she was sinking. *Broke* sent some of her men across to *Sparrowhawk* to save their lives. *Sparrowhawk* sent some across to *Broke*. Neither ship sank.

Eventually the two ships parted themselves, but as they did so another destroyer of the 4th Flotilla, the *Contest*, came out of the darkness and crashed into the stern of *Sparrowhawk*, jamming her rudder hard over, thus crippling *Sparrowhawk* both ends.

Broke then disappeared, and very much injured struggled back across the North Sea through a rising gale. Two German destroyers were met and engaged on the way back, but they broke of the action after a few minutes unaware of the crippled state of their opponent, and eventually the *Broke* sighted land at 5.0 p.m. on Saturday, the 3rd June; she had received her damage 65 hours before, at about midnight on Wednesday, 31st May.

Then the *Sparrowhawk*, *sans* bow, *sans* stern, lay off in the darkness, a helpless wreck, and waited for what fate might have in store for her. Fate played with her. A German destroyer, at about 2 a.m., came up to within 100 yards of her, and then stopped. The *Sparrowhawk*'s men prepared for a final fight using their one remaining gun before this destroyer should kill them, but suddenly, and for no apparent reason, the German destroyer started her engines again, gathered way, and disappeared into the darkness. For 3½ hours nothing more happened, but then, out of the misty half-light of the morning, a dim shape approached, which with despair was recognised to be that of one of the latest German light cruisers, and the *Sparrowhawk*'s again prepared for their end. 'Fellows went about sort of whispering that this must be the end of all things, and asked each other what it was like to be dead.' But their course was not yet run. The light cruiser started to heel over to one side, to settle down forward, then quietly stood on her head, and—sank.

Meanwhile *Tipperary*, a blazing wreck since the time of her first action at 11.30 p.m., with the ammunition at the forward guns exploding box by box at short intervals, and an occasional German closing her to fire a few rounds at her or at another time only to inspect her, at last reached her end, and about 2 a.m. sank by the bow.

A few of the survivors of her crew took to life-saving rafts— the boats had been smashed up by gunfire—and others just swam off to take their chance in the sea, for the rafts could not hold all who were left. Three hours later one of these raft loads came across a ship, or rather the remains of a ship, for it was what was left of the *Sparrowhawk*, the destroyer without bows or stern. 26 survivors of *Tipperary* were hauled aboard the *Sparrowhawk*. They had been recognised afar off by the tune they were singing, 'It's a long, long way to *Tipperary*,' although the officer with them on account of exposure, 'could not think of the words, and his music was all one note.' Eventually an undamaged destroyer, the *Marksman*, came across the *Sparrowhawk*, and the survivors of both ships were brought back in safety to Scotland.

But, alas, the casualties to the 4th Flotilla did not belong only to *Tipperary*, *Broke*, *Sparrowhawk*, or *Spitfire*. Stationed in rear of our battle fleet, the 4th flotilla happened to be directly in the path of the German squadrons steering from the scene of the day action towards Horn Reef, and one or another boat of the flotilla continued to be in action with enemy ships during most of the night.

H.M.S. *Fortune*, almost at the same time as *Tipperary* was damaged, was sunk by the concentrated gunfire of three or four German heavy ships, and not long afterwards H.M.S. *Ardent*, her sister ship, chummy ship, and subdivisional mate, was also sunk by gunfire. Of *Ardent*'s crew there were only two survivors, one of whom, the Captain, was rescued about six hours after her loss by the *Marksman*. Of *Fortune*'s crew of about eighty officers and men, only two raft loads of men were saved, these also by the *Marksman*. Other destroyers of the flotilla, the *Garland*, the *Porpoise*, the *Contest*, the *Ambuscade*, and others were sharers in much of this fighting, and had other adventures which have not been mentioned here. But more extracts would detract from the interest of the narratives given in the following chapters—*Broke*'s, *Garland*'s, *Spitfire*'s, *Sparrowhawk*'s, *Tipperary*'s, *Marksman*'s, and *Ardent*'s. They are printed in the order named, and narrate the adventures which fell to the lot of *Tipperary*'s Flotilla.

Narrative of the Navigating Officer of H.M.S. *Broke*

Half-Flotilla Leader of *Tipperary*'s Flotilla

From 6.15 p.m. onwards the 4th Flotilla, placed during the battle fleet action on the disengaged side of the battle line, had been steaming at full speed endeavouring to reach a position ahead of the battle fleet, but the continuous alterations of the battle line towards the enemy had prevented the desired position being reached. Our disappointment at not being able to get into a favourable position during the day action was very great, but somehow we all felt that our time would come after dark.

About 9 p.m., just as it was getting dark, we at last succeeded in getting ahead of *King George V.*, the leading battleship. She at once informed us that the battle fleet were forming night cruising order, and ordered us to take station 5 miles astern of her, course south and speed 17 knots. All firing in the battle fleet appeared to have ceased, and there was no sign of any enemy ships. Occasional flashes of gunfire were seen on the horizon to the south-west, which we assumed to be the battle cruisers still in action, but that was all.

On reaching our position 5 miles astern of *King George V.*, the flotilla turned to south and reduced to 17 knots. Captain D. formed the destroyers in single line ahead, *Tipperary* leading the 1st Half-Flotilla, with *Broke* in the centre of the line leading the rear four or five destroyers.

It was by this time about 9.30 p.m., and quite dark. Our chief anxiety was that we were unaware of the relative positions of any of our ships or squadrons except the battle fleet, and also we did not know the position of the enemy. From time to time flashes of gunfire were seen on the starboard bow, but it was impossible to estimate their distance, or from whom they came.

At about 9.50 a very violent explosion was seen almost right ahead, flames reaching a height of several hundred feet. For one moment the ship suddenly seemed to stop dead; then, giving a series of short heaves, she went on again. On the bridge we immediately thought that we had fouled some submerged obstruction, but the engine-room reported that it felt like an underwater explosion ; at all events, no damage was caused. We wondered if the battle fleet were being attacked. All officers and men were closed up at night action stations, as it was inadvisable to fall out any guns' crews owing to the likely proximity of the enemy.

Tipperary hit by a German salvo.

Tipperary Put Out of Action

Soon after 9.50 p.m. a ship was sighted coming up on the port quarter on a similar course to our own. After a great deal of gazing through glasses we made her out to be one of our light cruisers, and shortly afterwards *Tipperary* was seen to flash the challenge and get the correct answer. Owing to the darkness and mist, I noticed that her hull could not be seen more than of a mile away.

Some little time after this light cruiser had disappeared into the darkness, the outlines of three ships were made out on the starboard beam, also steaming in the same direction as ourselves. As far as we could make out, they appeared to be four-funnelled light cruisers,

307

and the Captain and both thought that they were one of our light cruiser squadrons. *Tipperary* was again seen to make the challenge, but this time, to our great surprise, it was answered by the simultaneous switching on of searchlights in all three ships. It became impossible to see their outlines any longer, but *Tipperary*'s hull was almost at once silhouetted against the darkness, getting clearer and clearer as each successive searchlight focussed itself upon her. For a moment one beam rested on us, but a second later it swung round ahead on to our unfortunate leader.

Almost simultaneously a heavy and accurate fire was directed on *Tipperary*. Splashes of the shells striking the water all round her could be seen, and in what appeared to be less than a minute she burst into flames. I still felt certain that these ships were our own cruisers, and so did the Captain, for without any hesitation he ordered me not to turn away and fire torpedoes until we could definitely establish the fact that they were Germans.

Fortunately, at this moment, one stray searchlight beam from the leading ship swept aft and rested on the rear ship of her squadron. Although it was only for an instant, it was time enough for us to recognise the ship as an enemy. The Captain at once gave the order 'Carry on,' and we turned away and fired the starboard after torpedo tube, increasing to full speed immediately afterwards. The necessary directions had been passed to the torpedo tubes immediately the ships were sighted, so there was no delay in firing once their identity was established. Nearly everyone on deck declared afterwards that we scored a hit, but on the bridge we were so occupied in keeping a look-out ahead to avoid ramming any of our own destroyers, that it was impossible to watch the course of the torpedo. At all events, the enemy almost immediately switched off all lights, and we did not see them again.

Broke's Action about Midnight

We now found ourselves steaming full speed into the darkness, with nothing in sight except a burning mass on the starboard quarter, which must have been the remains of the unfortunate *Tipperary*. The Captain accordingly ordered me to bring the ship back to the original course south and to reduce to 17 knots, the speed of the fleet, in order to have a look round and see if we could collect our destroyers together again. His intention was to attempt another attack on the three enemy ships before they had time to get too far away, and we hoped that the rest of our destroyers had fired torpedoes when we did, and would, therefore, not be far off. As we turned *Sparrowhawk* was sighted, and took station astern of us.

Almost as soon as the ship was steadied on her course south, the hull of a large ship was sighted on the starboard bow on a more or less parallel course, but this time well before the beam and not more than half a mile away. The Captain immediately gave the order to challenge, but almost as he spoke the stranger switched on a vertical string of coloured lights some green and some red, an unknown signal in our service.

'Starboard 20; full speed ahead both; starboard foremost tube fire when your sights come on; all guns—Green 40—a battleship,' and various other orders were simultaneously shouted down the various voice pipes on the bridge, but the German had evidently been watching our movements, and we were too late.

Within a few seconds of our seeing his recognition signal, he switched on a blaze of searchlights straight into our eyes, and so great was the dazzling effect that it made us feel quite helpless. Then after another interval of about a second, shells could be heard screaming over our heads, and I vaguely remember seeing splashes in the water short of us and also hearing the sound of our 4-inch guns returning the fire of this German battleship, which we afterwards had strong reason to believe was *Westfalen*. I then remember feeling the ship give a lurch to one side as a salvo hit us, and hearing the sound of broken glass and débris flying around, after which the searchlights went out, and we were once more in the darkness.[2]

Broke Collides with *Sparrowhawk*

At this moment I became conscious of the fact that I could get no answer from the quartermaster at the wheel, so shouting to the Captain that I was going below, I jumped down on to the lower bridge. There, in the darkness, I found complete chaos. The

---

2 An examination afterwards of the wheel and telegraphs showed that the pointer on the dial of the port telegraph was at 'Full speed,' while that of the starboard was still at 'Half-speed,' and the wheel indicator showed 15 degrees of starboard helm which appears to prove that the orders 'Starboard 20; full speed ahead both,' given immediately the hostile challenge was seen was not yet completely obeyed before the enemy shell hit us. This will give an idea of the rapidity with which the German ship switched on searchlights and opened fire.

quartermaster and telegraphman were both killed, and the wheel and telegraphs were shattered and apparently useless. I found our midshipman had followed me down to assist, and we were both just starting to strike matches to make certain that communication with the engine-room was gone, when I heard the Captain's voice down the pipe shouting, 'Full speed astern both.'

I looked up for an instant and saw a green bow light of some other ship just ahead of us, and then with a terrific crash the ship brought up all standing, and we were hurled against the bridge screens by the force of the collision.

On picking myself up I at once saw that we had one of our own destroyers bumping alongside, and an ugly-looking rent in her side abreast of the bridge showed where we had hit her. Steam was roaring out of our foremost boiler-rooms, and it was extremely difficult to see or hear anything. Our ship appeared to be settling by the bow, and at intervals gave unpleasant lurches from side to side, which for the moment made me feel that she might be sinking. I went down on the forecastle to try and find out the extent of our damage, and to see what had happened, and to my surprise found a strange officer standing there, who turned out to be the sub-lieutenant of the *Sparrowhawk*, the destroyer which we had rammed. He informed me he had been pitched on board by the force of the collision, and I afterwards found out that three of her men had had the same experience. I remember vaguely telling him that I thought our ship was not much use, and that he had better go and find out if *Sparrowhawk* could steam, as he said he did not think she had been hit by gunfire.

I then went in search of the Captain, and found him still on the bridge. After I had reported to him the name of the destroyer we had collided with, he ordered me to go aft and get the after steering gear connected, while he went to his sea cabin to dispose of the confidential books. Although the German battleship had ceased firing, we felt she might appear again at any moment. Getting aft was no easy job, as all the ladders were gone, and scalding steam was hissing out of the boiler-rooms from a dozen different places, but the 1st lieutenant and I together succeeded in getting there after a bit of a struggle.

Here I found the engineer officer, who, having been informed by a stoker that everyone on the bridge had gone, was very pleased to see us. He had stopped the engines on his own initiative, and was

Broke's upper bridge.

extremely cheering in his news that there was no damage aft, and
that, as three boilers were more or less all right, we could steam
slowly for the time being.

The after bridge was then commissioned, and as we were bumping very heavily against the *Sparrowhawk*, we went astern into the
darkness to clear her. It was not a moment too soon, for just as we
got clear another destroyer suddenly appeared out of the darkness,
and before we could give a word of warning came crashing into
Sparrowhawk's stern. I remember recognising her as *Contest* by the
number painted on her bows.

At the time we felt rather pleased that she had arrived, even in this
manner, for she would now be able to look after *Sparrowhawk*, for
whose condition we felt some responsibility.

The Passage Home

On getting clear we steamed to the northward at slow speed, and I
remember looking at my watch and seeing that it was a quarter past
midnight. Although most of the forward part was flooded, the ship
seemed quite seaworthy, and we speedily discovered that the bulkhead before the foremost boiler-room was sound, which seemed

311

very hopeful, and a party was thereupon sent down to shore it up. Reports from the engine-room, although a trifle gloomy at first owing to a shortage of fresh water, rapidly improved, and eventually the engineer officer said he thought we could maintain revolutions for 10 knots for a more or less indefinite time. The way in which he and his staff located the damage below and shut steam off the damaged boilers was really splendid.

The wounded, some 34 in number, including the sub-lieutenant and the paymaster who were both hit in the legs by splinters, were got below, while the dead, numbering 42, were buried as soon as possible. Our surgeon at this time was badly wanted, but I am sorry to say he was among the killed. Six men were found to be missing, and their fate remained unknown to us.

Day was now slowly breaking, and our hopes of getting away safely were fast rising, but at 1.15 they sank almost to zero when we sighted two German destroyers on our starboard quarter, steaming towards us at full speed.

We had only two serviceable guns left, and both of these were aft so we turned our stern to the enemy at once and increased speed to our utmost safe limit—about 10 knots. As they closed I remember a feeling of extreme disgust and disappointment at being thus caught after having been so lucky in making our escape from the other ships.

The Germans, however, appeared to be feeling even more scared than we were, which was saying a good deal. On approaching to within 500 or 600 yards they turned up together abreast of us, and the leader opened fire with his bow gun. We replied with our starboard after gun, which was the only one remaining that would bear, and to our astonishment and joy both ships put over their helms and disappeared into the early morning mist, leaving us alone, still above water. They had scored two hits amidships, but these fortunately did little or no damage.

After this somewhat unpleasant incident no more enemy ships were sighted, and we proceeded on our slow and somewhat tedious passage to the northward, turning up to N.E. at about 8 a.m., with the idea of heading up the North Sea, keeping fairly close to the Norwegian coast in case of accidents. We decided that shaping a course direct for the Humber or any other convenient port might land us into the midst of a fleet action, in which, needless to say, we were hardly likely to be of much use, and for which we had little ambition.

The remains of some charts were found forward and spread out in the ward-room, and with the assistance of the sub.'s sextant and the chronometers, which were undamaged, navigation became more or less simple.

Unfortunately our wireless gear was more or less out of action, but on one occasion during the night of the 1st of June a signal was got through to the C.-in-C. giving our rough position and condition, but after that all efforts at wireless communication proved ineffective.

During the day (June 1st) we were able to examine the damage done to the ship, both by shell fire and by the collision with *Sparrowhawk*. The damage due to shell fire, considering the very short time we were under fire, was enormous. The ship had been hit roughly a dozen times between the bow and the second funnel, though abaft that she was untouched there were indications that two hits must have been from 11-inch shells.

Several rounds burst in the coal bunkers, fortunately doing little or no damage, but one large shell exploded at the base of the fore-most funnel, and this caused the damage to the foremost boilers. Another shell burst on the starboard side of the lower bridge, and it was this one that had wrecked the bridge, chart-house, and steering gear, and been the cause of our collision with *Sparrowhawk*. The upper bridge had practically nothing left intact on it. Bits of the magnets from inside the compass binnacles were strewn about the deck, while the range-finder, searchlights, and semaphores were all smashed to bits. How any officers and men who were on the bridge escaped, it is difficult to imagine.

Another small shell burst on the foremost mess deck, and caused a large proportion of the casualties to our crew, and there was evidence that several men, rushing forward to escape, had avoided this shell burst, only to be immediately killed as the bows of the ship crumpled up in our collision with the *Sparrowhawk*.

During the night of Thursday to Friday, 1st to 2nd June, the wind and sea got up considerably, and by 4 a.m. on the 2nd it was blowing so hard from the N.W., and the ship was bumping so badly, that it became evident that our bulkheads would not stand it much longer. At about midnight our fore-mast rolled over the side, most of the rigging having been shot away. At 6 a.m. on the 2nd we were reluctantly compelled to turn round to the south-east, so as to get the sea astern, and during the whole of that day we remained thus, heading back towards Heligoland, but going dead slow so as not to close the German coast more than was absolutely necessary. Towards sunset, however, the wind and sea began to moderate, and we slowly hauled round to the westward bit by bit, like a sailing ship hauling off a lee shore, and at 8 p.m. that night decided to make for the Tyne.

At 5 p.m. on Saturday, 3rd June, land was sighted, much to every-one's relief, and shortly afterwards we were met by some of our destroyers from Rosyth and escorted into the Tyne, where, after discharging the wounded, we were berthed alongside the *Bon-aventure*. Here we were only too pleased to accept the hospitality of a bath and a good dinner, and the sleeping accommodation which the officers of that ship kindly gave us.

Narrative from the Engine-Room of H.M.S. *Broke*

At the time of the explosion, about 9.50 p.m., I was in the engine-room, and was thrown forwards and backwards several times by the shock of it, and as I did not hear any explosion I thought we had run into a submarine, and my engine-room artificer on watch was of the same opinion. Although coming from some other ship not even in sight of us, this shock was almost as strong as when we ran into the *Sparrowhawk* a few hours later. After this we had a fairly quiet time below until we met the *Westfalen*. I was in the engine-room again then, and felt the enemy's shells hitting us for'ard; not making much noise, but a distinct 'slap' as each shell hit the ship. We were then going full speed, and everyone in the engine-room was very cheer-ful, as we had had no reports from the stokeholds telling of any damage. But almost immediately after the hits we felt a great shock, and the starboard telegraph went to 'Half-speed,' the port remain-ing at 'Full.' I realised that we had hit something pretty hard, and after waiting below about half a minute went on deck to see what was happening. I found we had rammed the *Sparrowhawk*, and were pushing her in front of us; one of the men told me that the whole of the fore-part of the ship was carried away and all officers killed.

I hailed *Sparrowhawk* to try and tell him this, but owing to the noise of escaping steam I could get no answer, so went below, stopped both engines, and ordered steering gear to be changed over to the after position. Coming on deck again I met the 1st lieutenant, whom I was extremely pleased to see, as I did not feel very happy about navigating the ship back to England by myself. He told me the situation, and we went for'ard to examine the damage. Whilst he was shoring up the bulkheads I examined the boiler-rooms, and found it necessary to shut off all except the after three boilers, with which we continued steaming.

We then plugged what holes we could and tried to get the ship clear of water, but had hardly started when three Hun destroyers passed us a few hundred yards away and opened fire. They hit us a few times, rather further aft this time, but luckily did no damage to the engines or after boilers, and we carried on.

Most of the casualties to the engine-room staff had occurred to those off watch who were stationed on the fore mess deck as ammunition supply and fire parties. Almost all the men in the foremost stokehold were killed, but abaft this there were practically no casualties. As usual, we had a lot of trouble with the pumping arrangements, though they had been tried on leaving Scapa, but eventually we got rid of most of the water.

The actual action lasted such a short time that there was no time to realise anything in particular, and in a destroyer one is so close to the upper deck even when below that the feeling of being fastened down hardly enters into the question. Afterwards, on our way back, my men were very cheery, and were only too ready to go below for their watches.

H.M.S. *Garland*

The Destroyer next astern of H.M.S. *Sparrowhawk* at the commencement of the 4th Flotilla's Action, 11.30 p.m.

The story of our adventures in the *Garland* during the night of May 31st is written in four acts, the first commencing at 9 p.m. on the 31st., when the 4th Flotilla in single line were forming up in their night cruising station. We were in the middle of the line, which was just in the midst of a 16-point turn to starboard, when four destroyers were sighted ahead. At first I was under the impression that they were some of our own boats belonging to another flotilla, but after a good look at them with my night-glasses I suddenly realised that they were Germans. We had by this time started to turn in the wake of our next ahead, and, before there was time to get the guns trained on to the enemy and open fire, they apparently realised that we were British and turned away at full speed. The two leading boats each fired a torpedo at us, which, thanks to the fact that we were by this time almost end on to them, missed and passed up our starboard side a few feet away, making a great noise as the propellers broke the surface. The presence of the enemy was at once reported to our Captain 'D'; but they had already disappeared into the night and there was no sign of them left; and, indeed, a destroyer farther up the line, hearing the torpedoes pass him but seeing no enemy reported that it was a submarine that had attacked him. Thus ended Act 1, uneventfully.

The second act commenced at 10.35 p.m., at which time a cruiser gradually loomed up on our starboard beam. At first we could not make out what she was, but, as she gradually closed in, we made her out to be a German light cruiser of the *Graudenz* class. Our torpedoes, in preparation for firing at battleships, were set too deep to ensure hitting her, so we had to haul them back out of the tube, and reset them to run at a less depth. In the meantime we reported the presence of the enemy light cruiser to Captain 'D' in the *Tipperary*, and anxiously waited to hear from aft that the torpedoes were ready, expecting every moment that the enemy would open fire and blow us out of the water. It was really only a minute or two, but it seemed hours before the report from aft came through, and by then, to our disappointment, the German had apparently already realised who we were, and had sheered off into the darkness without firing a shot. However, we felt sure that she was not far off and expected every moment that we should sight her again, and our expectations were not in vain. At 11.25 p.m. four light cruisers were sighted on our beam, steering an almost parallel course, and this group did not hesitate, but straight away opened fire on the flotilla, and we replied with our 4-inch guns at our nearest opponent. Then we increased speed and turned away to bring our after torpedo tube to bear on her. The torpedo was fired and was seen by the tubes' crews to hit just beneath her mainmast, causing her searchlights to go out almost immediately; but on the bridge we were too occupied in keeping a look-out ahead to be able to see anything of this.

The *Tipperary*, our leader, must have been disabled during the first salvo, for she was now ablaze forward and was stopped. Our flotilla had all increased to full speed and had turned away to fire their torpedoes and get out of the enemy's searchlight beams, so that the difficulty now was to pick up our next ahead again out of the darkness. We cast about for some time, chasing dark objects which looked like destroyers, until we suddenly sighted a destroyer close on our starboard bow, steering at right angles to our course. We both of us just had time to put our helms hard over and start to swing, before we came alongside one another. For an instant one could have stepped across from deck to deck, but I believe we never actually touched; then we opened out clear of one another. This destroyer was the *Sparrowhawk*, originally our next ahead, but having thus turned away and avoided collision we lost sight of one another again. A few minutes later we sighted a black mass ahead, which we narrowly missed, but the *Contest*, following astern of us, apparently did not see us turn off to clear it, and ran into it. This was the last we saw of the *Contest* for some time. We afterwards discovered that the black mass was the *Sparrowhawk* again, now locked in collision with the *Broke*.

Shortly afterwards we managed to get into station astern of a ship which we thought at the time was the *Sparrowhawk*, but which turned out later to be the *Spitfire*, and we followed her back towards the *Tipperary*, hoping to find the remainder of our flotilla round about there. The German cruisers had by this time ceased firing, but the forepart of the *Tipperary* was one immense sheet of flame. *Spitfire* went on across her stern at high speed, so we slowed down in order to go up alongside her and render any assistance in our power, but when we were only a few hundred yards off there was a loud report and a flash close under our bridge, as if our foremost gun had fired. I leaned over the bridge rail and asked them what they were firing at without orders, and was surprised to be told that they hadn't fired; however, I soon discovered what it was. Two enemy ships, which we could only make out by the flash of their guns, had sighted us, lit up as we were by the burning *Tipperary*, and had opened fire at both of us. They made exceedingly good shooting at the poor *Tipperary*, but fortunately for us, the only damage we received was from the first salvo, one shell of which hit our whaler, while another, though it did no harm, burst right alongside. The only thing to do was to get away at our utmost speed as apparently we could do no good where we were, but were only drawing the enemy's fire on the *Tipperary* as well as ourselves. We were not in a position to use our torpedoes, and we therefore made off to the east and southward to endeavour to find the remainder of our flotilla. This may be called the end of Act 2.

Loss of H.M.S. *Fortune* and H.M.S. *Ardent*

After searching for about 10 minutes, we sighted a battleship on our port side, which we took to be one of our own fleet, and had no sooner turned off to avoid her than we sighted several destroyers; these turned out to be the remainder of our own flotilla. We just had time to settle down in our station between the *Fortune* and the *Porpoise*, when we found ourselves steaming *almost alongside* a line of big ships. They made a challenge of coloured lights, and getting no reply switched on their searchlights and opened fire. They were so close that it was quite easy to identify them as German pre-dreadnought battleships of the *Pommern* class. We immediately increased to full speed, turned, and fired a torpedo from our foremost tube at the nearest of them. Our next ahead, *Fortune*, was knocked out straight away, and our next astern was also hit. We managed to escape untouched, though how I do not know, for every salvo fired at us straddled our stern, and every time I felt sure that the next one must get us. But each salvo landed in exactly the same relative spot as the last, and when we turned away and got stern on to the enemy the shots still just missed us, falling close alongside on our starboard beam. The water between us and the enemy was so lit up by searchlights and gun-flashes that the track of a torpedo we fired was clearly visible, not only to us, but I believe to our next astern also. It hit the German right beneath her funnels, and as we disappeared into the darkness we could see this ship listing gradually over to port, but we were out of sight before she sank.

After this we searched in all directions for about half an hour for our flotilla mates, but without result. We were steering south, as we believed our fleet was going in that direction, when suddenly we sighted an extraordinary object straight ahead. The sea was flat calm and the night hazy, and this object appeared like a large fountain coming towards us. It was right on top of us before we realised that it was a destroyer, her bows badly damaged, throwing up an immense sheet of spray as she steamed at about 20 knots. She passed so close that I could read her number—it was *Contest*, our subdivision mate, which we had last seen ramming the black mass of

Broke and *Sparrowhawk.* I hailed her, but the only reply we got was a cheer from the men on her deck as she flashed by. We hoped that she would turn and follow us, but, as she did not, we turned and gave chase, and eventually gained touch with her, and she formed astern of us. This brought Act 3 to a close.

Daylight Action

We now cast about in various directions, hoping to find some of our own ships, but instead enemy destroyers kept on looming up, though only to disappear again as soon as they sighted us. This went on until daylight when we decided to make for the Tyne, as the *Contest* could only steam 20 knots, and by this time we had ascertained that the fleet was at least 40 miles south of us, and there was therefore no hope of catching up with them. Shortly after this, we sighted four destroyers steaming at high speed on our port bow, on an opposite course to us. We soon made them out to be Germans, and altered course across their bows. Seeing this, they altered onto a parallel course; but then, apparently thinking better of it, altered back to their original course. We, therefore, altered on to a parallel and opposite course to them and opened fire.

They got our range almost at once, but all their shots fell just over or just short, of us, and they never scored a hit, although some of their shots fell so close that we could see the white streak of the projectile under water, and others seemed actually to hit us under water. Apparently the enemy were intent on getting home to Germany, as they never turned but continued at full speed to the southward, whereas if they had cared to do so they could have steamed round us and would have been more than a match for us, being two to one. One of them (I presume in order to lighten his ship!) fired a torpedo at us at a range of about 3,500 yards, a range at which it was most unlikely to hit a destroyer. It was set to run on the surface, and passed several hundred yards astern.

This was the last we saw of the enemy, and we spent the remainder of the morning searching for the *Porpoise*, whose wireless signals, asking for assistance, we had intercepted. It was no easy matter finding her, as we were very vague as to our own position, but in the course of the forenoon we sighted a Danish vessel eastward bound from the Tyne, and from her we got a position. By making and receiving wireless signals to and from *Porpoise*, and also *Achates* which now was somewhere in the vicinity searching for *Porpoise*, we managed roughly to discover the latter's direction, and found her about noon (June 1st). She could only steam about 6 knots as she had had her main steam pipe damaged and was losing a lot of water, but she managed to last out until we made the Tyne next day. Then we went alongside her and towed her up the river to Palmer's yard. Here we collected some torpedoes and ammunition from other destroyers, had a most welcome night's rest, and sailed next morning to rejoin the fleet.

H.M.S. *Spitfire* and the Night Action of Jutland
31st May to 2nd June, 1916

The night was dark, and in the *Spitfire* we had absolutely no idea of where the enemy were, and only a very vague idea of the position of our own ships.

The flotilla was in single line ahead, Captain 'D' in the *Tipperary* leading, followed by *Spitfire*, *Sparrowhawk*, and some eight other destroyers, with *Broke* (half-flotilla leader) in the middle of the line. Our course at about 9.0 p.m. was south, speed 17 knots, and it was pretty evident to us that there would be something doing during the night, though we were very nervous that we might run into our own ships by mistake.

Between 9.0 and 10.0 p.m. a series of flashes and explosions were seen to the southward, and at about 9.45 p.m. the sudden blood-red flame of a violent explosion was seen in the distance. The shock to the ship which followed was so great that at first we thought we had fouled some submerged object. Personally, for a moment I thought we had struck a mine or been torpedoed.

About 10.15 p.m.[3] the last destroyer in the line reported three vessels closing us from astern, and shortly afterwards we could distinguish them is what appeared to be three four-funnelled cruisers steaming at high speed on our starboard quarter, course about south-west by south, which was nearly parallel to our course but closing in about 20°. Occasional flames from their funnels were seen, but their identity could not be established. As they kept

---

3 This time was actually between 11.15 and 11.30 p.m.

closing us and *Tipperary* did not challenge, we concluded that they must be British, but when they were in to, I should think, 500 to 700 yards' range and nearly abeam of us, *Tipperary* made the challenge. The reply was all three ships switching on one blaze of searchlights. The majority of these lights were trained on the *Tipperary*, and only a few stray beams lit on us and on our next astern. Then these lights immediately went out, and after an extraordinarily short pause were switched on again and at the same moment a regular rain of shell was concentrated on our unfortunate leader, and in less than a minute she was hit and badly on fire forward.

We immediately opened fire, and at the same time the Captain turned the ship away to bring the after torpedo tube to bear. We fired a torpedo, then waited until, much to our joy and relief, it was seen to get the second enemy's ship between the after funnel and. the mainmast, and she seemed to stop firing, heel over, and all her lights went out; but instead of the violent explosion we expected to see there appeared a kind of dull red glow, and then fire seemed to spread forward and aft from where she was hit. It struck me as exactly like a large set piece at a firework display; the fuse being lit, and the fire spreading along from one firework to the next all along the frame.

By this time we had been hit several times. The after guns' crew and the torpedo party were suffering the most casualties, but the latter luckily not until after they had fired our second torpedo, from the foremost tube, at the leading enemy ship, apparently their flagship. I believe however it passed ahead of her. Our helm was put hard a starboard, and we increased to full speed with the idea of hauling out the line to reload our torpedo tube with the remaining spare torpedo, which was kept on the upper deck. But at that moment we were hit by a salvo, and, as a friend in the next ship astern said to me afterwards, 'You seemed to disappear with a salvo hitting you amidships, one great sheet of flame.' I think, personally, that this was the salvo which hit us by No. 2 funnel, as afterwards a large shell hole was found through the base of this funnel, probably made by an 8-inch shell which had scraped the top of the boiler and gone out the port side. The after gun had been carrying on a rapid fire during the turn and after we were hit, but as it appeared to be drawing the enemy's fire on us and was of little use, it was ordered to cease fire, and we were instantly left alone by the enemy. But they must have kept us under close observation, for a few minutes later we momentarily switched on our recognition and steaming lights for fear we might be closing another British flotilla on our port beam, and as we did this a salvo was hurled at us, which, although short, was good shooting for direction.

German Cruiser tries to ram *Spitfire*

We now eased down and surveyed the general situation, taking the opportunity to order the after tube to be reloaded with the spare torpedo. But this proved to be impossible as the torpedo davit was broken up, the winch wires were splintered, and the majority of the torpedo ratings were wounded or killed. With the exception of these men and the after guns' crew, our casualties up to now were extremely small considering that we had been under the fire of big ships, at point blank range, for several minutes, which shows how difficult it is to hit a destroyer at night unless concentrated fire is brought to bear on her the moment she is seen. But as we were now unable to fire torpedoes, the Captain decided to return to the *Tipperary*, to see if he could help her in any way, and if necessary we could carry on action with our guns.

We closed the *Tipperary*, now a mass of burning wreckage and looking a very sad sight indeed. At a distance her bridge, wheel-house, and charthouse appeared to be one sheet of flame, giving one the impression of a burning house, and so bright was the light from this part that it seemed to obliterate one's vision of the remainder of the ship and of the sea round about, except that part close to her which was all lit up, reflecting the flames. As we neared the *Tipperary*, we saw a German cruiser hovering near. Suddenly the Captain realised that she had seen us, and was trying to ram us. She was coming at us full speed across our port bow. The Captain ordered, 'Hard-a-starboard: full speed ahead both,' and, leaning over the bridge screen, shouted, 'Clear the foc'sle.' It wasn't a minute too soon, as with an awful crash the two ships met end on, port bow to port bow, we steaming almost 27 knots, she steaming not less than 10 knots (perhaps 20 or more). You can imagine how the $1/_8$-inch plates of a destroyer would feel such a blow. I can recollect a fearful crash, then being hurled across the deck, and feeling the *Spitfire* rolling over to starboard as no sea ever made her roll. As we bumped, the enemy opened fire with their fo'csle guns, though luckily they could

Collision between *Spitfire* and German light cruiser.

not depress them to hit us, but the blast of the guns literally cleared everything before it. Our foremast came tumbling down, our for'ard searchlight found its way from its platform above the fore-bridge down to the deck, and the foremost funnel was blown back till it rested neatly between the two foremost ventilation cowls, like the hinging funnel of a penny river steamboat. The enemy, probably it was the cruiser *Elbing* that blew herself up at dawn next day, surged down our port side, clearing everything before her; the boats came crashing down and even the davits were torn out of their sockets, and all the time she was firing her guns just over our heads. But none of her shells hit us, except two fired from her fo'csle guns just before the ramming which passed through the canvas screens round the bridge. The Captain was standing on the bridge, but bent down, whether or not with an object I don't know, and the shell passed across the top of his head taking his cap with it, and left only a skin-deep though nasty wound. With the exception of the Captain, the coxswain, and one seaman, who later on were all extricated with much difficulty from the wreckage, everybody on the bridge was killed by these two shells. Eventually the cruiser passed down the length of us, cleared us astern and disappeared, leaving us still afloat, but drifting and in a somewhat pitiful condition.

Luck now turned against us as fires started breaking out forward, and to make matters worse all the lights were shortcircuited, so that anyone going up to the bridge received strong electric shocks. Moreover, all the electric bells in the ship were ringing, which made things feel rather creepy.

It was extraordinary the way fire spread, burning strongly in places where one thought there was hardly anything inflammable, such as on the fore-bridge and the decks, but flags, signal halliards, and the cocoanut matting on the deck all caught fire, and sparks from the latter were flying about everywhere. We thought the light would be sure to draw some enemy's fire on us, but fortunately it didn't. There was a large hole in the base of the second funnel through which flames were pouring out, and every single hose pipe in the ship seemed to be cut by splinters and useless. One got rather a nasty shock by walking one moment on a small fountain from the fire main and the next minute stepping on something smouldering or burning. The Downton pump (fire pump) had been sent hurling into the air, and had landed on top of the unfortunate chief stoker, but he was got out and the doctor attended to his injuries.

We rigged a voice pipe down to the engine-room from the compass aft, and for about half an hour steered by that. The doctor, a young surgeon probationer, did some fine work during this time. His chief success was amputating, singlehanded and without any anesthetic, an able seaman's leg, who with the coxswain was found lying amongst the wreckage on the bridge. While he was performing this operation the fire party were busy all round him with their fire hose. It was marvellous the way this young doctor moved about, eventually getting all the wounded into the ward-room and cabins, and he never left them or took any rest himself until we arrived in harbour 36 hours later.

The actual damage to the bows and ship's side was considerable. About 60 odd feet from our stem aft along the port side had been torn away, and in exchange the enemy had left 20 feet of her upper deck inside our mess deck. From examination of this it was decided that it was her fo'csle, as such anchor gear as cat davit blocks, cat pendant, etc., were found left behind. (There was considerably less than 20 feet by the time it was landed, as on our arrival in harbour a party of men with chisels and hammers came on board to collect mementoes.) The fact that the high fo'csle of a cruiser should be as low as the mess deck of a destroyer, indicated that the enemy must

Damage to *Spitfire*'s bridge. Caused by blast of German light cruiser's guns. Photo looking from aft.

previously have been badly damaged and must have been down by the bows when she rammed us. Along our side were indentations as far aft as the mainmast, but there was not much damage abaft the fo'csle. The mast was lying in three parts on the port side of the upper deck amidst a débris of wires, flags and matting, and twisted and broken stanchions, etc.

After an inspection of the engine-room and boiler-rooms, the engineers decided that the good ship was capable of steaming with three out of the four boilers, and up till now the bulkheads were holding all right, so the after steering position was connected up, we shaped course west speed 6 knots, and all began to feel happier. To our joy the Captain suddenly turned up, alive though rather badly knocked about, as he had been blown off the bridge on to the upper deck, a distance of about 24 feet. Also the Sub-lieutenant, who was the last to leave the fo'csle before the crash and who had been thrown off the fo'csle on to the upper deck, re-appeared, and so too did the Gunner. All the confidential books were destroyed, and we held a council of war as to our next movements.

The Passing of the Ship on Fire

Just at this time all our ship's company started to collect aft, owing to a misunderstanding in the order 'Connect up aft,' referring to the steering gear, being mistaken for 'Everybody aft.' Before the mistake was realised almost all the ship's company had collected aft, when suddenly there was a cry from nearly a dozen people at once, 'Look out!' I looked up, and saw a few hundred yards away on our starboard quarter what appeared to be a battle cruiser on fire steering straight for our stern. We thought that she was steering for us with the intention of cutting us in two, and we thought that we were done for; I believe the majority of us lay down and waited for the crash. But no crash came. To our intense relief she missed our stern by a few feet, but so close was she to us that it seemed that we were actually lying under her guns, which were trained out on her starboard beam. She tore past us with a roar, rather like a motor roaring up hill on low gear, and the very crackling and heat of the flames could be heard and felt. She was a mass of fire from foremast to mainmast, on deck and between decks. Flames were issuing out of her from every corner. She appeared to us to be a battle cruiser as her funnels were so far apart, but afterwards it transpired that quite possibly she was the unfortunate *Black Prince* with her two centre funnels shot away.

Soon afterwards, about midnight, there came an explosion from the direction in which she had gone.

The Return to Harbour

The remains of a chart were patched together, and we came to the conclusion that, being no further use as a destroyer, we had best steer to the westward at the utmost speed the bulkheads would stand—about 6 knots.

As we had no signalmen left, likewise no signalling lamps, we had to prepare to use an ordinary electric torch for replying to a challenge should this be necessary. Wireless, of course, was out of the question as the mast had gone, and we could get no result from a secondary aerial and set that was rigged up. Mess tables, collision mats, and shores, were used to try and fill up the gaping bow, but they were all washed inboard again time after time, as the wind and sea were now fast rising.

By dawn, June 1st, the sea had risen a good deal, and the wind was still freshening from the south-west, and about 8.0 a.m. we had to turn the ship head to sea and ease down. All store-rooms, shell-rooms, and lower mess decks forward being flooded, we began to get very anxious whether the fore boiler-room bulkhead would stand the strain. At dawn the Captain ordered a tot of rum to be served out all round, and must say that cheered up the men no end. Luckily the galley was not damaged, and we all got some food, the men in there and the officers in the after canopy round the wheel.

We held a very impressive funeral service for the seven men who had been killed. In accordance with the custom of the Service, they were lashed up in their hammocks, with a practice projectile at their head and feet, and laid on the quarter deck. Volunteers acted as bearers, and the Captain read the funeral service. The colours under which they had fought were half-masted, and we lowered their bodies as reverently as we could in to the deep; there was a big sea running. Then we turned to and cleared up the ship.

Two gun crews were organised and kept manned in case of meeting anyone, but except for one Norwegian merchant ship, which realising we were in a bad way offered to take us off, we met no one. We refused the Norwegian's offer, but made use of him to assist our navigation by shaping course along the track he had left, which we assumed would lead us to some port or other.

In the dog watches the sea got up and the wind increased so considerably that we had to turn to north to keep the sea on our quarter. We organised a complete but rather 'Harry Tate' signalling outfit. It consisted of bearing out spars lashed on to what remained of the bridge, and several flags cut up so as to make the flags we might urgently require, principally those for the 'challenges' for the next twenty-four hours.

Our hopes of getting home fell during that night (June 1st–2nd), as the weather gradually became worse and worse, and about 1.0 a.m. we decided that the only thing to do was to fire distress signals, estimating that we were about 60 miles from the English, or it might be the Scottish, coast.

As we were on the point of doing this, at about 2.0 a.m. (June 2nd), suddenly—it seemed like a miracle—the wind died down and the sea got smoother and smoother, until at 4.30 a.m. we turned to west-south-west and increased speed to about 10 knots. As the morning drew on we met a patrol drifter, which informed us we were 22 miles E.N.E. of the Tyne. After making such a land fall as this, we came to the conclusion that *the* best aids to navigation are a

Damage to *Spitfire* caused by blast of German light cruiser's guns.
Photo taken when entering the Tyne. Damage to side caused by the collision.

torn piece of a chart, a book-ease batten as a ruler, and the wake of the last met merchant ship as sailing directions! From then onwards I lost all idea of time, but we steamed into the Tyne with every single flag hoisted that we could think of as means of recognition, being frightened of the War Signal Station, and not being able to reply to her searchlight challenges.

We berthed at Jarrow by H.M.S. *Bonaventure*, whose officers and men showed us the greatest kindness. They sent over a party to tidy up the ship, and our entire ship's company went over to her for baths and a good square meal. We were all very glad of both.

CHAPTER XVI

TIPPERARY'S FLOTILLA
(Continued)

The Adventures of H.M.S. *Sparrowhawk*
Action about 11.30 or 11.45 p.m., in which *Tipperary* is Damaged

At about 10 p.m. violent gunfire was seen and heard on our starboard bow, which we concluded must be our 2nd Battle Squadron firing on enemy torpedo craft, and we prepared to deal with the enemy if opportunity offered. We distinctly saw three ships on fire during this action, the fires lasting for about 10 minutes, and the whole action for about 25 minutes.[1]

About half an hour later there passed us 9 or 10 destroyers, which closely resembled our Yarrow-built boats, and as we had no idea of where any of our squadrons were except the 2nd B.S., we concluded that these destroyers must be some of our own craft, so we took no steps to engage them. Probably however they were enemy, for a little later we intercepted a signal made from *Ardent* and others to *Tipperary*, reporting that they had had torpedoes fired at them.[2] This was annoying, as we felt we had lost an opportunity.

Until about 11.45 p.m. no further incident occurred, but then we sighted three ships on our starboard beam, steering approximately the same course as ourselves but steaming a little faster, and we reported these ships to Captain D., informing him that at least one of the three was a three-funnelled light cruiser. He replied that he thought them to be our 1st Light Cruiser Squadron—three-

---

1 This was probably the action of the 2nd Light Cruiser Squadron at 10.20 p.m. See Chapter XIV.

2 See narrative of *Garland*, page 315.

funnelled ships of the *Galatea* class. Our Captain, however, was sus-
picious that they were enemy, and he ordered both torpedo tubes to
be trained on the starboard beam ready for action, for the ships, whatever they were, were only about a mile away, and easy torpedo targets.

They slowly crept up past us, and when the leading ship was
abreast of *Tipperary*, Capt. D. challenged her. Immediately all three
ships switched on their searchlights and absolutely simultaneously
opened a very heavy and accurate fire upon *Tipperary* and *Spitfire*,
both of which had at once been 'picked up' in the searchlight beams.
A shell from the first salvo hit *Tipperary*, apparently on the bridge,
and a huge shower of sparks and flames shot up, absolutely envelop-
ing the ship from our sight. *Spitfire* disappeared also in a cloud
of smoke and spray, and we never saw her again. She was our
'chummy' ship, so we were rather worried about her safety. We also
were picked up by the enemy's searchlights, but were not hit by gunfire, although shells were falling all round us.

The glare of the searchlights was absolutely blinding, and on the
bridge we could see nothing clearly; but we turned away to port,
fired one torpedo, and then managed to get clear of the enemy's
searchlight. Just after we fired, one of the enemy's ships accidentally
switched his lights round on to one of his own ships, and we were
able to identify her as a battleship of the *Nassau* class, an early
dreadnought; at the same moment a huge column of flame shot up
amidships, and we knew that at least one torpedo had done its job.

A few minutes later our Torpedo Gunner came on the bridge to
report to the Captain that he had fired a torpedo, that he had
observed its track, and that he felt sure it had hit as he had timed the
run with a stop watch, and the explosion in the enemy ship had
occurred at the moment he had expected.

Collision with H.M.S. *Broke*

The enemy had by now switched off all his searchlights, and the
only ship to be seen was one about 3 miles away on our starboard
quarter, which was burning fiercely, and must we knew be either the
Tipperary or the *Spitfire*. Sounds of gunfire were coming from her,
and when we had recovered our sight in a respite from the glare of
the German searchlights, we eased speed and turned to close this
burning vessel, thinking we might find some German destroyers
hanging round her.

But we had only gone about a mile when we sighted the *Broke*, still hale and hearty, and we were ordered to take station astern of her. We reduced to 17 knots and turned to south, the course of the fleet for the night, relieved to find ourselves in company with another ship, for a single destroyer steaming about by herself after a fleet action is likely to be treated with equal disfavour by friend and foe, and sunk on sight. About now we were joined by others of our flotilla, *Contest, Ardent,* and *Fortune,* and, I think, two or three others.[3]

At about 12.15 a string of coloured lights suddenly appeared right ahead of *Broke*, and I remember saying to my Captain, 'My God, sir, there are those devils again!'

The lights were kept on for three seconds, then a blaze of search-lights was switched on to us from it seemed every direction, and from so close a range that they seemed to come from almost directly above us. At the same instant

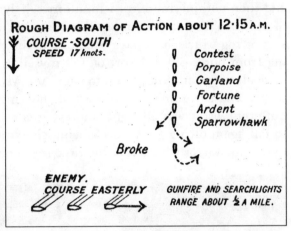

gunfire from apparently every direction burst out at us. The noise was terrific; the smell and fumes of bursting shell were simply chok-ing, and to add to it all there was the blinding glare of searchlights wherever one looked. Speed was at once increased to full, about 28 knots, the helm was put hard over to bring *Sparrowhawk* round to port, and orders were passed to fire the remaining torpedo.

Broke, ahead of us, had also put her helm over to steer out to port away from the enemy, but just as we were both turning I saw *Broke* hit by a salvo forward, and, to my horror, when she should have eased her helm and steadied on a course to fire a torpedo as we were doing, I saw that she was still swinging very quickly to

---

3 The order of the Flotilla is not certain: it is possible that not all these 7 destroyers were present in the line. But the relative position of *Broke* and *Sparrowhawk* to the enemy was as shown.

port as if her helm was jammed hard over, and was coming round straight for us.

We were only half a cable (100 yards) apart, and I saw that a collision was absolutely inevitable; there was no time to avoid it. So, in addition to the enemy's gunfire which was straddling us with every salvo, we saw *Broke* coming straight for our bridge, absolutely end on, at 28 knots. I remember shouting a warning to everybody in hearing to hold on, and cried out to the fo'csle gun's crew to clear off the fo'csle. Then I leant over the bridge and watched *Broke*'s bow coming absolutely dead straight for us. I really don't know why, but it was a fascinating sight; I clear forgot all about the Germans and their gunfire. Just as she hit us I remember shouting out 'Now!' and then nothing more till I found myself lying on the fo'csle, not of our ship, but of the *Broke*, illuminated in a bright light, but in a sort of fog which must have been due to the clouds of steam escaping from burst pipes. I sort of felt myself to see if arms and legs were all there, and then tried to stand up. My right leg hurt abominably, and I couldn't get any sort of movement into my right arm, but otherwise I was all right, and eventually I got up, though only to fall again owing to the deck being so extraordinarily slippery. I understood later why, but at the time it did not worry me.

Sparrowhawk and *Broke* in collision.

The whole of *Broke*'s foc'sle was an absolute shambles, but I crawled along until I came to a place where I could stand up. There was a perishing noise going on all the time, as the Germans were still endeavouring to sink the ship, and I could not see the *Sparrowhawk* owing to the clouds of escaping steam. As I was getting to my feet I met a fellow, who said, 'Who the hell are you?' I told him that I was the sub-lieutenant of the *Sparrowhawk*, and added that *Sparrow-hawk* had sunk, and that I was going to report to the Captain of the *Broke* to ask for a job. He told me that the Captain was on the remains of the bridge, and disappeared.

I eventually found a ladder up to the bridge and went up, picking my way over the wreckage of the lower bridge, and found the Captain, whom I knew slightly, and reported myself to him. He didn't seem to have realised that it was the *Sparrowhawk* he had rammed until I informed him of it. He told me to go back to my Captain and tell him that he had given orders for the crew of the *Broke* to be transferred to *Sparrowhawk*, because *Broke* was sinking, and I was also to ask for *Sparrowhawk*'s engines to be worked so as to endeavour to get the two ships apart, as they were now locked together and straining badly. I informed him that I was unable to see any sign of the *Sparrowhawk*, but he pointed her out to me, and I went to carry out his orders.

About this time the enemy ceased firing and switched off their searchlights, probably because the clouds of steam issuing from *Broke* and *Sparrowhawk* entirely hid them from sight.

I had to jump across a gap of about 6 feet from one ship to the other, and owing to my leg I didn't succeed in clearing it, but luckily caught the lower rail of *Sparrowhawk* with my left arm, and hung there with my body between the two ships. I holloaed out and somebody heard me and hauled me on board.

I found my Captain and gave him the message from the Captain of the *Broke*. His remarks were, 'But that's a pity, Sub., because I've sent across precisely the same message to him. This ship is also sinking fast!' The orders for the men to cross had actually been given, and about 20 of our ship's company went into *Broke* and about 15 men from *Broke* came across into us.

By this time the escaping steam had been got under control and the appalling noise stopped, and by means of megaphones the two Captains were able to communicate, the engines were worked, and the two ships drew apart with a sickening rending and crunching of steel plates. It was rather an anxious moment as we separated, for it was questionable whether the water-tight bulkhead would not be torn away as the ship's parted, and if it did we should sink. However, it was all right. *Broke* then disappeared stern first into the darkness, and we were left alone—not in a very healthy condition.

I was feeling at this period excessively cold, so as soon as I had nothing to do I went aft to my cabin to put on some more clothes. Much to my surprise when I got aft I found that we had no stern left, and was informed that *Contest*, shortly after our collision with *Broke*, had crashed into our stern, and cut it off absolutely clean for a distance of about 15 feet.

I then went forward to inspect the damage at that end, and found that the chart-house and bridge had gone over the side, together with the mast and foremost funnel, and the whole forward part from the foremost funnel to the stem was merely hanging on to the ship by one small steel plate, and was pointing out at right angles to the ship on our port side. The two ship's dogs, which lived forward at sea, could be heard howling somewhere behind the débris of this part, but it was quite impossible to get them out.

We then heard gunfire, and shortly afterwards two enemy destroyers passed us ahead, steaming fast, but made no attack. I distinctly saw these two ships, as I happened to be right forward at the time, but apparently very few other men saw them.

The bulkheads were now being shored up, as hopes were entertained of saving the ship, but my Captain instructed me to burn all the confidential books and documents in the boiler furnaces, which was quite a pleasing job as the night was bitterly cold. It had started to blow, and I could at least for a time keep warm at this job.

About 2 a.m. being on deck again, I saw, together with the most of the ship's company, a German destroyer come slowly up to us until, when about 100 yards off us, she stopped, and we prepared for one final scrap with her, with the one gun and one torpedo that were left in action.

Most of the officers and men were grouped round the after gun. In the hope of saving the ship, orders were given that the gun was not to fire until the enemy opened fire, and being determined to get some of his own back, the Captain took gun-layer, the 1st lieutenant was the trainer, and I was to look after the spotting. The gunner stood by with his last torpedo. The rest of the gun's crew was completed by various seamen, and those left without a job were ordered to lie down along the upper deck. We loaded, and waited for the flashes of gunfire from the German destroyer. But none came, and suddenly, just in the same way as she had appeared, she started her engines again, gathered way, and disappeared into the darkness— why we never discovered.

All this time *Tipperary* had been burning fiercely, much to our discomfiture as at times the flames lit us up distinctly, and we must have been visible for miles round. Just after the enemy destroyer had gone *Tipperary* sank.

Now we had nothing to do. We could not steam, as the *Contest* in the collision with us had jammed our rudder hard over, and no matter how we worked the engines we could not do anything except steam round in circles at dead slow speed, stern first. The engineers tried to cut through the bolts holding the rudder to the ship so as to drop the rudder off, but without success, and we were unable to make headway. Our wireless was, of course, altogether out of action, but one of our operators, a boy aged only 16½, worked very hard to produce a small temporary installation, but could not get it to go. However, it was a good effort, and deserved success.

Daylight, June 1st

Nothing more happened till about 3.30 a.m., when it began to get light. We had spent the remainder of the night keeping warm and cheering each other up.

A large shape, which we knew was a big ship, then moved up out of the mist. We just prayed that it was one of our own. Every man on board was straining his eyes to try and make her out, and some officers were using glasses as well. Our feelings, when we saw that she was one of the latest class of German light cruisers, may perhaps be imagined. Fellows went about sort of whispering that this must be the end of all things, and asked each other what it was like to be dead, etc. We had all been a bit worried by all the night show, and it was very early on a cold windy morning, so perhaps our feelings may be excused.

As yet the German cruiser could not see us, so we got as much ammunition as possible up from the after magazine and piled it round the after gun, for we jolly well meant, if we had to go, to take as many Germans with us as possible. Again the Captain ordered us not to be the first to open fire, as it was always hoped that some of our ships would arrive and help us to get our ship back to harbour. So we waited; just waited for the flashes of her guns and—thought.

I had some spotting glasses, and as it got light I tried hard to see men on her upper deck for she was only about a mile and a half away, and after a short time it had become really light. I thought she started to heel over to one side slightly. Then everyone else noticed it, until there was actually no mistaking it. She settled down forward, very slowly, and then quietly stood on her head, and—sank. We had seemed to be absolutely done, there had seemed to be no hope whatever, and then this happened; you can imagine what we felt like.

'It's a Long, Long Way to *Tipperary*'

The next incident occurred at 6.10 a.m., when somebody reported a submarine in sight, and once more the after-gun was manned at the run. Luckily the 1st lieutenant with his glasses made out the supposed submarine to be a carley life-saving raft full of men, for though they were only about half a mile away, the sea was so confused that we could only catch a glimpse of them now and again.

They saw us and put up a sheet as a sail. We tried to work the engines to steam towards them, but without much success. As they managed to paddle nearer we heard them singing 'It's a long, long way to *Tipperary*,' so we knew who they were, and incidentally jolly well agreed with them. It *was* a long way!

After about an hour and a half they finally managed to get alongside, but 16 out of the 23 collapsed. Poor fellows, they were

'It's a long, long way to *Tipperary*'

336

absolutely done. We managed to get them all on board with the exception of three, who were already dead, but five more died on our quarter deck. The rest amongst whom was one officer, the sub-lieutenant of the *Tipperary*, we dosed with brandy, and they soon recovered. They were all tremendously pleased to have reached something more substantial than their carley raft at last, but we thought that it was a case of 'out of the frying pan into the fire.' I remember the most cheery man of the lot was a fellow who had a hole quite as large as a half-crown right through one of his legs, but it didn't seem to worry him in the least. They told us that in the early morning a German lifeboat had passed them full of men, and that they had hailed them and asked to be taken on board, but they had been told to go to h—l. We presumed these Huns to have been part of the crew of the German cruiser that we had just seen sink, abandoning their ship.

About 6.45 a.m. a four-funnelled light cruiser appeared on the horizon and made the private signal to us, but we were unable to reply, having nothing in the world to do so with. We could not distinguish until she challenged whether she was English or German, because it was too misty, and the German light cruisers are very similar to ours, so the after gun was again manned. When she made the challenge we realised that she was English, but hoped that she would not open fire because we were unable to reply to it. She did not, but instead she steamed away and left us, perhaps because about half a mile away from us our bows were floating bottom up—they had dropped off earlier in the morning—and she may have mistaken this for the conning tower of a submarine. Whatever was the reason we were not reticent in voicing our opinions, for every moment the wind was blowing harder and the sea getting rougher, and our ship looked like sinking.

A Dutch trawler then appeared about two miles away, and we waved every available sheet, cloth, or coat, to attract her attention, for we badly wanted her to stand by us, but she took no notice. Whether she saw us or not I do not know, but she passed on out of sight; we cursed her good and proper.

Marksman Arrives

About 7.15 a.m. three columns of smoke appeared over the horizon, and soon afterwards three vessels came into view, which we quickly recognised to be English destroyers with a flotilla leader, the *Marksman*. They were steaming straight for us, and *Marksman* made the challenge. By this time somebody had been over the side and managed to get, from one of the signal lockers floating along-side, three flags which would make *Sparrowhawk*'s number, and these we hoisted at the mainmast: H flag, 61 pendants. They served their purpose, and *Marksman* increased to full speed and came up alongside. Her Captain ordered all our engine-room ratings, etc., to leave the ship in case we sank whilst being taken in tow, and informed my Captain that he intended to tow the remains of *Sparrowhawk* back to harbour, if she'd stand it, which was of course exactly what we all wanted. So we made fast two 3½-inch wires round the pedestal of the after gun, and then everybody was ordered to abandon the ship in case any of the bulkheads should give way.

Marksman then started to tow, having reported to the Com-mander-in-Chief that she had found the remains of *Sparrowhawk* and had taken off survivors. But after having towed the ship for about half a mile at 3 knots, both hawsers parted, one after the other in quick succession, owing to the state of the sea. At the same time signals were received by *Marksman* of the close proximity of enemy submarines. So a signal was made to the C-in-C. that the efforts to tow had proved useless, and instructions were asked for. The C-in-C. replied that the wreck was to be sunk and the survivors brought to Scapa Flow. Eighteen lyddite shells were then fired into the ship until she sank, the fore part going down first, and H flag, 61 pen-dants, and our colours, still flying from the mainmast. Thus was the end of the *Sparrowhawk*.

The officers and ship's company of the *Marksman* were most extraordinarily kind to us, giving us all that we wanted, and they told us many details of the action, of which we had seen so little.

We arrived at Scapa Flow on the Saturday morning, June 3rd, were sent to various depot ships, and finally sent south on the Monday morning.

Narrative of a Survivor of H.M.S. *Tipperary*

This description of the night of the 31st May to 1st June in the *Tipperary*, or afloat on her raft, is written nearly four years later,

partly from memory and partly from a brief account I wrote shortly
after the action.

The *Tipperary* was a large destroyer, which originally had been
built for the Chilians, but was taken over by our Admiralty in 1914
before she was completed. She was commissioned exactly a year
before Jutland, on 1st June 1915, but most of that year she spent in
dock as the result of two accidents. The first mishap was a bump
with one of our submarines off Harwich when a huge rent was torn
in her side, and within a few weeks of coming out of dock after that,
while leaving Harwich Harbour on a dark night in a strong tideway,
she went ashore to avoid collision with a light cruiser. She was then
in dock again until the beginning of May, 1916, when we joined the
Grand Fleet.

Her armament was more powerful than the average destroyer's,
consisting of three 4-inch guns on the foc'sle and three 4-inch right
aft, and a pair of torpedo tubes on either beam amidships. My station, as sub-lieutenant of the ship, was on a small platform aft outside the auxiliary wireless office, in charge of the three after-guns,
but the only communication which I had with the bridge was the
one gun-control voice pipe, through which all control orders had to
pass. I thus had little chance of finding out what was going on at any
time, except what I could see myself.

On the night of 31st May, I knew that the remainder of the
flotilla were in a single line astern of us, and, as far as I could
understand, we were steaming south at 17 knots, stationed 5 miles
astern of our battle squadron, with another flotilla stationed on
either beam steering the same course and speed as ourselves. We
were of course all closed up at our action stations, as it was by this
time quite dark.

Some short time after 11 p.m.—I remember the rough time, as I
had just previously asked the time of the petty officer telegraphist
in the W/T office—I saw some ships off our starboard beam steaming in the same direction as ourselves. I reported this to the bridge,
and receiving no reply, presumed that they were known to be
friends. Again a little later I saw the slight glare on the smoke above
the funnels of a ship on the starboard beam, but again got no information from the bridge.

At about 11.45 I suddenly saw and heard a salvo of guns fired
from some ship or ships to starboard at extremely short range. They
were so close that I remember the guns seemed to be firing from

339

some appreciable height above us. At almost the same instant the *Tipperary* shook violently from the impact of being hit by shells. (I was told afterwards that the first salvo hit the bridge, and it must have killed Captain (D) and nearly everyone there.)

I opened fire with the after guns as soon as the enemy opened on us. Proper spotting was out of the question, but crouching behind the canvas screen of my control position (I felt much safer with this thin weather screen between me and the enemy guns, though it wouldn't have kept out a spent rifle bullet) I yelled at the guns to fire. I don't think they heard me, but they opened fire all right. During this time both our starboard torpedo tubes were fired, but the enemy were so close that I think that the initial dive which torpedoes usually take as they enter the water made them go under the enemy ships. The enemy's second salvo hit and burst one of our main steam pipes, and the after-part of the ship was enveloped in a cloud of steam, through which I could see nothing. Losing all their steam, the turbines were brought to a standstill, and we dropped astern out of the action.

The three ships of the enemy that were firing at us could not have fired more than four salvoes before they gave us up as done for, and the whole thing had happened so suddenly and was over so quickly that I think we were all quite dazed. Aft we had been hit by only three shells, and only a few of the gun crews were wounded, but when the steam cleared away we found that the majority of the men stationed amidships were killed or wounded, including those ratings which had come up from the engine-room and stokeholds, while forward the ship was on fire, with flames coming out of the forward coal bunkers, and the bridge alight and an absolute wreck. The only two survivors that I saw afterwards of the people stationed forward were the first lieutenant, who was in the crow's nest up the foremast and in some miraculous way, in spite of the mast having been shot down, arrived aft, shaken but still alive; and the surgeon probationer, who came aft wounded in the leg.

For about hours two the ship floated in this condition, during which time we employed ourselves getting the wounded aft on to the quarter deck and covering them with officers' bedding from the cabins, and in putting out two small fires which commenced aft. We also collected all the confidential books, and placed those not already in steel chests into weighted ammunition boxes, ready to throw overboard in an emergency.

The patience and courage of the wounded was wonderful. On one of my expeditions forward, when I was passing a half-completed little sheet-iron structure which we had been building as an office, I heard a voice say, 'Do you think you could have me shifted out of this, sir?' I collected three men, and from the wreck of this shanty we lifted out and carried aft a stoker, badly wounded and apparently paralysed, but quite cheerful. He directed the operation of being got out himself.

At another time our L.T.O. (leading torpedo man), who was doing his best to administer first-aid, called me over and asked, 'What can I do with this, sir?' showing me a man with a large portion of his thigh missing. I merely covered the wound up with a large piece of cotton wool and put a blanket over him. 'Feels a lot better already, sir,' said the wounded man.

We could not cope with the fire forward, it being impossible to get along the upper deck, as the ready supply of ammunition for the forward guns was exploding box by box at short intervals. All the boats were completely smashed, but two life-saving floats which were undamaged were got into the water and kept alongside ready. We threw everything that could possibly catch fire overboard, in the hopes of stopping the fire spreading aft, and I think we got rid of far more things than was necessary, even throwing overboard the upper deck supply of ammunition by the after guns and the two port torpedoes. Perhaps we did it more to keep ourselves employed and our minds from thinking of the forward magazine, than with any idea of being useful.

Tipperary Sinks, about 2 a.m.

At one time during these two hours some ship opened fire on us for a short time, but luckily she did not hit us. Also two small craft, which we took to be enemy destroyers, closed us, asked who we were, and disappeared again into the dark.

Shortly before 2 a.m. the 1st lieutenant noticed that the ship was going, and gave the order, 'Everybody aft.' The ship heeled slightly to starboard, then the bows gradually went under. The 1st lieutenant ordered 'Everyone for themselves,' and we clambered over the side into the sea.

The small carley float had already left, and I have never heard of it being seen again. Those who were lucky enough to be in time, got on to the large carley float, the remainder just jumped into the sea. By the time I got to the rails the stern of the ship was well up in the air and the propellers were out of the water, so I slid down a rope on to the port propeller, and thence into the sea.

Unlike most people, I had kept my sea boots on during the last two hours, thinking that I should have plenty of time to take them off when the moment came, but this I quite forgot to do, and I found myself in the water with my sea boots still on, and only two breaths of air in my lifesaving waistcoat.

However, I found no difficulty in kicking the boots off, and the waistcoat was very comfortable for swimming. I started off trying to get clear of the ship, as I was afraid of being sucked down by eddies, but could make no headway for some time, probably because I was trying to swim to windward, and it was not until I swam round the stern of the *Tipperary* and pointed down to leeward that I got any distance from her. I heard a commotion behind me, and looking over my shoulder saw the last of the stern just disappearing, so I swam hard for a bit.

I now found myself some distance from the thirty odd other swimmers—amongst whom I noticed Peter, our 1st lieutenant's white-haired terrier—with the carley raft further to leeward. As I had little hope of being picked up, I swam slowly away from the others, preferring to drown by myself rather than with a crowd.

After swimming about for what I suppose was an hour, I saw two German pulling boats passing, and soon afterwards heard our men on the raft hailing them. I swam towards the raft, thinking now that there might be a possibility of being saved. As a matter of fact, the Germans passed by without taking any notice. The cold of the water had sort of numbed my brain, and I now had only one idea left—to reach the raft, and I eventually reached it. It was overcrowded, but they pulled me up on to it, an engine-room artificer on one side of me and a red-haired marine on the other side, and I had room to sit on the edge. The raft, supporting about 30 men, was about a foot under water—it's a hollow, copper, oval-shaped affair, with life-lines and things to hang on by—and as the night drew on a swell got up and the seas washed up and down over our middles, like the waves when one first wades out bathing, only much colder. We sang various popular songs, but I suppose because I had got colder swimming about than the others who had been on the raft all the time, I could not think of the words, and my music was all of one note.

When at last daylight gradually appeared we made out the shape of a small ship, apparently steaming round and round in circles. We were now all in a dull, comatose condition, in which one didn't care whether one lived or died; so much so that, although the destroyer was only a hundred yards from us, it was very difficult to get anyone to use the paddles and get there. When the men on one side of the raft paddled, the other side stopped, and we simply spun round in a circle. At last an ingenious petty officer, standing up on the board in the centre of the raft, held up a counterpane, and we sort of made sail towards the *Sparrowhawk*—for so we found the ship to be. Eventually we reached her about 5 a.m. and were hauled on board, and though her stern was cut off and her bows also were nearly off just by the bridge, she was Paradise itself to us compared to the carley raft.

Of the original 32 men who had been on the raft (I think there had been 32), 2 had died and dropped off during the night, and 4 were found to be dead when hauled on board the *Sparrowhawk*. Soon after we arrived on board the bows of the *Sparrowhawk* broke off and floated away, but eventually a destroyer-leader—the *Marksman*—appeared, and after trying to tow the *Sparrowhawk* and finding it impossible, took the crew and ourselves on board her, and sank what was left of the *Sparrowhawk*. We returned in the *Marksman* to Scapa Flow.

The only other survivors of the *Tipperary* of which I have heard, except those picked up with me from the raft, were the Surgeon and I think two ratings, picked up by one of the German boats. They were taken to Holland in a Dutch trawler.

Narrative of the Commanding Officer of H.M.S. *Ardent*[4]
One of the only two Survivors of the Ship

By about nine o'clock practically all firing had ceased, and the 4th Flotilla took station astern of the battle fleet in two lines, about a mile apart. We were all steaming to the southward towards the

---

4 This narrative was first printed in the *Britannia Magazine* of the Royal Naval College, Dartmouth, Christmas, 1916.

Heligoland Bight at about 17 knots. Various firings went on on either side of us, but I could not make out any ships. Once our line eased down for some reason and nearly stopped, when the *Fortune*, which was next astern of me, opened fire from the starboard side, and we clearly saw a submarine on the surface which fired a torpedo at the *Fortune*, but missed. We charged round at the submarine but she disappeared, and we didn't see her again.

It then became evident that the enemy were close at hand. We saw flashes and heard guns all round us, and several destroyers in our line opened fire. Then I clearly perceived four big ships on a nearly parallel but slightly converging course to us, on our starboard quarter. They challenged several times, and their challenge was not an English one. They then switched on their searchlights, picked up the *Fortune*, and opened fire on her. The leaders of my line appeared to increase speed and turn away to port. I could see the *Fortune* was hard hit, so altered round to starboard and fired a torpedo at the leading enemy ship. We could all see it hit most clearly, and there was an enormous upheaval of water right forward. Her foremost lights went out, and she turned away. By this time other searchlights were on us from the second ship, and fire was opened on us, but we got through and away with very little damage. We caught a last glimpse of the *Fortune*, on fire and in a sinking condition, but fighting still and firing her guns in a most inspiring manner. The *Fortune* had been in my sub-division for over two years, during which time we had always worked together, and her Captain, Lieut.-Com. F. G. Terry, was in my class in the *Britannia*, and a very great friend of mine. But the *Ardent* was not to survive the *Fortune* for long.

As we got away from this attack I could see that a most desperate action was being fought on our starboard hand, where our other line of destroyers were. A great flame suddenly went up and lit up the sea for a great distance round. This burning ship turned out to be the *Tipperary*, our Captain 'D.'s' ship. She burnt a long time.

It was now nearly midnight, and I found myself alone, and so resumed the course of the fleet and increased speed, hoping to pick up the rest of my division. Smoke was reported right ahead, which I thought would be theirs but as I got nearer realised that it was not our flotilla, but a big ship steaming on exactly the opposite course to us. I attacked at once, and from a very close range our remaining torpedoes were fired, but before I could judge of the effect the enemy switched on searchlights and found us at once. I then became aware that the *Ardent* was taking on a division of German battle-ships. However, we opened fire and ran on at full speed. The next moments were perhaps the most thrilling that anyone could experi-ence. Our guns were useless against such big adversaries; our torpe-does were fired; we could do no more, but wait in the full glare of the blinding searchlights for the shells that could not fail to hit us soon at such close range. There was perfect silence on the bridge, and not a word was spoken. It must only have been seconds, but it seemed like hours. At last it came, and as the first salvo hit I heard a seaman ejaculate almost under his breath, 'Oo-ooh,' as one does to a bursting rocket. Shell after shell hit us, and our speed diminished and then stopped; then the dynamo stopped, and all the lights went out.

Our three guns that had been barking away like good 'uns ceased firing one by one. I looked on to the forecastle and saw and heard the Captain of the forecastle exhorting the only remaining man of his gun's crew to 'Give them one more,' but that 'one more' was never fired, and I saw later both these brave souls stretched out dead. I myself was wounded by almost the first salvo, but felt no great pain or discomfort. The actual feeling when I was struck was as if I had been hit on the thigh with an iron bar, though eventually a piece of shell about as big as my little finger was taken out of me.

The enemy ships suddenly switched off lights and 'ceased fire.' I could feel the ship was sinking, and said so to my 1st lieutenant, who also was on the bridge, and told him to get out the boats and rafts, or what might be left of them. I tried to get down the starboard bridge ladder, but that was shot away. The port one was hanging by a shred, and I slid down that. The leading telegraphist came up to me in the quietest and most matter-of-fact way, and asked if he should make any report. I told him what to make, and he saluted, disappeared, and I never saw him again. The leading signalman came up and said in the most cheerful way, 'Well, the old *Ardent* done her bit all right, sir.'

The ship was nearly gone, so it only remained for us to try and save as many of the crew as possible.

H.M.S. *Ardent* Sinks (soon after Midnight)

A terrible scene of destruction and desolation was revealed to me as I walked aft (with some difficulty). All boats were in pieces. The funnels looked more like nutmeg graters. The rafts were blown to bits, and in the ship's side and deck were holes innumerable. In the very still atmosphere, the smoke and steam poured out from the holes in the deck perfectly straight up into the air. Several of my best men came up and tried to console me, and all were delighted that we had at length been in action and done our share. But many were already killed and lay around their guns and places of duty. Most of the engine-room and stokehold brigade must have been killed outright.

I walked right aft and sat down on the ward-room hatch. I could do no more as my leg was very stiff and bleeding a lot. My servant and another seaman, both of whom had been with me over two years, came aft to look for me and to help me. I sent them forward and told them to pass the word for each man to look out for himself. For a moment or two I was quite alone; the smoke cut me off from those further forward, and there was absolute quiet and stillness. Then all of a sudden we were again lit up by searchlights, and the enemy poured in four or five more salvoes at point blank range, and then switched off her lights once more. This would be about ten minutes from the time we were first hit.

The *Ardent* gave a big lurch, and I bethought myself of my 'Gieve' waistcoat. I blew and blew without any result whatever, and found that it had been shot through. Another lurch, and the ship heeled right over, and threw me to the ship's side. I could feel she was going, so I flopped over into the sea, grabbing a lifebuoy that was providentially at hand. The *Ardent*'s stern kept up a few moments, then she slowly sank from view. As the smoke and steam cleared off I could see many heads in the water—about forty or fifty I should think. There was no support beyond life-belts, lifebuoys, and floating waistcoats, so I was afraid that few of us could possibly survive, especially as I realised that all the destroyers had, gone on, and that no big ship would dare to stop, even if they saw us in the water.

I spoke to many men, and saw most of them die one by one. Not a man of them showed any fear of death, and there was not a murmur, complaint, or cry for help from a single soul. Their joy was, and they talked about it to the end, that they and the *Ardent* had 'done their bit' as they put it. While there were still many alive, a German came close and fired a star-shell over us. I could see her distinctly, and was all for giving her a hail, but the men all said 'No': they would sooner take the remote chance of being saved by an

English ship than be a prisoner in Germany. I was nearly done-in once or twice in the first hour by men hanging on to me in the last stages of exhaustion, and I was separated from my lifebuoy and was pulled right over in the water, but managed to recover myself and the buoy. None of the men appeared to suffer at all; they just seemed to lie back and go to sleep.

After a long weary while the sun came up, and then I was feeling much more comfortable than two hours previously. I found a skiff's oar floating past, and put it under my arms. I began to feel very drowsy, and dropped off into a sort of sleep several times, only to be awakened again by waves slapping into my face. There was quite a swell, but the surface of the water was smooth, owing to the masses of oil floating about from sunken ships. I woke again, after what I felt to be a long time, to hear a shout, and could see ships a long way off. I took a sort of detached interest in them, heard and gave an answering shout to 'Stick it, *Ardent*'s!' to someone in the water near by, but whom I could not see, and watched the ships disappear again without much interest, and dozed off again.

Once more I woke to find a flotilla leader—the *Marksman*—close alongside me. I sang out for help, and in reply got a welcome and reassuring shout, 'You're all right, sir; we're coming,' and once again relapsed into unconsciousness, and have no recollection at all of being actually got on board. The time I was picked up was just after six o'clock.

I began to take an interest in the outside world again about 7.30, and from that moment, with the exception, of course, of my leg, which was very stiff and painful, and also a few odd scratches and cuts, I felt absolutely no ill effects whatsoever from my long period in the sea. We had rather a rough passage back, but they were very kind to me in the *Marksman*. I got quite a start once when the fore-castle guns right over my head opened fire, but I got a reassuring message the same moment from the Captain to say that they weren't in action, only sinking the *Sparrowhawk*, which had been so badly damaged in collision that it was impossible to tow her back. I was placed on board the hospital ship *China* on June 2nd, and was oper-ated on that night.

I could not finish a narrative like this without a word about my crew. They were really a splendid lot, and all through the long, weary months of waiting, they were as cheery and contented as possible. I always felt that their great spirits, confidence, and the alacrity with which they tackled every job was a much greater source of inspiration and help to me than anything I did was to them. I was lucky, too in my officers. The 1st lieutenant, Lieut. Egan, on that last great night, was calmness personified. The torpedo gunner (Mr. Livermore) seemed almost as much pleased that his torpedo, which scored the first hit, hadn't 'broken surface' (a great matter for professional pride with gunners (T)) as that it had hit. The artificer engineer and his staff did just what was wanted, and faithfully fulfilled every order from the bridge till death overtook them. All hands fought the ship with the utmost gallantry, and in a most tenacious and determined manner, till she sank beneath them, and then met their death in that composed and happy spirit that I am convinced comes to all those who do their duty to the end. May they rest in peace.

Narrative of H.M.S. *Marksman*
The Flotilla Leader which rescued Survivors of
H.M.S. *Sparrowhawk, Fortune, Ardent*, and *Tipperary*

The night left one with a confused memory of guns, searchlights, sudden bursts of firing and ships on fire, of which we seldom knew whether we were witnessing a friend or an enemy in trouble as we had little or no information as to the relative position of ourselves to the other ships and squadrons of the fleet. During the later part of the night we were detached, and soon after daybreak, the weather being hazy, we found ourselves in the neighbourhood where the *Tipperary* and others of the 4th Flotilla had received such severe handling. We first saw a shape appearing, which we hoped would prove to be a crippled German, but it turned out to be the *Sparrowhawk*, with her bow off and a small section of her stern removed, exposing the inside of her tiller flat. She was a pitiful sight. Grouped in her after part were her own crew and the survivors of the *Tipperary* with their sub-lieutenant. As far as I remember these survivors of *Tipperary* had made the *Sparrowhawk* in a raft; all were loud in their praises of their sub-lieutenant's pluck and conduct on this occasion.

We transferred all hands aboard us, and then tried to tow the *Sparrowhawk* stern first, but after several attempts the idea was abandoned, and we asked the Commander-in-Chief by wireless for permission to sink her by gunfire, which eventually was approved.

I cannot quite recollect whether it was before or after we sighted the *Sparrowhawk* that we observed and picked up two raft-loads of the *Fortune*'s men, including their chief artificer engineer. The whole sea for a large distance round was a mass of oil, and it was also in this area that we came upon the Captain of the *Ardent*, who had been in the water some five hours, and was in the last stages of exhaustion. I believe that he and one other rating were the only survivors of the *Ardent*. There were quantities of bodies floating around in the vicinity, mostly British, but all dead. When we first arrived on the scene we saw the bow of a destroyer sticking up about 50 feet out of the water, but it shortly afterwards disappeared. After sinking the *Sparrowhawk*, we calculated that we should soon be sighting one of the main bodies of our fleet coming up from the southward, which, sure enough, we did do, and we joined up with them for our passage back to Scapa Flow.

CHAPTER XVII

OTHER INCIDENTS OF THE NIGHT

Two Actions of H.M.S. *Castor*, about 10.04 p.m. and
12.15 a.m.; Loss of H.M.S. *Turbulent*, about 12.25 a.m.

The three most fiercely fought actions during the night of
Jutland were those of the 2nd Light Cruiser Squadron, of
Tipperary's (4th) Flotilla, and of the 12th Flotilla at daybreak.

But, in addition to these three actions, certain other engagements with enemy ships did occur, notably those of the *Castor*,
and of the 13th Destroyer Flotilla. In the latter action one of
our destroyers, the *Turbulent*, was lost with all hands. During
H.M.S. *Castor*'s two engagements at about 10 p.m., and again
at about 12.15 a.m., she was in company with and leading
some boats of the 11th Destroyer Flotilla, but she seems to
have been the only ship actively engaged with the enemy,
although in the first engagement torpedoes were fired by some
of the destroyers, which it was hoped may have caused damage or loss to the enemy. In the second engagement, the
Castor's think that they sank a German destroyer by gunfire at
point-blank range. Of this not much description can be given.
They fired into the German, and hoped that they sank her,
and that's all about it. Whether the Germans had adventures
of the same nature as some of our badly damaged destroyers,
one does not know.

Accounts then from officers of H.M.S. *Castor* and of
H.M.S. *Marne* of the 11th Flotilla, and of H.M.S. *Petard* and
Nicator of the 13th Flotilla, will describe these incidents
which were taking place concurrently with all the other night
actions; and we may place here also the conclusion of the narrative of H.M.S. *Malaya*, battleship of the 5th B.S., which
will indicate the feelings of the men in big ships during the

hours of darkness, when the light of searchlights, gun-flashes, and of ships blowing up or on fire was constantly illuminating the horizon to the northward of them, but without giving them any opportunity to share in the fight.

Narrative from H.M.S. *Castor* (Night Action)
Continuation of H.M.S. *Castor's* Narrative from Part II., page 203

Soon after dark we saw three ships loom up to starboard, and as we challenged they switched on searchlights and opened fire. They fired only at us, being apparently unable to see our destroyers, which were painted black. We were hit direct four times; one shell hit the forecastle just under the bridge and, bursting inside, made a hole about 5 feet in diameter, and the splinters from it wounded a large number of men in the fore ammunition lobby; one shell went right through the fore mess deck and burst outside the disengaged side of the ship; one hit the motor barge, a brand new boat which had only done one trip with Capt. (D), bursting in her and setting her on fire; another shell hit the disengaged side of the fore-bridge and wiped out everybody in the way of signalmen, messengers, etc., who had gathered there, with the exception of one man. This man had a miraculous escape, the 4-inch shell bursting practically between his legs, but all the force of the explosion must have gone on in the direction in which the shell was travelling, for it blew a large hole in the deck of the bridge, and through this the man fell. He landed on another man who had been killed by that same shell, but he himself was practically unhurt. Besides these direct hits, the ship was covered with splinter dents from shells which burst on hitting the water short, and several men at the midship guns were laid out by them. We fired a torpedo at the leading Hun, and the two after 6-inch guns, which were not being directly fired at, were making very good practice at the enemy. But the Germans soon altered course away, thereby avoiding the torpedo we had fired, and we then did the same, missing collision with one of the second half-flotilla boats by inches only.

We soon collected ourselves again after this little brush, and temporarily repaired all minor damage, such as electric leads cut, etc.

Two or three times during the night we saw heavy firing some 2 or 3 miles ahead, but we were not able to ascertain who it was. Suddenly a German destroyer appeared quite close, steaming slowly. We tried to ram, and got within a few yards of her, but she was too quick and avoided us. However, we fired several shots into her at point-blank range, but it was impossible to tell if she sank. That was the last we saw of the enemy, and we then set about trying to regain touch with our own battle fleet, as it was still possible that the action would be renewed at daybreak, but it was 9 o'clock in the morning before we found them.

On 22nd November, 1918, the day after the High Seas Fleet surrendered, I was one of the inspecting party of the German light cruiser *Koln*. In her there was a memorial to '14 officers and men of the light cruiser *Hamburg*, killed at the Battle of Skaggerack.' The *Hamburg* was the leading ship of the three Germans which were in action with us at 10 p.m. on 31st May, 1916, so it seems we gave as good as we got. We had 16 killed and about 40 wounded.

H.M.S. *Marne*, of 11th Destroyer Flotilla
In Company with H.M.S. *Castor*

The 11th Destroyer Flotilla, including *Marne*, left Scapa Flow at 10.30 p.m. on 30th May, in company with the battle fleet, and proceeded towards the Skaw, screening the 2nd Battle Squadron. During the day action the flotilla was stationed on the disengaged bow of H.M.S. *King George V.*, the leading battleship in the line, but we had practically no share in the action. Twice we went out to attack German destroyers, but they refused to accept battle, so each time we withdrew without having got into action.

After dark the 11th Flotilla took up night cruising stations, and shaped a course to the southward at 17 knots.

About 10.30 p.m., what appeared to be three light cruisers were sighted about 1,500 yards away on the starboard beam. Before they could be identified as friend or foe, they had switched on searchlights and opened fire on the flotilla with every available gun. Apparently *Marne* was the first ship they made out in the darkness. Telegraphs were put to 'Full speed ahead,' but for some reason unknown there was a temporary stoppage and the ship lost her way—most fortunate as it happened, for it caused all the enemy's salvoes to fall in the water just ahead of us. Everyone on the bridge thought that we had been hit aft, but our stoppage apparently was only due to a hang up in the signals to the engine-room. *Castor* then came up between *Marne* and the enemy, incurring a heavy gruelling herself, but probably saving *Marne*. One hit that the enemy scored on *Castor* set one of her boats afire, and, burning fiercely, it lit up the whole ship. She was a most impressive sight, racing along past us with this fire in her and at the same time engaging the enemy with her starboard broadside.

Fortunately *Marne*'s stopping was only momentary, and we then darted ahead again. *Castor* drew clear, and she and *Marne* and *Magic* each discharged torpedoes. One of these must have found its target, for an explosion occurred amongst the enemy ships. The hositle vessels then extinguished their lights, and nothing more of them was either seen or heard. The gun-flashes and the searchlights had been so intensely glaring during this short action, that for some few minutes after firing ceased one felt almost completely blind in the ordinary darkness. *Marne* had a lucky escape in this skirmish, as most of the enemy shells fell ahead of her and only one 4-inch struck her, and that one aft without exploding.

All night long gun-flashes were visible. A burning vessel was in sight for quite a long time, believed to have been *Tipperary*. Later a terrific explosion occurred, undoubtedly some capital ship (? *Lutzow* or *Black Prince*) blowing up.

Dawn found *Marne* still with her flotilla, and she took station 5 miles on the starboard beam of *Castor*. A British light cruiser, most likely *Dublin*, was met and she asked her position as all her own records had been shot away. *Marne* joined up with the main body of the Grand Fleet about 8 a.m., and eventually returned to base without further incident.

Loss of H.M.S. *Turbulent*
About 12.25 a.m.

Continuation of the narrative of H.M.S. *Petard*, destroyer of the 13th Flotilla, after that flotilla's torpedo attack on the German battle cruisers at about 5 p.m., during the battle cruiser run to the north (see Part I., page 56).

. . . About 7 p.m. we seemed to turn to south, remaining still astern of the 5th B.S., with the 4th Flotilla on our starboard beam. We proceeded like this till about 9.30 p.m., when on our starboard bow searchlights were switched on, and an engagement took place for several minutes. This was also repeated about 10.30 p.m., and one could tell that it was our 4th Flotilla, because their tall foremast funnel and two short after ones were clearly visible, lit up in the searchlight rays. One did not know at all what was going on, but could tell there were several destroyers on fire, the peculiar white light given off by the burning oil being most distinct. About 11.30 p.m. there was a similar disturbance for a few moments on our starboard quarter, and then darkness again.

At 0.15 a.m. our flotilla's course was altered from south to southwest by west. At 0.25 we sighted a dark mass about 5 or 6 points on our starboard bow, steering S.E. about 600 yards away. On looking at her closely there could be no doubt at all what she was, as at the angle we sighted her at we could see clearly large crane derricks silhouetted against the sky, and only German ships have these fittings. At the same moment the German battleships switched on recognition lights, consisting of two red lights over a white one.

The *Petard* had fired all her torpedoes in the day attack, there was nothing we could do but get away, so we increased to full speed and altered course about a point to port to clear the enemy's stem.

As soon as we had passed ahead of her she switched her foremost group of searchlights on to us, but they just missed our stern on being switched on, though they were trained round to the right directly, and then illuminated us perfectly. Immediately afterwards we saw flashes of the enemy's secondary armament being fired, and on the bridge we felt the ship tremble slightly, and guessed we had been hit aft. They seemed to give us another salvo, and then the second ship in the line—we could now see four—also joined in; this second salvo struck us further forward in the ship, but luckily missed the bridge and the midship guns' crew.

At this moment the foremost group of German searchlights were switched off us and trained round to port all together on to the *Turbulent*, my next astern. Immediately afterwards, according the the evidence of some of my ship's company aft, she was rammed and sunk by this leading German battleship, but I personally did not see this. We escaped without any further incident.

Petard had been hit six times. One shot penetrated the roof of No. 2 stokehold and cut an oil fuel pipe, setting this oil alight, so that it flared up out of the shell hole and lit up the whole ship perfectly. Luckily, the engine-room department were able to shut off the oil to the broken pipe and extinguish the fire in a few minutes. The enemy's first salvo had hit the after part of the ship, and had killed or severely wounded the whole of the officers and crew of the after 4-inch gun; this salvo also wrecked all the officers' cabins, and unfortunately killed the surgeon probationer just at the moment when his services were most required.

That was all we saw of Jutland, as having one boiler disabled and being short of oil, we were detached with *Nicator* to return to Rosyth at 6.30 a.m. However, we were not quite free of the Germans yet, for about 4.0 p.m. on June 1st, just as we made the coast off the Farne Islands, we were attacked by a German submarine. But the torpedo missed, passing between the two destroyers, and apparently sank and exploded on the bottom of the sea, as we all felt the explosion immediately afterwards.

Continuation of Narrative of H.M.S. *Nicator*
(Of the 13th Destroyer Flotilla, Rosyth Force)

Continued from page 65

We eventually joined up with our flotilla again at 'Windy Corner,' just as the Grand Fleet were deploying, which was a truly wonderful sight. The contrast between the calm manœuvring of the battle fleet followed by the battle cruisers and 5th Battle Squadron, as compared to the seeming confusion of the small craft was extraordinary. It seemed like Piccadilly Circus with the policemen on strike, and the motor 'buses pushing their way through all the smaller vehicles.

During the night we took station astern of the *Petard*, and with all the destroyers following the *Champion*, were in the line between the battle fleet and the battle cruisers and 5th Battle Squadron. Throughout the night, up to the time the enemy broke through the line we had noticed spasmodic actions going on, beginning right away on our starboard bow, and gradually working aft, and closing us as we altered course.

Some time after midnight, I cannot remember the exact time, the signal to alter course to S.W. came. For some time there had been a long lull between these intermittent busts of firing, which we took to be a flotilla attacking, when suddenly we saw challenging going on, and some ship, I do not know which, switched on its fighting lights for a second or two and then off again, apparently by accident. Then without any warning searchlights were switched on abaft our starboard beam, and settled on the *Petard*, ahead of us. We saw three or four big ships, obviously Germans, silhouetted for a moment; then a burst of fire, followed quickly by another, and the light went out. The *Petard* was badly hit, and suffered a lot of casualties. Then all lights switched on again, this time on us for a fraction of a minute during which time we thought we were in for it too, but they trained aft on to the *Turbulent*, two ships astern of us and as far as I can remember, the tail of the line of destroyers. She appeared to be at absolutely point-blank range, and in a few second a ripple of fire seemed to run the whole length of her. It looked as if she were blown right out of the water. It all happened so suddenly that we hardly realised what was taking place, and it somehow did not strike us that this was the German fleet breaking through the line, unluckily at the weakest point, just between the battle fleet and battle cruisers. When daylight came we sent our surgeon probationer on board the *Petard*, as their surgeon had been killed with the first salvo. With only a destroyer's medical outfit and no anæsthetics he performed wonders, and undoubtedly saved a number of lives.

By this time we were running very short of oil, as we had been out on patrol the night before and had had no opportunity of replenishing before we had to joint up with the battle cruisers, so we were told off to return to base with *Petard*.

Continuation of the Narrative of a Turret Officer, H.M.S. *Malaya*
(5th Battle Squadron)

Continued from page 130

Of the results of the day action I can say very little. I cannot definitely say that I saw any big ships sink, but only one light cruiser and one destroyer. My impression at the time, however, was that the enemy were in a very bad way when they disappeared in a cloud of smoke. They were certainly very disorganised, and several were seen to fall out. On each occasion, when I had a good view of them after the arrival of the Grand Fleet, they seemed to be more disorganised than before.

Our disappointment at the intervention of the mist may readily be imagined, when one considers that we knew the High Seas Fleet was already beginning to feel the strain and that the disposition of our own ships was so nearly ideal.

Several time during the day action I had looked for my brother's destroyer, the *Nicator*, but could never distinguish her amongst all the other boats. I felt fairly confident as to his safety, for I had not seen any daylight action by our torpedo boat destroyers, except the repulse of the half-hearted German attack. I little knew that he had followed Comdr. Bingham at about 4.30 p.m. to within 3,000 yards of the High Seas Fleet, and had only escaped by the greatest good fortune and his Captain's wonderful handling of the ship.

German star shell showing up a night attack.

We steamed south during the night, which was full of incident. Officers and men remained at their action stations, for the enemy were very near, and close action might be expected at any moment. About 9.0 p.m. I remembered that I had not eaten for some time, and was very glad of a sandwich of tinned salmon, which was served out—nothing warm could be obtained, as the galley was out of action. The men managed to get a little sleep during the night, but I was not so fortunate, my perch not being very comfortable. Also,

I hardly dared sleep, for it seemed so necessary to be absolutely ready.

We heard and saw several destroyers' attacks on the Germans. One especially we had an extremely close view of, some of the German shells fired at our destroyers actually falling around us. I have a very vivid impression of those destroyers dashing into the blinding searchlights and star shells, and into a perfectly furious fire. The leading boat was hit badly, and was soon ablaze stem to stern. The others seemed to make good their escape after having fired their torpedoes. On this occasion, as during other attacks, we heard and felt heavy explosions, as though a torpedo had hit, and one ship was actually seen to sink. One of the explosions lit up the whole sky.

It seemed absolutely impossible to know what was going on all round us, and where was friend and where was foe. But, as so much was happening, we thought it absolutely certain that we should meet in the morning. It is not easy to express our feeling when with dawn down came the mist; we could see no more than 2 miles, and not a German was in sight. We cruised about until nearly noon, hoping against hope that the weather would clear and allow us to complete yesterday's work. At noon I was not sorry to be able to get out of my turret for lunch, for I had had no rest and no food for the last 24 hours, and I was quite ready for both. The next and most trying duty was to discover the casualties of my division, which had suffered heavily. The majority of the wounded were unconscious, for they had been dreadfully burnt, but those to whom I spoke only wanted one to write to their people saying that all was going well, and to know about the action. Several of them afterwards died.

At 8 p.m., June 1st, the most mutilated of the dead were buried at sea.

I need hardly say that the behaviour of the men was perfectly splendid. From the shell-room to the gun-house and 'control cabinet,' they all did their jobs with the utmost cheeriness, often under very uncomfortable conditions. They could feel the ship being hit and take up an unpleasant list, but they had no other thought than to keep the guns going and thereby eventually annihilate the whole German fleet.

CHAPTER XVIII

12TH FLOTILLA ATTACK AT DAYBREAK

The torpedo attack carried out by the 12th Destroyer Flotilla upon a German battle squadron at daybreak (approximately 2 a.m.) on June 1st was one of the most successful enterprises of the Battle of Jutland. It resulted in one German battleship being sunk, and another one being hit and badly damaged, whilst the attacking flotilla escaped without the loss of any ship, and received material damage to only one destroyer, H.M.S. *Onslaught*, whose Captain and 1st lieutenant were killed.

The British ships present in the attack were the flotilla leader, H.M.S. *Faulknor*, and eight destroyers—*Obedient*, *Mindful*, *Marvel*, and *Onslaught*; *Maenad*, *Noble*, *Nessus*, and *Narwhal*.

Narratives from officers in four of these ships, describing the incidents of this attack, are included here. The report of the attack made by the Commander-in-Chief in his despatch was as follows:—

'(Para. 23). The attack carried out by the 12th Flotilla (Captain Anselan J. B. Stirling) was admirably executed. The [German] squadron attacked, which consisted of six large vessels besides light cruisers, comprised vessels of the *Kaiser* class [dreadnought battleships], and were almost completely surprised. A large number of torpedoes was fired, including some at the second and third ships in the line; those fired at the third ship took effect, and she was observed to blow up. A second attack, made twenty minutes later by *Maenad* (Commander John T. Champion) on the five vessels still remaining, resulted in the second ship in the line being also hit and blown up.[1]

The destroyers were under a heavy fire from the light cruisers on reaching the rear of the line, but *Onslaught* was the only vessel which received any material injuries. In *Onslaught*, Sub-lieutenant Harry W. A. Kemmis, assisted by Midshipman Reginald G. Arnot, R.N.R., the only executive officers not disabled, brought the ship successfully out of action and reached Rosyth.'

Narrative of H.M.S. *Obedient*
(Leading Ship of 1st Division)

BY AN OFFICER ON HER BRIDGE

About 10.30 p.m. *Champion* and four destroyers appeared on our starboard beam, and whilst there heavy firing took place in that direction, many shells falling close to the flotilla. A ship, too, was seen to be on fire in the same direction. At 11.20 p.m. there was further heavy firing on the starboard bow, and three big explosions were seen, and again a ship was seen to be on fire, which continued to burn for a long while; in fact, could still be seen astern for a full hour later, although below the horizon.

At 12.10 a.m. the flotilla was subjected to heavy gunfire from the direction of the starboard beam, which necessitated altering course to east, and later to north-east, before resuming our southerly course at 12.30 a.m.

Just about an hour later, at 1.43 a.m., as daylight was appearing, a line of ships were sighted on our starboard beam, steering apparently a parallel course to us, about east-south-east. Owing to the mist we could not at once determine whether they were enemy ships or not, but our doubts were very soon dispelled by one of them challenging us. She flashed the letter 'K' in morse code, but this was not the correct challenge for the night, so obviously the ships were German.

We were the division nearest to the enemy, and at first we thought that Captain (D) in *Faulknor* was not aware of them, and so ran

---

1 Probably this ship did not sink.

alongside his ship to tell him by megaphone. Our captain then decided to attack with our division, and we altered course to starboard to do so, but just afterwards we observed that the enemy had turned away together about 6 points (67 degrees), and, as we noticed that our flotilla had increased speed to prepare for an attack, we turned back to rejoin the *Faulknor*. By the time we had rejoined she had increased to 25 knots, and holding on to her course until 2.0 a.m., then altered course 16 points to starboard (180 degrees), and we, with our division, took station astern of her.

The enemy were now clearly visible on our port side, dreadnought battleships leading and pre-dreadnoughts following, a long line of them. Conditions were nearly ideal for an attack, as it was too light for searchlights to be of much use to the enemy big ships, and yet, with the mist as an added cloak, it was sufficiently dark to make the laying of guns on fast-moving targets difficult. The *Faulknor* led the flotilla into attack.

It is difficult to write clearly of the details of the attack, for one was too busy at the time to take note of what was happening all round. One only watched the enemy ships come looming up out of the mist at regular intervals apart and momentarily expected to see the flash of their guns break out. At 2.05 a.m. we fired our first torpedo, being then abreast what appeared to be the fourth ship of their line, at a range of about 2,000 to 3,000 yards. At the same moment fire was opened upon us from all the enemy ships visible and with all calibres of guns, turrets and secondary (5.9-inch) guns. This fire was very accurate; indeed, so accurate as to save us, for

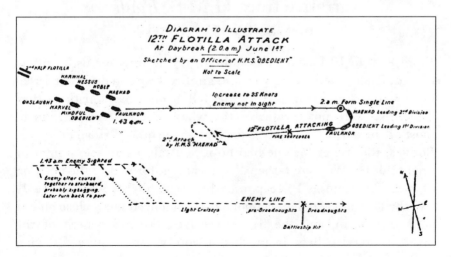

salvo after salvo fell within a 50-yard circle of us, and many of our guns' crews were drenched by the splashes, yet no shells hit us.

Just as it seemed that we must be hit, and when we thought our torpedo must have missed, there came our reward. Right amidships on the waterline of the ship that we had fired at—the *Pommern*, now on our port quarter—appeared a dull red ball of fire. Quicker than one can imagine it spread fore and aft, until reaching the foremast and mainmast it flared upwards, up the masts in big red tongues of flame, uniting between the mastheads in a big, black cloud of smoke and sparks. Then one saw the ends of the ship come up as though her back was broken, before the mist shut her out from view. In the silence that followed, a voice on our bridge was heard to say, 'Pity the poor devils, they ain't drawn their month's money.'

A heavy fire continued to be directed at us, and the *Nessus* and *Onslaught* astern were hit. We increased to full speed and commenced to zig-zag, which undoubtedly saved us from being hit. Further torpedoes were fired at the enemy line, but nothing could be seen of the result owing to our speed and the mist which quickly shut out the ships, now on our quarter, from view.

During the rest of the morning nothing further was seen of the enemy, except that after we had joined up with part of the 1st B.S. (*Revenge*, *Agincourt*, and *Hercules*), at about 4 a.m., a Zeppelin was sighted. All ships fired at her with guns ranging from 15-inch turrets to .303-inch Maxims.

Narrative from H.M.S. *Faulknor*
(Leader of the 12th Flotilla)

From 9.30 to 10.15 p.m. was rather a trying time for us, as intermittent flashes were being seen and gunfire heard in different directions without it being possible to tell from what squadron they came. We were not certain of the whereabouts or disposition of most of the battle fleet, and as for that of the other British destroyer flotillas, the writer for one had no idea at all where they might or might not be. We were rather disagreeably informed of the position of some of them at 10.15 p.m., when searchlights were suddenly switched on and a violent cannonade commenced fairly close on our starboard beam, and the flotilla received the full benefit of the 'overs' and ricochets from this action without quite knowing whether we were being attacked or not, which made this period about the most unpleasant time we had.

The gunfire continued violently for some few minutes and then receded. As it passed away a light cruiser suddenly came crashing through the flotilla, narrowly avoiding collision with several destroyers, and again several of our boats had to go full speed astern in a hurry.[2] I believe that the ship was one of our light cruisers which had just been attacked by several German destroyers, but luckily no damage resulted, although the contretemps had the effect of further delaying the flotilla and upsetting our disposition.

Meanwhile, further away to the westward, firing could be heard and the reflection of searchlight flashes was visible in the sky, but about 11 p.m. these disappeared, and only a dull glow as if from a burning ship remained, which subsequently we supposed to have come from the *Tipperary*. Soon after this, at 11.30 p.m., a very distinct shock was felt throughout the *Faulknor*, and the noise of a distant explosion was heard, which appeared to us to be like a large ship blowing up, but again no one knew what ship it might be. Soon after midnight, or thereabouts, the *Faulknor* and the 4th Flotilla appeared to run out of the scene of action, and only occasional searchlights in the distance remained visible. The opportunity was now taken by some officers to inspect the ship, but the damage discovered consisted only of one little hole in the upper deck, with a dent to the engine-room skylight and hatch, which really was rather wonderful, considering that the ship had been under direct or indirect fire for over six hours.

Shortly after half-past one in the morning a division of battleships were sighted off our starboard bow, their shapes being clearly seen, although it was dark. The flotilla was immediately ordered to increase speed, and we turned away to port in order to get ahead of these battleships unobserved. After a few minutes on this course a turn to starboard was made by the *Faulknor*, followed by the flotilla, in the order, *Faulknor*, *Obedient*, *Onslaught*, *Marvel*, and *Narwhal*, with, I think, the *Maenad* a short distance astern, and about 1.55 a.m. the battleships were again in sight on the starboard bow. Speed was at once increased to 25 knots and course altered so that the flotilla were approaching the ships at an angle of about 45 degrees.

---

2 The 12th Flotilla had had the same experience at 'Windy Corner' during the day action (*vide* page 133).

Torpedoing of *Pommern* at dawn. (From a painting)

It was now evident that they were Germans, but apparently they had not seen us yet, as there was no sign of searchlights or challenges.

The Captain gave orders for the torpedoes to be fired as the sights came on, and at 2 a.m. turned on to a parallel and opposite course to the Germans. At 2 minutes past 2 the *Faulknor* fired her first torpedo, which probably passed ahead of the second enemy ship as the director officer fired rather too early and allowed too much for the enemy's speed.

About two minutes later the second torpedo was fired, but almost simultaneously with this the Germans sighted our flotilla, and all their battleships opened fire, together with the light cruisers astern of their line who poured in a particularly heavy fire on us. The sea seemed to be alive with bursting shells and the air with the whistle of passing projectiles. The range was if anything under 1,500 yards, and 'overs' much predominated. Suddenly a huge explosion took place in the third German ship, and with a deafening noise and shock she seemed first of all to open out, then to close together, then to go. Evidently somebody's torpedo had hit, but as explosions were taking place all round from bursting shells and guns were firing, a torpedo explosion was almost impossible to distinguish until the ship herself blew up. But when this did happen, even amidst the inferno that was going on, the explosion stood out alone, and we knew that our attack had at least done for one German big ship. Our own small 4-inch guns were firing right royally against I do not know how many inches of armour, but at point-blank range, so I hope that they strafed a few Huns.

About 2.10 a.m. a dull flash from astern told us that the flotilla were not getting through scot-free. We considered afterwards that this flash was from a shell exploding on the *Onslaught*'s bridge, from the effects of which their 1st lieutenant was killed, their Captain mortally wounded and the bridge demolished. The *Onslaught* herself appeared to turn straight towards the enemy, but then turned back and came on apparently safe.

The *Faulknor* now went on to full speed until by a quarter past two all was over, and we were out of range unscratched. Seventeen torpedoes we found had been fired by the flotilla, but at what cost at the time we were unable to tell, for as daylight slowly showed up or following there was only *Obedient*, *Marvel*, and *Narwhal* still with us. Later, a wireless came from the *Maenad*, telling us of her safety, but of the *Onslaught* we heard nothing until we reached Scapa Flow on the morning of 2nd June, when we found that she, too, was safe. We had, therefore, lost none of our destroyers in this successful attack.

Narrative of the Senior Surviving Officer of H.M.S. *Onslaught*
(Rear Ship of the 1st Division, 12th Flotilla)

At dark all our destroyers collected and formed under the orders of *Castor*, 5 miles astern of the battle fleet. During the night all sorts of little odd scraps seemed to be taking place about every hour; searchlights would suddenly switch on, there would be a burst of light gunfiring for a few minutes when one could hear odd shells whistling by, then the searchlights would suddenly switch off, and all would be quiet once more. In our ship we could not make out what was happening. Once our fo'csle was pierced by a stray splinter of shell; and once two red lights were switched on by a ship close on one quarter without anything further happening or anyone knowing who had done it.

About 1.30 a.m. our flotilla increased to 20 knots and started altering course; then we saw vague forms of ships to starboard. In single line following our leader, the *Faulknor*, we altered to a course parallel to these ships, and increased to 25 knots to get ahead of them. As we passed them we could plainly make out their silhouettes to be those of German heavy ships, and what surprised one so much at the time was that they seemed to be blind to our existence. When ahead of them the *Faulknor* led us (the first half-flotilla) round 16 points in single line ahead, so that we came down to attack on opposite courses to the enemy with our torpedo tubes trained to port. The German squadron consisted of at least three battleships of the *Kaiser* class (dreadnoughts), one destroyer, and two battleships of the *Heligoland* class (pre-dreadnoughts), steaming in the order named in single line ahead.

We fired all our four torpedoes at the second and third ships of the line; and one apparently hit, as there was a big explosion and a sheet of flame went up, as if we had got her in the magazine. Just at this time one of the *Heligoland*'s switched on searchlights and started firing at us. We turned 8 points away, and sent a messenger down to the engine-room to tell them to make a smoke screen to hide our movements, and as we were turning the *Nessus* just ahead of us was hit. A second messenger was sent down to the engine-room on the same errand as the first, and shortly afterwards I went down myself to find out what the delay was about making the smoke screen. I left the bridge with the Captain, 1st Lieutenant, and Gunner there, all congratulating each other on having got a hit with a torpedo on a German battleship. As I arrived down the ladder on to the upper deck something happened which seemed like a firework display on the bridge, and at the same time our smoke screen started. I went back to the bridge and found we had been hit by a shell on the port side of it; the Captain was badly wounded, the 1st Lieutenant, coxswain, and one signalman was killed, and the Gunner was nowhere. As the last order on the telegraphs was 'Full speed ahead both,' and no one was steering the ship, I tried the wheel, but found that all the rod gearing had been shot away, so I went aft and the engineers quickly connected the after steering position. A fire which had started in the chart-house amongst the charts and confidential books there was quickly put out by the chief stoker and an emergency fire party, but the place and its contents were practically destroyed.

We remaining officers (the 1st Lieutenant was killed and the Captain mortally wounded), with the exception of the Surgeon probationer who was busy with the wounded, having got things going again, held a Committee of Taste and decided that, as we were no more good to the fleet, had no torpedoes left, only two guns, and a much reduced complement of officers, we should ask permission to return to base.

Our wireless was nearly intact, and we signalled the *Castor* for approval by it, to which we received an affirmative reply about 5 a.m. As all our navigational records had been destroyed on the bridge, we had to ask the *Mindful* for her dead-reckoning position. With this position, and using an old general chart of the North Sea, which was kept in the ward-room for reference purposes, and a book and a set square for parallel rulers, we laid off a course for the Firth of Forth, to which we altered, and increased speed to 30 knots. We chose the Firth of Forth, May Island to be exact, as being a nice central landfall to make for, for if we missed it to the northward we had all Scotland to pick up, and to the southward were several hundred miles of English coast. We had not much faith in the accuracy of either our compass, our position, or our course!

On the way back we met several of our own destroyers which had become separated from their flotillas during the night, and we had some difficulty in answering their challenges, as one of our signalmen had been killed and the other had lost an eye, and we had no means of answering them except by semaphore hand flags.

I am sorry to say that our Captain died about noon on this day, in spite of all the Surgeon probationer could do for his wounds.

On account of a rising head sea we had to ease speed to 15 knots at 11 a.m. on June 1st, but were able to increase again about 5 p.m. to 25 knots. At 4 p.m. we sent a wireless signal stating that we expected to arrive off May Island at 7 p.m., and at that time we did actually sight land, which the Engineer-Lieutenant-Commander recognised as being Arbroath, and so it proved to be, as we shortly afterwards sighted the Tay Bar buoy. From here we altered course down for May Isle. A coastguard station ashore was very insistent challenging us, but as the secret replies had been destroyed in action, and in any case we had no means of visual long-distance signalling, we took no notice. A small oil torpedo boat met us off May Isle, and having ascertained who we were, led us through the obstructions, which had been considerably altered since I was last in the Forth. We anchored off Port Edgar about 9.30 p.m. on June 1st, and a hospital boat came at once and took off our dead and wounded; the doctors there told us of the loss of the *Queen Mary* and our other battle cruisers, which we had not known of, and we in turn told them the little we had seen of the action, which seemed to cheer them considerably.

Two days later the ship was ordered to Leith for repairs, and the Captain of another destroyer was detailed to take her there. But he very sportingly protested that, as we had managed to get back across the North Sea alone, surely we ought to be able to go round the 15 miles to Leith. This was allowed, tugs and pilots being ordered to meet us off the entrance to Leith, but they were not used, and we arrived in the repairing basin unaided.

Narrative from H.M.S. *Maenad*

(Leading Ship of the 2nd Division of 12th Flotilla)

The following is an account of the attack carried out by 12th Flotilla on a division of the German battle fleet in the early morning of 1st June:—

Maenad was leading the 2nd Division of the first half of the 12th Flotilla, and was stationed on the port quarter of *Faulknor* (Captain D.), the 1st Division being on starboard quarter of *Faulknor*. The other destroyers in the 2nd Division were *Narwhal*, *Nessus*, and *Noble*. The 12th Flotilla's course was south, speed 17 knots, and we were stationed approximately 10 miles astern of the 2nd Battle Squadron, Admiral Burney's.

The short night had been very dark and full of excitement, as flashes, explosions, searchlights and star shells had been constantly visible from various points to the west and north of us, and since all hand had been at action stations since 6 p.m. on the evening before, nerves were at 'concert pitch.' The flotilla had been well 'strafed' by some presumed enemy cruisers astern of us about midnight, but though many shots had fallen between the lines and alongside, fortunately no one was hit. Course had been altered to north-east and speed increased to 25 knots for some time to draw clear, then the original course and speed had been reverted to after the firing ceased.

Suddenly about 2 a.m. some dark objects loomed up on the starboard beam and there was much speculation as to what they were, for it was, of course, possible that we had unknowingly closed on our own battleships.

They were exciting moments. Jane's *Fighting Ships* was on the chart table ready for reference, and the Captain, 1st Lieutenant, and Midshipman consulted it eagerly to determine what vessels these might be, but the ships soon showed themselves to be enemy by giving recognition signals quite different to those used in our service.

Faulknor ordered speed 25 knots, and went on to this speed as soon as the signal had been passed to us, at the same time altering course to port to open out from the enemy; our original courses were converging, and the distance we had closed to was about 400 yards. *Maenad* stuck close to *Faulknor*'s port quarter, determined not to lose touch with her. The Captain ordered both tubes to be trained on the starboard beam as soon as the first division received orders to attack, and this was done. On we went, the noise of the guns firing, etc., being drowned by the roar of the engine-room fans as steam was raised for full speed. The eagerness of the stokers was so great that soon too much pressure was raised, the safety valves lifted, and all other noises were drowned in the deafening roar of steam escaping at 250 lbs. pressure close by the bridge.

We followed *Faulknor* round, but the turn came unexpectedly, and try how they would, the torpedo tube's crews could not train as fast as the ship turned, and only one torpedo was fired. The order was, therefore, passed to train the tubes to starboard in preparation for another attack, which the Captain said he intended to carry out. While this was being done a big explosion occurred as a result of the flotilla's attacks (since thought to have been the *Pommern*). We then turned a complete circle to starboard, though how we passed through the remainder of our division without collision we don't know, as *Narwhal*, *Nessus*, and *Noble* were all astern of us.

Second Attack by H.M.S. *Maenad*[3]

About 2.25 a.m. the enemy, consisting, as far as we could see, of five *Koenig* or *Kaiser* class battleships, were sighted again, and course was altered parallel to them when about 2,000 yards off. The enemy

3 A further narrative from H.M.S. *Maenad* will be found on pages 416-424.

were firing hard at us, and their shots were falling short and over, and certainly felt as if they were passing close to our heads, but, in spite of it all, *Maenad* was not hit anywhere.

We fired two torpedoes in this second attack and then turned away under full helm, and while still turning, right astern, there was a terrific explosion, which at any rate showed that one of our torpedoes had hit an enemy. It was rapidly getting light at the time, and in a few minutes it was broad daylight, and we came across *Marksman*, who asked where the enemy were. They had disappeared in the fog, however, and after a time the idea of finding them was given up.

About 5 a.m. that morning we came across a float with eleven men on it, who were picked up, and were found to belong to *Fortune*. Not far off were dead bodies covered in oil, which we discovered belonged to the *Ardent*. Other ships picked up her Captain and one seaman, who were the only ones there left alive.

After searching all day, we received orders to return to Rosyth, but only arrived there the following evening, owing to various searches for crippled ships which we were ordered to make *en route*. Fresh torpedoes and ammunition were taken in, and in four hours' time the ship reported ready for sea again.

THE RETURN TO HARBOUR

And now there are few incidents of Jutland left which have not been already described by some eye-witness in the British fleet. It remains only to speak of the aftermath of the battle and— one cannot help it—of the bitter disappointment of that dawn of June the 1st, 1916, when the German fleet was found to have escaped to its harbours.

The dawn broke grey and misty, and very slowly to the British fleet. It relieved the strain of the night, but it brought with it nothing else of satisfaction. Concentrated, intact except for two battleships (the *Warspite* and *Marlborough*), and practically undiminished in fighting power, the British fleet could anticipate a renewal of the action with reasonable confidence. It had appeared to them overnight that they had the full measure of their opponents, and given a full day's daylight they could expect victory, a complete victory, worthy of their standards.

So at 2.47 a.m. on June 1st the Battle Fleet turned to the north, sent out the light forces ahead and on the wings to gain touch with the enemy, and the crews of the fleet, though tired after the strained watching and waiting of the night, closed up with eagerness at their action stations, making all those little final preparations which, after long waiting, one makes when the moment of the test approaches. But there was to be no test. June 1st was to bring only a maturing disappointment, a gradual realisation that, as the dawn widened to day and the full visibility gave no more concessions to hope than had the first streaks of morning light, that there was to be no completion of yesterday's work. As no reports came from the scouts spread ahead and on the flank, as no fresh ships were sighted except an occasional British straggler rejoining the fleet after being separated during the night, as nothing but the familiar silhouettes of our own ships could be seen on either hand, gradually it was borne home to the British fleet that the Battle of Jutland was finished. The scouting forces could find no enemy ships about, no sign of the German battle fleet, for the German battle fleet were past them, to the eastward of them, making their way down the swept channel off Schleswig Holstein towards Cuxhaven. Only two or three straggling German light craft were sighted in the very early hours of the morning, and they quickly disappeared into the mist, and after that no other surface ship was seen, only a Zeppelin which was fired upon, but not hit.

One can appreciate the feelings of the fleet at dawn from the narrative of the midshipman in the foretop of the battleship *Neptune*:—

'At about ten minutes to midnight a messenger came into the gun-room looking as dirty and weird as a traveller from the infernal regions, to report that all hands would go to action stations again at 2 a.m.. At 2 a.m. we were all back at our action stations, the same lot of us in the top as yesterday.

Shortly before three we heard heavy firing to the eastward. The visibility was quite good, and gave promise of a better day; we had plenty of ammunition left, and felt that, given the chance, we could make short work of what remained of the enemy. Was this the chance? All quarters were warned. The guns had been left loaded all night, and were as ready as we were to start again.

The silhouette of our battle cruisers became faintly visible, but there was no sign of the enemy. We searched the horizon all round with glasses, hoping to find some target, but there was nothing.

About 3 a.m. a Zeppelin suddenly appeared out of the morning haze, and steered towards us until the ensign trailing from its car could be seen. I had never seen a Zeppelin before, and regarded it curiously. An order was passed to "X" turret to fire one round at it at maximum elevation. Our round went off, and for a brief second I could see the projectile in the air, but then the airship lifted its nose

'Great smears of oil and wreckage.'

disdainfully to the morning breeze and disappeared to the south-
westward, and a signal was received ordering us not to waste ammunition. Not until the Zeppelin was out of sight did I realise the full
significance of this early morning visit. It meant that the Germans
now knew exactly where we were; we should not see the High Seas
Fleet that day.'

The British fleet turned to the north at 2.47 a.m., and swept
up and down over their track of the night and over the area of
yesterday's fleet action, until 1.15 p.m., but no enemy ships
were to be found. There were relics of the fight. Patches of oil,
with in the centre some wreckage or even the bows of a ship
still sticking up, and floating bodies around. It was even possible in a very few cases to rescue a man here or there from the
wreckage still alive, but very few were these, for the cold of the
North Sea waters is soon numbing in its effect, and humans
floating in it mercifully soon lose their senses, become drowsy,
and then drown. 'None of the men appeared to suffer at all;
they just seemed to lie back and go to sleep.'

Where *Tipperary*'s flotilla had fought in the night the
patches of wreckage were frequent.

'During the two or three hours succeeding daylight we passed
through large quantities of floating wreckage, hammocks, bodies,
etc. An alert signalman reported he saw a hand waving from a spar

373

some distance away, and on closing we were fortunately able to rescue a stoker belonging to the *Tipperary*, who informed us that his
ship had been sunk some four or five hours perviously. . . .

Later in the morning we found the disabled *Sparrowhawk*, or
rather what remained of her, as she had been cut in two. . . .'

[Narrative of H.M.S. *Dublin*.]

'Then following a day of search, while we sat and dozed at our stations, and the only signs of the enemy were hundreds of their
drowned bluejackets in their life-saving waistcoats, floating near the
great smears of oil and wreckage that marked the grave of some
ship, with also large numbers of dead fish floating near these
patches of wreckage, apparently killed by the explosion.

At 6.0 p.m. on June 1st we dispersed from action stations, went
into cruising stations, and returned to our base.'

[Narrative of H.M.S. *New Zealand*]

So the battle fleet gave up the search for the enemy at 1.15
p.m., 'being reluctantly forced to the conclusion that they had
regained their bases' (Jellicoe), and shaped course for Scapa
Flow. The return to harbour was uneventful.

Though it had apparently been part of the German's strate-
gical scheme to have a quantity of submarines stationed off
the British East Coast harbours to attack our fleet on coming
out to battle, and on the return after action, no large scale
attack was made. A few British ships, chiefly destroyers, had
torpedoes fired at them when approaching the English and
Scotch harbours, and one or two ships on their passage across
the North Sea were also attacked by submarines, but the
intensity of these attacks was no more than was customary to
the fleet when steaming in the North Sea, and they were not
successful.

A more important factor in the experience of most ships was
the bad weather which sprang up early on June 1st. Struggling
back across the North Sea on June 1st, June 2nd, and even on
June 3rd, there were half-a-dozen or more crippled British
ships, some in the tow of another ship or some in tow of
another cripple—*Onslow* and *Defender*, for example—almost
all with their wireless shot away, their navigational appliances

gone, and for many their seaworthiness dangerously impaired by the damages received in action. *Marlborough*, *Warspite*, *Southampton*, *Broke*, *Spitfire*, *Onslaught*, these and a number of other damaged ships were struggling back, some at no more than 4 or 5 knots speed, or some even, as was the *Broke* on account of her bows being smashed up, forced to turn stern to sea and making back on June 2nd towards the coast of Germany, before the dying down of the gale allowed her to make good some ground on a westerly course.

The narrative of H.M.S. *Spitfire* typically describes the anxieties of the damaged ships struggling across the 300 miles from the Jutland bank to the English coast:—

'Mess tables, collision mats, and shores were used to try and fill up the gaping bow—but they were all washed inboard again, time after time, as the wind and sea were now fast rising.

By dawn—June 1st—the sea had risen a good deal, and the wind was still freshening from the south-west, and about 8.0 a.m. we had to turn the ship head to sea and ease down. All the store-rooms, shell-rooms, and lower mess decks forward being flooded, we began to get very anxious whether the fore boiler-room bulkhead would stand the strain. The Captain ordered a tot of rum to be served out all round at dawn, and I must say that cheered up the men no end. Luckily the galley was not damaged, and we all got some food, the men there, and the officers in the after canopy round the wheel. . . .

Two guns' crews were organised and kept manned in case of meeting anyone, but except for one Norwegian merchant ship, we met no one.

In the dog watches the sea got up and the wind increased so considerably that we had to turn to about north to keep the sea on our quarter.

Our hopes of getting home again fell during that night (June 1st–2nd), as the weather gradually became worse and worse, and about 1.0 a.m. we decided the only thing to do was to fire distress signals, estimating that we were about 60 miles from the English, or it might be the Scottish coast.

But about 2.0 a.m.—it seemed like a miracle—the wind suddenly died down and the sea got smoother and smoother, until at 4.30 a.m. we turned to west-south-west, and increased speed to about 10 knots

As the morning drew on we met a patrol drifter, which informed us we were 22 miles E.N.E. of the Tyne. . . . We entered the Tyne and berthed at Jarrow by the *Bonaventure*, whose officers and men showed us all the greatest kindness. They sent a party over to tidy up our ship, and our entire ship's company went over to her for baths and a good square meal. We were all very glad of both. . . .'

All across the North Sea on the morning of June 1st were being committed to the deep the bodies of those who had given their lives in the fight—committed to the deep wrapped in their hammocks in the traditional manner of the seaman, as Sir Francis Drake was laid to rest three hundred years ago.

'Drake he's in his hammock an' s thousand mile away,
(Capt'en art tha' sleeping there below?)
Slung 'atween the round shot in Nombre Dios Bay,
An' dreamin' arl the time o' Plymouth Hoe.'

But of the 6,800 men who died at Jutland more than half already lay on the Jutland banks around the wreck of a ship thay had manned. They were buried 'in one great cloud of flame and smoke,' during the fight.

'We have fed our sea for a thousand years,
And she calls us, still unfed,

.   .   .   .

For that is our doom and pride.'

376

Part IV

Points of View

(Being Further Narratives principally from the Battle Cruiser
Fleet)

PART IV

POINTS OF VIEW

We have now read of the fighting of Jutland as witnessed or experienced by men of the British fleet, from practically the first to the last shot of the battle. It is only proposed to add here some few further accounts which have been omitted from their chronological position in the book, because of the undesirability, either of lingering too long over any one period of the battle, or of grouping together too many accounts from any one squadron.

Although it may refer to a period of the battle that has already been described, each separate account seems to contain fresh interest of its own, and to possess an historical value of its own by virtue of a colour that individual experience gives to it. Particularly noticeable is the 'point of view' which people engaged in some specialised work carry away with them of a battle. Some minor incident which influenced their particular work will probably be impressed on their memory more clearly than some major incident of the battle. Perhaps it is natural that a trickle of boiling water down your back (or the loss of your trousers from the blast of a gun) should influence you more strongly than an enemy ship sinking six miles away from you. One observes this point of view in the difference between two shipmates' narratives.

And there are in a modern fighting ship, both literally and figuratively, a great number of watertight compartments, separating the work of one party of men from the sight or interest of another party. The healing work of the medical staff, the destructive (to the enemy) work of the gunnery staff, the keeping-the-engines-going-to-orders work of the engineers, and so forth, are different kinds of work creating different perspec-

378

tives to men so employed. The different parties in action are self-contained, largely unaware one of the work of the other. except when efficiency or inefficiency of one party, or the chances of war, influence the work of another party.

The following accounts show something of the individual experiences of different specialist officers—using the term in its general and not its strictly naval sense—and the point of view of the battle these experiences engendered. A medical account is by the medical officer of H.M.S. *Princess Royal*, the ship next astern of the *Lion* throughout the action; a gunnery account by the gunnery officer of the battle cruiser *Tiger*, and there is also the completion of the narrative of the control officer of H.M.S. *Lion*. The engineer's account is by the engineer officer of H.M.S. *Warrior*, the ship of Admiral Arbuthnot's 1st Cruiser Squadron which suffered such severe damage at the 'Windy Corner' period, and whose eventual loss on 1st June has already been narrated in Chapter VIII.

All these three ships were heavily engaged with the enemy; the *Warrior* for her terribly fierce ten minutes at about 6.15 p.m., the *Lion* and *Princess Royal* for, on and off, more than four hours, and all three accounts therefore are full of battle incidents. It is worth while remembering, however, that probably eight-tenths of the men of the British fleet were engaged throughout the Battle of Jutland in carrying on quietly with their own particular job; in doing it without hitch and without particular battle incident; so that eight-tenths of the fleet can now find little to recall about the Battle of Jutland beyond the fact that they were there, did their job, and came back from doing it safely.

One ought to emphasise, therefore, that these points of view that follow are those of officers in ships which were more heavily engaged with the enemy than were the majority of the British fleet. The narratives are principally from battle cruiser personnel, because, as the Admiralty communiqué of the action stated, 'the brunt of the fighting fell on the battle cruiser fleet.'

The chapter, and the book, concludes with the narrative from a destroyer, H.M.S. *Maenad* of the 12th Destroyer

Flotilla, which, accompanying the battle fleet from Scapa Flow, came into the action at about 6.15 p.m., was a spectator of the battle fleet action until 9.0 p.m., and during the night was stationed with the other destroyer flotillas astern of the battle fleet. The 12th Destroyer Flotilla, as we have read, carried out the torpedo attack on a German battle squadron at 2 a.m. in the morning of June 1st, and sinking one pre-dreadnought battleship, fought the last engagement with heavy ships of the battle. As H.M.S. *Maenad* was the last destroyer of her flotilla to attack these enemy, her narrative, read in conjunction with H.M.S. *Lion*'s narrative or H.M.S. *Tiger*'s, which describe the action from 4.0 p.m. onwards, provides a review of practically the whole battle from start to finish. It may be convenient to read them together accordingly.

Jutland, as seen from H.M.S. *Lion*
(Flagship of the Battle Cruiser Fleet)

At noon, G.M.T., on 31st May, 1916, the British Battle Cruiser Fleet and the 5th Battle Squadron were in the eastern North Sea, steaming in the direction of the Skaggerack. The force was commanded by Vice-Admiral Sir David Beatty, who flew his flag in the *Lion*. The British Battle Fleet, together with the 3rd Battle Cruiser Squadron and the remainder of the Grand Fleet from Scapa Flow, were also at sea, but to the northward of us, under the Command of Admiral Sir John Jellicoe; it was the intention that Sir David Beatty's force should rendezvous with the battle fleet later on in the afternoon if the sweep to the east was uneventful.

It was a glorious day, and being a 'Make and Mend,' a naval half-holiday, many of the *Lion*'s officers had settled down on deck to enjoy the sunshine, little suspecting that before tea-time they would be engaged in the one big naval battle of the war.

At about 2.30 p.m. the *Galatea*, scouting to the eastward, reported five enemy battle cruisers in sight. At first this report was hardly credited as German heavy ships had not been heard of at sea for quite a long time, and many of us went to action stations in our thin summer clothing, never dreaming that we should remain there for the rest of the day and through the following night. Doubts of the

Signalmen sending a message by searchlight.

truth of the reports, however, were soon removed when the enemy appeared over the horizon.

After the receipt of the first enemy report, Sir David Beatty altered course to the south-eastward and increased to full speed, with the intention of cutting off the enemy from their base, and incidentally of making quite certain of bringing him to action. Hitherto the enemy had always steamed for home as soon as he became aware of our presence near him, so that the surest way to force an action was to place our fleet between him and his front door.

Sir David's course proved a good one, and it was not long before we were in range of the enemy, and at about 3.45 p.m. both fleets opened fire. The *Lion* led the battle cruisers into action at a speed of about 24 knots. It was a wonderful sight to see these great ships with their battle flags flying, their guns cocked up at high elevation trained on the enemy, funnels smoking and huge bow and stern waves being thrown up, straining to the uttermost to obtain a lead upon the enemy. My own particular station was on the fore-bridge, which, from the point of view of seeing the show, might be described as the front row of the stalls. I think that all officers and men felt complete confidence in their leader, and a real fighting spirit permeated the whole squadron.

At first it was quite difficult to realise that we were under fire, the only indication being huge columns of water, like giant water spouts, which appeared to form all round the ship. The noise of the enemy's guns and the shriek of their shells was completely drowned by the noise of our own guns firing in salvoes and the multifarious

Damage to deck, *Lion.*

Damage to funnel, *Lion.*

382

ship noises which accumulate at sea, especially when steaming at high speed. The effect of shells striking the ship was so local that only men in the vicinity of the explosions knew that we were being hit at all.

Shortly after opening fire a shell struck 'Q' turret (situated between the second and third funnels), at the junction between the front and roof armour, lifting the latter clean off, like the lid of a sardine tin. All the men in the gun-house were killed outright, with the exception of Major Harvey, Royal Marines, who had both his legs shot away, but managed to crawl to the voice pipe and give the order to close the magazine doors. Immediately after this he died. Meanwhile the fire in the gun-house spread down to the working chamber below, and set alight the cordite which was waiting in the loading cages. The flash from this cordite then passed down the trunk to the magazine handing-room (the space outside the magazines somewhat resembling the hall of a house, the magazines corresponding to the rooms opening off the hall), but by this time, thanks to Major Harvey's order, the magazine doors had just been closed, so that the cordite flash, instead of penetrating into the magazines, escaped up to the mess deck. But the magazine crews, after performing their final duty of closing the doors, had not time to escape, and were found dead in the handing-room.

Meanwhile the opposing squadrons were proceeding on a southerly course at a speed of 24 knots hotly engaged, the range being about 17,000 yards. At about 4.0 p.m. the *Indefatigable* was struck by a salvo and blew up. Half an hour later the *Queen Mary* suffered the same fate. Fortunately these two disasters were not observed by the ship's company of the *Lion*, as the majority were all under armour and fully occupied with their duties, but those of us on the bridge were not so lucky. The *Queen Mary* was only a short distance astern of us, and her end was a sight which is indelibly stamped on the minds of all who witnessed it. The first sign that something was wrong was clouds of grey smoke, which appeared to emerge from her sides. They increased in volume, and finally rose to a huge column about 600 feet above the sea, totally obscuring the ship, and when this gigantic cloud moved away there was no sign of the great battle cruiser which, only three minutes previously, had been steaming along at full speed with all her guns in action. The *Tiger*, being the next ship astern of the *Queen Mary*, had no time to alter course clear, and was compelled to steam through the dense smoke cloud of her next ahead's explosion, which must have been a very trying experience for her.

A pleasing little incident occurred in the *Lion* at about this time. A signal boy happened to observe a large unexploded German shell lying close to some burning paint-work on the upper deck, and reported to the signal officer: 'It doesn't seem right to me, sir, that that there shell should be so close to that there fire, and with your permission, sir, me and Boy—— would like to push it out of the way.' Of course, instructions were immediately given for its removal, and a little party of signalmen and boys rolled the projectile over the side.

The Turn to the North

The battle continued on a southerly course until 4.40 p.m., when the masts of the German High Seas Fleet came clearly into sight over the horizon directly ahead of us. The sea at this point appeared to be black with ships, and Sir David immediately turned the battle cruisers 16 points to starboard, and set a course to the northward to lead the enemy towards the British Grand Fleet, which was now proceeding south at full speed in the hopes of making contact with the enemy.

Shells falling near *Lion*.

384

The enemy battle cruisers followed our movements, and the battle recommenced on a northerly course, at closer range and with even greater intensity than before. Shortly after turning to the northward we met the 5th Battle Squadron, lead by Admiral Evan Thomas, steaming to the southward. This squadron, after passing us on opposite courses, also followed the general turn to the north, forming astern of our squadron, and in this position drew on themselves the enemy's fire and relieved the strain on us to such an extent that, from our point of view, the enemy's fire appeared to slacken considerably.

The visibility between 5.0 and 6.0 p.m. was not good, and very often the enemy ships were totally obscured by smoke and mist, but the firing continued intermittently on both sides till 5.55 p.m., when, to our great joy, we sighted the British Battle Fleet in six columns steaming towards us. Sir David then proceeded at full speed to the eastward to take up his position at the head of the battle fleet, the position allocated to the battle cruisers after deployment by the Grand Fleet battle orders.

We reached this position before the Battle Fleet had deployed into line, but were slightly hampered in our movement by the congestion caused by the various flotillas and light craft also taking up their stations in the van. This was a very trying moment for those responsible for handling the ships, for so close were the ships to one another that there appeared to be no sea room at all at one time and, to make things more lively, enemy shells were falling all around, but the damage done to our ships was comparatively slight.

This phase of the battle is generally referred to as 'Windy Corner,' because, to complicate matters still further, a general turn to the eastward and southward to bring all our battle line into contact with the enemy, was being executed at the same time.

But we were soon clear of this entanglement and at a closer range to the enemy, who, being now somewhat demoralised, were turning away to the southward towards their base.

Sir Horace Hood, with the 3rd Battle Cruiser Squadron, here saw his opportunity and led his force across the van of the enemy. It was a most inspiring sight to see this squadron of battle cruisers dashing towards the enemy with all guns in action, and all of us who saw it felt like cheering them on, as we were certain that the decisive moment of the Battle had arrived. Our feelings, however, underwent a sudden change, for, just when the defeat of the enemy appeared certain, the *Invincible* was hit by a salvo, blew up by her midship turret, and split in two. It happened, literally speaking, in a flash: one moment she was the flagship leading her squadron, full of life, to close and it seemed likely annihilate the enemy battle cruisers; the next moment she was merely two sections of twisted metal, the fore end and the after end of her floating apart on the water.

After she was gone, the remaining two battle cruisers of the squadron, *Inflexible* and *Indomitable*, held their position, supported closely by the *Lion, Tiger, Princess Royal*, and *New Zealand*. Sir David then led his force to the southward in an attempt to head off the enemy. As we passed close to the wreck of the *Invincible* we observed a small company of survivors standing on a raft, who cheered us as we passed, indicating that, in spite of their terrible experience, their spirit remained unshaken, although their hope of being rescued must have been slight.

At about 8.0 p.m. the enemy began to emerge through the smoke screen which had hitherto obscured him, and we immediately re-engaged him at a range of about 11,000 yards and inflicted terrible punishment. His main consideration now appeared to be to escape out of our clutches, for there was little attempt to reply to our fire, and from this time till dark no damage was received by the British battle cruisers at all, but we were continually hitting the German ships.

June 1st

After dark we were ordered to conform to the movements of the Battle Fleet, which was steaming south towards the Heligoland Bight, with a view to re-engaging the enemy at dawn. During the night we remained at our action stations, expecting every moment to be attacked by destroyers, but no exciting incident occurred with the exception of various alarms, and many indications that other portions of the fleet were not having such a peaceful time as we were.

The following day our squadron made many attempts to locate the enemy, but with no success, and we finally came to the conclusion that he had managed to slip in behind his mine-fields during the night.

As there seemed to be no further chance of coming to grips with the enemy, we were able to take stock of the damage and also obtain some food, which most of us had not seen for nearly 24 hours. I shall never forget my own feelings when I left the bridge and endeavoured to find my way to the ward-room. Between decks everything was in total darkness, and the atmosphere was thick with cordite fumes, blending disagreeably with the smell of burnt paint, burnt flesh, and chloroform. I groped my way along the mess decks and narrowly escaped falling down several great yawning chasms in the deck—places where shells had burst. Finally I observed a lighted room, and thought 'Thank Heaven, here is the wardroom and food at last,' but it was actually the Captain's cabin, which the Fleet Surgeon was using as an operating theatre, and I hastily retreated. On finally reaching the wardroom, I could hardly believe my eyes, the contrast after the havoc and disorder of the mess decks was so extraordinary. The table cloth was still on the table, and the crockery of yesterday's meal was still undisturbed.

Similarly, several cabins were quite untouched, whilst others were entirely wrecked, which shows how local the effect of high explosive shells can be. The Navigating Officers' cabin, for example, was an extraordinary sight, a heavy shell having burst inside it, and everything was completely burnt away with the exception of the heads of his iron golf clubs. They lay in a little heap in the corner where his bag of clubs had previously rested, and formed his only remaining possession.

At 1.30 p.m., June 1st, it was considered that the enemy had returned to his base, so the whole fleet left the scene of the operations, and we, in the Battle Cruiser Fleet, set course for Rosyth with mixed feelings; considerable relief that the battle was over, combined with a strong feeling of disappointment that the Hun had once more escaped us. There was very little elation evident anywhere.

After quarters that night we buried our dead at sea. Sir David Beatty came aft, and the funeral service was read in the presence of the whole ship's company, the band playing the 'Dead March.'

Early next morning we reached Rosyth, and were loudly cheered by the Forth Garrison, but our response was not very enthusiastic, for we were conscious of the gaps in our line—three out of eight battle cruisers in action had been lost—and the silent little company of women waiting on the quay filled one's heart with sadness. There was no time for sentiment, however; the moment we had secured to our buoy the ship was alive with dockyard and Admiralty officials, who proceeded to prepare us for the next battle; while all of us who could do so lay down to get some sleep.

Battle Cruiser Force moored in Firth of Forth immediately after arrival.

Narrative of the Gunnery Control Officer of H.M.S. *Lion*

From 6.0 p.m. to the End of the Action
(Continued from Chapter VI., page 115)

Battle Cruisers during the Battle Fleet Action

At 6.03 the ship having made an alteration of course to starboard in the direction of the enemy, a three-funnel light cruiser is sighted fine on the starboard bow, and one salvo is fired at her with a guessed range of 8,000 yards. The salvo falls very short, but as the cruiser is apparently stopped, certainly badly on fire, and probably out of action, the turrets are swung back on to the beam bearing, where it is expected that the capital ships will again be sighted when the atmosphere clears or when the courses have converged sufficiently.

Just after this the 1st Cruiser Squadron passes ahead of the battle cruiser line, pouring forth a volley of hate at the light cruiser, and then passes down towards the rear of the battle cruiser line on the enemy side. Beyond the fact that they crossed the line on which look-out is being kept and are firing very rapidly, they are not regarded with special interest nor followed to the rear. [H.M.S. *Defence* blew up at 6.16 p.m., within 4 or 5 miles of H.M.S. *Lion*.]

At 6.14, after a 13-minute interval, capital ships are again sighted in the mist on the starboard beam at a range of about 10,000 yards, and between 6.16 and 6.21 ten salvoes are fired at the supposed leading ship, whereupon she again retires, and for four minutes is out of sight, our own ship altering course to starboard to regain touch. The battleships of the Grand Fleet had been sighted from the battle cruisers at 6.06, and had deployed at 6.16, so that during this last burst of firing—6.16 to 6.21—the battle cruisers must have been coming into position ahead of the line of battle. Six minutes later, 6.27, the target is again visible, and is engaged until 6.31½, when the recorders note 'very misty and much smoke,' and half-a-minute later, 'target obscured.'

A further long interval now commences, which continues until 8.19, except for a short three-minute burst at 7.13. At 7.05 the battle cruisers make an appreciable alteration of course to starboard, during which one of the control staff took the opportunity to look quickly down the line of battle cruisers, now fine on our quarter, and after counting six ships remarks, 'Well, we are all here all right.' He did not realise that *Queen Mary* and *Indefatigable*, out of the original 1st and 2nd Battle Cruiser Squadrons, had been lost three hours ago, and that *Inflexible* and *Indomitable* had joined the battle cruiser line about 6.50 p.m. after the loss of *Invincible*, bringing the total back to the original six again.

During this lull a large ship sinking is passed, the bow of which is pointing up nearly vertically out of the sea. The shape of this ship's forefoot and the colour of the anti-fouling composition on the bottom, not recognised as being British, causes a remark to be made 'That is a Hun ship.' This wreck must have been the *Invincible*, sunk a few minutes previously.

Between 7.13 and 7.16 the enemy are again sighted and four salvoes fired at them, but two destroyers stationed on their engaged bow put up a most efficient smoke screen by emitting very dense clouds of black smoke from their funnels, which completely obscures the capital ships steaming into the area the other side of it. Thus screened, the capital ships alter course away, and additionally hide themselves behind their own smoke. At 7.20, and again at 7.45, the battle cruisers alter course towards the enemy, but there is an interval of an hour during which no target is in sight, and not until 8.19 is a three-funnel ship sighted 20 degrees before the starboard beam at a range of about 10,500 yards. She immediately alters away, retiring into the mist, and only one salvo is fired at her.

At 8.22 p.m. capital ships come into sight 10 degrees abaft the beam, but by now daylight is fading, and the mist and smoke are no better, so that the conditions for aiming and observation of fire are thoroughly unfavourable. Nevertheless, between 8.22 and 8.28, 14 salvoes are fired at the leading ship at a mean range of 10,000 yards. At this close range, and in a light which is almost dusk, the 'effect of hits' on the enemy can clearly be seen—there is no question of mistaking the flash of the enemy's gun for our shell bursting, which observers are so inclined to do, for *the effect* of hits can be seen. I cannot describe it more exactly.

At 8.28, in gathering darkness, this last target falls away, showing very obvious signs of having received severe punishment, as was bound to be the case after being engaged at 10,000 yards whilst she herself is apparently incapable of returning the fire. She is badly on fire, smoke and steam well up at numerous points in her hull, the upper works are wreathed in a cloud of thin, grey-yellow vapour from which the masts and funnels stand up in disordered array, and every few minutes a darker patch of smoke is added to the general mist on her upper deck, or a yellow column of fire plays up out of the ship, the effect presumably of a shell or shells which have hit her a few seconds or perhaps a few minutes before.

From 8.28 till 9.24 p.m. the battle cruisers continue their course to the S.W., and then alter to south for the night, in agreement with the general movement of the fleet. Accurate reports as to the exact amount of ammunition expended, and as to the general state of the armament, are received in the control position and communicated to the Captain. One turret is definitely and finally out of action, but the other three are in all respects ready to continue the action at daylight.

During the night the hands remain at their night action stations, which in a battle cruiser provide for the manning of the secondary, the anti-torpedoboat armament, and the gun control staff spend the night in the top. When not doing their turn at look-out they sleep soundly, stretched out on the deck.

At very early dawn an alarm is given consequent upon sighting a 'shape' just before the starboard beam, but it turns out to be one of our own light cruisers. With daylight come the sounds of gunfire from a direction astern, but this proves to be only the anti-aircraft guns of ships at the rear engaging a Zeppelin which they have sighted. Enemy surface ships are not sighted.

Point of View of a Medical Officer
Narrative from the Medical Officer of H.M.S. *Princess Royal*

In all the battle cruisers there are two main 'Dressing Stations,' one in the fore and the other in the after end of the ship. The fore dressing station is below the main deck, and is surrounded by about 9 inches of armour. Here the majority of instruments and dressings are kept, since it is the most protected and convenient locality for operations.

It is situated just on the starboard side of the centre line of the ship, almost directly below one of the turrets, and in size is about 10 feet by 15 feet, plus an entrance space where a hatchway leads down from the main deck. Through this hatchway the wounded are passed down, but in the *Princess Royal* its narrowness was really the principal defect of the station. There were two bunks against one bulkhead, or wall, of the station for bad cases; a small medical store-room adjoined one corner, and a folding operating table, with another small table for the tray holding the instruments, was rigged in the centre of the station. The Surgeon-Commander was stationed here with a party of ten hands, which included the stretcher party. A similar party under the next senior surgeon was stationed in the after dressing station, which was aft on the port side of the mess deck, unprotected by armour, but possessing the advantages of accessibility, an X-ray apparatus, and hot water led to it.

In other parts of the ship there were collections of dressings, for example in the turrets, engine-room, shell-rooms, etc., where also were stationed various members of the first-aid party. This first-aid party, all told, was about thirty strong—three medical officers, the chaplain, five sick berth ratings, and about twenty ship's police, stewards, and writer ratings, who were trained in first-aid duties but had no skilled medical knowledge. The two senior medical officers, as mentioned, were respectively in the for'ard and after dressing stations, each with a party of ten men, and the junior surgeon was in one of the turret shell-rooms. Each turret had two of the first-aid party, with a supply of tourniquets, bandages, and simple dressings.

As all our main arrangements had been completed shortly after the outbreak of war, and were left always ready for action, there remained little to be done on going to action stations, except to muster the first-aid parties, test communications, and see that the instruments, stretchers, etc., were ready.

About 2.30 p.m. it first became generally known on board us that enemy light cruisers had been reported, and that a seaplane had been sent up to examine them, and we then immediately went to 'action stations.'

After seeing everything correct, I went on deck to try and see what was happening. With glasses it was easy to make out five large enemy ships on our port bow, and away on our port quarter, but apparently much further off, were our own 5th B.S. Shortly afterwards the enemy opened fire, and I saw two distinct salvoes fired, but was quite unable to see where the shell pitched. I then returned to the foremost dressing station, and not many minutes seemed to elapse before a terrific crash was felt, and several of the party made a somewhat violent acquaintance with the deck. All lights were immediately extinguished which led to some confusion in the sudden darkness. After lighting two oil lamps which were kept for emergencies, and taking a look round, we found only one casualty amongst the party, this a fairly large scalp wound, but whether from a fall or from a fragment of shell I do not know. Probably the latter, as next day about 3 lbs. weight of shell fragments from an 11- or 12-inch shell were swept up from the deck of the station.

The light from the oil lamps was very poor, and vision was further obscured by the heavy whitish fumes which began to descend into the compartment, and which could not be cleared away as the ventilation fans were always, by order, shut off in action, owing to the danger of flooding compartments below the water level. The atmosphere became very unpleasant, the fumes being irritating to eyes and throat. The gauze respirators in use at that time (1916) were ordered to be put on, and were distinctly useful for a time, but later on the atmosphere became so unbearable that I sent a message to the Flag Captain asking for permission to take up our stations on the port side of the foremost 4-inch battery, situated on the upper deck under the forecastle. Whilst waiting for permission, the first-aid party dressed casualties as they occurred.

Not much work was entailed by the change of station, as only dressings in first-aid bags were taken up to the battery, everything else being left in the dressing station, as we hoped to return there later (which we did). In the battery we dressed several cases, chiefly of burns occurring amongst members of the fire and repair parties—parties which appear to me to have perhaps the most exposed and dangerous job of any in action; they certainly did wonderful work under their respective officers, and I am afraid they suffered many casualties. After shifting our station it was possible to gather roughly that a shell had entered through the Admiral's pantry and exploded in the Admiral's port cabin, blowing away a respectable portion of the deck at its after end, and it was evidently fragments of this shell which had found their way down the hatchway into the dressing station.

In the meantime other casualties began to arrive, and amongst them a gun-layer from the after turret, which had been put out of action by a direct hit. He, poor fellow, had a foot nearly blown away, but had been very skilfully dealt with by the first-aid party in the turret and carried in a stretcher to us from right aft. This gun-layer had developed German measles about two days previously, and should by rights have been landed, but owing to the mildness of his complaint, and because he was an important rating, he had been kept isolated on board and permitted to come to sea. Later on I amputated his leg, from which he ultimately made a good recovery, and he is, I believe, still serving.

The atmospheric conditions in the fore dressing station having improved, and several cases requiring operative treatment, we proceeded to get them down from the 4-inch battery back to the station. We were still without electric light, and the oil lamps were very poor, so this fact and the uncertainty of what was likely to happen in the immediate future made me hesitate to start operating at once: moreover, assistance was required to give an anaesthetic. So I despatched a message to the surgeon stationed in the turret shell-room to join me in the fore dressing station. In the meantime I decided to visit the after dressing station, where the 2nd surgeon was stationed, to see how they were faring there. I found them very busy amongst casualties—chiefly burns, but also some serious wounds from a shell which had penetrated the upper deck in rear of the mid-ship turret on the port side. The surgeon himself and several of the party had been knocked down by the explosion and were suffering from concussion, but were all carrying on.

On returning to the fore station I found that the surgeon had arrived, so I proceeded to operate on a Blue Marine[1] who had been brought down bleeding seriously from a punctured wound of the face. As the light was still very bad, one of the first-aid party, who, besides previous experience at Heligoland and Dogger Bank, had been present at the Bombardment of Alexandria in 1882, volunteered to assist. He was a stout fellow, and of great value in keeping up the spirits of everyone. I always remember him saying at Heligoland on 28th August, 1914, when other members of the party were new to this class of entertainment, 'Lor' bless you sir, they fires a lot, but they never 'urts each other!'—this somewhat contemptuous opinion of the gunnery world being based on his experiences at Alexandria.

We had hardly started operating before rapid firing developed, and the tray with all my instruments was deposited on the deck. However, with a fine disregard of modern aseptic principles, we carried on, and having dealt with the above-mentioned marine, proceeded to operate on the gun-layer. The light was most trying, the securing of arteries during the operation being particularly difficult; however, in the middle the electric light was again switched on, and everything then became comparatively easy. The dressing of large numbers of burns, some very extensive ones, now fully occupied the time of the whole staff, and when this was completed and the casualties made as comfortable as possible, hot soup, etc., was supplied.

Most of the wounded, who numbered altogether exactly 100, of which between 70 and 80 were seriously burned or wounded, were collected into two groups; one on the main deck in the lobby outside the Admiral's cabin, and the other on the mess deck aft on the port side, near the after dressing station. They lay on mattresses on the deck, or on bedding laid on mess tables. Two of the men who had been operated upon occupied the two bunks in the fore dressing station, and one or two others were in canvas cots on the deck or on the mess tables. The first-aid party worked hard attending to them, helped by a stoker who was on the sick list at the time of the action, and who afterwards was promoted by the Captain to leading stoker for the valuable assistance he gave to the first-aid party in this action.

About 11 p.m. we had things in fair order, and I was able to go to the ward-room for some food, where I learnt from a naturally some-

---

1 *i.e.*, a man belonging to the Royal Marine Artillery.

what excited group of officers that a signal had been received from the Admiral Commanding Battle Cruisers, saying that we should probably meet the Germans again on the following morning and proceed to annihilate them. As an individual, nothing was more pleasing than the prospect of blowing up as many Huns as possible, but as a medical officer I could not but reflect on what was likely to be the fate of our casualties, now numbering some 100, exposed as they would be in further action.

During the night we steamed slowly south, but at dawn nothing of the Germans was to be seen. During the next day we buried the dead at sea, and arriving in the Forth on the Friday morning, June 2nd, discharged our wounded in about 2½ hours to the hospital ship *Plassey*.

On thinking over the experiences of being in action at Jutland and elsewhere, I have been struck with the distinct manner in which a modern ship in action is divided into two separate worlds; the one stationed in conning tower, control positions, and turrets, directing the actual fighting and movements of the ship; the other between decks in the engine-rooms and stokeholds, in the shell-rooms or magazines, and here and there between decks working as fire parties, repair parties, or first-aid parties, serving, as it were, the other world of the ship.

As far as my experiences go, the one world is much cut off from the other, and nothing impressed itself more on my memory than the absolute absence of authentic news reaching us between decks. At Heligoland and Dogger Bank actions I heard nothing till the action was over. At Jutland the only news was bad news, whispered to me about half-hour after the action had commenced by the Master-at-Arms, who was in my party, that the *Indefatigable* had been sunk, and shortly afterwards that the *Queen Mary* had blown up.

The absence of news and the enforced idleness at the commencement of an action, when one can simply hear the ship firing and neither know what enemy is being engaged nor what course the action is taking, is undoubtedly very trying to all concerned. Later, when work arrives, conditions become easier, though no doubt the sight of maimed individuals is very trying to the non-medical ranks and ratings of the first-aid party.

At Jutland the conduct of all the wounded was splendid. From the large number of severely injured who must have suffered considerable pain and discomfort for at least 48 hours, and who must have realised what a bad time they would have had in the event of further action—not a complaint was heard. I confess to a much greater admiration for all ratings than before the war, and also feel that officers and men were brought much closer to, and had a better understanding of each other after being in action together than they did before—at least this was certainly so in the *Princess Royal*.

Narrative of a Gunnery Officer

Notes on the Battle of Jutland, as seen by the Gunnery Officer of
H.M.S. *Tiger*, 1st Battle Cruiser Squadron

On the afternoon of the 31st May, 1916, the 1st and 2nd Battle Cruiser Squadrons were out on one of the usual weekly cruises towards the Fisher Banks. The 3rd B.C.S. had gone up to Scapa Flow for target practice, and the 5th Battle Squadron had come down to join us in the Forth in their place. It was the first time the 5th B.S. had come out with the battle cruisers from the Forth.

During the afternoon watch we had heard that our light cruisers ahead had sighted submarines and possibly a German light cruiser, but when action stations were sounded off, whilst we were at tea, I felt somewhat aggrieved at not having been warned, so that I might be ready for the range-finder exercise which I expected would take place during general quarters. However, on going on the bridge, I found that more news from the light cruisers had come in, from which it was evident that there were enemy about: so we were at general quarter stations in earnest: soon everything was ready from the gunnery point of view. I was stationed in the 13.5 gun control tower with alternative choice of going to the top if the weather was very clear. I had a spotter in the top in direct communication with me, and the 6-inch control was also aloft as the 6-inch armoured positions were very cramped.

The order of the battle cruisers was *Lion, Princess Royal, Queen Mary, Tiger*, with *New Zealand* and *Indefatigable* astern. The 5th B.S. dropped astern on our starboard quarter after we increased speed to 25 knots at about 3.30 p.m.

At this time we received the signal to prepare for immediate action, and soon afterwards the *Lion* reported enemy battle cruisers in sight to the N.E.

At 3.45 we sighted enemy ships, apparently battle cruisers, five in number, which I estimated to be *Hindenburg, Lutzow, Derfflinger, Seydlitz,* and *Moltke.* (I was wrong; the *Von der Tann,* not the *Hindenburg,* was there). Their bearing was approximately north, on our port bow; the weather was misty in patches, the visibility varying from 12 to 6 miles; wind west, force 3[2]; sea calm. I gave the target as 4th ship from the right. At 3.46 the range-finders gave a first range of 21,300 yards.

At 3.49 the enemy opened fire. The first salvo I saw drop was quite 2,000 yards short of us, and did not seem to have a very small spread. 3.50 *Lion* opened fire, and we opened fire. Target 4th ship from right, range 18,500. Our first salvo missed for deflection, second salvo was over. The submarine screen of destroyers on our engaged bow were causing great interference with their funnel smoke, and the enemy line was covered in cordite smoke from their guns firing. The smoke and flashes of the enemy salvoes when coinciding with our fall of shot made spotting very difficult. The enemy were firing very rapidly. The top reported that the funnel smoke of our battle cruisers ahead made their view very bad, so I did not shift my position to the top. I think that at this time all the battle cruisers except 'P.R.' had under-estimated the rate; we had.

3.52 The Germans were firing rapidly and getting our range; I saw splinters fly from our fo'csle past the gun control tower.

3.53 'Q' and 'X' turrets did not come to the 'ready.' I had felt the concussion from hits on our armour, though I did not know for some minutes that both these turrets had been penetrated. 'X' turret came in again after missing two or three salvoes, though with only one gun except at long intervals. Spotting was very difficult, but I increased the rate of fire as much as possible, firing double salvoes. We received several more hits; but the transmitting station reported some good range-finder ranges received, so I came to range-finder range and fired as rapidly as possible using double salvoes separated by small corrections. The enemy ceased to hit and her fire slackened. I do not think we were ever seriously hit by the enemy battle cruisers after 4.0 p.m.

4.5 *Indefatigable* blew up; I did not know it at the time. We continued rapid fire. About 4.10 I had the greatest difficulty in making sure of my target, as the enemy had a ship ahead of their line,

[2] A measure according to the Beaufort scale by which 0 represents a calm and 10 a gale.

Officers controlling the fire aloft.

probably a large light cruiser, which was sometimes there and sometimes not, and was making volumes of smoke. For some minutes
about now, we counted her as a battle cruiser, and so engaged No. 3
instead of No. 4 of the enemy line. I thought we were doing well.
The enemy fire had slackened as far as we were concerned, but the
smoke and gun-flashes of the enemy still made spotting difficult,
and the decreased visibility had made the range-finder readings few
and far between. I knew 'Q' turret was badly hit and had flooded a
magazine, but the enemy fire was not effective, and although conditions were difficult I thought we had got the better of the Germans.

At 4.24 I felt a concussion ahead, and looking forward saw an
enormous sheet of flame and a cloud of black smoke—the *Queen
Mary* had blown up. We steamed on into the cloud. It was pitch
black, we could not fire, so I used the opportunity to 'line up dire-
tor.'[3] Before this was finished we were clear of the smoke cloud, and
I got the order to shift target to 3rd battle cruiser from the right, as
we were now 3rd ship in the line. We fired a couple of salvoes in
gun-layer firing before getting back into director. The enemy fire
was still feeble, and as the visibility had become good for a few minutes, we made real 'battle practice' for some time. 200 yards' corrections were taking the salvoes from short to over, and this was one

---

3 Lining up the director is the method of checking that the electrical receivers of the
director firing system, in each turret, are all in step with the master instrument aloft. All
instruments, including the master instrument, are run down to zero (or to a special lining
up mark). When all are together at this mark all will be in step with one another.

of the few occasions when I was able to see the splashes of overs between the enemy funnels. One of the enemy battle cruisers lost her place in the line, and came dropping back. It was either the leading or second ship I thought, and when she became No. 3 we had a nice shoot at her, but the visibility was not keeping good.

4.25, Enemy destroyers attacked and our 6-inch battery had five minutes at them, but at long range.

4.30, The enemy battle cruisers were out of sight in the mist or smoke screen, and we checked fire, but about ten minutes later a squadron of enemy battleships came into view on our port bow, and just then *Lion* turned 16 points to starboard, and we followed her round. I think they hit us with a few 12-inch in the forecastle and funnels—we gauged the size from bits of shell afterwards. Then the 5th B.S., which came past us on our port side directly after we turned, engaged them, and we lost sight of them.

4.40, We were now going back on our tracks, and there was a lull with no enemy in sight. I got permission to go and see the condition of 'Q' and 'X' turrets and see if I could assist them. The following was their condition, although I did not find it all out until later:—

'X' Turret.—An 11-inch shell had hit the barbette, level with the upper deck. It had penetrated the 9-inch plate, killed the centre sight-setter, and was found intact, except for its nose and fuse, in the gun-house exactly in the geometrical centre of the turret, between the two guns and between the upper and lower floors of the gun-house. No other damage was done except the cutting of the main director firing circuits and the temporary jamming of the gun-loading doors by fragments of shell and of armour, and the smashing of one firing dynamo.

'Q' Turret had been hit on the roof in the centre sighting hood, the shell appearing to have burst there, blowing a large hole in the roof plate. Two men in the gun-house were killed and several wounded, including the midshipman of the turret, who died of his wounds next day. All sights were destroyed, and the director firing circuits were cut. The right gun-loading cage was jammed, but luckily in the 'down' position so that it did not interfere with the hand loading. The left gun-loading cage was temporarily jammed, the range-finder and lookout periscope smashed, but the officer of the turret was unhurt. He got up his spare crew from below, cleared away the dead and wounded, got his left gun into action with director training and laying, and fired with the sound of the other turrets'

399

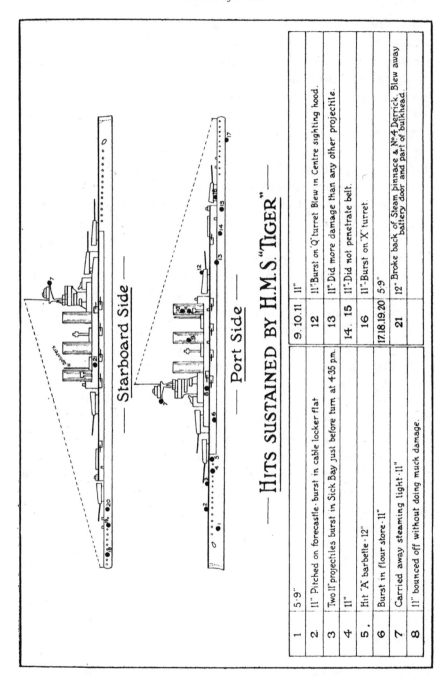

— Starboard Side —

— Port Side —

HITS SUSTAINED BY H.M.S. "TIGER"

1	5·9"	9. 10. 11	11"
2	11" Pitched on forecastle - burst in cable locker flat	12	11" Burst on "Q" turret. Blew in Centre sighting hood.
3	Two 11" projectiles burst in Sick Bay just before turn at 4·35 p.m.	13	11" Did more damage than any other projectile.
4	11"	14. 15	11" Did not penetrate belt.
5	Hit "A" barbette - 12"	16	11" Burst on "X" turret.
6	Burst in flour store - 11"	17. 18. 19. 20	5·9"
7	Carried away steaming light - 11"	21	12" Broke back of Steam pinnace & Nº 4 Derrick. Blew away battery door and part of bulkhead.
8	11" bounced off without doing much damage.		

400

firing. Also, after a lapse of a few minutes, he got the right gun going with hand loading with his spare crew.

4.50 p.m., I had just got on to the roof of 'X' turret and was talking to the officer of the turret, when the turret began to train, and I saw the other turrets doing the same, and then an enemy salvo arrived near the ship. I did record time back to the gun control tower, and found my assistant had everything ready and guns trained on the enemy flashes, but there were no enemy visible. They appeared soon, and I was surprised and annoyed to see that they were apparently our old friends the battle cruisers, and that there were still five of them. I thought the one dropping astern had been done for. We opened on the third from the left, which I could distinguish as having a large red centre funnel. The enemy were in irregular order and soon turned away and were out of sight, but as by now I knew of the loss of the *Indefatigable* and the *Queen Mary*, I realised that we had lost two ships and the enemy none, and although I felt that the enemy were badly knocked about—their fire was nothing compared to what it had been during the first ten minutes—this state of affairs made one very angry. I knew the 5th B.S. were engaging the enemy battle fleet astern of us, but I knew nothing of the position of our battle fleet except that it was out in the North Sea.

At 4.58 we sighted the enemy and re-engaged the same ship as before, the 3rd from the left, distinguished by a red centre funnel. The light was much better, and we had a good run at her, almost as good as our shoot just after the *Queen Mary* sank, and she appeared to drop out of line. As she dropped astern we engaged the new ship, which had now become No. 3 from the left.

At 5.10 we lost sight of the enemy in the mist. Our speed was now 24 knots. Checked the ammunition used, and found that 'B' turret, which as far as I know never missed a salvo throughout the action, had fired five or six common shells, as the shell-room parties had not been able to get the armour-piercing shell into the cages quickly enough. This accounted for the spread for direction which I had noticed earlier in the action, and for which I had lined up the director and found it correct. We lined up again; all correct. 'A' turret reported right gun temporarily out of action with a fractured runout valve box, to which a most skilful repair was made later on.

5.42, Sighted the enemy battle cruisers again, and our ships opened fire. We again had a good light and a good run, but later on spotting became harder. The enemy reply was extremely feeble as far as we were concerned. There were very large splashes, presumably 15-inch salvoes from our 5th B.S., falling near the rear enemy battle cruisers.

At 6 o'clock the visibility became poor and the firing very intermittent.

At 6.5 we sighted the mass of our battle fleet on our port bow, and I was very glad to see them. . . . I then realised that our Admiral had led the enemy to our fleet; but I did not know that we were circling round the enemy and that we were getting between him and his ports.

At 6.7 a disabled German light cruiser appeared on our port bow, and one of our torpedo boat destroyers appeared to 'loaf' up to her and torpedo her—our destroyer appeared to be half-disabled herself too (this was the *Onslow*). The light cruiser was down by the stern and burning. I did not think she was worth 13.5 ammunition, of which we had used a good deal, but we put the 6-inch guns on to her to prevent her firing torpedoes or guns at us as we passed, and they had a very nice run at her. From reports afterwards, I gathered she

Battle Cruiser Force seen from two miles to the eastward, showing the difficult target they presented.

must have been the *Wiesbaden*, which later received fire from the battle fleet.

6.19, Visibility was poor; and there was a lot of smoke about. We sighted a line of battleships, *Konigs*, I thought, and opened fire on the third from the left. In about four minutes we were having a good run at her.

6.29, Enemy out of sight. Smoke and mist.

6.32, Fired a couple of salvoes through a hole in the enemy smoke screen at an enemy stern on.

6.35, *Defence* class cruisers crossed our bows, steaming towards enemy and firing on both sides. The enemy battle cruisers were just visible on our starboard bow, and apparently not firing, but there was a squadron on our starboard beam, from which gun-flashes only were visible, concentrating a terrific fire on the advancing *Defence*, now on our starboard bow. The leading cruiser, the *Defence* herself, blew up with an explosion very similar to that of *Queen Mary*.

There was the sound of heavy fire astern, and I thought our battle fleet must be in action all along the line.

6.36, German torpedo boat destroyers emerged from the smoke on our starboard beam, presumably to attack ships astern of us, and we engaged them with our 6-inch guns, and appeared to sink at least one of the leading boats.

A sudden alteration of course to avoid a torpedo, which I did not see, was made at 6.39. The 13.5s reported the amount of ammunition expended, totalling about 250 rounds.

7.17, Enemy squadron of four ships re-appeared—our old friends the battle cruisers, I thought, but their fire now was feeble or non-existent. We opened fire on 3rd ship. Their line was confused, and one ship was lagging astern.

7.20, Enemy made dense smoke screen from destroyers and turned away. We checked fire, and I could hear no firing astern.

7.53, Tested director on one of our light cruisers on port bow. All correct. Checked ammunition expended.

8.20, Sighted a group of ships on starboard bow and opened fire on 3rd from left, a three funnelled battleship of *Heligoland* class. Conditions for control easy, except for deflection which was upset by the enemy apparently slowing down, and we appeared to be doing well. The enemy scarcely replied, and was burning fiercely, which we could see plainly in the gathering dusk.

8.40, Lost sight of enemy in smoke and dusk. I was surprised to see it getting dark and asked the time, thinking it about 5.30 p.m., and was amazed to hear that it was nearly nine o'clock

8.45, I felt a heavy shock, and thought we had been torpedoed, but nothing happened.

Night.—We had eased speed, and, as it became dark, prepared for the night and the chance of meeting the enemy. We served out food for the men, and I sent my messenger to bag the remains of the ward-room tea from the ward-room, on which we feasted in the gun control tower. I dared not leave the control to see the damage, and anyhow I knew the turret officers, armourers, hydraulic E.R.A.s, and electricians would do everything that could be done, and so well did they do it that by daylight every gun in the ship was in full working order except the right gun and the sights of 'Q' turret. These two jobs were dockyard work, and we could do nothing at sea.

As a matter of fact nothing happened to us during the night, and I had great difficulty in keeping awake.

Morning.—When daylight came the visibility was low—a thick mist on the sea. Our Squadron altered course 16 points, and I felt a feeling of mean pride in that—apparently—the *Tiger* was the only one of the 1st or 2nd B.C.S. whose turrets were all training. A Zeppelin appeared, and some ships—wisely—unloaded their guns at her. After that I had little hope of seeing any more enemy. Not that I felt at all keen to meet fresh enemy battleships—if there were such things—I knew now the extent of the damage to our ship and our squadron, but I was sure that the enemy battle cruisers were badly hammered, and we should have liked a full revenge for *Queen Mary* and *Indefatigable*. I was not yet sure of the loss of *Invincible*, though I could see she was not with the 3rd B.C.S., which had joined us. As a matter of fact, when we had passed her wreck the previous evening, I had thought she was a German, and had passed word below that we were passing a sunken German ship.

Now came the time of clearing up and repairs. As it was still thick I could not leave the control position, and I did not see the worst of this, but I attended the burial service on the upper deck in the drizzle and spray. The wind had got up a little by the afternoon. It was most impressive. At this time, I had no idea that the fleet had engaged in one of the great actions of the war. I thought that it had been just a cruiser action like the Dogger Bank. Gradually reports came in from the battle fleet, and we were elated by news of German losses. We were surprised on arrival in harbour to find that the public were prepared for news of a defeat, and asked our people why we had not sunk the Germans at last. But we were well received by the local inhabitants.

Arrival in Harbour.—When we got into harbour we tackled the repairs again, and were ready for sea very soon. But a worse job was the writing of the reports. Evidence was hopelessly conflicting as regards the enemy, and the fire control table records were the only really reliable data. But reports had to be made, and in a hurry, as well as the repairs executed, and I fear that the reports were far from complete. It was very hard to know which officers and men in the gunnery department to recommend for special recognition when all had done so well. I have said little about the personnel in this narrative, for in my duty I saw little of them during the action, except just my gun control tower crew. They were perfect. But from the way orders were carried out I knew it must be same throughout the ship. The reports from the officers of turrets, transmitting station, the 6-inch control and 6-inch guns confirmed this. No praise can be too high for the officers and men.

Control Notes.—Most of my experiences I have described in these notes, but there are a few other non-technical points which may be of interest. The enemy shorts frequently wetted the top control position: I commenced by using 12 power glasses, but soon changed to 6: I did not experience any eye strain.

Blast from our own guns was not as severe as I had expected; blast from enemy shell was non-existent in the G.C.T., and for all I could tell the enemy might have been using practice projectiles. The enemy shell could clearly be seen after they ricochetted short, but I saw none before they ricochetted. Until dusk, I could not see our 13.5-inch shells burst—we were using armour-piercing shell—but I did see the 6-inch high explosive bursting. Few of our overs could be seen. It was very hard to judge the inclination of the enemy, except of the leader of the enemy line, who was generally far clearer of smoke than any of the others. The total number of rounds we fired was:—13.5-inch, 304; and 6-inch, 140. We were hit 21 times— viz., 2, 12-inch; 11, 11-inch; and 5, 5.9-inch hits. At the time I knew nothing about the hits which were not on armour, except for seeing some splinters fly from the forecastle, but the hits on the armour jolted the whole ship.

The Engine-Room of H.M.S. *Warrior*
(Armoured Cruiser of Rear-Admiral Arbuthnot's Cruiser Squadron)

A Narrative of Experiences between Decks during the Action of the 1st Cruiser Squadron, and afterwards when the *Warrior* had been crippled.

Wednesday, May 31st, 1916.—In the morning we carried out the usual programme, still uncertain of our destination though we continued to steam E.S.E., and were told to prepare for higher speed. As the afternoon wore on we made all preparations for battle, went to action stations, and then fell out and went to tea. About 5.30 we began to see the smoke and to hear the firing on our starboard bow, and then the buglers sounded off 'Action' and we went to our quarters. The telegraphs were rung to full speed, and I made a tour through the stokeholds to see that everything was all right and to say a word of encouragement to the men. They all seemed keenly on the alert, and gathered round me eagerly as I passed along telling them not to get excited over the sounds of bursting shells, as those that burst in the water alongside produced a louder concussion on the hull of the ship than those that actually burst inside.

Just as I returned to the engine-room ladder-way (at 5.55 p.m.) we opened fire, and it seemed impossible to believe that this was going to be other than the ordinary procedure of target practice. The measured thuds of our guns going off continued as I descended the ladder, and indeed, with one exception, they were the heaviest explosions I heard throughout the action. When I reached the starboard engine-room platform everything was in first-class order. The electric lights shone brightly on the polished steel, and the engines were running perfectly at 135 revolutions a minute, which, in view of the facts that the sea was flat calm and the ship's bottom clean after the recent docking, meant that she was making a clear 22 knots through the water, though her normal full speed was 21. Everyone was doing his utmost, and I felt that at least the thing that I had been working for for the last four years was being achieved for the first time. Thinking I would go and have a look at the port engine-room, where 'M.', the Senior Engineer Lieutenant, was in charge, I went up the ladder, and before going down the other side I thought

I would try and get a peep up on deck and see what was going on. Just as I got through the armour door on the main deck, I was met by some other people, including the Boatswain, running back, as they said we were being straddled by 11-inch shell, and they thought it wasn't very healthy out there. As I turned back I perceived that a shell had come in on the marines' mess deck, from which I had come. A brown smoke was hanging about, and the men of the fire brigade were carrying away three or four poor fellows and laying them down, looking dazed and frightened. I therefore went straight down to the port engine-room to see if anything had happened there. 'M.' told me that they had heard an explosion overhead, and some of the lights had gone out, but apparently there was no serious damage done below. Finding everything going splendidly down there, I decided to return to the starboard engine-room, and I looked into the Engineers' office at the top of the ladder on the way. There, for the last time, I saw my Stoker Secretary sitting at his books as if nothing unusual were happening, but he pointed out to me that they had had a shell in a bit further forward, and going out on to the mess deck I found a great gaping rent in the deck overhead, with the daylight falling weirdly through it.

However there was neither time nor temptation for speculation, and I hurried below again to the starboard engine-room. Shortly afterwards, at about 6.15, I heard a tremendous explosion at the after end, a heavy jar went through the whole fabric, and most of the lights went out. Immediately afterwards there was a heavy roar of water and steam, and my impression was that we had been torpedoed. Several men came running forward from that end, one of them with blood streaming down his face. In that moment I realised fully what cold drawn funk is like. But I had to make a decision, and advancing towards the after end, I tried to gauge the extent of the damage. The engines still went on running, which seemed to show that the cylinders had not been hit, but in the dim uncertain light I perceived what appeared to be Niagara at the after end of the engine room, though whether the sheet of water was rising up from below or pouring down from above I couldn't be sure at the time. Anyhow, a blast of steam on my face warned me that I hadn't long to think about it, and I soon made up my mind that no pumps could deal with the quantity of water that was coming in, and that the only thing to do was to get the men out as quickly as possible. Not knowing that the other engine-room also was damaged, I gave the order to open the water-tight door on the mid-line bulkhead and to go through to the other side, intending to take charge and control the working of the department from there myself. But the door was screwed hard down and the sprocket chains were greasy, and it struck me that by the time the men had got it open and gone through, the water might be above the sill and would flood the other engine-room before they could get the door closed again, so I ordered all hands up on deck at once. The artificers asked if they should ease or stop the engines, but I said 'No,' as I guessed that the Captain would want to keep going as long and as fast as possible, and the main steam valves could be shut off from the mess deck if necessary. At first the men didn't know what to do, as the ladders at the after end were inaccessible, but I shouted to them to go up the midship ladder, and hustled all towards it in front of me. As soon as it appeared that they had all gone up, I followed them myself, but by that time all the lights had gone out, and it was pitch dark.

When I got to the top, knowing it was useless to go aft, I turned forward and felt my way by the handrails along the platform at the tops of the cylinders towards the door at the fore end, which communicated with the port engine-room and with the mess deck. When I got there, however, a stoker told me that we could not get through there, as the mess deck was on fire, and when I tried to do so I was met by a rush of thick smoke and blinding fumes that drove me back. At this moment with this in front and the roar of steam behind me I felt like a trapped rat, for there seemed no possibility of lifting the heavy armour hatches overhead, and a spasm of sheer terror came over me; but just then I realised that the man was calling my attention to a glimmer of light above, and the next minute I found myself climbing out through a torn rent in the deck—the extension of the shell hole I had seen previously from outside our office.

When I got out and looked round, the first thing I saw was a group of men behind the shelter of one of the after turrets trying tentatively to open a fire-main valve on the upper deck. Then I noticed that there were yellow flashes followed by angry reports coming from some ships away on our beam, and shells were whizzing and screaming through the air just above my head, and I decided that this was no place for me. At all costs I must get down to the port engine-room and take charge there, and to that end I made my way to the main deck hatchway; but before I could get half-way down it I was nearly choked with hot, stinging smoke, and had to retreat. I then went further aft and got down to the half-deck, which was partly wrecked, and tried to get through the armour door to the mess deck, but with the same result. Through the smoke and flame I saw a brilliant display of fireworks, where the circuits were fusing in festoons of electric arcs.

Finding this route hopeless, I went along the upper deck again and tried to reach the mess deck from the fore side, but here again any attempt to approach the burning compartment was completely frustrated. I then endeavoured to collect my scattered wits with a view to putting out the fire, but I found that I had the greatest difficulty in getting my brain to work at all. I have heard other fellows say that they have been seized with this temporary mental paralysis, which seems to last for ages, but really lasts for moments only. On such occasions when it is difficult to originate anything, evolutions rehearsed at drill work automatically, and at this moment I found my subordinates readier than myself in carrying out measures that I had myself devised.

By this time some of the forward section of the fire brigade had arrived—nearly the whole of the after section of the brigade were knocked out in the burning compartment. It then occurred to me that I had better let the Captain know how things stood, and if possible get him to communicate with the port engine-room and tell them to keep the fire engines going full bore. As I got up to the conning tower I perceived that we were practically alone on the sea, and steaming along at about 15 knots.

It was now a little after half-past six, and for the next two hours we fought and struggled to put that fire out. It had got a firm hold in the gunnery office, where the papers, desks, and shelves burned fiercely till the steel partitions were red hot, and the paint on the sides and the corticene on the deck outside were all flaring. The heart of the fire was inside, round a corner where no hose could reach it, and to enter the compartment was like going into an oven, and you simply could not get there. One of the most heart-rending experiences was when I passed along the half-deck on one occasion by the wrecked hatchway, and one poor fellow, who was lying there wounded, held out his arms to me and begged me to help him out. But I dared not stop. We didn't know when the ship might go down under us, and it was my job to keep her afloat if possible. So I had to pass on, hoping that someone else would give him a helping hand.

By this time volumes of steam were roaring out of the ventilators to the port engine-room, and the agonising conviction came over me that 'M' must be done for, since, as I told the Captain, nobody could be alive down there now. We had lifted some of the upper hatches, but before we could climb down to open the lower ones into the engine-room we were met with smoke and fire, and could not get near them. The steam from the engine-room also blew across the entrance to the mess deck, further impeding all access to the fire. In fact, we couldn't get at the fire because of the steam from the engine-room, and we couldn't get at the engine-room because of the fire, which was becoming a furnace, and at last I went to the Captain and asked permission to draw the fires in the stokeholds and shut off the boilers from there.

Even so, it was a long time before we could put the fire under on the mess deck, and it was eventually checked by a man climbing down the ship's side and playing the hose in through the hole made by the shell that had caused the fire! It was about 9 o'clock before we could lift one of the armoured hatches, and then, to our amazement, we heard people shouting. I rushed round to the engine-room ladder way, and there I found 'M.' who had just been helped out. I helped him along to the ward-room and put him in an armchair and gave him my brandy flask, which he wanted badly, while he told his story.[4]

He told me that the shell which had driven us out of the starboard engine-room came through both engine-rooms and burst at the mid-line, leaving most of its gas in the port engine-room, where he was. He was knocked down by the concussion, but got up and tried to see what could be done. He found it impossible to escape by any of the ladders, and as they were getting choked by the fumes and the steam, he tried and succeeded in doing what I had tried and failed to do—namely, to open the mid-line door to the starboard engine-room just after we had gone up. By the time they had closed the door they found, by the glimmer of the sole remaining oil lamp, that the water was coming over the floor plates, and the crank pits were full up and the cranks were swishing round in the middle of it. He said that he had not realised the fact that we were making water fast until a cold feeling round the ankles awoke him to the true state of affairs.

---

4 What follows has been supplemented slightly from the report of his experiences which he wrote after the action.

Not realising the full extent of the damage here, he first tried to put the pumps on, but soon found that hopeless. Then he tried to ease the engines and shut off steam, fearing further accidents, but by this time the water was breast high over the floor plates, and he decided that the only thing to do was to clear out. But by this time the ladders were inaccessible as the floor plates were dislodged and there was every chance of being drawn into the swirl of the racing cranks. They climbed up over pipes and condensers, holding hands to prevent the swirling water carrying them away. Unfortunately their chain was twice broken, with the result that several men were jammed somehow and drowned. The remainder climbed from one vantage point to another as the water rose till they reached the upper gratings, but by this time it was quite dark, and having no purchase anywhere they could not dislodge the gratings overhead, and found themselves apparently doomed to certain death. Not only were they expecting to be drowned, but escaping steam almost suffocated them, and they kept splashing the oily water over their faces to keep them from being peeled. Some men had wrapped scarves round their heads to protect themselves, and all kept as much of their bodies as they could in the water. The surprising thing was that the engines went on working till the water was half-way up the cylinders, and only stopped then because the boilers were shut off. And this agony of terror went on for nearly two and a half hours in pitch darkness and apparent hopelessness before they were rescued. How 'M.' himself behaved I can only shrewdly guess, but there was one other man there, a stoker petty officer named 'K.,' who absolutely refused to recognise the horror of the situation, and kept talking and cheering them all up to the very end. At the start there were about eight of them, and they kept hold of each other to save their lives as long as possible, but one by one they kept dropping off and getting lost and drowned in the water, till at the last there were only three of them left. 'M.' himself would have been lost, having slipped from his hold and finding himself being drawn down into the machinery, but 'K.' held on to him and kept him up until he recovered somewhat. They thought at one time that the ship had been abandoned, but the click of a valve being worked conquered their fears of that. Then they felt a noticeably cold stream of water coming in, which they stirred up as much as possible, and from this apparently they had the idea that the ship must be under weigh, and therefore in tow of someone, which encouraged them.

A fire party.

At last they heard some order being 'piped' round the ship, and they all shouted together, and this led to their rescue. And, by Jove, I was thankful to see 'M' when they got him out.

Meanwhile, I had to go back and look after the ship, which was now being towed by the *Engadine* at a speed of about 8 knots. As soon as we got into the engine-rooms we found that they were both full up, and the water was rising. There was nothing further to be done there, so the only thing was to locate the damage and prevent the adjoining compartment from filling also. The fire was not yet out, and the steam fire engines, of course, were now out of action, but some of the men opened up a coaling scuttle close to the burning corner and most courageously went down in smoke helmets and used buckets of water that were passed down to them from above. The whole place was strewn with corpses, some fearfully mangled among the twisted girders, and the stench was indescribable. I went down to the after boiler-room just in front of the flooded engine-rooms, and found the water coming in through a certain number of leaks, which, however, could be dealt with, so I sent a warrant officer down with a few artificers to stop these up. We had to keep the forward hand pumps going to prevent the water accumulating in the bilge, and this took a considerable number of hands.

Abaft the engine-rooms things were not so satisfactory, as the decks and bulkheads had all been strained and buckled by the explosion, and we found the adjoining compartments were filling up one after another. There was only one portable hand pump available, and the rest had to be done by baling with buckets. All through the night we struggled on, trying to keep pace with the water by strenuous exertion all round. About midnight we all met in the wardroom, where the messman had managed to produce a ham and a loaf or two of bread. Everybody was wonderfully cheerful, though personally I couldn't do much in the eating line. I mumbled a few pieces of dry bread in a dry mouth, but I couldn't go on with it. And the only thing we could find to drink was one bottle of port. We were astonished to find that the only casualty among the officers was the Carpenter, who was killed outright by a shell on the mess deck at the beginning of the action. The 1st Lieutenant was wounded in the leg by some small splinters, but he limped about most of the night assisting with the work. There were 66 men killed and 35 wounded, of whom 4 have since died. They kept the doctors busy all through the night patching them up.

Thursday, 1st June, 1916.—We could gauge the sinkage of the ship very accurately by noting the rise of water inside in the engine-room, from step to step of the ladder. By 2.0 a.m. we had stopped the further entry of water and were keeping it down with the pumps, and at 4.0 it had not gained anything, but after that a new difficulty arose, which ultimately defeated us. The weather, which had been flat calm for a whole week before, began to freshen, and the upper deck in parts was simply riddled and torn to ribbons. Consequently, when the seas began to break over, it was absolutely impossible to keep water from pouring down below in tons and flooding the mess deck and flats. We tried to construct cofferdams with mess tables and canvas awnings, but the plates and girders were twisted into all sorts of shapes, with great yawning gulfs where decks and cabins ought to have been, so that it was hopeless. The men, too, were getting utterly worn out with their exertions at the pumps and baling, and the sea was getting distinctly worse.

At about 4 o'clock the day broke, in what we all agreed was 'a hopeless dawn,' and indeed as we looked around our shattered deck under a threatening sky, with still forms lying where they had been deposited under blood-stained sheets or flags, we felt that there was very little chance of bringing the old ship in, even if she were not torpedoed by a submarine, which was a highly probable contingency.

413

Soon after 6.0 a.m. I realised that she was rapidly losing her stability, and by the way the water was rising, I knew she could not last much longer. When I went up to report my opinion to the Captain, I found that he had just come to the same conclusion, and at that very moment the Commander came up and made the same announcement. Consequently the skipper waited no longer, but signalled to the *Engadine* to cast off the tow and come alongside.

This was a lengthy business under the circumstances, and we made preparations to abandon ship. Our work was finished, so I went to my cabin, which was knee deep in water, and looked round with a hopeless feeling at the things I must leave behind. However, whether I fetched up in an English harbour or a German prison camp, I thought it would be just as well to be clothed as befitted my rank, so I pulled off my wet and filthy overalls and put on a respectable uniform suit which was hanging up. Looking into a drawer, I saw a spectacle case, a card case, and a pair of nail nippers, which I thrust into my pocket. I was the only officer who left the ship with visiting cards!

After two attempts, the *Engadine* succeeded in running up alongside, and then began the agonising business of getting the wounded across. The smaller vessel was plunging heavily up and down, and some of the poor fellows in the stretchers got rather roughly handled. The head of the stretcher would be passed in and seized by willing hands, but before the operation could be completed the ships would roll apart, and the flimsy contrivance, supported only at one end, would droop downwards to a perilous angle before it was drawn into safety. One poor beggar *did* slip out through the foot of the stretcher, and fell down into the water between the ships. His right foot had been amputated at the ankle, but he made a plucky attempt to swim in spite of cold and exhaustion. It seemed an awful time before they could get a rope, and then they could not get it round him. At last one of their flying officers, the one who first sighted the enemy, went down with a tow-line, but just before he reached the man the latter fell backwards in the water, frothed at the mouth, and died. 'R.' however, got the rope round him and steadied him with his legs, himself holding on only with his hands while they were hauled up. It was a hideously slow process, and every moment we expected to see them both squashed to a jelly where the two ships' sides kept grinding together. After a seemingly interminable interval they were hauled over the bulwarks, but only one was alive.

By this time we had all followed, each with a carefully considered jump, assisted by many outstretched hands from the other side. The sea was getting rapidly worse, and if we hadn't got off when we did we should never have got off at all. The skipper and 'H.B.' were the last to leave the ship, and the former waited till he thought everyone had gone before he jumped, but the wily 'H.,' having determined to filch the honour, stepped back again, and by so doing nearly lost his own life, for the gap widened and he jumped short, and was only pulled in by someone holding on to him by one hand. The Navigator of the *Engadine* took charge of me, and conducted me to his cabin, which he told me to make my own. As I had dragged my uniform on rather hurriedly and under difficulties, I was glad of the opportunity of readjusting my toilette. Meanwhile the *Engadine* had let go and backed off, and then steamed ahead past the old ship, whereupon the men gave three cheers, and then broke into our old pantomime song, 'It's a long, long way to the *Warrior.*' And that was too much for me. I was thankful that I was inside a cabin where no one could see me, for then I quite broke down. . . .

The *Engadine* fellows were awfully good to us. They gave up all their cabins to us, where we were billeted in twos and threes, and the ward-room was made into a hospital. Being such a much smaller ship, they couldn't possibly give us proper meals, but they first provided us with biscuits and whisky *ad lib.*, and afterwards with basins of soup and cocoa. I lay down on the bunk and rested till mid-day. In the afternoon, our Captain sent round orders for us all to write rough reports, as far as we could remember, of all that had occurred while it was fresh in our memories. In the dog watches the ship's company were mustered by the ledger, which the paymaster had dutifully brought with him, and when our men came up I went along to the table to witness the last roll call. It was a sad business. At times for each one that answered there were four or five blanks, for most of the casualties were in our department. We entered the Forth about midnight and anchored behind May Island at 2.0 a.m. At last we were safe.

Friday, 2nd June, 1916.—In the morning, after a rather uncomfortable night sleeping in one's clothes, we steamed up to Rosyth, and we went alongside a jetty about 9.0 a.m. Before leaving the ship all hands were fallen in on deck, and the officers with the Captain on the upper bridge. The latter then made a simple but impressive speech, opening with the earnest words—'I am proud—*very proud*—to have commanded such a ship's company as the *Warrior*'s.' He recalled some of the leading incidents of the fight, and of the struggle that followed it, expressed a hope that it might be his privilege to command us all together again in another ship, and finally read out a preliminary and provisional list of officers and men who were conspicuous for meritorious service, and whom he should recommend for promotion and other recognition. We were all much moved, and everybody cheered wildly.

After that the Parson stood up and read a short Service of Thanksgiving for those who had survived, and a Burial Service for those who had gone down with the ship. We then disembarked, and the ship's company was divided up and quartered for the time being on board the *Crescent* and the *Dreadnought*, which were lying in the dockyard.

'A Destroyer of the 12th Flotilla in the Day and Night Actions'

Narrative from H.M.S. *Maenad*

The 31st of May started off as a very dull, hazy day, the visibility being only about 2 miles at the most. This got better later in the day and the sun came out, but it was never very clear. I had the afternoon watch, and everything seemed quite peaceful. One or two signals came through letting us know that the German fleet was at sea somewhere to the southward, but we had heard that yarn before, and it left us rather cold.

At 4 p.m., just as I came off watch, things brightened considerably as the fleet increased to 20 knots, and everyone went to action stations and prepared for instant action. We then heard that the battle cruisers were actually engaged with the enemy, but even then that had happened before, and we expected that the enemy, with the battle cruisers in chase, were steaming as fast as they could back to Germany, and a good deal faster than the battle fleet could pursue them.

However, things turned out differently, and we heard they were coming northwards; when quite suddenly, and, to myself at any rate, very unexpectedly, we heard heavy gunfire quite near, and then sighted the battle cruisers appear out of the haze steaming very fast, firing rapidly, and with shell splashes shooting up at intervals round them. This, I think, was probably the most impressive sight I saw during the whole show, partly I suppose because it was the first sight I had had of any ship in action during the war. The time was about 6.0 p.m.

In the destroyers we had nothing active to do at the beginning of the battle fleet action—no enemy ships within range of our guns, nor a target for our torpedoes. We were simply spectators, with ample time for our minds to wander from one possibility to another. A first impression was that our battle cruisers must get beaten into a cocked hat, due to seeing our ships being fired on heavily, while one could see no sign whatever of the enemy. I could not bring myself to realise at first that the Germans were getting just as good a pounding as our ships, and probably a worse one. That thought passed away very quickly as I caught sight of some of our battle-ships quite near, and turned my head to have a look at the battle fleet—a wonderful sight, steaming at 20 knots in cruising formation, all in beautiful station, a much bigger fleet than ever appeared at any review. This gave one a feeling of absolute confidence in everyone and everything.

The battle cruisers passed across the bow of the fleet from starboard to port, and the fleet then deployed to port, falling in astern of the battle cruisers. Our flotilla dropped from our screening stations ahead of the 1st B.S., the starboard wing division, to our battle station which was on the starboard beam of the rear division of the line, so putting us between our fleet and the enemy, which was a very nice position for seeing things going on but rather too apt to be among the enemy's short shots for comfort. Almost as soon as the fleet deployed at about 6.30 they commenced to open fire, and I remember well getting a bit of a shock as the *Revenge* fired a salvo of 15-inch bang over our heads at quite a short distance from us. But this was compensated for by the feeling of 'that'll shake 'em,' as you thought of the shells dropping on or near a Hun at the other end.

Shortly after the fleet had formed into battle line the 5th B.S., which had been following the battle cruisers, came up and formed astern of the fleet. We had a splendid view of the *Warspite* as she got hit aft, and with her helm jammed over while going fairly fast she turned a complete circle towards the enemy. Owing to turning at speed with full helm she took up a heavy list, and then appeared to get a full salvo right into her, which covered her in smoke. As the smoke cleared away I saw her with this list, and not realising what actually was happening, my heart came into my mouth, as I thought she was going down. We had just had a rumour that one or two of the battle cruisers had already been sunk, so were all very relieved when we saw her carry on as though little or nothing had happened, and take up her station in the line again.

It was not until after the deployment that we could see anything of the German fleet except for occasional gun-flashes, but now we could see their ships at intervals, sometimes quite clearly when the mist seemed to lift, though usually only faintly through banks of mist or through the smoke. It was weird and curious how it struck one on seeing these German ships, which we had been waiting to see ever since August, '14. The whole thing seemed very unlike a naval battle just then. Right aft, at the after gun, which was my action station, we had got everything ready that we could think of, and we had now only to wait for our turn and watch the big ships have theirs. We all sat down or lay down on the deck, this being in our opinion the best way of avoiding shell splinters, and to anyone who did not know what was going on we must have looked rather as though we were having a smoke and stand-easy in the middle of an ordinary tactical exercise. I must admit that at the beginning, when the Germans were firing at our fleet and occasional shots fell short and round us, I felt uncommonly frightened. If you watched a shell drop and then looked at the water just afterwards it looked as though there was a shower of rain with enormous drops all round. As it happened, I don't think a soul was touched or any splinters found on board except one, which, some weeks later, was found embedded in the ship's side when we were scraping the paintwork.

It did not take long to get over that feeling of unsafety and then try and strain one's eyes to see what actually was happening to the German fleet. It was quite easy to see that our fleet were all right, but to make anything definite out in the German line was impossible. I could see they were having a pretty rotten time, as now and then you would see a flash in one of their ships, which was certainly not a gun-flash, and then sometimes a dull red glow for a few seconds or perhaps half a minute, which was evidently a fire of some kind that had broken out. All this was very encouraging, but, of course, one was 'seeing' a lot of things which never happened or became very much magnified and glorified because one wanted them to happen.

418

Then came the terrible sight when we watched the *Defence* blow up. She came steaming from the head of the line apparently going towards the rear of the enemy, until she got hit by a salvo. This must have damaged her badly, but the smoke cleared away and she steamed on as though unhurt, but almost immediately afterwards she was hit by another salvo, and there was an enormous cloud of smoke and a sheet of flame hundreds of feet high, also huge bits of débris in the air. When this cleared there was nothing. She had literally gone up in a puff of smoke.

At about 7.30 we saw a German light cruiser drop out of the line and sink. I have forgotten her name, which we learnt later, but it cheered us up immensely to see something definite of that sort. And about ten minutes later a German destroyer was disabled, apparently one taking part in the big torpedo attack they made. This destroyer lay helpless between us and the enemy until the 1st Division of our flotilla were sent out to finish her off.

We then lost sight of the enemy, who, as far as I could see, immediately after their attack made a heavy smoke screen and turned away from us, so that it appeared to me we were both steaming in opposite directions for a short time, the enemy to the westwards and ourselves in a south-easterly direction. We, of course, lost sight of the enemy, but turned again soon afterwards, and at 8.10 steered west by north, which must have meant we were practically following in their track.

The Night Action

The action now broke off, and everything was quiet, and we had a short time to think of more personal things. About the first thing we all realised was how true it was that one cannot fight on an empty stomach! So we collected such food as we were able to find, some bread and corned beef, and some boiling water, with which we made tea. After this meal I was sent for by the Captain on the bridge, where also were the 1st Lieutenant and the Midshipman, and we had a talk about what had happened and compared notes on what we had seen. I was very glad to hear what they had gathered in the way of news, as they naturally had a better view from the bridge than I had aft, where one is only 6 feet above the water-line.

Our discussion was abruptly finished at 8.40, when we altered course to south, and heard firing on the starboard bow, which

419

turned out to be one of our cruiser squadrons in touch again with the enemy. This lasted for a short time, but from our position we could see very little of what had taken place. This state of knowing that something was going on but being unable to find out any details of the result was the most trying thing of all, and was twenty times accentuated when night came on.

We were now steaming a rather irregular course in a southerly direction at about 18 to 20 knots. The light was beginning to fail, and the fleet was taking up their night cruising stations. We took station astern of the 1st Battle Squadron, and had other flotillas on either beam. At 9.25 we were steering south at 18 knots, and 9.50 reduced to 12 knots, due, we found out later, to the 1st B.S. not keeping up the speed of the fleet owing to their flagship, *Marlborough*, being a lame duck. *Marlborough* eventually dropped out, having transferred her Admiral to the *Revenge*, and returned to Newcastle for docking.

It was now quite dark, and I think I spent most of my time praying for daylight. One felt very lost in the darkness, and kept wishing you were in some other place in the ocean to see what was going on there, what gun was that that had just fired, etc. One felt so helpless, not seeing anything or being able to do anything. I spent most of my time sitting wedged in between two empty ammunition boxes near to my gun, with a mackintosh over my head to prevent the light of my cigarette or pipe from showing. Nearly everyone was smoking continuously all day and night—I got through 100 cigarettes and a ¼-lb. tin of tobacco in just over 12 hours.

At 10.4 p.m. we heard firing on our starboard beam and saw searchlights switched on, and at 10.20 the same kind of thing happened—the 2nd Light Cruiser Squadron being in action with some enemy light forces. On all these occasions one worried tremendously, because you knew, saw, and heard something going on but couldn't see any result.

At 11.45 firing started on our starboard quarter quite close at hand. I immediately turned over to the Captain—I had been looking out on the bridge for an hour to give him some rest—and went aft again. Things now got rather beyond a joke, as the enemy ships seemed to be large ones, and their searchlights were directed all round us, and some of their shells were falling quite close. We increased to 20 knots, and slowly drew clear of the firing, when we realised that it was not us that the enemy were engaged with at the moment, but some other ships. Just after we were clear we saw first one and then another dull red glow start and get brighter. The feeling that came over one then that one was really watching a human bonfire, and not knowing whether it was friend or enemy—in either case it was bad enough—made it rather a horrible sight.

12th Flotilla's Attack at Daybreak

After this engagement was over, we had practically two hours during which nothing of interest that I can remember occurred. We were steaming on various courses between south and east at 17 to 18 knots. That was from midnight till 1.55 a.m. I was aft at my gun at this time and had nothing to do; one smoked a good deal and dozed occasionally.

At 1.55 we altered course to South 30° East, went on to 25 knots, and the word was passed to close up properly at action stations. Our flotilla leader, the *Faulknor*, had sighted some German heavy ships, and turned so as to steer in the same direction as them, to get ahead of them. Things then got very exciting as we left the German ships and lost sight of them, while we took up a position for attack, knowing that in a few minutes we should turn and go straight for them from ahead.

At about 2.15 a.m. we turned, and everyone was at pretty high tension waiting to sight the Germans as they appeared out of the haze. At 2.20 we sighted them and attacked. As soon as the attack started, one lost all sense of excitement, because things were *happening*. The Germans opened a fairly heavy fire on all of us, and right at the beginning hit the *Onslaught*, which was quite close to us. We fired one torpedo at a German battleship of the *Konig* class about 4,000 yards off, but I do not know whether we hit. One torpedo from the flotilla certainly found a mark. The whole attack only lasted about five minutes, by which time we had passed this division of German ships and lost sight of them.

After the attack our Captain, having only had time to fire one torpedo, decided to attack again, so he turned and left the flotilla, increased to full speed, and off we went after the Germans. It did not take long to find them, and at 2.28—only 8 minutes after the first attack—we sighted them again and fired two torpedoes. During

'Ready!' (4-in gun's crew)

this and the previous attack there had been nothing for the guns' crews to do, and, as they were very keen, I opened fire with the after gun at a German battleship; rather ridiculous to fire against their armour with 4-inch shells, but it gave us a lot of satisfaction, particularly as the gun-layer swore he saw some shell explode on their superstructure. I'm afraid, however, that this firing rather disconcerted the Captain, as he thought it was our ship being hit aft instead of our gun firing.

Just before we turned away and lost sight of the Germans we had the satisfaction of seeing one of our torpedoes take effect on one of the Germans, and a most splendid explosion resulted, sending a flame well up to her masthead. At the time we, of course, thought she would sink, but unfortunately we found out later that they got her back into harbour.

When that was over we turned away and found ourselves alone, not far from the Horn's Reef light vessel, roughly 20 to 30 miles S.W. of it. At 2.45 we turned to the northward, hoping to run across our flotilla again. We saw no sign of them, but met two of the 13th, the Rosyth Flotilla, *Moresby* and *Obdurate* I think they were, so joined up with them. A little later we picked up *Marksman*, our flotilla half-leader, and then *Champion*, the light cruiser carrying Captain 'D.' 13. We all joined up and formed a small detached squadron of our own. We steamed to the north and north-west, but saw nothing until 3.30, when we sighted two German destroyers on our starboard bow; we opened fire on them, and they fired several torpedoes at us, neither side scoring any hits. They were quickly lost in the haze and we did not follow them up, as we sighted in the distance a large ship screened by many more destroyers, and we had not sufficient torpedoes left to make an attack.

This attack only lasted ten minutes, and at 3.40 we altered to N.N.W., and were on that course until 5 o'clock, when we ran into a lot of oil and wreckage. We also saw many dead bodies bobbing about, but could not tell what nationality they were. We stopped by the wreck of one ship to search for any survivors, and the *Marksman* found one, the Captain of the *Ardent*—I believe he was practically the only survivor of his ship. He had been in the water five hours, and was nearly done for. After a good search for any other survivors we went on, and shortly afterwards sighted some survivors on a 'Carley' raft. These belonged to the *Fortune*. Just as we were getting near to pick them up we sighted a submarine's periscope, and then a torpedo passed just under our stern, so we left the raft and steamed round and round at high speed for a short time, and then stopped to pick up the men. We got eleven on board us, and one of the other destroyers got a few more. Unfortunately one of our survivors died after being on board a short time. I enquired of our survivors about the 1st Lieutenant of the *Fortune*, Lieut. R. E. Paterson, whom I knew very well, and gathered he had last been seen swimming away from an overloaded raft, so as to give the other men a chance. He was never seen again.

At 5.45 we proceeded and steered north, and were on this course or roughly so until 8 a.m. During this time I took the opportunity of getting a little sleep, and I think most of the others on board did so too. We were all tired out, and unless there was some immediate work to busy oneself about, one could hardly keep one's eyes open.

We sighted the disabled *Sparrowhawk*, and the *Marksman* was detached to stand by her, but after trying to tow her stern first *Marksman* eventually had to give it up, remove the crew, and sink the ship.

The remainder of us spread out in line abreast to make a wide sweep, and so sight any straggling ships, wteckage, survivors, etc. At 8.0 a.m. we altered to south again to make a further sweep. I got some breakfast then and went on the bridge to keep the forenoon watch. We realised that there now seemed little chance of seeing the Germans again.

At 9.0 we altered to S.E., and at 10 back again to N.W., having sighted nothing. I was alone most of the time on the bridge, and my mind wandered back over the happenings of the last 12 hours, but the details I cannot remember, as I was half-asleep most of the time. We carried on our sweep up the battle ground of the previous day, but saw nothing. The other two destroyers with us were sent back to Rosyth in the forenoon, as they were getting short of oil, which left ourselves and the *Champion* to go on. We swept up towards the entrance of the Skaggerack, and at about 3.30 in the afternoon turned to west, our course for the Firth of Forth.

We arrived in the Forth at about 4 p.m. on the 2nd of June, filled up with oil, took in ammunition, torpedoes, and provisions, and were ready to go out again by 8 p.m. Luckily we did not have to go out, but had a good night's rest.

It was rather a shock in the morning on turning out to discover what time it was. Apparently Summer Time was in force at Rosyth, though we never used it when at Scapa Flow, and breakfast that morning was at 11 a.m.!

Message from His Majesty the King

Sent to the Commander-in-Chief of the Grand Fleet in reply to a message of 'humble duty and respectful and heartfelt wishes on His Majesty's Birthday,' ☙ ☙ ☙ telegraphed on June 3rd, 1916. ❧ ❧ ❧

'I am deeply touched by the message which you have sent me on behalf of the Grand Fleet. It reaches me on the morrow of a battle which has once more displayed the splendid gallantry of the officers and men under your Command.

I mourn the loss of brave men, many of them personal friends of my own, who have fallen in their country's cause. Yet even more do I regret that the German High Seas Fleet, in spite of its heavy losses, was enabled by the misty weather to evade the full consequences of an encounter they have always professed to desire, but for which when the opportunity arrived they showed no inclination.

Though the retirement of the enemy immediately after the opening of the general engagement robbed us of the opportunity of gaining a decisive victory, the events of last Wednesday amply justify my confidence in the valour and efficiency of the fleets under your command.

GEORGE, R I.'

THE BRITISH CASUALTIES, 31st MAY TO 1st JUNE, 1916.

SHIP	KILLED		WOUNDED		PRISONERS OF WAR		REMARKS
	Officers.	Men.	Officers.	Men.	Officers.	Men.	
H.M.S. ACASTA, - - -	1	5	...	1	...	...	
,, ARDENT (sunk), - -	4	74	1	1	...	...	
,, BARHAM, - - - -	4	22	1	36	...	...	
,, BLACK PRINCE (sunk),	37	820	...	...	...	...	Includes 5 civilians.
,, BROKE, - - - -	1	46	3	33	...	...	
,, CALLIOPE, - - -	...	10	2	7	...	...	
,, CASTOR, - - - -	...	13	1	22	...	...	
,, CHESTER, - - -	2	33	3	39	...	...	
,, COLOSSUS, - - -	...	...	...	5	...	...	
,, DEFENCE (sunk),	54	849	...	...	...	...	Includes 4 civilians.
,, DEFENDER, - - -	...	1	...	2	...	...	
,, DUBLIN, - - -	1	2	...	24	...	...	
,, FORTUNE (sunk), -	4	63	...	1	...	...	
,, INDEFATIGABLE (sunk),	57	960	...	...	...	2	Includes 5 civilians.
,, INVINCIBLE (sunk), -	61	965	...	...	...	...	Includes 5 civilians.
,, LION, - - - -	6	93	...	43	...	...	Includes 2 civilians.
,, MALAYA, - - -	2	61	...	33	...	...	Includes 4 civilians.
,, MARLBOROUGH, - -	...	2	...	...	...	...	
,, MOORSOM, - - -	...	...	...	1	...	...	
,, NESSUS, - - - -	2	5	...	7	...	...	
,, NESTOR (sunk), - -	2	5	...	...	5	74	
,, NOMAD (sunk), - -	1	7	...	...	4	68	
,, ONSLAUGHT, - -	3	2	...	2	...	...	
,, ONSLOW, - - - -	...	2	...	3	...	...	
,, PETARD, - - - -	2	7	1	5	...	...	
,, PORPOISE, - - -	...	2	...	2	...	...	
,, PRINCESS ROYAL, -	...	22	1	77	...	...	Includes 2 civilians.
,, QUEEN MARY (sunk),	57	1209	2	5	1	1	Includes 5 civilians.
,, SHARK (sunk), - -	7	79	...	2	...	...	
,, SOUTHAMPTON, - -	...	35	1	40	...	...	Includes 1 civilian.
,, SPARROWHAWK (sunk),	...	6	...	...	...	...	
,, SPITFIRE, - - - -	...	6	3	16	...	...	
,, TIGER, - - - -	2	22	...	37	...	...	
,, TIPPERARY (sunk), -	11	174	...	2	...	8	
,, TURBULENT (sunk), -	5	85	...	...	...	13	
,, VALIANT, - - - -	...	...	...	1	...	...	
,, ,, WARRIOR (sunk),	1	70	2	25	...	...	Casualties sustained prior to the loss of the ship.
,, WARSPITE,- - - -	1	13	3	13	...	...	Includes 3 civilians
Totals, - - - -	328	5671	25	485	10	166	

Grand total, 363 Officers + 6322 Men = 6685.[1]

---

[1]*Note.*—The British casualties at Trafalgar, 21st October, 1805, totalled 1663 killed and wounded.

APPENDIX B

TABLE SHOWING THE AUTHORITY OF THE NARRATIVES

The following table is compiled for the purpose of indicating to historians, students, etc., the probable degree of reliability that can be attached to the accuracy of details in the various narratives. Without reflecting upon the several authors this appears to be necessary, for it is a well-established fact that time dulls accurate memory of events, and that few men in the confusion of battle can obtain an accurate impression of events which did not come immediately under their personal notice.

The position and duty of the author during the action, and the date at which notes or the narrative itself were written, are, therefore, tabulated. In all cases, the authors were actually serving during the action in that ship by which the narrative is named. The narratives were written in their present form in 1920 unless otherwise stated.

NARRATIVE.	AUTHORITY OF AUTHOR.
Abdiel, - - - -	Letter written from memory.
Acasta, - - - -	Written from memory by the Commanding Officer.
Agincourt, - - - -	Author's action station was as an 'Observer.' Made notes accordingly. Narrative written in 1920 from these notes.
Ardent, - - - -	A copy of a narrative written by the Commanding Officer and printed in pamphlet form in late 1916.

427

Badger,	-	-	-	-

Written from memory by an Executive Officer.[1]

Bellerophon, - - -

Written by an Executive Officer stationed aloft from ship records made during the action and notes made directly afterwards.

Broke (pages 306-314), - -

Written from navigation notes made during the action and personal notes made afterwards by the Navigating Officer of the ship. Checked by the Commanding Officer.

Broke (pages 314-315), - -

Written from memory by the Engineer Officer.

Calliope, - - - -

Written from memory by an Officer stationed on the forebridge.

Caroline, - - - -

Written by an Executive Officer immediately after the action.

Castor, - - - -

Written by an Executive Officer from notes made 2 or 3 days after the action.

Chester, - - - -

Written by the Navigating Officer from notes made during the action, and combining a Narrative of the Engineer Officer. Checked by the Commanding Officer.

Cochrane, - - - -

Written from memory by an Executive Officer.

Colossus, - - - -

Narrative written by an Executive Officer from his own and several other Officers' notes. Times according to the Official Observer's record.

Conqueror, - - -

Written by an Officer in a turret from notes made during and immediately after the action.

---

[1]An Executive Officer indicates an Officer of the Executive Branch as opposed to the Engineering, Medical, or Paymaster's Branch.

Defender, - - - -	Written from memory by an Executive Officer.
Dublin, - - - -	Written from memory by an Executive Officer.
Duke of Edinburgh, - -	By an Officer stationed aloft. Elaborated from notes made during the action. Narrative is practically a copy of an account written immediately afterwards.
Engadine (pages 169-172), -	Written from memory by the Commanding Officer.
Engadine (pages 172-173), -	Written from memory by an Officer of the R.N.A.S.
Falmouth, - - -	Written by an Officer stationed as Observer from notes made during the action.
Faulknor, - - -	Written by an Officer stationed on the fore-bridge from notes made directly after the action. Checked by the Commanding Officer.
Galatea, - - - -	Written from notes made during and directly after the action.
Garland, - - - -	Written by an Officer on the forebridge, from memory.
Indomitable, - -	Written by an Officer of a 12-inch turret, from a note-book kept in the turret through the action (see page xxx).
Inflexible, - - - -	Written from memory by the Gunnery Officer, who was stationed aloft during the action.
Lion (pages 380-387), - -	Written from notes by an Officer stationed on the fore-bridge.
Lion (pages 92-98, 108-115, - and 388-391),	Written from records kept in the Gun Control Top and Official records made in the Transmitting Station during the action.

Maenad (pages 368-370),			-	Written by an Officer stationed on the fore-bridge from ship records.
Maenad (pages 416-424),			-	Written by an Executive Officer from notes made at the time.
Malaya (pages 115-122, 356-358),			-	Written by a Turret Officer from notes made immediately after the action (see page 115 for details).
Malaya (pages 99-104),			-	Written from memory by a Midshipman stationed in the Torpedo Control Tower.
Marksman,	-	-	-	Written from memory.
Marlborough,	-	-	-	Elaborated from notes made during the action, the author being stationed aloft.
Marne,	-	-	-	Written in 1920 from notes made in a diary immediately on return to harbour after the action.
Moorsom, -	-	-	-	A letter written by an Executive Officer shortly after the action.
Neptune, -	-	-	-	Written from notes made immediately after the action by a Midshipman stationed aloft.
Nestor,	-	-	-	Extract from the book, *Falklands, Jutland, and the Bight,* the author of which was the Commanding Officer of H.M.S. *Nestor.*
New Zealand (pages 33-36),			-	Written from notes and ship records by the Gunnery Officer, who was stationed aloft.
New Zealand (pages 37-40, 51-52),			-	Narrative made from an account written by the Navigating Officer shortly after the action, and checked by navigation notes. Some notes of the Torpedo Officer are included. Both Officers were stationed in the Conning Tower.

Nicator, - - - -	Written from memory by an Executive Officer. Checked by letters written directly afterwards.
Nomad, - - - -	Written from memory.
Nottingham, - - -	Written from navigation notes and a personal journal, by the Navigating Officer.
Obedient, - - - -	Written by an Officer stationed on the fore-bridge from notes made after the action. Checked by the Commanding Officer.
Onslaught, - - -	Written from memory.
Onslow, - - - -	Written by an Executive Officer of the ship from action notes and reports. Checked by the Commanding Officer.
Petard, - - - -	Written from notes by an Executive Officer.
Princess Royal (pages 28-33), -	Written from notes and reports made by Recorders and Turret Officers, etc., during and directly after the action.
Princess Royal (pages 391-396),	Written by the Medical Officer of the ship from memory.
Queen Mary, - - -	Written about three weeks after the action by a Petty Officer who was stationed in the after-turret, and was rescued after the explosion by H.M.S. *Petard*.
Southampton (pages 77-80, 265-267, and 288-293),	A re-written version of an account written immediately after the action by the Torpedo Officer of the ship, whose station was in the Conning Tower during the day action and on the fore-bridge during the night action.
Southampton (pages 80-84, 294-299),	Extract from the book. *A Naval Lieutenant*, 1914-18, the author

			of which was stationed in the after gun control position in the day action, and was on the upper deck during the night action.
Sparrowhawk,	-	-	Written by an Executive Officer stationed on the bridge from notes made directly after the action.
Spitfire,	-	-	Written from memory by an Executive Officer. Checked by the Commanding Officer.
A Submarine,	-	-	Written from memory by an Executive Officer.
Tiger (pages 40-43),	-	-	Written by the Torpedo Officer who was stationed in the Conning Tower, from memory.
Tiger (pages 89-92),	-	-	Written by the Engineer Officer of the ship, from memory.
Tiger (pages 86-88),	-	-	Written by the Turret Officer of the damaged turret, from memory.
Tiger (pages 396-406),	-	-	Written by the Gunnery Officer of the ship from notes made by himself and recorders during the action. Particular endeavour made to use these notes without alteration and to avoid post-battle impressions.
Tipperary,	-	-	-	Written by an Executive Officer survivor partly from notes and partly from memory.
Warrior (pages 161-169),	-	Written from reports made to the Commanding Officer immediately after the loss of *Warrior* by all heads of departments of the ship.
Warrior (pages 406-416),	-	Written by the Engineer Commanding of the ship. Narrative is practically a copy of a personal journal written immediately after the action.

Warspite (pages 139-150),   -   Written by the Executive Officer of the ship. Narrative is a copy of an account written immediately after the action, omitting some personal and irrelevant details. Description of the helm jamming incidents at Windy Corner checked by the Commanding Officer.

Warspite (pages 130-133),   -   Written from memory by a Midshipman stationed in the torpedo control tower.

Yarmouth,   -   -   -   Written from navigation notes made during the action by an Officer stationed on the bridge.

APPENDIX C

CONTENTS.
Brief Explanation of the Course of the Action.
Chronology of Events.
Summary of Strength and Losses of the Two Fleets.

Brief Explanation of the Course of the Battle.[1]

At 2.30 p.m. on 31st May, 1916, a British battle cruiser force from Rosyth was at sea in the Heligoland Bight, about 200 miles north of the German coast. The force was under the command of Sir David Beatty. Sir John Jellicoe, with the main British battle fleet from Scapa Flow was in support of the Rosyth force, roughly 60 miles to the northward.

Unexpectedly, at 2.30 p.m., one of the Rosyth light cruisers reported enemy ships in sight, and Sir David Beatty steered to intercept them. After an hour and a quarter's steaming, 5 German battle cruisers were sighted, and at 3.48 p.m. Beatty's 6 battle cruisers opened fire at a range of 18,500 yards—10½ land miles. The Germans were to the eastward of the British battle cruisers, and both forces steamed to the south at high speed, fighting a fierce gunnery duel. At 4.4 p.m. H.M.S. *Indefatigable* blew up and sank. At 4.26 p.m. H.M.S. *Queen Mary* blew up, but the four remaining British battle cruisers continued the action with the five German ships. The range varied from 6½ to 9 miles.

Ten minutes later (4.37) a large force of German battleships was sighted coming up from the southward, and at 4.45 p.m. Sir David Beatty turned right about, to the northward, and was imitated a

---

1 This account is not authoritative but is based upon second-hand sources only. It is hoped that it is sufficiently accurate to indicate truly the main course of the battle. Von Scheer's book, 'The High Sea Fleet,' and Lord Jellicoe's book, 'The Grand Fleet, 1914-16,' together with the narratives of eye-witnesses, are the principal authorities used.

few minutes later by the German battle cruisers. The duel was then continued on a northerly course. At about the same time the 5th Battle Squadron, four powerful ships of the *Queen Elizabeth* class, which had been following the battle at their utmost speed, formed up 2 miles to the southward of the battle cruisers and engaged the van of the German battle fleet and the rear German battle cruisers.

Sir John Jellicoe at 5.0 p.m. was now about 40 miles to the north-ward of the action, steaming at full speed to the southward with his 24 Dreadnought battleships, in the hope of joining the battle. Admiral Von Scheer, the German Commander-in-Chief, with 22 German battleships,[2] was 10 miles south of our battle cruisers, and was pursuing to the north, to keep in support of his own battle cruisers and to finish off any damaged British ships that might drop astern out of the action.

The battle-cruiser duel, with the 5th B.S. fighting the van of the German battle fleet, continued from 5.0 to 6.0 p.m. on a northerly course, periods of calm being alternated with periods of fierce fighting. No British or German ships were sunk during this hour, but several capital ships on both sides received severe damage from shell-fire.

The British Battle Fleet Arrives

A few minutes before 6.0 p.m. Sir David Beatty's battle cruisers made junction with the leading ships of the British battle fleet. Sir David Beatty turned sharply to the eastward, was joined by three more battle cruisers detached from the Grand Fleet, and forced the five German battle cruisers to turn away to the south-eastward. At 6.33 one of the reinforcing British battle cruisers, H.M.S. *Invincible*, flying the flag of Rear-Admiral Hood, was hit in a turret, the magazine blew up, and she sank.

At 6.15 p.m. Sir John Jellicoe, in the battleship *Iron Duke*, sighted the leading ships of the German battle fleet, and deployed his battle

---

2 Possibly only 21 Battleships, but probably 22:—16 Dreadnoughts and 6 pre-Dreadnoughts. The relative Forces therefore were:—

      Germans, -   - 22 Battleships; 5 Battle Cruisers.
      British, -   - 28 Battleships; 9 (reduced by 5.0 p.m. to 7) Battle Cruisers.
Information of the Light Forces present is less certain, but probably was, very approximately:—

      Germans, -   - 11 Light Cruisers; about 70 Destroyers.
      British, -   - 33 Cruisers or Light Cruisers; about 80 Destroyers.

fleet from cruising formation into battle line.[3] Their immediate course was roughly north-east, swinging round to south-east, one ship following in the wake of her next ahead. They opened fire as they deployed, the enemy battle line bearing roughly south of them.

The British battle fleet from 6.0 to 6.30 p.m. formed a curved line like the outer side of a crescent, and were firing at the German battle fleet, disposed in an irregular or in a curved line on the inside of the crescent. The rear of our line was nearer to the enemy than were the van. Apparently the German battle fleet turned a complete circle together to starboard at about 6.20 p.m., then resumed their easterly course with the leading ships swinging through south-east to south; then turned together to the west at about 6.35 p.m., and back to the eastward quarter of an hour later. But at no time was more than a portion of the German battle fleet visible to any one part of our battle line, and for most of the action three or four big ships, or occasionally five or six, was the maximum number in sight. It is probable that the Germans similarly were able to see only a fraction of our battle line at any one moment.

Between 7.0 and 7.30 p.m. torpedo attacks were launched by German destroyer flotillas, and the British battle fleet altered course away from the enemy to avoid the torpedoes. The two principal attacks appear to have been launched at 7.10 and 7.25 p.m., but in addition individual German ships probably fired torpedoes from the vicinity of their battle line at any time from 6.15 p.m. onwards. H.M.S. *Marlborough*, flagship of the 1st Battle Squadron, was hit by a torpedo at 6.54 p.m., but held her place in the line until after dark.

About 7.20 or 7.30 p.m. the German ships made a heavy smoke screen, and under its cover altered further away to the westward, and the British battle fleet lost touch with them. By 9 p.m. all firing had finally died down, the day action was ended, and both battle fleets were left practically intact. The British fleet was to the south-eastward of the Germans, between them and their bases.

The Night Action

At 10 p.m. night fighting commenced. It was a still but cloudy night, very dark. The German fleet in three groups steered to the south-

---

3 To deploy technically means to alter from a closed up cruising formation into a single line or other open formation in which all guns can be brought to bear on the enemy.

eastward, *en route* for a lightship called Horn Reefs, which marked one of the two mine-swept passages to the German harbours.[4] Sir John Jellicoe ordered a mine-layer to lay mines near to the light vessel, and himself steered with all his fleet to the southward at 17 knots to make ground towards Heligoland, so as to deny the enemy the other swept passage to Germany, and to place himself in such a position that he might bring the enemy to action at daylight.

The British destroyer flotillas were stationed astern of the battle columns to guard the rear from night torpedo attacks. Between 10 p.m. and 2 a.m. the German fleet steered across the path of the British flotillas, were attacked with torpedoes, and one or perhaps two German battleships were sunk. Also, two or three German light cruisers and one destroyer were sunk. Five British destroyers were lost during these attacks. The British battle fleet, being 5 to 10 miles to the southward, ahead of the destroyer flotillas, did not encounter any enemy ships during the night, but they continuously saw astern of them the gun-flashes, searchlights, and explosions of the flotillas in action.

At dawn on June 1st, at 2.47 a.m., the British battle fleet turned to the north, and swept up and down until past noon seeking for the German fleet. But the Germans had all passed through or passed across the rear of the British fleet before 2.30 a.m.,[5] had some of them gone across the British mine-field by Horn Reef, but had lost only one ship in doing so,[6] and were now steaming down the coast of Schleswig Holstein in safety behind their own mine-fields, towards the final security of their harbours. They were sighted by British surface ships only once again before they came to surrender themselves off Rosyth 2½ years later.

The British battle fleet returned to Scapa Flow on the afternoon of June 1st, and Beatty's battle cruisers returned to Rosyth.

---

4 There was another swept passage which ran along the northern German coast, by the Friesian Islands, and gave exit to the west or north-westward, but as it was nearly 150 miles distant from the battle it need hardly be taken into account.

5 Accurate information of the German positions is not yet public, but according to his own book the German C.-in-C. passed Horn Reef L.V. at 3 a.m.

6 Possibly she was only damaged; accurate intelligence is not yet public. It is stated that the ship was the battleship *Ostfriesland*.

Chronology of Principal Events.

(**Note**.—These times are not based upon authentic records, but are taken from the Jutland despatch, checked with narratives, Jellicoe's *Grand Fleet, 1914-1916*, and Von Scheer's *High Seas Fleet*.)

PHASE I.—Battle Cruiser Action,   Roughly 4.0 to 6.0 p.m.
PHASE II.—Battle Fleet Action, .   Roughly 6.0 to 9.0 p.m.
PHASE III.—Night Action,   .   Roughly 10 p.m. to 2 a.m.,
                                         June 1st.

2.20 p.m. *Galatea* reports enemy ships in sight.
           Rosyth battle cruiser force steer to intercept enemy.

2.40 p.m. Grand Fleet raise steam for full speed and prepare to join Rosyth Force.

3.8 p.m.   *Engadine's* Seaplane is hoisted out and commences reconnaissance flight.

3.25 p.m. Rosyth battle cruisers sight 5 enemy battle cruisers bearing north-east. Range, 23,000 yards (11½ sea miles). Course, E.S.E.

3.25 p.m. 13th Destroyer Flotilla takes station ahead of battle cruisers, near to 2nd L.C.S.; 1st and 3rd L.C.S. are astern—*i.e.*, to the northward of battle cruisers. 5th Battle Squadron (4 ships *Queen Elizabeth* class) are about 5 miles astern of battle cruisers.

3.48 p.m. *Lion* opens fire. *Princess Royal, Queen Mary, Tiger, New Zealand, Indefatigable*, following astern in single line, also open fire.

4.4 p.m.   *Indefatigable* sunk.

4.8 p.m.   5th B.S. open fire; range 20,000 yards (a very long range).

4.26 p.m. *Queen Mary* sunk.

About 4.15   13th Destroyer Flotilla attack enemy battle cruisers
to 5 p.m.   with torpedoes, engage enemy destroyers with gunfire, and eventually attack enemy battle fleet.
             Nestor and *Nomad* sunk. Two German destroyers sunk.

4.38 p.m. 2nd Light Cruiser Squadron (*Southampton, Nottingham, Birmingham, Dublin*) ahead of *Lion*, report enemy battle fleet in sight.

4.46 p.m. Rosyth battle cruisers alter course 16 points to starboard in succession on to northerly course.

438

4.52 p.m.   German battle cruisers alter course 16 points to port (outwards) in succession on to northerly course.

4.57 p.m.   5th Battle Squadron pass our battle cruisers, then turn 16 points, and form up about 2 miles astern—*i.e.*, to the southward of them. Course North. They engage van of German battle fleet.

5.0 p.m.   Grand Fleet is approximately 40 miles north-north-west (true) from H.M.S. *Lion.*

5.0 to   Four remaining battle cruisers—*Lion, Princess Royal*
6.0 p.m.   *Tiger, New Zealand*—continue gunnery duel with 5 German battle cruisers on a northerly course, range about 13,000 to 18,000 yards. There are intervals during which fire is checked; enemy are periodically obscured by mist.

   5th B.S. engage German battle crusiers and van of German battle fleet.

About   Hood's battle cruiser squadron (*Invincible, Inflexible,*
5.30 p.m.   *Indomitable*), having been detached from Grand Fleet at 2.30 p.m. to support Rosyth battle cruiser force, sight gun-flashes.

About   Light cruiser *Chester* engages enemy light cruisers, and
5.40 p.m.   soon afterwards other ships under Admiral Hood come into action.

5.59 p.m.   *Shark* sunk.

About 6.0 to 9.0 p.m. BATTLE FLEET ACTION.

About   Arbuthnot's Cruiser Squadron, *Defence,* etc., com-
5.50 p.m.   mence action with German light cruiser.

5.56 p.m.   *Marlborough*, western wing battleship of Grand Fleet, sights *Lion.*

About 5.55 to 6.25 p.m.   Windy Corner period.

6.5 p.m.   *Onslow* attacks German light cruiser, then battle cruisers, then battle fleet. Is damaged, and about 7.15 p.m. is towed out of action by *Defender.*

6.14 p.m.   Battle Fleet deploys. Immediate course as they deploy E.N.E. ships then altering course in succession to S.E. by E. *King George V.* leading 2nd B.S. in the van; *Iron Duke* with 4th B.S. in the centre; *Marlborough* with 1st B.S. in the rear. 5th B.S. form astern of 1st B.S.

6.16 p.m. *Defence* blown up, *Warrior* disabled.

6.17 p.m. Battle fleet opens fire, 1st B.S. in the rear commencing. German light cruiser *Wiesbaden* set on fire, sinks soon afterwards.

6.20 p.m. *Warspite*'s helm jams.

6.21 p.m. Hood's battle cruisers form ahead of *Lion* and engage enemy battle cruisers at about 8,000 yards range.

6.25 p.m. 3rd Light Cruiser Squadron (*Falmouth*, etc.) attack enemy battle cruisers.

6.30 to 7.20 p.m.   Battleships in the centre and van firing at enemy.

6.33 p.m. *Invincible* blows up.

6.38 p.m. Battle fleet deployment complete; fleet in single line ahead steering S.E. by E.

6.47 p.m. *Acasta*, lying disabled, is passed by *Iron Duke* and the battle fleet.

6.54 p.m. *Marlborough* (4th battleship from the rear) hit by a torpedo.

7.0 to
7.14 p.m. Six British battle cruisers in van, hauling round through south to a south-westerly course, regain contact with enemy, which had been lost; range 15,000 yards. British battle cruisers are roughly 5 to 7 miles ahead of leading battleship.

7.10 p.m. 1st German destroyer attack on battle fleet.

7.0 to
7.40 p.m. Course of battle fleet south, with periodical alterations to the eastward to neutralise torpedo attacks.

7.12 p.m. Rear ships of battle fleet (*Colossus*, *Neptune*, etc.) engage enemy battleships or battle cruisers.

About
7.20 p.m. Rear ships of battle fleet dodging torpedoes.

About
7.25 p.m. Second German destroyer attack. German battle line makes large turn away under cover of this attack and of smoke screen. Probably two German destroyers sunk.

7.45 p.m. *Obedient, Marvel, Mindful,* and *Onslaught* sink a German destroyer, flying a Commodore's pendant, that lay damaged between the fleets.

7.45 p.m. Battle cruisers lose touch with enemy.

About 1st and 3rd L.C.S. locate head of enemy's line again.

8.20 p.m. Battle cruisers on a westerly course regain touch. Enemy appear to suffer heavily from gunfire.

8.22 p.m.   4th Light Cruiser Squadron (*Calliope*, etc.) engaging
              enemy.

9.5 p.m.   *Caroline* fires torpedoes at enemy battle cruisers.

9.0 p.m.   Battle fleet course south; speed, 17 knots; take up night
              dispositions.

              Day action finished.

9.32 p.m.   *Abdiel* detached to lay mine-field off Horn Reefs. Lays
              mines about 1.0 a.m.

10 p.m. to 2 a.m.   NIGHT ACTION.

10.4 p.m.   H.M.S. *Castor* and part of 11th Destroyer Flotilla in
              action (*Castor*'s 1st Night Action).

10.20 p.m.   Light cruiser action of 2nd L.C.S. (*Southampton,
              Dublin, Nottingham, Birmingham*) with German light
              cruisers.

              German light cruiser *Frauenlob* sunk by torpedo from
              Southampton.

About   Actions of *Tipperary*'s (4th) Flotilla commence.[7]

11.30 p.m.   Rough chronology was:—

              About 11.30 p.m.; 4th Flotilla in action at close range
                  with German cruisers. *Tipperary* is
                  set on fire. *Spitfire* is damaged.

              About 11.45 p.m.; *Ardent, Ambuscade, Garland,* and
                  Fortune engage enemy big ship;
                  Fortune is sunk.

              About 11.30 p.m. *Spitfire* closing the burning *Tipperary*
                  is rammed by a German cruiser.

              Soon after   Burning ship, possibly H.M.S. *Black
              Midnight.   Prince*, passes close by *Spitfire*.

              About 12.15 p.m.[8] *Broke*, followed by *Sparrowhawk* and
                  others, in action with German
                  battleship. *Broke* collides with
                  Sparrowhawk.

---

7 It is probable that during these actions one or more German cruisers or battleships were sunk by torpedoes, but there is not sufficient evidence upon which to base a definite statement.

8 Available evidence is conflicting as to whether the time of this action was just before midnight or just after.

Soon after Midnight.	*Ardent* sunk by German battleships.
About 2 a.m.	*Tipperary* sinks. Survivors take to rafts.
About 3 a.m.	*Sparrowhawk* sights German light cruiser. German light cruiser sinks.
About 4 a.m.	*Garland* and *Contest* engage four German destroyers
About 5.0 a.m.	Survivors of *Tipperary* on a raft reach H.M.S. *Sparrowhawk*.
8.0 a.m.	H.M.S. *Sparrowhawk* is sunk. Her crew with survivors of *Tipperary* are taken on board H.M.S. *Marksmen*.

12.15 a.m. H.M.S. *Castor*'s 2nd night action (one German destroyer probably sunk).

12.30 (?) Part of 13th Destroyer Flotilla (*Petard*, *Nicator*, etc.) in action with German battleships.

H.M.S. *Turbulent* rammed and sunk.

> *Note.*—Sometime during the night or early morning H.M.S. *Black Prince* foundered.

German battle cruiser *Lutzow* was abandoned and sank as result of damage received during day action. One German light cruiser, perhaps two, also sank during the night.

June 1st.

1.45 a.m. 12th Destroyer Flotilla (*Faulknor*, *Obedient*, etc.) sight enemy battle squadron. Manoeuvre into position of torpedo advantage.

2.0 a.m. Attack. One German battleship hit by torpedo and sunk. H.M.S. *Onslaught* damaged, but no British ship lost.

2.45 a.m. H.M.S. *Maenad* turns back and delivers a second attack by herself. Probably one of her torpedoes hit.

2.30 a.m. Vice-Admiral Sir C. Burney, Commanding 1st Battle Squadron, transfers his flag from *Marlborough* to *Revenge*. *Marlborough* proceeds to England.

2.47 a.m. Grand Fleet Battle Squadrons, accompanied by cruisers and a few destroyers, turn to north. German battle fleet at this time was passing or past Horn Reefs, which bore roughly north-east 40 miles from I*ron Duke*.

3.0 to 6.30 a.m.	Several cruisers or destroyers sight enemy light craft disappearing in the mist. No action is fought.
3.30 to 4.0 a.m.	Zeppelin in sight from various British ships.
7.30 a.m.	H.M.S. *Warrior* abandoned. *Engadine* takes off crew.
1.15 p.m.	British Battle Fleet shapes course for Scapa Flow.

June 1st. **Damaged Ships proceeding Home Independently—**

BATTLESHIPS.

H.M.S. *Marlborough*.

H.M.S. *Warspite*.

DESTROYERS.

H.M.S. *Onslow* in tow of H.M.S. *Defender*.

H.M.S. *Acasta* in tow of H.M.S. *Nonsuch*.

H.M.S. *Broke*.

H.M.S. *Spitfire*.

H.M.S. *Garland*, with H.M.S. *Contest* and H.M.S. *Porpoise*.

H.M.S. *Onslaught*.

German battle cruiser *Seydlitz* very badly damaged in the day action, reaches Cuxhaven, but (it is believed) sinks or is purposely grounded at the entrance. She is later salved.

German battleship *Ostfriesland* (?) strikes a mine in the vicinity of Horn Reefs.

June 2nd.

8.0 a.m.	H.M.S *Marlborough* arrives safely in the harbour.
Forenoon.	Battle fleet returns to Scapa Flow.
9.45 p.m.	Battle fleet refuelled and reported ready for sea.

June 3rd.

About 8.0 p.m.	*Broke* enters the Tyne. All damaged British ships now back in harbour.

SUMMARY OF STRENGTH AND LOSSES OF THE TWO FLEETS

STRENGTH.

BRITISH.

28 Battleships.
 9 Battle Cruisers.
33 Cruisers and Light Cruisers.
 1 Seaplane Carrier.
 1 Minelayer.
79 Destroyers.

GERMAN.

22 Battleships.
 5 Battle Cruisers.
11 Light Cruisers.
About 72 Destroyers.

LOSSES.

(British losses are known; German losses are estimated only but probably are correct).

BRITISH.

3 Battle Cruisers.
3 Cruisers.
8 Destroyers.

GERMAN.

1 Battleship.
1 Battle Cruiser.
4 Light Cruisers.
5 Destroyers.

INDEX

Page references in *italics* refer to illustrations.

Abbreviations
A/B = Able Seaman; Br = British; Cdr = Commander; Cdre = Commodore; CPO = Chief Petty Officer; Flt/Lt = Flight Lieutenant; Ger = Germany; HMS = His Majesty's Ship; L/S = Leading Seaman; Lt = Lieutenant; P/O = Petty Officer; R/A = Rear-Admiral; RM = Royal Marines; V/A = Vice-Admiral

445

Contest, HMS *map* 124-5, 304, 306, 311, 318-19, 331, *map* 331, 334
Cordelia, HMS 20, *map* 124-5, 138
Crescent, HMS 416
Cromarty 167-8, 171, 174

Defence, HMS 102, 108, 135-7, 157, *map* 158, 161-4, 168, 174-8, *map* 175, 227, 244, 264, 274, 278
  class 268, 403
  loss of 15, 59, 127, 129-31, 137-8, 150-1, *map* 158, 159-61, 181, 184, 193, 198, 198*n*, 244, 275, 389, 403, 419
Defender, HMS *map* 124-5, 202, 248, 253-4, 255-8, 374
Derfflinger (Ger) 251*n*, 265, 274, 397
  class 117, 182, 199, 205-6, 227, 273
Deutschland class (Ger) 272
Dogger Bank, battle of 30, 89, 394-5, 404
Dreadnought, HMS 416
Dublin, HMS *map* 74, 78, *map* 124-5, 244, 287, 290, 294-5, 299-301, 353, 373-4
Duke of Edinburgh, HMS *map* 124-5, 157, *map* 158, 159-61, 174-8, *map* 175, 278

Egan, Lt 348
Elbing (Ger) 323, *323*
Engadine, HMS *map* 21, 24, 26, *26,* 28, 33, 62, 161, 165, 167-73, *170,* 248, 412, 414
  abandonment of 177
Epworth, Mr 58
Erin, HMS 104, *map* 124-5
Evan-Thomas, R/A 51, 83, 98, 106, 157, 223, 385
Ewart, Lt 46-7

Falmouth, HMS *map* 21, 19-20, *map* 124-5, 159, 265, 273-5, 274, 276
Farie, Captain J U 52
Faulknor, HMS *map* 124-5, 133-5, 208, 359-66, *map* 361, 368-9, 421
Fearless, HMS *map* 124-5, 138, 221, 221*n*, 237
Fifth Battle Squadron 61, 75, *map* 76, 79, 83, 98-9, 105-6, 115-22, *map* 124-5, 126-31, *132,* 136, 151, 157, *map* 158, 169, 179, 192, 204-5, 208, 223, 265-7, 293, 350, 354-5, 380, 385, 392
  see also Barham, Malaya, Warspite, Valiant
Firth of Forth 172, 293, 367, 395
Fitzgerald, CPO 37
Formidable, HMS 213
Fortune, HMS 318, 331, *map* 331
  loss of 15, 305-6, 344, 349, 370, 423
Francis, P/O E 43-50, 59

Galatea, HMS *map* 18, 20-4, *map* 21, 56, 106-8, 115, *map* 124-5, 137-9, 139, 215, 226, 237, 238-9, 264
  class 330
  sights German battlecruisers 33, 99, 264, 380-1, 396
Garland, HMS *map* 124-5, 306, 315-20, *map* 331

Gaunt, R/A E F A 183
Gloucester, HMS *map* 124-5, 159, 274, 277
Goodenough, Cdre 288
Goshawk, HMS *map* 124-5
Grand Fleet (Br) *map* 16, 51-2, 75, 78, 84, 122, 126-7, *128,* 131-3, 137, 145, 149-424, *180*
  see also Jellicoe *and individual ships*
Graudenz class (Ger) 316
Green, Captain John 37

Hamburg (Ger) 351-3
Hampshire, HMS *map* 124-5
Harvey, Major (RM) 92-4, 382
Hawkesley, Cdre J R P 202-3
Heath, Admiral 177
Heligoland *map* 16, 21, 177, *map* 282, 283, 288, 300, 314, 344, 386, 394-5
Heligoland class (Ger) 203, 269, 366, 403
Hercules, HMS *map* 124-5, 194, *map* 211, *map* 215, 362
High Seas Fleet (Ger) *map* 16, 15, *map* 74, *75,* 76, 80-1, 106, 119-20, 131, 137, 141, 159, 174, 193, 205, 259, 357
  sighted 36, 51, 68, 70-3, 75-8, 115-16, 264, 384
  see also individual ships
Hindenburg (Ger) 397
Hipper, Admiral von 22-4, 27-30, 33-5, 38-40, 42-3, 46, 51, 70, 83
Hood, R/A Sir Horace 192, 223, 230-1, 235, 247, 268, 276, 385
Horn Reef Light Vessel *map* 16, *map* 282, 283-4, 305, 422
Hydra, HMS *map* 124-5

Inconstant, HMS 20, *map* 124-5, 138
Indefatigable, HMS 28, 33-4, 51, 98, 396
  loss of *map* 18, 15, 27, 32, 34, 37-9, *38-9,* 42, 61-2, 73, 77-8, 101, 141, 278, 382, 389, 395, 397, 401, 404
Indomitable, HMS *map* 124-5, 192, 202-3, 206-7, 223, *map* 224, 226-7, 229, 235, 238-44, 273, 276, 386, 389
Inflexible, HMS *map* 124-5, 192, 202-3, 223, *map* 224, 225, 226-30, 235, 239, 241, 276, 386, 389
Invincible, HMS 177, 192, 223, *map* 224, 226-7, 233, 235, 239-40, 259, 276
  loss of 15, *map* 124-5, 184, 189, 194-6, 199, 202, *map* 224, 225, *228,* 229, 239-41, *240,* 244-6, 268-9, 271-2, 275, 279, 386, 389, 404
Iron Duke, HMS 39-40, 79, *map* 124-5, 179, 204, *map* 215, *map* 220, *map* 224, 236, 244, 260, 271, *map* 282, 301

Jellicoe, Admiral Sir John 79, 126, 153, 161, 203-4, 208, 214, 216, 219, 222-3, 225, 230, 234-6, 265, 267, 338, 359-60, 374, 380
  see also Grand Fleet, *Iron Duke*
Jerram, V/A Sir Thomas 179, 202